LEADERSHIP

Communication Skills for Organizations and Groups

LEADERSHIP

Communication Skills for Organizations and Groups

J. Kevin Barge
Baylor University

ST. MARTIN'S PRESS
New York

Editor: Suzanne Phelps Weir
Managing editor: Patricia Mansfield-Phelan
Project editor: Diana Puglisi
Production supervisor: Joe Ford
Art director: Sheree Goodman
Text design: Leon Bolognese & Associates, Inc.
Cover design: Kay Petronio

Library of Congress Catalog Card Number: 92–62789
Copyright © 1994 by St. Martin's Press, Inc. All rights reserved. No part of this book may be reproduced, stored in a retrieval system, or transmitted by any form or by any means, electronic, mechanical, photocopying, recording, or otherwise, except as may be expressly permitted by the applicable copyright statutes or in writing by the Publisher.
Manufactured in the United States of America.
8 7
f e d c b

For information, write:
St. Martin's Press, Inc.
175 Fifth Avenue
New York, NY 10010

ISBN: 0–312–08117–0

ACKNOWLEDGMENTS

Acknowledgments and copyrights are continued at the back of the book on page 275, which constitutes an extension of the copyright page.

Box 1.2, adapted from Karl Weick, "The Spines of Leaders" in *Leadership: Where Else Can We Go?* (1978), eds. M. W. McCall and M. M. Lombardo. Copyright © 1978 by Duke University Press. Reprinted by permission.
Figure 2.1, courtesy of A. G. Jago and *Management Science.*
Box 2.1, James C. McCroskey, *An Introduction to Rhetorical Communication,* 6th edition. Englewood Cliffs, NJ: Prentice-Hall, 1993, p. 37.
Figure 2.2, The Leadership Grid Figure from *Leadership Dilemmas—Grid Solutions,* by Robert R. Blake and Anne Adams McCanse (formerly the Managerial Grid Figure by Robert R. Blake and Jane S. Mouton). Houston: Gulf Publishing Company, p. 29. Copyright © 1991, by Scientific Methods, Inc. Reproduced by permission of the owners.
Box 2.3, courtesy of F. E. Fiedler.
Figure 2.3, courtesy of F. E. Fiedler.
Table 2.1, reprinted by permission of publisher, from *Organizational Dynamics,* 19, #1, 1990. All rights reserved.
Box 2.5, reprinted by permission of publisher, from *Organizational Dynamics,* 18, #3, 1990. All rights reserved.
Table 3.1, adapted from V. D. Miller and F. M. Jablin, "Information Seeking during Organizational Entry: Influences, Tactics and a Model of the Process," *Academy of Management Review* 16 (1), 1991.
Table 4.3, courtesy of R. M. Hogarth and S. Makridakis, "Forecasting and Planning: an Evaluation." *Management Science* 27, #2, 1981.
Table 5.2, courtesy of R. Y. Hirokawa, "The Role of Communication in Group Decision-Making Efficacy: A Task-Contingency Perspective," presented at CSSA, 1988.
Box 5.2, adapted with the permission of The Free Press, a division of Macmillan, Inc. from *Crucial Decisions: Leadership in Policymaking and Crisis Management* by Irving L. Janis. Copyright 1989 by The Free Press.

PREFACE

Contemporary organizations are in the midst of several trends that are making their environments more complex and chaotic than ever before. An emerging global economy is presenting new business opportunities in new markets and challenges associated with greater competition. Novel organizational structures are being created as businesses forge new linkages and joint ventures to create innovative products. Communication technologies are being introduced into the workplace to enable organizations to make decisions and develop products more quickly. The diversity of the work force is increasing, as women and various ethnic groups continue to enter organizations in greater numbers and in higher-status managerial positions. These and other recent trends require that the contemporary organization successfully manage its ever-changing, diverse, and complex environment to survive.

Leadership has always played an important role in managing the organizational environment. Today's leaders, however, need to be more flexible, adaptable, and innovative to manage the changing and complex business environment. Leadership involves much more than telling workers what to do and when to do it. In contemporary organizations, effective leadership means mastering a broad repertoire of behaviors that can be adapted to various kinds of situations.

Leadership: Communication Skills for Organizations and Groups adopts the view that leaders' adaptability is best explained by viewing leadership as a form of mediation. That is, leadership mediates among the information present in the organizational environment, the actions of employees, and the organizational outcomes. It provides a medium that helps organizational members accurately interpret information and take appropriate actions for removing obstacles and achieving goals. For leadership to be effective, then, it must be as complex as the information environment of which it is a part. If it fails to meet this requirement, leadership is unable to help organizations meet challenges and goals. The primary purpose of leadership is to develop an organizing system that helps organizational members coordinate their actions, recognize and analyze obstacles, and meet objectives.

The key to more complex leadership behavior and more adaptability to new situations is good communication skills. Unlike most other leadership texts, this book views leadership as inherently rooted in the communication process. Leadership, then, is effective to the degree that it can adapt its messages to the constraints of a situation. Leaders skilled in competent communication are able to adapt or modify their messages to meet the needs of particular situations. Leadership communication may need to be simple, clear, and direct in some situations but complex, ambiguous, and subtle in others. Effective leaders possess a large repertoire of communication skills that they draw from to adapt their messages to a variety of situations. The ability of leaders to interpret others' messages and to construct messages for others is a key to effective leadership. *This text identifies the communication skills that leaders need to help manage the information environment and the collective actions of organizational members.*

THE PLAN OF THE BOOK

The book is organized into three parts that parallel the following three assumptions:

1. *Leadership is a form of mediation.* To mediate between a sophisticated complex environment and organizational members' action, leadership must be equally as sophisticated and complex.
2. *Leadership is best explained by communication skills.* Communication skills are related to two qualities of mediation: object mediation and action mediation. *Object mediation* refers to the ability to form accurate and in-depth impressions of the information environment and to draw valid inferences about the nature of obstacles present in that environment. *Action mediation* refers to the ability to take actions that will remove obstacles from the environment. It requires leaders to make decisions, manage relational issues, and articulate powerful messages aimed at motivating employees to act in desired ways.
3. *Leaders' communication competence can only be assessed in the context of the organization.* All organizations structure their own norms for assessing the relative effectiveness and appropriateness of leaders' communication. Thus, it is only within this context of the organization that a leader's communication competence can be assessed.

Part I: The Nature of Leadership and Communication

Chapters 1 and 2 of the text outline a communication skills model for leadership and discuss it in terms of other, competing perspectives. Trends that have made the business environment significantly more complex are identified and some traditional views of leadership are presented in Chapter 1. The need for leadership to be as complex as its information environment is also explained.

Chapter 2 overviews many traditional and contemporary theories of leadership. It examines such traditional leadership theories as trait theory, Blake and Mouton's (1985) managerial grid, participative management, Fiedler's (1967) contingency theory, and situational theories (for example, Hersey and Blanchard's [1982] life-cycle theory). Several more innovative, contemporary leadership theories are also discussed, including the substitutes for leadership, transformational, and leader-member exchange theories. The text compares and contrasts the various theories with the communication skills model of leadership.

Part II: Communication Skills and Leadership

Chapters 3 and 4 concentrate on the communication skills associated with object mediation. Chapter 3 examines the relationship between networking and collecting information. For leaders to understand the nature of their environment, they must first expose themselves to it and then construct communication networks that will provide the information inputs they need to make sense of the environment. An exciting integration of how leadership relates to task, personal, cultural, and innovation networks is presented. The skill of networking is described in depth, including examples of how leaders may acquire information through mentoring relationships and information-seeking strategies. Information, however, cannot be accepted uncritically. Chapter 4 overviews the challenges associated with collecting and analyzing information. Biases arising from the use of simple decision-rules and how to employ the communication skill of data splitting to counteract the tendency toward bias are explained.

Chapters 5 and 6 focus on leadership's role in decision making and relational issues. An overview of the kinds of decisions made by leaders and organizational members is provided in Chapter 5. Constraints that arise from the nature of the task, the personalities of organizational members, and the need for consensus are identified as the causes of poor decision making. The concept of vigilant decision making and the communication messages and strategies associated with it are also presented. Relational management, covered in Chapter 6, involves how leaders can help manage the relationships among employees and the organization. A case study involving W. L. Gore & Associates is a major focus of the chapter and provides concrete examples of the theoretical concepts. Role development, motivation, conflict management, and feedback are also discussed.

For leaders to help employees meet the challenges of the environment, they must be able to articulate motivating messages. Chapter 7 emphasizes the social influence of leadership—how to articulate messages that motivate employees to comply with particular decisions or actions, how to create visions for organizations, and how to employ linguistic elements to advantage in different situations.

Part III: Managing the Complexities of Leadership

Leaders attempt to manage the complexity of the information environment in a competent manner. Chapter 8 addresses how leaders may deal with paradoxes within the organization. There are several types of paradoxes present in organizational life, including the paradoxes of trust, disclosure, regression, and others. Paradoxes pose complex challenges that the leader must manage. Their relationships to such issues as employee membership, assimilation, growth, and innovation are discussed.

Chapter 9 focuses on competent leadership communication. Although most other leadership texts discuss competent leadership and competent communication as separate issues, *Leadership* joins the two related concepts to define what constitutes competent leader communication. The book takes the position that competent leader communication is both effective at achieving goals and appropriate given the organizational culture. Competing definitions of organizational effectiveness and appropriateness are also discussed in the chapter. Finally, an examination of competent leadership communication is undertaken in terms of several different organizational cultures: the tough-guy macho culture, the work hard, play hard culture, the bet-your-company culture, the process culture, and the total quality management culture.

ACKNOWLEDGMENTS

While writing *Leadership,* I quickly discovered the writer's paradox: To write a high-quality text, one must first fail in order to succeed. I was fortunate to have the help of a professional team at St. Martin's Press to guide me through this paradox. I am indebted to Cathy Pusateri, for the opportunity to write this book, and to Jane Lambert, for her ongoing encouragement of the project. In addition, I would like to thank acquiring editors Nancy Lyman and Suzanne Phelps Weir, project editor Diana Puglisi, and copy editor Wendy Polhemus-Annibell.

To the reviewers who critiqued early drafts of the manuscript, I am grateful for their thoughtful and useful comments, which helped me to improve the text tremendously: Terrance Albrecht, University of South Florida; Elizabeth Goering, Indiana University–Indianapolis; Dennis Gouran, The Pennsylvania State University; Iris Hicks, Baylor University; Margaret McLaughlin, University of Southern California; Renee Meyers, University of Wisconsin–Milwaukee; Eileen Berlin Ray, Cleveland State University; David Seibold, University of California, Santa Barbara; Vincent Waldron, Arizona State University–West; and Theodore E. Zorn, University of North Carolina.

I also thank Cal W. Downs of the University of Kansas, Randy Y. Hirokawa of the University of Iowa, and Kenneth M. Johnson of Syracuse University for their feedback and constructive criticism of my thoughts on leadership. Their input, friendship, and support helped shape the book in significant ways.

Finally, without the support of my family and close friends I would have had neither the motivation nor the time to complete this project. I am grateful to Denise Barge for her unending support and encouragement. Our evening talks about what it means to be a leader provided many useful insights into the topic. I thank my parents, Jim and Silvey Barge, for providing, through their professional, personal, and community lives, examples of what it means to be a leader. To my family, who encouraged me to pursue and complete the project, I dedicate this book.

J. Kevin Barge
Baylor University

CONTENTS

LEADERSHIP

Communication Skills for Organizations and Groups

Part I

THE NATURE OF LEADERSHIP AND COMMUNICATION

Chapter 1

Communication and Leadership

> Leadership is primarily viewed as a vitally important skill to obtain commitment and motivation and to energize people to accept the worthwhileness of a new strategy or other major change. But in organizations with highly interdependent and dynamic parts, all of which are in flux, accomplishment takes more than commitment. It is not that commitment is unimportant; rather, it too is dependent on the leader's ability to build a system worth committing to.
>
> *(Sayles, 1993, p. 227)*

It is undeniable that leadership plays an important role in helping people coordinate their ability in organizations and groups. One of leadership's primary responsibilities is to help create systems of organizing that allow companies to provide services and goods to customers and to achieve goals and quotas. While the primary responsibility of leadership has not changed greatly over the years, the means and manner by which individuals performing leadership roles accomplish these tasks has been subject to debate and discussion. This discussion was particularly pronounced during the 1980s and 1990s as business people became increasingly concerned over their lack of competitiveness against both domestic and international business opponents. Buzzwords such as *empowerment, Total Quality Management, charisma, vision, benchmarking, world class,* and *best practice* became incorporated into the vocabulary of leaders as they struggled to reverse their declining fortunes. The feeling was that the leadership of the past was not working and that new ways of leading were required to manage the future.

The traditional view of organizational leadership was based on two assumptions about work and workers that have shaped business thinking since the early 1900s (Case, 1993). First, jobs should be broken down into their basic components and should be engineered to be as simple as possible. Duties and responsibilities should be highly compartmentalized and should be sequenced in ways that allow for the efficient production of goods and services. Second, all workers require close supervision and discipline. Since duties and written protocols specify appropriate worker behavior, the primary role of leaders is to ensure that the workers successfully discharge their assigned duties. From this perspective, leaders are the people who tell people what to do and when to do it. Leaders are the disciplinarians and naysayers who punish employees when they don't obey company rules. Leaders are the rule-givers who set company policy. Leaders are the accountants and "bean-counters" who closely monitor performance indicators and take action when employees deviate from performance goals and quotas. Leaders are a select class of individuals in organizations who make a difference to the organization's bottom line.

This view of leadership was adequate so long as economic conditions in the United States were stable. Any inefficiencies or flaws produced by this kind of leadership were hidden by the fact that for the early part of the twentieth century companies were able to provide services and products that achieved reasonable profit margins. So long as businesses continued to be profitable and make money, the impetus for reexamining and changing organizational leadership styles was diminished.

However, the once-stable work environment has been replaced by an environment of turbulence, change, and unpredictability. Greater domestic and international competition has increased the volatility of the market and has stimulated a need for increased innovation and product development, requiring work systems to be reconfigured on an ongoing basis to meet customer needs. A new emphasis on bringing new products to market quickly, efficiently, and cheaply is required if organizations are to maintain and increase their market share (Cushman & King, 1993). Technology use and sophistication also have increased. The growth of information technologies, as well as the increased sophistication of robotics and automation, require companies to continually integrate new technical processes into their systems for organizing work. At the same time, diversity within the work force has increased as more and more women and minorities have entered the job market (Johnston & Parker, 1987). Organizations must take into account the diversity of their employees' cultural backgrounds as they construct work systems to get the job done.

What is the ultimate outcome of these trends? As Stratford Sherman (1993) points out:

> Bit by bit, the forces of technology and economics are destroying the artificial constructs—such as rigidly hierarchical schemes for organizing work—that since the 19th century have limited the ability of people, organizations, and markets to behave in natural ways. The next few years of transition will be brutal for all concerned, but the result promises to be worth some suffering. The workplace will be healthier, saner, more creative, and yet more chaotic—like nature itself. (p. 51)

What is the implication for leadership? What kind of leadership is required to successfully manage these changing conditions? The purpose of this first chapter is to highlight the kinds of communication skills that contemporary leaders need to manage their increasingly chaotic and unpredictable business environment. As the workplace becomes more complex and today's business emphasizes continual improvement in work effectiveness, individuals must develop and broaden their repertoire of leadership skills. To do so, they must understand leadership in a historical context—and how the traditional view of leadership has failed to recognize the complexity of leadership skills and behavior.

THE NATURE OF WORK AND LEADERSHIP

For several hundred years, managers, chief executive officers, and organizational scholars have asked the same deceptively simple question: "What is leadership?" The diversity of their answers demonstrates the bewildering complexity of the concept of *leadership*. For some analysts, a leader is a person who possesses certain personality and physical traits. Many people, for example, would consider such famous personalities as Napoleon, Indira Gandhi, Winston Churchill, Mother Teresa, and Hitler leaders because they had or have particular traits that distinguish them from nonleaders. Others characterize leadership as consisting of a unique set of behaviors that individuals perform in the course of interaction. People such as Mary Kay, of Mary Kay Cosmetics; Lee Iacocca, former CEO of Chrysler; Steven Jobs, founder of Apple Computer; and Bill Gates, president of Microsoft, are considered leaders because of their ability to articulate and inspire a vision that other organizational members believe. Still others define leadership as a special type of relationship between leaders and followers. In this view, leaders are individuals who cultivate close relationships with their followers and personalize those relationships to make each follower feel special and unique. It is difficult to arrive at a single agreed-upon definition of leadership—over 300 definitions have been offered during the past thirty years (Bennis & Nanus, 1985).

Despite the diversity of opinion on what leadership is, most leadership theories reflect our conceptions of how work has traditionally been performed in organizations. The influence of the traditional view of organizational work can be seen in three common assumptions about leadership.

Assumptions about Leadership

Assumption 1: Leadership is equated with a person or a group of persons who perform a particular role in an organization and are typically members of the formal hierarchy. The traditional notion of work in organizations emphasizes an organizational hierarchy, with individuals supervising those below them in the hierarchy. Viewing work as a hierarchically organized system predisposes organizational members and theorists to attribute leadership to a specific individual or group of individuals, and, moreover, implies that leaders in organizations are primarily members of the management hierarchy (Fiedler, 1967; Hersey & Blanchard, 1982; Hosking, 1988; House, 1973). This perspective minimizes the contribution of other employees toward accomplishing a particular goal or task. Moreover, in this view, to study effective leadership one only needs to identify the qualities of an organization's most effective managers. This "managerial" bias toward leadership has recently been criticized because it ignores the possibility that leaders may not be managers and that managers are not necessarily leaders (Zalesnik, 1990).

This underlying assumption of many leadership theories may actually decrease rather than increase employees' motivation by minimizing the importance of their skills and abilities. Nonleader skills and abilities are viewed as unimportant, and employees are viewed as being unable to make a significant contribution to the organization. This kind of attitude can ultimately lead to ineffective work performance.

> An insurance-company clerk confessed to Barbara Garson, author of a book about work, that she OK'd a store owner's policy calling for $5,000 protection against fire and $165,000 against vandalism—exactly the reverse of what she figured the right numbers were. "I was just about to show it to Gloria [the supervisor]," the clerk admitted, "when I figured, Wait a minute! I'm not supposed to read these forms. I'm just supposed to check one column against another. And they do check. So it couldn't be counted as my error." Garson says she must have looked disapproving, because the clerk suddenly got mad. "Goddamn it! They don't explain this stuff to me. I'm not supposed to understand it. I'm supposed to check one column against another." (Case, 1993, p. 82).

Leaders are assumed to be the ones who are accountable for work performance. The unfortunate byproduct of this assumption is that employees may come to view their contributions to the organization as inconsequential and meaningless, and may take less care to do their jobs well.

Why do some experts assume that leadership is confined to a small, select group of individuals within an organization? One reason is that people tend to attribute the effectiveness and performance of an organization to a particular person, rather than to an abstract concept such as organizational structure, organizational policy, or technological innovation. As Pfeffer (1978) and Calder (1977) point out, we sometimes credit leadership for an organizational outcome even when other explanations for the outcome are possible. This type of simplification is inappropriate when it ignores larger situational factors that may enhance or diminish the contribution an individual leader makes to an organization. For example, in a study on the degree to which newly elected mayors were actually responsible for enacting changes in their city government, Salancik and Pfeffer (1977) found prior budgets to be a better predictor of city budgets than the actions of the mayor. In another study comparing the impact of individual leader behavior on the productivity of a small group with the impact of the behavior of the group as a whole, Barge (1989) found that the entire group's behaviors were more accurate predictors of group productivity than the behavior of the individual leader. Both studies suggest that the success or failure of an organization should be attributed not to a single individual's leadership but to certain organizational concepts such as structure.

Assumption 2: Leadership can be reduced to a small set of behaviors or traits that are equally effective across all situations. The traditional view of work has been to identify the key components of a task and to break it down into critical behaviors that must be performed. Similarly, one perspective on leadership aims at simplifying the job known as leadership into a few simple behaviors to be performed. Moreover, if organizational work is clearly defined, compartmentalized, and does not change over time, then leadership may also be viewed as a set of stable traits and behaviors that cut across people, tasks, and situations. Just as workers were viewed as being replaceable within organizations, leaders became interchangeable so long as they either possessed certain traits or mastered particular behaviors associated with that organizational role.

This simplification is typically done in two steps. First, leadership is simplified by classifying several types of individual leadership behaviors under a few categories or styles of leadership. In the 1950s, the Ohio State Leadership Studies attempted to identify the behaviors that consistently characterize leadership. Several hundred leadership behaviors were identified, including scheduling, maintaining performance standards, enforcing work deadlines, offering encouragement, and "needling" subordinates (Schriesheim & Kerr, 1974). Rather than focus on the unique aspects of these individual behaviors, the researchers grouped them into two global dimensions—task orientation and consideration—in an attempt to capture the major dimensions of a leader's behavior. The behaviors mentioned earlier were grouped under task orientation. People-oriented leadership behaviors were grouped under consideration, and included accepting others' ideas, expressing feelings, and praising the contributions of others. When researchers discuss the behaviors of leadership, they often refer to the two dimensions of task orientation and consideration, rather than to the individual behaviors that comprise these two factors.

Second, these reduced dimensions are then tested to see if they are equally effective across different situations. Theorists search for a style or pattern of leadership behavior that is universally acceptable in a variety of situations. For example, the forerunners of participative management, Lewin, Lippit, and White (1939), contend that there are three basic styles of leadership: *autocratic,* in which power and decision making are centralized in the role of the leader; *democratic,* which emphasizes shared decision making and equal power between leaders and followers; and *laissez-faire,* in which little concern is displayed for finishing a job. Of these three styles, the authors consider democratic leadership to be the most effective form of leadership. More recently, Blake and Mouton (1985), in advancing their Managerial Grid, have argued that a leadership style emphasizing a high concern for both task completion and maintenance of positive interpersonal relationships is superior to all other styles. This style, known as Team Management, allegedly is equally effective and equally applicable in all situations.

Leadership behavior is assumed to remain constant over time as leaders perform particular sets of behaviors within and across situations. While it is intuitively appealing that leadership can be boiled down to a core set of behaviors, leadership behavior is much more complex than that. Effective leaders are characterized not so much by their performance of a particular behavioral function, but by the variety of behaviors they exhibit and the messages they send. One of the leadership qualities of President Ronald Reagan, for example, was his concern for people. But to characterize Reagan simply as having been "high in consideration" ignores the various ways in which he manifested this concern. Whether he was answering personal correspondence to citizens, speaking to individual families at the memorial service for those who died in the explosion of the space shuttle *Challenger,* or helping old friends with problems, Reagan was displaying his concern for people at all times. The variety of his behavior was caused by the need to adapt people-oriented behavior to changing circumstances.

Similarly, leaders often change their approach to problems when their initial course of action fails. President John F. Kennedy, for instance, dramatically changed the way he approached the Cuban missile crisis based on his experiences in the failed Bay of Pigs invasion (Janis, 1982). The manner in which Kennedy conducted meetings and organized his advisers during the Cuban Missile Crisis was different from his style during the Bay of Pigs invasion. Thus, to define leadership as a small set of critical behaviors that remain constant across situations discounts the broad behavioral repertoire of skills and abilities leaders often must use to adapt to different situations.

Assumption 3: Changes in needed leadership behaviors and traits can be modeled using a few key situational variables. In response to the charge that traditional models failed to account for situational differences in leadership, theorists began to address leadership's complexity by constructing situational leadership theories. *Situational leadership theory* assumes that leadership behavior must adapt to the situation in order to be effective. From this perspective, a model of leadership is constructed that accounts for changes in leadership behavior that result from the situation. It requires researchers to define the parameters of a situation and to specify what kind of leadership behavior is necessary to manage a particular situation successfully. Some of the situational parameters that researchers have used include the nature of the task (House & Dessler, 1974), the follower's maturity level (Hersey & Blanchard, 1982), and the quality of the leader-follower relationship (Fiedler, 1967).

Whether one can accurately model the complexity of leadership behavior is an issue of debate because of the difficulty in choosing which situational variables to include and which to exclude in the model. According to Fisher (1986):

> The situational contingency approach to leadership is similar to the "it-all-depends" hypothesis. Which leadership function is most effective? It all depends. What is the best style of leadership? It all depends. And it depends on a bewildering array of different variables associated with the situation, the leader, and the other group members. For example, either the leader or the followers could represent one or more of over two thousand different personality types. The task situation of the group could be any one of twenty different task types. The number of potential elements in the physical setting and in functions associated with interactional behavior could also be in the thousands. In short, the contingency approach to leadership seems intuitively reasonable. However, the number of variables which are potentially contingent on leadership and the possible combinations of those variables of situation, leader, and followers are virtually impossible to comprehend. (pp. 203–204)

Given the infinite variety of possible situational factors and the impossibility of including all of them in the model, modeling leadership's complexity is difficult.

Box 1.1
The Case of Texas Wildcat Trucking

You are the head of the Human Resource Department for Texas Wildcat Trucking, referred to as Wildcat for short throughout the southwestern United States. Wildcat has experienced phenomenal growth during the last ten years, expanding from seven hubs in Texas to over twenty-four hubs now located in Texas, New Mexico, Louisiana, Alabama, Oklahoma, and Arkansas. The work force has expanded from roughly seven hundred employees to four thousand employees.

Currently, the company is in the process of adopting a team-based approach to management. Incorporating this approach into the organization means that you will need to train your employees in leadership and select certain employees to serve as team leaders. You are in the midst of creating a leadership training program, and to this end have solicited proposals from several consulting groups. Following are excerpts from these groups' proposals:

Stylemasters, Inc. At Stylemasters, our philosophy is that any employee has the potential to become a leader but must first master the style of a leader. Our program of leadership will train your team leaders in one style—Team Management. Ideally, we feel that you need to identify the one or two team members who are to be the leaders in the company. Our emphasis is on training leaders in how to be leaders, not on how to teach followers to be followers. Once your company selects the employees perceived as leaders, we will work to teach them the principles of Team Management. This style of leadership gives team leaders the ability to treat all problems and situations with an eye toward maintaining good interpersonal relationships and achieving goals. We change the old saying, "Once you've seen one, you've seen them all," to "Once you've mastered our leadership style, you've mastered them all."

Managers 'R Us. The backbone of any organization is management. Without effective managers, organizations cannot succeed. The view of Managers 'R Us is that training should focus on the managers of work groups and work teams. In our training program, we will first identify those managers in your company who are consistently effective. We will then determine the traits and behaviors those managers possess that distinguish them from ineffective managers. Finally, we will custom-tailor a leadership program for your managers based on the characteristics of the effective managers in your organization.

Leadermetrics. The founder of our company, an avid photographer, believes that it is necessary to have good equipment to take a beautiful picture. We apply this philosophy to the teaching of organizational leadership. We have developed a series of highly sophisticated questionnaires, surveys, and interviews that we use to identify effective leadership within an organization. These tools are aimed at answering the question, "What is effective leadership in your company?" We come during a time period selected by your organization to administer our surveys and conduct our interviews. Based on

Box continued

the information we collect, we construct a model of effective leadership that characterizes your company. We then create a training program based on that model.

Strategic Leadership in Companies (SLIC). The function of any organization is to work in order to make a profit. At SLIC, we believe that leaders must help the organization and its members work better. Our training program is unique in that it assumes effective leaders must adapt their leadership behavior to the work at hand. Thus, we have developed a model of leadership that assumes leaders encounter tasks within the organization that vary from being very simple to very difficult. The goal of our program is to teach leaders different strategies—those that are effective for managing simple tasks and those that apply to managing difficult tasks.

ASSIGNMENT 1

Choose what you consider the best proposal for the Human Resource Department. What are the relative strengths and weaknesses of each proposal? If you could combine certain aspects of the proposals, what would they be? Write a brief (one-page) recommendation to the president of Wildcat Trucking.

ASSIGNMENT 2

Each of the proposals conveys its own philosophy about leadership and the functions of leaders. How does each consulting firm manage the complexity of leadership? Does it simplify leadership's complexity, equate leadership with management, attempt to model leadership's complexity, or use a combination of all three? Write a brief (one-page) analysis comparing and contrasting the four statements of philosophy.

(See Box 1.1.) While valuable for recognizing that leadership changes according to the situation, such a perspective has difficulty accounting for the infinite variety of situations that confront leaders. In fact, it poses the exact opposite problem of the first two assumptions. It has the advantages of embracing leadership's complexity, but has the simultaneous problem of trying to account for all the nuances of the leadership situation.

EMBRACING LEADERSHIP'S COMPLEXITY

The changing, chaotic, and complex environment of contemporary organizations requires a view of leadership that is adaptable and flexible. A view of leadership that can treat its complexities is required. Yet our conception of how work is performed in organizations and its influence on our conceptions of leadership in part causes us to simplify leadership as opposed to examining its complexities. The emphasis on breaking down work and leadership into their component parts and then coordinating the parts to produce goods and services equates them with machines. The traditional approach to leadership relies heavily on a mechanistic metaphor that characterizes leadership as another cog in the organizational machinery. Without leadership, the organizational "machine" cannot function. Assuming leadership is performed by only a few organizational members reduces leadership to a part of the machine. The complexity of that part is further reduced by standardizing the types of operations the part performs. Like the regulator of a car engine, leadership is expected to perform a limited and standardized set of functions regardless of time and location, according to the perspective that views leadership as a universal set of behaviors. Once we know the specific kind of machine, as in specifying key situational variables that affect leadership, it is easy to identify the type of part required. The nature of the machine dictates what parts are critical for it to function successfully. Thus, the assumptions discussed above tend to characterize leadership as a process of finding a reliable part that fits into the existing organizational machinery.

Viewing Leadership as a Medium

To understand leadership as a complex behavioral process, Weick (1978) suggests using a *leader-as-medium* metaphor. In this view, leadership mediates between an organization's actions and its performance. Leadership is aimed at helping a company organize its collective action to make sense of its environment and attain desirable goals. Thus, leadership helps organizations mediate information. Within organizations, the sources of information, the meanings assigned to that information, the numerous ways individuals act on that information, and the multiple goals that individuals pursue are all extremely varied. According to Weick, leadership's primary function is to help the organization make sense of its environment through the creation of an organizing system. For example, it is important for the marketing department of an international manufacturing firm to monitor the success of advertising and sales campaigns, but it would be difficult for one person to oversee and monitor the marketing strategy both within the U.S. and in foreign markets. To address this problem, leaders could create a system of organization by assigning members of the marketing department to monitor certain geographical regions and to report their results to the larger group during weekly staff meetings. Such an organizing system could help reduce the complexity of the incoming marketing information and allow the marketing group to make informed decisions.

For leadership to be an effective medium, and for employees to organize themselves into an effective system, leadership must be as complex as the information it is expected to mediate. Ashby's (1968) law of requisite variety, in its simplest version, holds that "only variety can regulate variety." As information becomes more complex, the processes that must be undertaken to make sense of that information and to take necessary action on it also need to be more complex. Tom Peters (1989) puts this idea into lay terms by suggesting organizations "must be as wacky as the environment if [they] are going to survive." The law of requisite variety can be illustrated through an analysis of how a professional golfer and an amateur golfer make sense of the golf course and play the sport. What separates the professional golfer from the amateur is the greater complexity of the former's skills. When encountering a particularly difficult or complex course, the professional is likely to have many more skills on which to draw than the amateur. For example, the professional may be better able to make sense of how wind and other weather conditions can alter a shot and how to adapt the shot to the course. When we say that a professional golfer has "mastered" a course, we mean that the person's knowledge, skills, and abilities exceed the demands presented by the course. Thus, the golfer is in a sense more complex than the course. Similarly, leadership is an effective medium when the complexity of the processes used to collect, interpret, and act on available information is as great as the complexity of the information being processed.

Weick (1978) contends that two types of mediation are instrumental to effective leadership: object mediation and action mediation. *Object mediation,* which is the ability to make sense of information within the environment and to thereby arrive at reasonable and plausible interpretations of it, requires leadership to be "externally constrained," with attention and focus directed toward the environment. Weick emphasizes that the focus of leadership must be directed outward in order for leaders to collect and form detailed impressions about the environment.

Object mediation is like using a contour gauge to make imprints of the environment. A good example of the use of a contour gauge is when locksmiths use wax or clay to take impressions of a key that reflect its contours. Whether leadership is functioning as a good object mediator depends on two factors: (1) the number of elements comprising the gauge and (2) the independence of the elements. A high number of independent elements tends to improve one's ability as an object mediator. Imagine that you are a leader and are asked to conduct a performance appraisal of one of your employees. Your appraisal will depend on several factors—the number of criteria you employ, the performance areas you evaluate, and the relative importance you give to each area. To evaluate an employee's work performance, any number of evaluative criteria may be employed; these may include getting along with co-workers, prompt completion of assignments, managing paperwork, initiative, and amount of absenteeism. Which criteria are employed will directly influence the impression the leader forms of the employee. Moreover, if the various criteria are strongly related, the evaluation may be biased. For instance, if you believe an employee's level of initiative is strongly influenced by how many times that person has been absent from work, little information will be gained about other factors contributing to the level of initiative. The absenteeism rate of the individual directly colors your view of the person's initiative. To avoid bias and create more detailed impressions, it is important to include many elements in the medium and to ensure that they are relatively independent of each other. Object mediation is particularly important because, as the leader-as-medium metaphor maintains, what you believe in is ultimately what you will see. That is, your method of interpretation dictates how you will view a particular situation. Therefore, in order to form accurate impressions and make informed decisions, many loosely related elements are required.

The other form of mediation, *action mediation,* refers to behavioral actions aimed at removing environmental obstacles. To be an effective action mediator, leadership requires a broad behavioral repertoire from which to draw. At this point, leadership shifts from being "externally constrained" to being "internally constrained." Attention shifts from the environment and the forming of impressions to decision making, particularly in regard to actions that need to be taken to manage demands faced by the organization. Similar to object mediation, the key to effective action mediation is possession of a large behavioral repertoire from which leadership can draw. Leadership is not marked by the performance of a particular act; rather, it is characterized by the variety and complexity of the acts it performs. As the situation becomes more complex, leadership also needs to become more complex in terms of its actions, messages, and functions. (See Box 1.2.)

Communication and Leadership

When leadership is viewed as a form of mediation, it is difficult to identify clearly a single style of leadership that is effective across all situations. It is also difficult to distinguish between leader and nonleader functions, and to define leadership as a set of particular traits. Rather, in this view, *leadership* is an interactional process that helps people in organizations manage their environment. Leadership facilitates organizational members' understanding of the obstacles they may face as well as the planning and selecting actions that help the organization accomplish desired goals.

Our particular definition has several implications for the study of leadership. First, leadership is viewed as a behavioral process, with a focus on the overt messages that transpire among members of an organization. The focus for researchers is on studying how individual messages or patterns of messages function to manage the amount of ambiguity within the environment. Second, leadership complexity varies according to the complexity of the environment. To manage complex environments, more complex messages and patterns of messages are required. Leadership's complexity is marked by the number of messages, the variety of functions that individual messages serve, and the variety of message sequences. Third, leadership aims at fulfilling two broad processes: helping the organization make sense of its environment, and helping the organization select actions for pursuing desired goals.

The nature of communication. The mediation view of leadership emphasizes the importance of communication. Leaders must not only know what problems face the organization, they also must be able to communicate their knowledge in a way that is understandable to others. For leadership to be effective, communication must help organizational members reduce the ambiguity of the situation and plan and select actions that help the organization achieve its goals. Individual

Box 1.2
Changing the Image of Leadership

Leaders are typically viewed as being in control of themselves and others, dynamic, and "in charge" of events. These are the images created by definitions of leadership that characterize leaders as decisive and persuasive, able to direct the actions of others and to dominate people within the organization. However, the leadership-as-medium metaphor has different implications for how we view leaders. Karl Weick (1978, pp. 49–58) highlights some of these implications for the behaviors and training of leaders.

1. *The good leader is docile.* Docile people tend to be more externally constrained and more focused on the external environment. By being less decisive and less committed to a course of action, they become better mediums because they are more perceptive.

2. *Docile leaders provide more diverse images to their followers.* Being aware of the variety present in an environment provides leaders the basic inputs to present differing images of organizational life, explanations for previous events, and interpretations of the meaning of organizational activities. According to Weick (1978), "to the extent that those followers thrive on seeing themselves engaged in interesting activities housed in interesting worlds, this leader should be influential" (p. 50).

3. *It is a handicap to be a natural-born leader.* Those who have long viewed themselves as leaders will have little, if any, experience as followers. The result is that these leaders are more limited in their perceptions of the environment and the kinds of images they can create than leaders who also have experience as followers.

4. *Leaders who are good mediums have shorter time horizons.* Good mediums are rooted in the "here and now" and are not as focused on the future. This allows leaders to collect rich impressions of the current environment.

5. *The docile leader is a better controller.* Being docile allows leaders to become better mediums because they are more attuned to listening and receiving information. By being better listeners and receivers of information, they are less likely to give irrelevant or inappropriate directions to employees.

6. *Leadership improvement may involve training in data splitting.* Good leaders have good perception skills; that is, they are able to distinguish between the qualities of the object and the qualities of the medium that may be coloring their view of the object. The ability to distinguish between the qualities of an object that are due to the object itself and those that are due to the medium used to observe it is the basis of the concept of *data splitting.*

7. *Self-acceptance improves medium qualities.* The quality of a medium is degraded when leaders are unable to accept themselves. By deny-

Box continued

ing aspects of their own being and personality they limit the ways in which they can acquire and understand information.

8. *Poetry enhances medium qualities.* Poetry provides insights into the human condition and experience that we are not usually able to articulate or understand. Poetry often juxtaposes images that we ordinarily would not have considered together. In essence, poetry decouples phenomena and allows us to think of elements independently. Thus, reading poetry can improve the quality of the medium.

9. *Medium management is a leadership tactic.* The leadership-as-medium metaphor views medium management as a powerful means of control that is accomplished by "intentionally expanding or reducing the number of elements" present in the medium (Weick, 1978, p. 56). Leaders are able to control the perceptions and actions of others by limiting or enlarging the number of elements used for object and action mediation. The ability of a leader to use medium management depends strongly on the richness of the leader's own medium.

10. *Viewing the leader as a medium intersects crucial issues in organizational theory.* Organizational theory is increasingly concerned with how organizations process and utilize information. The main issue for organizational theorists is determining how organizations can become good mediums in order to comprehend and manage their environment successfully. How leadership helps organizations become better mediums, and how leadership's medium qualities are related to the organization's medium qualities, are important points of intersection between leadership and organizational theory.

messages and interlocked sequences of messages become the primary means through which leadership is exercised. Their primary purpose is to manage the uncertainty and equivocality within the environment. This communication perspective is consistent with that of theorists who define communication as a process of managing uncertainty. Stemming from information theory, this view was first articulated in *The Mathematical Theory of Communication* by Claude Shannon and Warren Weaver (1949). The authors argue that the primary function and defining characteristic of communication is its ability to manage uncertainty.

Communication is the process of managing uncertainty. Although a variety of definitions have been offered for communication, this particular one is useful for several reasons. First, it is sufficiently broad to encompass numerous other definitions. Frank Dance and Carl Larson (1976) document at least 126 definitions of communication that differ in terms of the key components included. Theorists differ in their focus and view of communication in many ways, such as in their views as to whether people share meaning when communicating or whether the message sender really intends to send a message. Viewing communication as an uncertainty-managing process subsumes many competing definitions and diminishes the importance of certain characteristics. For example, the issue of whether communication is intentional diminishes in importance, because uncertainty may be managed knowingly or unknowingly. Second, managing instead of reducing uncertainty allows for communication both to increase and decrease equivocality within the environment. Early information theorists focused on the role communication played in reducing uncertainty. However, there are times when communication is needed to raise the uncertainty level. Eisenberg (1984) points out that, in certain circumstances, communication needs to raise uncertainty in order to encourage creative and innovative thinking among organizational members. Managing rather than reducing uncertainty means that it can be increased or decreased for a particular situation and to a manageable level. Furthermore, the definition is not restricted to managing uncertainty in either task situations or interpersonal relationships. Rather, it recognizes that uncertainty occurs in, and must be managed successfully in, both the task and the relational realms of an organization.

Communication skills. What mechanisms or devices can be used to describe the variety of messages individuals may select from when attempting to manage their environment? Since all situations possess unique characteristics, how can we account for the process through which individuals adapt their messages to a particular situation? The answer involves the concept of *skill.* However, there are many different definitions of skill. Brian Spitzberg and William Cupach (1989) suggest that skill can be thought of at three different levels of abstraction:

1. *Molecular level:* Skill at the molecular level is defined as a single microbehavior that performs a specific function. We can assess an individual's skill level by determining whether that person conveys or does not convey a particular message during interaction. We can say an individual possesses the skill of asking open-ended questions during team meetings if he or she is able to direct such questions toward other team members.
2. *Molar level:* At the molar level, a number of molecular skills are categorized as part of the same general type or class. For example, the molecular skills of asking team members for clarification or elaboration of comments, and of soliciting others' opinions, can be grouped under the general molar skill of seeking information.
3. *Process level:* Unlike the molecular and molar skill levels, which focus on the overt performance of a skill during actual discussion or interaction, the process level of skill examines cognitive and behavioral processes both before and during the performance of a skill.

This book adopts the view that *skill* is the specific ability required to perform a given task competently. A comprehensive explanation of skillful performance must include the types of communication processes, strategies, and messages that leaders may employ to help the organization make sense of and adapt to its environment. It is not enough for leaders to have the ability to assess and determine what actions they must execute to facilitate goals; they must also be able to perform those actions. Skill encompasses the notion that leaders must be knowledgeable about decoding and encoding information within organizations. *Decoding* refers to how individuals obtain information and diagnose situations, whereas *encoding* points to how individuals convey messages to aid the group in overcoming environmental obstacles. Leaders must also have a broad behavioral repertoire from which to draw when constructing messages aimed at helping others encode and decode information.

The Nature of Organizations and Organizing

Leadership is a process of helping organizations adjust to their environment. This view of leadership raises two questions: (1) What is an organization? and (2) How does leadership help an organization adapt to its environment?

Traditionally, the organization has been viewed from a systems perspective; that is, as a distinct whole comprised of smaller but related parts. The smaller parts, which make up the larger organizational system, include small groups of people—work teams, task forces, committees, and ad hoc committees. Sometimes called subsystems, the smaller parts are composed of even smaller parts—people who are linked together to form a distinct whole known as a dyad. The use of the term *organization* connotes a structure that can be easily identified. However, as Weick (1974) contends, such structures are really patterns of behavior and events: "The word, *organization,* is a noun and it is also myth. If one looks for an organization one will not find it. What will be found is that there are events, linked together, that transpire within concrete walls and these sequences, their pathway, their timing, are the forms we erroneously make into substances when we talk about an organization" (p. 358). In this sense, then, organizations are characterized by repetitive, interlocked sequences of behaviors and events.

Leadership helps an organization adapt to its environment by eliminating ineffective patterns of behavior and creating new ones that aid in the processing and managing of information. In addition, the relationship between individuals and groups within the organization must be addressed. Leadership must help individuals and groups create systems of organizing that contribute to the overall ability of the organization to manage its environmental challenges. According to systems theory, changes in lower-level systems (individuals and groups) can have dramatic effects on higher-level systems (organizations). For example, organizations that have adopted an autonomous work-team approach, in which groups are in charge of their own goals and of the methods for accomplishing them, find that allowing groups to create their own schedules has tremendous impact on the overall productivity of the organization.

The focus of this book is on how leadership and individuals performing leadership roles help the organizing process of people within organizations. On the one hand, leadership maintains an outward focus, as it must be attuned to information about the organizational environment. On the other hand, leadership must look inward—to groups of organizational members—in order to help coordinate the activities of organizational members and thereby to make sense of and act on the information obtained.

A COMMUNICATION SKILL MODEL OF LEADERSHIP

Researchers who view leadership as a form of mediation attempt to explain how individuals become more complex and skillful organizers. Metcalfe (1982) suggests that leaders may become skillful organizers by being highly perceptive and open-minded about various situations (object mediation) and by enlarging their behavioral repertoires (action mediation). As a result, leadership as a form of mediation focuses on the basic decoding and encoding skills that allow individuals to act in a more complex and skillful fashion. In this case, the task is helping the organizing process of groups and organizations to overcome environmental obstacles. The general assumption is that competent leaders are skillful performers who decode and encode messages that help an organization achieve its goals.

Consistent with Weick's (1979) model of organizing, a comprehensive leadership model must address the two broad processes of decoding and encoding aimed at completing the task of organizing. The leader's competence ultimately will be determined by the leader's performance—the degree to which others perceive the leader's communication as appropriate and effective. The general processes of encoding and decoding are associated with specific skills that facilitate the collection and interpretation of information and the construction of a system of work that allows the organization to achieve its goals. This model of leadership is illustrated in Figure 1.1.

It is important to remember that leadership is an interactional process that involves all organizational members. A reciprocal relationship must exist between leaders and followers in order for their relationship to be meaningful. Those in leadership positions must recognize that their purpose is to help organize the collective participation of all organizational members. This model may be interpreted as outlining the necessary skills and processes that individuals in leadership roles must possess. Leaders need to assess the situations they face and encode messages to help the organization remove environmental obstacles. In addition, leaders must recognize that they need to involve other organizational members in the decoding and encoding process for the collective system to make sense of its environment. It is this process of ongoing participation by leaders and followers that comprises leadership.

Decoding and Organizing

Leaders are good object mediators when they are sensitive to the information environment and are able to process that information effectively. In order to gauge the information environment successfully, leaders must be exposed to or in contact with the organization's values, beliefs, and norms; be sensitive to the nuances of organizational events; and be able to examine organizational events from different perspectives.

Networking. *Networking* involves establishing relationships with other organizational members. Initially, effective leaders must construct imprints of

FIGURE 1.1 Model of Communication Skills and Leadership

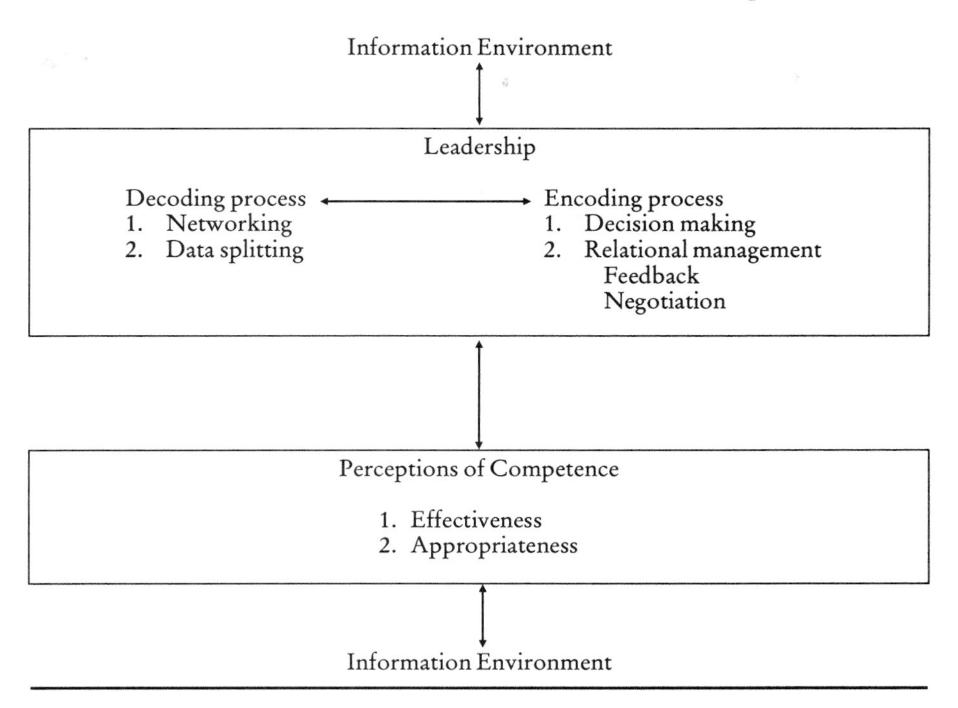

their environment in order to identify the obstacles that may impede the organization's goals. Networking is a skill that facilitates the gathering and processing of information. By successfully networking with others in the organization, leaders are able to collect valuable information about the problems confronting the organization and the actions that may be taken to solve them. Networking also encourages leaders to enlarge their knowledge of the organizational environment and its members as well as to understand the processes that are considered appropriate within the organization (Hosking, 1988). This enhanced knowledge base thereby allows leaders to identify problems, develop solutions, and select and implement policy efficiently and effectively.

Effective networking is strategic in the sense that leaders gain knowledge of central problems in need of resolution, enabling them to make sense of organizational activity and to distinguish between genuine and "pseudo" problems. This distinction is critical to organizational effectiveness, as treating a "pseudo" problem as a real problem can lead to negative consequences. For example, an organization may traditionally experience a decrease in profits during the summer quarter. The leader of a work team who lacks experience and is not well socialized might view this as a pressing problem and attempt to remedy it. The more experienced team members may resent the leader's actions because they recognize that the company's profits are cyclical and tend to be lower in the summer.

For them, a temporary drop in the company's profits is a "pseudo" versus a real problem.

Data splitting. *Data splitting* is a skill that helps leaders attend to the individual, fine-grained details of a situation. Leaders exhibit this skill when they are critical of new information and its relationship to the existing scheme of organizational activity. Leaders "split" the incoming data into smaller units to account for the uniqueness of the situation.

Through data splitting, leaders can often avoid problems associated with using routine ways of decoding information within the organization. Individuals use "scripts" to form interpretations of organizational events. During their membership in the organization they develop personal scripts for interpreting events and planning subsequent actions. These scripts are then used to help both individuals and groups within the organization make sense of the environment. Some organizations have so-called "hazing rituals," whereby the more experienced members tease the newcomers. Such rituals may become part of the initiation and socialization process of an organization. Organizational members who are aware of the hazing ritual may use the script governing it to interpret the teasing as a short-term hurdle rather than a personal affront.

Although scripts can be useful in reducing the complexity of decision making, their overuse can cause leaders to neglect the subtle differences among particular problems or situations (Gioia & Poole, 1984). Leaders who rely too heavily on organizational scripts tend to overlook the uniqueness of events and thereby fail to interpret and classify those events adequately. In a study of the effects of implicit leadership theories or prototypes, it was found that people tend to attribute certain types of behaviors to leaders even when those behaviors are not exhibited, provided the leader performs some behaviors characteristic of leadership (Cronshaw & Lord, 1987; J. S. Phillips, 1984; Phillips & Lord, 1981, 1986). For example, some followers view leaders as supportive and as asking many questions. If the followers classify a person as a leader, they may errroneously perceive that person as being supportive and as asking many questions. They may attribute these traits to the leader even if he or she does not exhibit the behaviors because the association between leadership and these behaviors is a fixed expectation in the followers' minds. Similarly, leaders who rely on predetermined organizational scripts may tend to encode strong interrelated images about organizational activities. This, in turn, may lead to assumptions about what elements to examine in a situation, the causal relationships among elements, decision making, appropriate actions, and the ordering of elements. Leaders may wrongly attribute certain qualities to a situation or problem, or they may classify a problem on the basis of a few details and neglect to consider the unique characteristics of that problem. By using data splitting, leaders can avoid such pitfalls.

Encoding and Organizing

Weick (1978) argues that, in order to form rich and diverse impressions of their environment, effective leaders should initially focus on object mediation.

Networking and data-splitting skills can assist leaders in forming complex and differentiated impressions. Once leaders analyze and make sense of the situation, they can focus on action mediation—selecting actions that will facilitate the removal of obstacles. In order to be effective action mediators, however, leaders must possess two important skills: decision making and relational management.

Decision making. Leadership helps the organization determine the actions it must take to accomplish tasks and overcome environmental obstacles. Action mediation involves choosing from various alternative courses of action those that will maximize potential task completion. As Mumford (1986) points out, leadership always involves making decisions that will contribute to attaining certain goals.

It is the leader's job to help the organization make appropriate decisions. Leaders must help fulfill five basic functions that lead to effective *decision making:* (1) establish a set of operating procedures, (2) analyze problems, (3) generate solutions, (4) evaluate solutions, and (5) determine methods for implementing solutions. If the leader encodes messages that help the organization fulfill these basic decision-making requirements, the organization is more likely to make appropriate decisions.

Relational management. A key component of leadership, *relational management* involves managing the interpersonal relations among fellow workers. As organizations develop, conflicts arise over the kinds of roles people will assume in the organization and over the ways to deal with problems. Leaders must help other organizational members to *negotiate* their roles and to resolve the conflicts that emerge. Sometimes these conflicts may cause workers to become less motivated and to lose their sense of loyalty and commitment to the organization. Leaders should be prepared for this possibility. In order to manage the relational aspects of groups successfully, leaders need to be able to manage conflict and to provide *feedback* regarding an individual's actions.

Assessing Leadership Competence

Ultimately, leadership is enacted through communication. Although the processes of decoding and encoding information help leaders identify behaviors that facilitate goal achievement, leaders may not be skilled at performing those behaviors well. Their inability to translate a selected behavior into appropriate action may be due to a lack of practice, inexperience, or fatigue (McFall, 1982). For example, many organizations promote morale and comradeship among employees through award ceremonies and other special occasions geared toward recognizing high-performing workers. Leaders who are inexperienced or fatigued may not be able to conduct these ceremonies in a way that is meaningful to employees.

When we speak of a competent leader or competent leadership, we typically mean that the individual is able to perform a particular behavior successfully. Skilled behavior is marked by two qualities: it is appropriate and it is effective.

Theorists define inappropriate behavior as behavior that is unnecessarily abrasive, intense or bizarre, and nonsocial. In contrast, skilled behavior that is *appropriate* conforms to the existing organizational norms, myths, and metaphors. For example, the computer manufacturer Data General encourages so-called "skunkworks"—small work teams that literally "hide out" from the formal organization, typically at an isolated location, and are expected to develop innovative products under severe time restrictions. Within such organizations, it is acceptable to obtain needed resources by bypassing the established hierarchy and contacting sources outside the organization to obtain parts and personnel. Leadership in a "skunkwork" is considered appropriate when it violates the normal rules and procedures of the organization. However, in most organizations, leadership is expected to conform to established procedures in order to accomplish goals.

The other quality of skilled behavior is *effectiveness.* Organizing serves an instrumental function by facilitating individuals, groups, and organizations toward achievement of goals, and is consistent with interpersonal definitions that characterize effectiveness as the achievement of interpersonal goals (Argyris, 1968; Spivack, Platt, & Shure, 1976; Breen, Donlon, & Whitaker, 1977; Foote & Cottrell, 1955; Fitts, 1970). From an organizational perspective, leadership may be considered effective when it allows the organization to achieve any of a number of valued organizational outcomes, such as profit, high return on investment, customer satisfaction, efficiency, and productivity. Hence, for leaders to be perceived as skilled, their actions must be both appropriate and effective.

THE ARTFUL NATURE OF LEADERSHIP

The stable and predictable business environments of the early to mid-twentieth century have been replaced by volatile, complex, and chaotic environments. The trend toward increasingly complex environments shows no signs of abating, and leaders can only anticipate that the challenges and obstacles they will face in years to come will be greater and more diverse as opposed to fewer and simpler. In this situation the primary task of leaders will be to continually refine, develop, and modify the organizing systems if their companies are to maintain their viability. To some people, these challenges may appear overwhelming and incapable of being managed successfully. In fact, people both within and without organizations are already voicing their frustrations in dealing with their complex environment. The following letter typifies these feelings.

> Dear Ann Landers:
>
> I am a 23-year-old college graduate (business major). I don't feel pressure to speak for my generation, but I know what I feel.
>
> People wonder about us. They say we are materialistic, just out for ourselves. They say we are apathetic. It must go deeper than that. Teens are committing suicide in record numbers. What is wrong with us? Just look around.
>
> The media reach far and wide, bringing stories from all over the

> world. We have overpopulation, the environment is being destroyed, our natural resources are dwindling. People are oppressed, starving and killing each other. There are enough weapons to blow up the world we live in 40 times! AIDS continues to spread and there is no vaccine and no cure.
>
> On the home front, the United States is faltering. The national debt is at a noncomprehensible level. Homeless people freeze to death on the streets. Gang violence, alcoholism and drug abuse are rampant. Teens are having babies out of wedlock and many will never get off welfare.
>
> Not many people my age will be able to own a house, no matter what their educational level or whom they work for. Takeovers and mergers ruin the hopes of job security. Many of us expect to have a lower standard of living than our parents. The U.S. is losing its edge in the world market.
>
> It could be hopeless. But I love this country, and I think there is hope. I don't believe my generation is apathetic. We just don't know where to start.
>
> —Waiting for Guidance in California

To deal successfully with the problems of the future, leaders are going to need to be more complex in their behaviors. They are going to have to be on the lookout for shifts in their environment, and they are going to have to incorporate the lessons they have learned from the past and develop new ways of leading based on past experiences.

The key to the leadership of the future will be the ability to coordinate diverse groups of people over differing tasks in a changing and unstable environment. Leadership is a complex process that requires individuals, groups, and organizations to be as complex as the environment of which they are a part. As a result, leadership cannot be defined merely as a list of step-by-step techniques that will always be successful. Although it may appear from the preceding discussion that the information environment, decoding, and encoding entail a list of steps leaders must follow to be perceived as competent, this arbitrary ordering of topics was selected merely for ease of presentation. Figure 1.1 illustrates how the four elements of leadership are interconnected. For example, the organizational environment influences encoding, decoding, and standards for assessing competent performance. The environment, as reflected in the organization's myths, stories, and culture, provides data that influences how information is decoded. An organization's culture structures its priorities, particularly the kinds of actions it takes and the decisions it makes. An organization's environment sets its standards for evaluating performance in terms of profit, efficiency, commitment, and satisfaction. Similarly, how we make sense of our environment directly influences decision making by clearly formulating the nature of the problem, as well as influencing performance. A parallel can be drawn between individual leadership performance and the leadership performance of an entire organization. If organizations have not made good sense of their external environment, they may perform poorly. Bourgeois (1985) notes that organizations tend to be more productive when top-level management perceives the external environment accurately. The recent troubles IBM has incurred, for example, are due in part to a misperception of the business environment. By believing that what customers wanted was faster and more powerful mainframe computers, IBM neglected a lucrative market in personal home computers.

Leadership in many ways is like the art of painting. When confronted with a blank canvas, the artist has a vision or an image of what is to be portrayed on that canvas. The artist begins to apply paint to create that image, selecting certain colors, mixing and combining those colors, and brushing the shapes onto the canvas. During this process, an earlier application of color may not please the artist's eye, so a new color or shading may be added. Once the painting is completed, others may assess its beauty and aesthetic value. Although most people cannot match the artistic level of a Van Gogh, Picasso, Cézanne, or Monet, everyone has the ability to obtain the basic raw materials used by such artists and to master some of the basic skills of painting. Similarly, leadership is difficult to master and some leaders are better than others; however, all potential leaders can master some basic leadership techniques. Such mastery does not guarantee effectiveness. The master artist is separated from others by the ability to create a variety of patterns.

The purpose of this book is to familiarize you with some of the communication skills that enable leaders to be more effective. It is important to remember that learning a skill is not the same as mastering a particular behavior to perform in a given situation. Learning the skills of networking, data splitting, decision making, feedback, and negotiation is not to be confused with mastering a particular style or behavior. Rather, truly skillful performance depends upon initially selecting a message, technique, or strategy that is adapted to the requirements of a given situation, and subsequently changing it if it fails to resolve the problem at hand. The presentation of skills and their associated messages and techniques is descriptive as opposed to prescriptive. The goal is to outline some of the options leaders may select from when leading organizations and groups. The underlying premise of this book is that through the development of a broad repertoire of encoding and decoding skills, leaders will be better able to adapt their behavior to the unique challenges of a given situation.

The basic organization of the book reflects the model of leadership presented in Figure 1.1. Chapter 2 provides a review of the existing approaches to the study of leadership. Chapters 3 and 4 examine how leadership may facilitate the decoding of information. In Chapters 5 and 6, issues regarding how leadership mediates actions to resolve problems are addressed. Chapters 7 and 8 then focus on how power and uncertainty within organizations can influence leadership. Finally, assessing leadership competence is the focus of Chapter 9.

SUMMARY

The current business environment is more chaotic, volatile, and complex than ever before. As such, it requires leadership that is highly adaptive, innovative, and flexible. The business environment also requires views of leadership that emphasize its complexity and adaptive nature. However, most traditional perspectives of leadership view its complexity as a problem rather than as a strength that can be exploited. Some theorists attempt to manage leadership's complexity by simplifying it. When such theorists equate leadership with management, identify a specific set of behaviors that characterize effective leadership in all situations, or try to classify the variety of behaviors that leaders use by means of a few select dimensions, they simplify the complexity of leadership. Conversely, when theorists match a specific set of leadership styles to a specific situation, they are trying to model the complexity of leadership. Unfortunately, providing a general theory that identifies a specific leadership style for a particular situation is difficult because of the numerous personality, task, and organizational factors that influence the acceptability of a given leadership style.

Rather than attempt to simplify or model the complexity of leadership as a means of understanding it, this book adopts the view that a new perspective of leadership is needed—one that embraces its complexity. This book views leadership as a form of mediation. That is, leadership mediates among an organization's environment, the collective action of employees, and performance outcomes. Leaders create a system of organizing that allows organizational members to recognize and make sense of obstacles present in the environment, as well as to take appropriate action to overcome those obstacles. For leadership to be a successful medium, it must be as complex as the environment it attempts to manage. If the environment is more complex than the organizing system developed by leaders, the organization will fail to survive.

Leaders must develop communication skills that allow them to vary their behavior according to the situation. They must be skilled in both object mediation and action mediation. Object mediation involves collecting information to form impressions of the environment. For leaders to become skilled at object mediation, they must initially expose themselves to their environment and then try to make sense of the information they collect. By networking and using other techniques that allow data to be split apart and examined, leaders can become better object mediators. Action mediation occurs when leaders take actions that allow them to remove obstacles present in the environment. To be effective action mediators, leaders must make decisions and manage relational problems that surface in the organization. Decision making, feedback, and negotiation are the skills that make leaders effective action mediators.

It is important to remember that only variety can regulate variety. In other words, leadership is effective only when it is as complex as its environment. The communication skills discussed in this chapter are not precise specifications of what leaders should convey in a given situation. Rather, as the following chapters point out, leaders need a variety of message strategies that they can choose from when networking, data splitting, making decisions, or managing relational issues. While the core skills presented provide some general guidance as to the kinds of behaviors that allow leaders to manage their environment successfully, it is not possible to specify the specific message strategy that will always be associated with a specific skill. The complex nature of leadership requires leaders to develop a repertoire of message strategies that can be adapted to the unique qualities of different situations.

QUESTIONS AND APPLICATIONS

1. On a blank piece of paper, brainstorm as many adjectives as possible to describe a leader. How many of the adjectives are active? How many reflect the docile nature of leadership? Explain why you view leadership as an active or a docile activity.

2. To improve the quality of leadership in area business and volunteer organizations, the local Chamber of Commerce is sponsoring a year-long seminar on leadership. It is limited to twenty-five citizens. As part of the application process, you are asked to answer the following question: "Briefly describe what leadership is to you." How would you answer this question?

3. Think about situations in which you find it (a) relatively easy to lead and (b) difficult to lead. What factors make the first situation easy? What factors make the second situation difficult? Why are certain situations more complex in terms of leadership than others?

4. For a situation in which you find leadership difficult, list the steps you think you would need to take to be a more effective leader. Then do the same for a situation in which you find leadership relatively simple. Compare the two lists. Do you need to talk to more people in one of the situations? Is one more complex than the other?

5. Assume you are preparing a networking training program for leaders, part of which will include a handout with the headings shown on the next page. How would you complete the handout? How would you define the global concept of networking? How many different behaviors can you list that help or hurt networking? How do these behaviors relate to skill level? Which portions of the handout tap into the molar and molecular skill levels?

LEADERSHIP AND NETWORKING

Definition of networking:

Behaviors that help networking:

Behaviors that hurt networking:

Chapter 2
Traditional Views of Leadership

> It was announced that the Center was to present a world premier of a new piece of music. Had you been a member of the audience that night, here is what you would have seen.
>
> When the curtains opened, a man walked on stage carrying a glass box supported by four legs, set the box down, and walked off stage.
>
> A man then walked on stage with a can of paint and a paint brush and painted a musical staff on each side of the box. He then painted the words *arco, pizzicato, fortissimo,* and *pianissimo* on each side, and then walked off.
>
> A man then walked out with a pitcher of water, poured the water into the glass box, and walked off.
>
> Four men in tuxedos walked out on the stage, two of them had violins, the third had a viola, and the fourth a cello. They also carried folding chairs. They opened the chairs, sat down on them, and each man faced a different side of the glass box.
>
> A man then came on stage with a can and poured its contents into the glass box. The can contained six black goldfish. As the goldfish started to swim around inside the tank, they lined themselves up with the music staff through which the musicians were looking. The musicians played the notes they saw as the fish were moving, and that was the new piece of music.
>
> *(Weick, 1989, p. 243)*

Leadership facilitates peoples' understanding of the goals and problems facing organizations and coordinates their joint activity to meet those challenges. The process of leading is similar to the actions performed by the men who set the stage for the musicians. The man who placed the music staff and score on the box provided a system to help the musicians interpret the subsequent movements of the goldfish. Without the interpretive act of drawing the musical staff and indicating the way in which the notes were to be played, there would have been only a clear box filled with water and black goldfish swimming about. The man who poured the goldfish into the box provided the prompts for the musicians to play their notes and to weave those notes into a piece of music. The example illustrates that leadership may be performed by different individuals. It also demonstrates how leadership helps people interpret an environment by providing messages that coordinate a group's activity.

In both music and leadership, notes or messages guide us along a path toward accomplishing an overall objective—whether that is completing a piece of music or achieving some goal. Intuitively, it makes sense that communication is the medium through which leadership occurs. Without communication to aid us in interpreting our environment or to move us toward our final destination, leadership cannot occur. This view of leadership emphasizes the importance of communication as the primary mechanism through which leadership takes place. However, the full potential of communication—as a force that creates and shapes our environment and that allows us to coordinate our actions—has not been fully explored in many contemporary theories of leadership. To understand the complex relationship between leadership and communication, we must first examine how existing leadership theories view communication.

A FRAMEWORK FOR VIEWING LEADERSHIP

Although it is difficult to identify the similarities and differences among existing leadership theories because of their large numbers, Arthur Jago (1982) provides a useful system for classifying them according to two central assumptions. First, the theories can be distinguished by the type of explanatory device they use to define leadership. Leadership theorists typically use traits or behaviors to explain leadership. *Traits* are underlying physical, cognitive, social, or communicative characteristics with which individuals are born and that remain with them throughout life. Theorists who rely on traits to define leadership suggest that certain people become leaders because they possess specific traits or qualities. *Behaviors* are the overt messages uttered or transmitted by leaders. From this perspective, individuals become leaders because they perform certain unique leadership behaviors.

The other assumption that Jago (1982) uses to differentiate leadership theories is whether they view leadership as universal or situational. Leadership theories are considered universal when they assume that a particular set of leadership traits or behaviors will remain effective across situations. A single set of traits or behaviors characterizes leadership because situational factors are not believed to influence the kinds of traits and behaviors required to manage others. In contrast, leadership theories are situational when they maintain that leaders possess different traits or adapt their behavior to different situations. In other words, who a leader must be or what a leader must do changes according to the situation. A leader may need to exhibit more task-oriented behavior when the task is ambiguous or more relationally oriented behavior when the task is clear.

The two assumptions yield the four leadership perspectives illustrated in Figure 2.1: (1) universal trait theory, (2) universal style theory, (3) contingency trait theory, and (4) situational behavior theory. In addition, since Jago's review, a

FIGURE 2.1 Typology of Leadership Perspectives

Context and Leadership	*Explanation for Leadership*: Traits	Behaviors
Universal	Universal Trait Theory	Universal Style Theory
Situational	Contingency Trait Theory	Situational Behavior Theory

Source: Adapted from A. G. Jago (1982), Leadership: Perspectives in theory and research, *Management Science, 28,* 315–336.

fifth leadership theory has emerged that is not readily captured in this typology—transformational theory (see page 52).

Universal Trait Theory

The *universal trait theory* of leadership was particularly popular during the 1930s and 1940s, when many studies attempted to identify the personal attributes of leaders. Their goal was to uncover the physical, personality, and social characteristics as well as the knowledge, skills, and abilities that enabled individuals to acquire and maintain leadership roles. Effective leaders possessed not only a higher number of particular traits than followers, but the proper "balance" of traits as well. This meant that leaders needed to have an appropriate amount of a given trait. For example, Ghiselli (1963) found that effective leaders were moderately intelligent, whereas ineffective leaders had either very low or very high intelligence. Furthermore, the proper balance of traits was viewed as the possession of two or more traits that served to moderate one another. A highly aggressive leader, for example, would need a high level of interpersonal sensitivity to moderate the aggressiveness. Otherwise, the leader would act aggressively without concern for the feelings of others. Conversely, leaders would be viewed as a "champion" of followers' beliefs and causes when they adopted an aggressive stance that took into account the feelings of their followers.

Early research on leadership traits focused on identifying the abilities and characteristics of leaders. General abilities—such as intelligence, knowledge, and technical competence—along with personality characteristics—such as alertness, emotional control, extroversion, initiative, insightfulness, integrity, originality,

Box 2.1
Is Universal Trait Theory Valid?

Several researchers contend that it is premature to dismiss the contributions of universal trait theory to understanding leadership. Summarizing numerous trait theory studies, Lord, De Vader, and Alliger (1986) argue that the traits of dominance, intelligence, and masculinity-femininity consistently predict leadership emergence. Kenny and Zaccaro (1983) reinforce the importance of leadership traits, arguing that "persons who are consistently cast in the leadership role possess the ability to perceive and predict variations in group situations and pattern their own approaches accordingly. Such leaders may be highly competent in reading the needs of their constituencies and altering their behaviors to more effectively respond to these needs" (p. 683). It is the ability to read and react to social situations that interests those who study communication. It is important to articulate those traits that allow persons to decipher communicative cues within a variety of situations and construct actions that are consistent with situational demands. One trait that may influence a leader's ability to encode and decode communication is communication apprehension. James McCroskey (1993) defines *communication apprehension* as the fear or anxiety associated with real or anticipated interactions. Complete the following Personal Report of Communication Apprehension-24 (PRCA-24), which is intended to measure an individual's degree of communication apprehension.

INSTRUCTIONS

This instrument is composed of twenty-four statements concerning your feelings about communication with other people. Please indicate in the space provided the degree to which you agree or disagree with each statement—by noting whether you:

5 strongly disagree
4 disagree
3 are undecided
2 agree
1 strongly agree

There are no right or wrong answers. Many of the statements are similar to other statements. Do not be concerned about this. Work quickly in order to record your first impressions.

_____ **1.** I dislike participating in group discussions.
_____ **2.** Generally, I am comfortable while participating in a group discussion.
_____ **3.** I am tense and nervous while participating in group discussions.
_____ **4.** I like to get involved in group discussions.
_____ **5.** Engaging in a group discussion with new people makes me tense and nervous.

Box continued

_____ 6. I am calm and relaxed while participating in group discussions.
_____ 7. Generally, I am nervous when I have to participate in a meeting.
_____ 8. Usually, I am calm and relaxed while participating in meetings.
_____ 9. I am very calm and relaxed when I am called on to express an opinion at a meeting.
_____ 10. I am afraid to express myself at meetings.
_____ 11. Communicating at meetings usually makes me uncomfortable.
_____ 12. I am very relaxed when answering questions at a meeting.
_____ 13. While participating in a conversation with a new acquaintance, I feel very nervous.
_____ 14. I have no fear of speaking up in conversation.
_____ 15. Ordinarily, I am very tense and nervous in conversations.
_____ 16. Ordinarily, I am very calm and relaxed in conversations.
_____ 17. While conversing with a new acquaintance, I feel very relaxed.
_____ 18. I'm afraid to speak up in conversations.
_____ 19. I have no fear of giving a speech.
_____ 20. Certain parts of my body feel very tense and rigid while I am giving a speech.
_____ 21. I feel relaxed while giving a speech.
_____ 22. My thoughts become confused and jumbled when I am giving a speech.
_____ 23. I face the prospect of giving a speech with confidence.
_____ 24. While giving a speech, I get so nervous that I forget facts I really know.

SCORING

The PRCA-24 allows you to compute an overall communication apprehension score and provides a summary of your apprehension in four specific communication situations: group, meeting, dyadic, and public.

Group = 18 + scores for items 2, 4, and 6; – scores for items 1, 3, and 5.
Your group score = _______

Meeting = 18 + scores for items 8, 9, and 12; – scores for items, 7, 10, and 11.
Your meeting score = _______

Dyadic = 18 + scores for items 14, 16, and 17; – scores for items 13, 15, and 18.
Your dyadic score = _______

Public = 18 + scores for items 19, 21, and 23; – scores for items 20, 22, and 24.
Your public score = _______

Overall Communication Apprehension (CA) = Add your group, meeting, dyadic, and public scores.

Overall CA score = _______

INTERPRETING THE SCORE

Low CA Overall score is less than 55. Low CAs talk a great deal; they even talk with people when they are not particularly motivated to talk.

High CA Overall score is greater than 83. High CAs are more withdrawn in conversation and appear tense and shy.

Moderate CA Overall score is between 55 and 83. Moderate CAs recognize that there are times to talk and times when they should not talk. Their level of participation in conversation varies.

DISCUSSION ISSUES

1. What is the relationship between communication apprehension and leadership? Are effective leaders low, moderate, or high in CA? Is flexibility in communication associated with low, moderate, or high levels of CA? How does communication apprehension influence the acquisition and production of communication?
2. Do communicative traits such as apprehension overcome the limitations associated with universal trait theory? Explain.

Source: J. C. McCroskey (1993). *Introduction to rhetorical communication* (6th ed.). Englewood Cliffs, NJ: Prentice-Hall.

self-confidence, and a sense of humor—represent some of the traits investigated during the early twentieth century. More recently, as Gary Yukl (1989) observes, the focus of trait theory has shifted from documenting personality traits and general intelligence to identifying the motivations and specific skills of leaders. The new focus of research suggests that leaders are motivated by strong needs for power and achievement and to a lesser degree a need for affiliation (McClelland & Boyatzis, 1982; Stahl, 1983). This combination of needs prompts leaders to empower rather than dominate followers, to build up rather than tear down the organization, and to value rather than downplay the contributions of followers. Dianne Hosking and Ian Morley (1988) contend that effective leaders must be skilled at networking and decision making, whereas Boyatzis (1982) argues that leaders must be technically skilled to execute their role appropriately. In a review of trait theory, Shelly Kirkpatrick and Edwin Locke (1991) contend that drive, motivation, honesty and integrity, self-confidence, cognitive ability, and knowledge of the business do matter for contemporary leaders. Despite the shift in focus, the traits and skills identified by recent studies are remarkably similar to those from past studies. Effective leaders are still viewed as self-confident, highly motivated, emotionally mature, and able to tolerate stress. (See Box 2.1 on pages 31–33.)

Universal Style Theory

In 1990, Tom Landry, the first head football coach for the National Football League's Dallas Cowboys, was unceremoniously fired. Amid the uproar and controversy, several associates and fans paid tribute to Landry's leadership and coaching. One of the most eloquent tributes was offered by Tex Schramm, former president of the organization.

> Class is created and perpetuated by the individuals who established it. You can go out to the Cowboy Complex and say, "Boy, this is a great place." But the feeling for the organization comes from the people inside that complex.
>
> It's one thing to be a winner. A lot of teams become winners and they come and go. It's great to have that as your goal. But it's something special to be a winner and accomplish this with a special sense of style and class. That's what makes one team unique and another just a winner. That *style* and class was personified by Tom Landry. (St. John, 1989, p. 24)

Schramm felt that what distinguished the Dallas Cowboys from other winning teams was Landry's leadership style, which inspired great performance, loyalty, and commitment among his players.

The *universal style theory* of leadership focuses on a set of individual styles or behaviors that are further classified into more generalized dimensions or groups. Landry's style was a hands-on approach in terms of the amount of personal attention and detail he devoted to player recruitment, training, and performance. Although behavioral styles may be influenced by personality traits and intellectual abilities, the focus of the universal style approach is to characterize patterns in people's behavior. For example, the individual behaviors of smiling, maintaining good eye contact, and nodding when listening to someone talk characterize an attentive communication style. Leadership styles refer to conventional patterns of behavior, such as task-oriented versus relationally oriented behavior. A universal style approach contends that a single leadership style can be equally effective across situations. Over the past sixty years, five lines of leadership style research have emerged.

Functionalist views of leadership. The basic premise of the *functionalist* view is that leaders perform particular behavioral functions that help organizations accomplish goals. A functionalist view attempts to identify the particular functions that enable people to create and maintain leadership roles. Moreover, functionalists argue that these leadership functions remain the same regardless of different personality types, groups, and tasks. The search for functions unique to leadership has generated a number of typologies for functional leadership behavior. Despite the functionalist belief that leadership functions can be identified, the number of leadership functions varies greatly among researchers. For example, the number of behavioral functions identified by researchers ranges from four to twenty-six (Cartwright & Zander, 1968; Bowers & Seashore, 1966).

Regardless of the number of leadership functions, they may be classified into three general categories. First, behavior can be characterized as performing a *task function*. Behaviors serving task functions facilitate the work of a group or organization. In a classic study of group roles, Benne and Sheats (1948) identify such functions as initiating, seeking and giving opinions or information, elaborating existing ideas, and orientation. Second, behaviors may serve a *relational function* by maintaining an appropriate interpersonal atmosphere within the group. Relationally oriented behaviors can provide encouragement, harmonize group feelings, set standards, and coordinate participation by team members in activities and discussion. Finally, certain behaviors emphasize the *individual roles* that members play in the group. Such behaviors inhibit discussion and diminish the organization's ability to accomplish its task. Benne and Sheats observe that individuals who block discussion often assume the role of the aggressor and openly attack other members' ideas and opinions. Other individual roles include seeking self-recognition at the expense of the entire organization and playing the role of the "joker" during discussion.

The functional approach to leadership is useful in predicting leadership emergence. Individuals take on leadership positions when they help orient the group to a particular problem, suggest procedures for organizing the discussion, and provide summaries of the group's progress (Knutson, & Holdridge, 1975; Schultz, 1974, 1986). However, the functional approach fails to identify consistently the behavioral functions that allow individuals to maintain leadership roles over time. Aubrey Fisher (1986) suggests that it is too difficult to explain how individuals carry on their leadership role over time because the functions of leaders differ dramatically according to the stage of a group's development. John Geier (1967) notes that, while appearing decisive and being highly verbal initially allow individuals to be considered as candidates for leadership roles, the same behaviors hurt their chances during later stages of the group's development. An alternative explanation for the inability of functionalist leadership theories to explain how individuals maintain leadership roles over time is the difficulty of identifying those behavioral functions uniquely associated with leadership. Lloyd Drecksel (1984) contends that leadership is characterized not by the performance of a particular function or set of functions but by the performance of a variety of behavioral functions. Despite its difficulty with identifying unique leadership functions, the functionalist view of leadership remains popular in leadership studies.

Ohio State Leadership Studies. During the 1950s, Ralph Stogdill and his associates at Ohio State University (OSU) conducted a number of studies aimed at identifying leadership behavioral characteristics. Stogdill believed leadership could be defined according to the types of behavior leaders exhibited, rather than their collection of personality and intellectual attributes. Beginning with a questionnaire measuring subordinates' perceptions of 150 leadership behaviors, the OSU researchers discovered that leadership behaviors could be characterized by two global dimensions (Fleishman, Harris, & Burtt, 1955; Halpin, 1957). The first dimension, *consideration* or relationship orientation, includes leadership behaviors that signal trust, respect, warmth, and interest in two-way communication. The other dimension, *initiating structure* or task orientation, is characterized by behaviors that facilitate the achievement of goals. The two dimensions are independent, which allows leaders to create styles that combine different levels of consideration and initiating structure.

A key question emerged during the OSU leadership studies: What is the optimal combination of these two dimensions for effective leadership? Early studies revealed that leaders high in consideration and initiation structure were viewed as more effective (Fleishman, 1957; Fleishman & Simmons, 1970; Halpin, 1957; Hemphill, 1955; House, Filley, & Kerr, 1971). This finding also has been found to be true in other cultures, such as Japan (Misumi, 1985; Misumi & Peterson, 1985). These early studies set the stage for later theories, which assumed that effective leadership behavior could be explained by the two factors of consideration and initiating structure. The optimal leadership style was referred to as "hi-hi," meaning effective leaders should exhibit high amounts of both types of behaviors.

Managerial grid theory. One of the most popular contemporary leadership theories is Robert Blake and Jane Mouton's (1985) managerial grid theory. According to this theory, managerial behavior is characterized according to two dimensions: (1) concern for people (or people orientation) and (2) concern for production (or task orientation). Using a grid with these two factors as axes (see Figure 2.2), Blake and Mouton identify a variety of possible styles exhibited by leaders:

Impoverished management (1,1). Leaders using this style exert minor effort toward accomplishing the task at hand. With little concern for either production or people, the leader makes broad assignments to subordinates and leaves subordinates to "fend for themselves." Such leaders believe that subordinates who are left alone will be better able to execute their jobs because they know their jobs better than anyone else.

Country club management (1,9). Leaders provide emotional support by conveying confidence in the subordinate's ability to accomplish the task, by complimenting successful performance, and by utilizing an open-door policy to listen to subordinates' concerns. Work assignments are suggested rather than stated directly. The emphasis is on creating an environment in which employees can relate well to co-workers and enjoy their jobs.

Middle-of-the-road management (5,5). This style of management emphasizes accommodating the subordinate's concerns and goals. Leaders make assignments while keeping in mind what subordinates view as acceptable or unacceptable. If a subordinate is unable to meet a target date for an assignment or feels pressured, the leader tries to reduce the workload. Such leaders try to balance production and people concerns.

Authority-compliance (9,1). The heavy concern for getting the job done

FIGURE 2.2 The Leadership Grid Figure

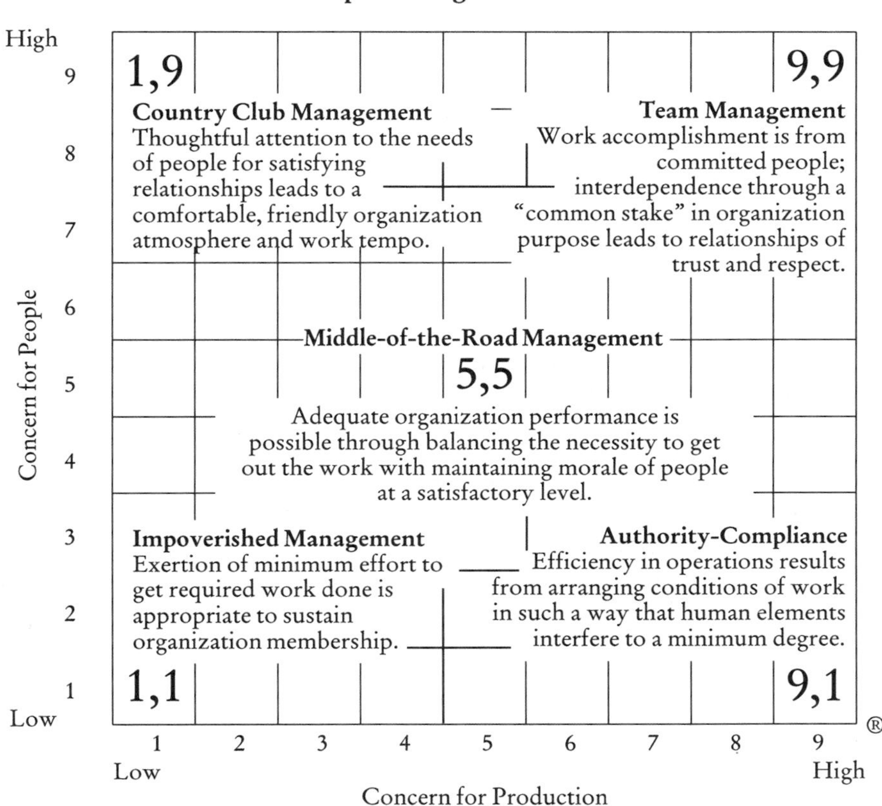

Source: The Leadership Grid® Figure from R. R. Blake and A. A. McCanse, *Leadership Dilemmas—Grid Solutions* (formerly the Managerial Grid Figure by Robert R. Blake and Jane S. Mouton). (Houston, TX: Gulf), p. 29. Copyright © 1991 by Scientific Methods, Inc. Reproduced by permission of the owners.

causes leaders to specify the work group's goals and to lay out specific procedures for accomplishing those goals. Leaders using this style closely monitor work performance. When performance lags behind or deadlines are not met, they criticize and assign blame to subordinates.

Team management (9,9). Leaders utilizing this style simultaneously emphasize production and people concerns. They aim to bring together members of the work team and jointly formulate goals, schedules, and responsibilities. Follow-up on work assignments is performed jointly with subordinates to determine and alleviate problem areas. At the completion of a task, a team manager, along with the other team members, assesses how the job was performed and generates improved methods for future jobs.

From Blake and Mouton's perspective, team management is the ideal leadership style. With its dual concern for people and production, it can empower followers and lead to heightened productivity, motivation, and commitment.

Iowa Child Welfare Studies and participative leadership. Another universal style approach views leadership as a form of decision making, distinguishing styles according to the type of participation, input, and involvement followers have in the decision-making process. This approach to leadership emerged during the Depression of the 1930s, when Kurt Lewin led a team of researchers investigating the influence of three types of leadership styles on group productivity and satisfaction (Lewin, Lippitt, & White, 1939):

1. *Autocratic leadership style:* Leaders are central authority figures who retain a high degree of control and power over their followers. Leaders make the decisions, whereas followers' participation in decision making is minimal. Leaders use one-way communication.
2. *Democratic leadership style:* Leaders and followers make decisions together and jointly determine courses of action. They are viewed more as equals because two-way communication exists between leaders and followers.
3. *Laissez-faire leadership style:* This style of leadership is best characterized by leaders who are not involved with the group's decision making. Very low levels of behavioral activity are present in leaders. Group members make work assignments and evaluate task completion among themselves.

In Lewin's study, preadolescent boys at a summer camp were each exposed to one of the three types of leadership. Each boy was assigned to a cabin and each cabin had a head counselor trained in behaviors designed to create one of the three leadership climates. Lewin discovered that the most satisfied campers were those in the democratic-style cabins, whereas the most dissatisfied campers were found in the autocratic-style cabins. Contrary to expectations, however, no difference was found between the productivity of campers exposed to autocratic or democratic leadership. (See Box 2.2.)

Lewin's research was followed by a series of studies that characterized leadership as a form of decision making. Tannenbaum and Schmidt (1958) describe four basic leadership styles ranging from "Tell" and "Sell" to "Join" and "Consult." They argue that effective leaders use the highly participative style of joining, which is characterized by democratic decision making. In the 1960s, democratic leadership continued its popularity as evidenced by a variety of employee participation plans, such as Likert's (1967) System IV and Scanlon plan. In the 1970s and 1980s, the bandwagon for participative forms of management continued to grow and was reflected in the call for organizations to use Japanese management techniques, such as quality circles, to empower employees (Kouzes & Posner, 1990; Ouchi, 1981; Peters & Waterman, 1982).

Democratic leadership is judged to be superior to autocratic leadership for

Box 2.2
The Case of the Overwhelmed Worker

Assume that TransAmerica Airlines is an international air carrier that provides service between the United States and Europe. Reservations on TransAmerica Airlines are made at one of several reservation centers within the United States. Service agents enter the reservations on a computer system, which keeps track of flights, available seats on flights, and rates for each flight. Agents are managed by team coordinators or TCs. Each TC has twelve agents under his or her control. Supervisors lead five TCs and the agents under their control.

One of the TCs, Mel, has recently encountered a problem with the amount of work she does at TransAmerica. Mel respects her supervisor, Alice, and has commented to many of her co-workers that "Alice is just the right kind of leader for the reservation center." Frustrated with her workload, however, Mel approaches Alice.

Mel: I need to talk to you. I feel like I can't keep on like this. I'm not sure what the most important part of my job is.

Alice: What's worrying you? If something is bothering you, get it off your chest. Let's talk about it.

Mel: I feel I've reached the end of my abilities. I feel I can't take on any more special projects. I'm neglecting my TC responsibilities.

Alice: Tell me some of the things that are above your responsibilities as a TC.

Mel: I feel I'm not spending enough time with the people and that I'm spending too much time coordinating special projects with Julian in Special Travel Services. I feel that my highest priority is to develop the skills of my reservation agents.

Alice: Before you take on things not passed through me, you've got to learn to say no for two reasons. First, you physically can't do all these projects, and second, it's not your responsibility to say yes. If I find out you're doing all these, I'll get upset. Julian knows he's supposed to call me first, but he calls you because he knows you'll say yes.

Mel: I know that, but if we don't do that, it won't get done.

Alice: Just remember you're important to me. Remember that one of your responsibilities is to delegate responsibilities to others.

Mel: But I feel I can't take agents off the desk.

Alice: Well, try to use their strengths. You need to prioritize the things you've got to get done in the amount of hours you've got. Forecast your projects, complete one job at a time, and then go on to the second.

Mel: Okay.

Alice We're aware you're very frustrated and need help. But remember about the four agents in training. Look at your trainees and remember they can do things like post rate updates. My suggestion is to reevaluate your train-

Box continued

ing program. Don't look at those four people as your trainees, but look at them as capable of updating rates. This is important because we're giving better service to the customer. This will help you get your work caught up. That's why we've got four people in training.

Mel: I don't need any more trainees, I need someone to help me.

Alice: We'll also try to arrange your position so it's better for you by letting you handle the special projects. However, we don't have approval and we'll need to justify it and get it approved.

Mel: Okay. When do you think all this will happen?

Alice: Maybe in a couple of months. Just remember, explain the situation to the senior agents and delegate them some responsibilities.

Mel: I'm concerned about the quality and integrity of the system. Things are getting out of hand. We don't have time to follow-up and help our agents solve problems. I feel we're starting to lose our integrity.

Alice: Well, even though you're a perfectionist, sometimes you'll have to grin and bear it.

DISCUSSION ISSUES

1. What key functions—functional, relational, individual—do you see Alice performing in this conversation?
2. How would you describe the task and relational orientation of Alice? Using the leadership grid shown in Figure 2.2, identify Alice's leadership style.
3. Is Alice's style of leadership autocratic, democratic, or laissez-faire? Why? What communicative cues characterize her style?

several reasons. First, followers are provided an opportunity to express their views, allowing them a say in their future and helping them meet their personal needs. The result is a high level of commitment to the organization. Second, the quality of decision making is improved in the democratic style. Decisions that are difficult to make and that have many possible solutions require increased participation in the decision-making process. Multiple perspectives are generated about a problem, ideas and viewpoints are challenged by others, and increased scrutiny of proposed solutions occurs. Finally, the implementation of a solution may be eased by involving those whom the decision will most directly affect.

Several popular management texts provide case studies showing that democratic leadership improves employee productivity and satisfaction (Bradford & Cohen, 1985; Kanter, 1979; Kouzes & Posner, 1990; Peters & Austin, 1985; Peters & Waterman, 1982). Although participative or democratic leadership can enhance organizational satisfaction and productivity, no consistent relationship between democratic leadership and satisfaction and productivity has been documented. In an early review of the participative management literature, Edwin Locke and David M. Schweiger (1979) discovered that only 22 percent of the studies found democratic leadership to be superior to autocratic leadership, and an equal percentage (22 percent) indicated that autocratic leadership was superior to democratic leadership. Fifty-six percent of the studies indicated that neither autocratic nor democratic leadership had a systematic impact on productivity. Democratic leadership's ability to stimulate higher work group satisfaction was better supported. Sixty percent of the studies demonstrated that democratic leadership was more positively associated with work group satisfaction than autocratic leadership. Still, 30 percent of studies were equivocal. More recent research does not support the view that democratic leadership is uniformally superior to autocratic leadership (Cotton, Vollrath, Froggatt, Lengneck-Hall, & Jennings, 1988; Miller & Monge, 1986; Schweiger & Leana, 1986; Wagner & Gooding, 1987).

Styles of operant conditioning. Although leadership styles are typically depicted according to task or relational behavior, rewards and punishments represent an equally important but often neglected class of leadership behaviors. Psychologists and motivation theorists alike recognize that rewards and punishments powerfully influence people's behavior (Hamner, 1979; Kazdin, 1980; Porter & Lawler, 1968; Skinner, 1969). From this perspective, leadership involves shaping others' behaviors by controlling the consequences associated with those behaviors.

The most comprehensive approach to examining how leaders use rewards and punishments to motivate subordinates is offered by Phillip Podsakoff and associates. In examining the relationships among leader reward, punishment behavior, and organizational outcomes, Podsakoff and his associates identify four general classes of behavior (Fahr, Podsakoff, & Cheng, 1987; Podsakoff & Todor, 1985; Podsakoff, Todor, Grover, & Huber, 1984; Podsakoff, Todor, & Skov, 1982):

1. *Performance-contingent reward behavior (CR):* This class of behavior focuses on whether leaders present rewards based on subordinate performance. It includes such behaviors as providing positive feedback when an employee performs well and quickly acknowledging improvement in work quality.
2. *Contingent punishment behavior (CP):* This class of punishment behavior involves the degree to which leaders punish subordinates based on their performance. This class of behaviors includes closely monitoring subordinates' performance and, when their performance is below standard, holding the employees accountable and expressing displeasure over work quality.
3. *Noncontingent punishment behavior (NCP):* This group of behaviors measures the degree to which leaders indiscriminately punish subordinates. There is no direct link between administering a punishment and subordinate performance. A manager is just as likely to punish subordinates when they are performing well or are performing poorly.
4. *Noncontingent reward behavior (NCR):* This category relates to leaders' tendency to reward subordinates indiscriminately. There is no

direct relationship between the rewarding behaviors and subordinates' performance; for example, leaders exhibiting this type of behavior may commend and praise a subordinate even when the employee is performing poorly, or they may rarely become upset with a subordinate whose performance is poor.

The different classes of behavior are assumed to be linked to employee productivity and satisfaction. Early thinking on how reward and punishment behaviors should be linked to organizational outcomes generated four proposed relationships: (1) *contingent rewards* should enhance employee productivity and satisfaction; (2) *noncontingent punishment behaviors* should be negatively associated with satisfaction and performance; (3) *contingent punishment behavior* should be negatively associated with satisfaction and positively associated with performance; and (4) *noncontingent positive rewards* should be positively associated with satisfaction and negatively associated with employee performance. Most research demonstrates that leaders using CR increase subordinates' productivity and satisfaction (Fahr, Podsakoff, & Cheng, 1987; Podsakoff, Todor, Grover, & Huber, 1984). The same studies also show that CP and NCP are not linked to higher levels of performance and satisfaction. Therefore, in order to motivate subordinates, leaders should praise and compliment good performance when it occurs.

Contingency Trait Theory

In the 1960s, theorists began recognizing how situational elements influence the desirability and effectiveness of a particular leadership trait or style. A growing number of theorists adopted the rather commonsense notion that effective leaders recognize situational demands and obstacles, sense opportunities present in the situation, and strategically adapt their behavior to cope with the situation. Several situational factors, such as role ambiguity, the nature of the task, followers' personality characteristics, and a leader's formal authority, have been hypothesized and tested to see how they influence the acceptability and effectiveness of leadership traits and behaviors. *Contingency trait theory* recognizes that the situation moderates the relationship between a leader's trait and effectiveness. If the leadership traits do not match the needs of the situation, leadership will be ineffective at helping organizations achieve goals. Fred Fiedler (1967) is the major proponent of contingency trait theory.

Fiedler's contingency theory of leadership effectiveness (1967; 1993) is an extension of universal trait theory. The premise underlying his "Leadermatch" program is that leaders are more effective and productive when their personality is congruent with the "favorableness" of a situation. To assess whether a leader's personality matches the situational needs, three pieces of information are required: knowledge of a leader's personality, a clear definition and assessment of the nature of the situation, and an explanation of how situational variables moderate the relationship between leadership traits and effectiveness.

A leader's personality ranges from being primarily concerned with getting the job done to emphasizing the need to maintain good interpersonal relationships. Personality can be measured using Fiedler's Least Preferred Co-worker (LPC) scale (see Box 2.3). Individuals use the LPC scale, which consists of sixteen 8-point bipolar adjective pairs, to describe the co-worker with whom they work least well. An LPC score is created by summing the responses across items, which results in a range of LPC scores from a low of 16 to a high of 108. Individuals scoring above 63 are classified as high LPC leaders, whereas those scoring below 56 are classified as low LPC leaders. High LPC leaders describe their least preferred co-worker in positive and favorable terms, while low LPC leaders describe their least preferred co-worker in negative and unfavorable terms. Fiedler argues that the LPC scale reveals a leader's motive hierarchy. High LPC leaders are relationally oriented because they are motivated by a need for affiliation. Low LPC leaders are more task oriented because they are driven by task-achievement needs. Rice (1978) suggests that low LPC leaders are more task-oriented because they value success to a greater degree than high LPC leaders. In addition, high LPC leaders are relationally oriented because they value interpersonal success. Both explanations highlight how a leader's personality affects his or her preference for certain leadership behaviors.

A leader's personality presumably remains stable across situations. The primary task for contingency theory is to identify the situational conditions that favor a leader's personality. Fiedler (1967) contends that the following situational factors influence the appropriateness of a leader's personality:

1. *Leader-member relations*—the degree of confidence and trust that followers place in a leader.
2. *Task structure*—the degree to which (a) the duties of a job are clearly stated, (b) problems can be solved by a variety of procedures, (c) decisions can be verified, and (d) an optimal solution exists.
3. *Position power*—the level of power vested by an organization in a leader's hierarchical position.

These factors are dichotomized into either good/poor, high/low, or strong/weak, yielding eight possible conditions of leadership ranging from very favorable to extremely unfavorable. At one end of the continuum, an extremely unfavorable situation could be characterized as involving poor leader-member relations, low task structure, and low position power. At the other extreme, conditions of leadership can include having good leader-member relations, high task structure, and high position power. Figure 2.3 illustrates the various combinations of situational factors and their relative degrees of favorableness.

According to Fiedler (1967), a leader is effective when a good fit exists between the leader's personality and the favorableness of the situation. Low LPC leaders are most effective in extremely favorable or unfavorable situations. High LPC leaders are most effective in moderately favorable or unfavorable situations. Intuitively, it makes sense that task-oriented leaders would be effective in highly unfavorable situations because followers require strong task leadership to make the best of a bad situation. In moderately favorable situations where group conflict exists, it is important to have more relationally oriented leadership to

Box 2.3

Fiedler's Least Preferred Co-worker Scale

INSTRUCTIONS

Think of a co-worker with whom you worked least well or who you did not enjoy working with. Rate the person using the following scales. Compute a sum score across all the scales.

Pleasant	--- 8	--- 7	--- 6	--- 5	--- 4	--- 3	--- 2	--- 1	Unpleasant
Friendly	--- 8	--- 7	--- 6	--- 5	--- 4	--- 3	--- 2	--- 1	Unfriendly
Rejecting	--- 1	--- 2	--- 3	--- 4	--- 5	--- 6	--- 7	--- 8	Accepting
Tense	--- 1	--- 2	--- 3	--- 4	--- 5	--- 6	--- 7	--- 8	Relaxed
Distant	--- 1	--- 2	--- 3	--- 4	--- 5	--- 6	--- 7	--- 8	Close
Cold	--- 1	--- 2	--- 3	--- 4	--- 5	--- 6	--- 7	--- 8	Warm
Supportive	--- 8	--- 7	--- 6	--- 5	--- 4	--- 3	--- 2	--- 1	Hostile
Boring	--- 1	--- 2	--- 3	--- 4	--- 5	--- 6	--- 7	--- 8	Interesting
Quarrelsome	--- 1	--- 2	--- 3	--- 4	--- 5	--- 6	--- 7	--- 8	Harmonious
Gloomy	--- 1	--- 2	--- 3	--- 4	--- 5	--- 6	--- 7	--- 8	Cheerful
Open	--- 8	--- 7	--- 6	--- 5	--- 4	--- 3	--- 2	--- 1	Guarded
Backbiting	--- 1	--- 2	--- 3	--- 4	--- 5	--- 6	--- 7	--- 8	Loyal
Untrustworthy	--- 1	--- 2	--- 3	--- 4	--- 5	--- 6	--- 7	--- 8	Trustworthy
Considerate	--- 8	--- 7	--- 6	--- 5	--- 4	--- 3	--- 2	--- 1	Inconsiderate
Nasty	--- 1	--- 2	--- 3	--- 4	--- 5	--- 6	--- 7	--- 8	Nice
Agreeable	--- 8	--- 7	--- 6	--- 5	--- 4	--- 3	--- 2	--- 1	Disagreeable
Insincere	--- 1	--- 2	--- 3	--- 4	--- 5	--- 6	--- 7	--- 8	Sincere
Kind	--- 8	--- 7	--- 6	--- 5	--- 4	--- 3	--- 2	--- 1	Unkind

Source: F. E. Fiedler (1967). *A theory of leadership effectiveness.* (New York: McGraw-Hill), p. 41.

FIGURE 2.3 Fiedler's Contingency Model of Leadership Effectiveness

Power	Weak				Strong			
Nature of the Task	Unstructured		Structured		Unstructured		Structured	
Leader-Member	Poor	Good	Poor	Good	Poor	Good	Poor	Good

Highly Unfavorable — Moderately Favorable/Unfavorable — Highly Favorable

SITUATIONAL FAVORABILITY

Source: Adapted from F. E. Fiedler (1967). *A theory of leadership effectiveness.* (New York: McGraw-Hill), p. 34.

provide support for followers and create a positive interpersonal climate. It does not make sense, however, that low LPC leaders would necessarily be more effective in highly favorable situations. Fiedler suggests that highly favorable situations are typically low in pressure. Therefore, when leaders are confronted with high pressure situations, they employ their dominant style as measured by the LPC. In low pressure situations, they utilize their secondary style, which is the opposite of their dominant style. Low LPC or task-oriented leaders thus adopt a relationally oriented approach in low pressure situations, one that meets the needs of the situation.

The contingency theory model has been extensively tested. Fiedler (1964; 1978) has performed several studies that support the predicted pattern of relationships. In a recent review of contingency theory, Peters, Hartke, and Polhmann (1985) generally affirm the relationships predicted by the contingency model. However, critics continue to question its validity because several studies do not support Fiedler's view or the LPC scales. Despite the continued criticism, contingency theory remains one of the most empirically tested and widely applied leadership theories in business and industry.

Situational Behavior Theory

Leaders often adapt their behavior to the nature of the situation. *Situational behavior theory* contends that leaders must adapt their behavior to meet the demands of the situation successfully. Unlike contingency theory, which focuses on traits, situational leadership theory focuses on a leader's behavior. Five situational leadership theories have emerged.

Path-Goal theory. Path-goal theory, originating with Robert House and associates, represents one of the earliest situational theories to emerge from the behavioral-style perspective (Evans, 1970; House, 1971; House & Mitchell, 1974; Filley, House, & Kerr, 1976). It views the primary function of leadership as clarifying the routes subordinates must travel to achieve personal and work goals. Since subordinates are goal-oriented, providing information and guidance on the paths they must take to achieve their goals helps improve their performance and satisfaction. Two underlying propositions frame path-goal theory. First, followers view a leader's behavior as acceptable and satisfying when it provides immediate satisfaction or facilitates future satisfaction. Second, leadership behavior causes followers to expend greater effort at their work when they can meet their needs only by performing at high levels.

House and his associates also hypothesize that followers are more satisfied with unstructured or ambiguous tasks when leaders provide direction and guidance. The opposite is also true: When followers perform clear and unambiguous tasks, they become dissatisfied when leaders provide guidance and direction. It is only when followers are unclear about how to proceed that they require direction to achieve their goals and are likely to appreciate the leader's guidance. However, if they already know how to perform a task well, and the leader's directions provide no new information, followers are more likely to perceive the leader's actions as an irritating intrusion. A leader's level of consideration for others is positively correlated to follower satisfaction when performing a highly structured task. Given that followers know what steps they need to take to achieve a task, all they require is encouragement. If the task is ambiguous, however, consideration does not help followers achieve goals and they become dissatisfied.

Although path-goal theory is intuitively sensible, limited support has been presented for its hypotheses. According to Chester Schriesheim and Mary Ann Von Glinow (1977), 50 percent of studies using path-goal theory indicate that directive behavior is positively correlated to follower satisfaction when the task is ambiguous. Directive behavior is also negatively correlated to follower satisfaction when the task is clear and straightforward. They note that slightly over 50 percent of studies demonstrate followers are satisfied when leaders use relational behavior in regard to clear tasks.

What accounts for the limited support of path-goal theory? Gary Yukl (1989) offers one potential reason for the lack of empirical support: a lack of specificity regarding what contributes to directive and relational leadership. The initial propositions of path-goal theory were formulated on the basis of broad behavioral categories, such as directive and consideration behavior. Yukl argues that the likelihood of finding strong correlations between such categories and specific performance outcomes is very low. He suggests that directive leadership should be broken down into more specific task-oriented behaviors, "such as clarifying roles, setting specific objectives, giving contingent rewards, planning the work, problem solving, and monitoring" (Yukl, 1989, p. 264). By specifying the particular types of directive and consideration behaviors that exist, it becomes more likely that the hypotheses of path-goal theory may be confirmed.

Life-cycle theory. Paul Hersey and Paul Blanchard's (1982) life-cycle theory of leadership assumes that leaders alter their style based on the maturity level of their followers. Follower maturity combines job and psychological maturity. *Job maturity* refers to an individual's ability to perform a specified task, whereas *psychological maturity* points to the individual's willingness or motivation to perform the task. Therefore, mature followers possess both the ability (knowledge and skills) and the motivation to perform a task. Immature followers possess neither the ability nor the motivation to perform a task.

Life-cycle theory identifies four leadership styles that may be used by leaders on the basis of followers' maturity level. A delegating style is characterized by leaders providing little direction or support to subordinates. A leader may identify a particular project or task for subordinates, but ultimately places responsibility on the followers for its completion. A participating style is characterized by two-way communication, active listening, supportiveness, and shared decision-making responsibility. Leaders using a selling style provide high levels of support and direction to followers. In the selling style, leaders identify the kinds of actions they want followers to perform and attempt to persuade followers to perform them. In the telling style, leaders provide intense direction to followers, telling them what roles to assume, what tasks to perform, and so on.

The appropriateness of any one style is contingent on the maturity level of individual followers. For those who are highly mature and confident in their ability, a delegating style is most effective because these followers do not require intense direction or the support of leaders. A participating style should be employed with followers whose maturity is moderate to high. Although these followers may be able to perform a task, they are unwilling to do so alone because of fear of failure. A participating style provides the needed support for overcoming this insecurity. Followers with a low to moderate level of maturity may be willing but unable to perform a task. In this case, a selling style allows leaders to provide the needed direction and to persuade followers to conform to the suggested direction. Finally, a telling style is used when follower maturity is low because these followers are both unwilling and unable to perform a task. Hersey and Blanchard (1982) assert that leaders should use a telling style in this situation because followers must be equipped with clear and precise directions in order to accomplish a task.

Studies that have directly tested the propositions underlying life-cycle theory indicate mixed support. Some studies find no support for the theory (Blank, Weitzel, & Green, 1986). In the most extensive test of life-cycle theory, Robert Vecchio (1987) found partial support for its propositions, particularly in instances involving followers with a low maturity level. He suggests using a telling style with immature followers; otherwise, leaders who support the inadequate performance of low-maturity followers only reinforce the behaviors that are preventing followers from performing the task well.

Regarding the types of leadership styles that work best under conditions of moderate and high maturity, life-cycle theory has received little or no support in the research. Despite this lack of empirical support, the life-cycle theory of leadership remains popular in management training and is emphasized in most leadership texts.

Normative decision theory. Beginning with Lewin, Lippit, & White (1939), one of the rich traditions in the universal style approach characterizes leadership on the basis of decision-making style. Growing out of this tradition, Victor Vroom and Phillip Yetton (1973) sought to determine the decision-making styles that lead to high-quality decisions in particular situations. They developed the normative decision model, which characterizes leadership according to three general decision-making styles. They also identified a set of rules for leaders to follow when selecting among the leadership styles. The three decision-making styles are as follows:

1. *Autocratic decision-making style:* Power in decision making is centralized in the leader. Subordinates may provide needed information for the decision, but they do not generate solutions to remedy a problem.
2. *Consultative decision-making style:* A leader asks followers to generate possible solutions for problems, but still retains the right to make the final decision. The final decision may or may not reflect follower input.
3. *Group decision-making style:* In this style, participation by all group members is emphasized and the role of the leader is that of facilitator. The leader facilitates and coordinates the group discussion and accepts the decision developed by the group.

Following are the rules that Vroom and Yetton suggest leaders should follow to select a leadership style. Note that, unlike the assumption underlying participative management theory, democratic or shared decision making is not considered inherently superior. Rather, a number of factors may influence the relationship between the appropriateness of a given decision-making style and decision quality and acceptance.

1. *Fairness rule:* Does the problem have a quality requirement?
2. *Leader information rule:* Does sufficient information exist to make a high-quality decision?
3. *Unstructured problem rule:* Is the problem structured?
4. *Acceptance rule:* Is acceptance of the decision by subordinates important for effective implementation?
5. *Acceptance priority rule:* If the leader were to make the decision alone, can one be reasonably certain that it would be accepted by subordinates?
6. *Goal congruence rule:* Do subordinates share the organizational goals that will be met by solving this problem?
7. *Conflict rule:* Is conflict likely among subordinates over the preferred solutions?

Vroom and Yetton (1973) also provide a decision tree for leaders that incorporates the specific decision rules. After answering the questions on the decision tree, leaders are guided to a set of styles appropriate to the given situation. A recent revision of the model provides additional criteria for identifying the single best procedure for a given situation (Vroom & Jago, 1988).

In the research, support for normative decision theory has been strong. Several studies indicate that the prescriptions in the decision tree lead to improved decisions, increased employee satisfaction, and greater employee productivity (Margerison & Glube, 1979; Vroom & Jago, 1978). In the research focusing on the validity and importance of the conflict rule, Crouch and Yetton (1987) suggest that the applicability of the rule is influenced by a leader's conflict management skill. They argue that managers who possess weak conflict management skills should not employ a group-oriented style. In addition, Dean Tjosvold (Tjosvold, Wedley, & Field, 1988) suggests that a leader's ability to manage conflict may be more important than following the decision tree in helping groups make better decisions. He found that constructive controversy—discussing opposing viewpoints and ideas—was nine times as important in predicting decision effectiveness as adhering to the rules of the decision-making tree. Although there is support in the research for some areas of the normative decision-making model, other areas need future investigation. (See Box 2.4.)

Leader-member exchange theory. Leader-member exchange (LMX) theory views leadership as a special type of relationship existing between leader and follower. The focus of LMX theory is on how leaders and followers coordinate and organize their actions to accomplish goals (Graen & Scandura, 1987). Leadership is thus viewed as a dyadic process of organizing, whereby "organizational members accomplish their work through roles" (Graen, 1976, p. 1201). The role relationship, which is negotiated by leaders and followers, is the key mechanism for explaining how leaders and followers organize themselves. Two general types of role relationships may exist:

1. *In-group exchanges:* The leader-follower relationship is characterized by high levels of trust and support. In addition, a high level of interaction and increased use of rewards mark in-group exchanges.
2. *Out-group exchanges:* The leader-follower relationship in out-group exchanges tends to be characterized by a lack of trust and support. Moreover, interaction and rewards are limited.

In-group and out-group exchanges are viewed as having multiple dimensions (Dienesch & Liden, 1986). In addition, leader-member exchanges are seen as varying in the degrees to which leaders and followers (1) like one another (affect), (2) are willing to defend each other (loyalty), and (3) participate with one another (contribution to the exchange). Arranging such exchanges along these three dimensions allows for a fuller accounting and greater specification of the kinds of relationship that leaders and followers cultivate.

LMX theory is situational in the sense that leaders develop unique relationships with followers; that is, leaders treat subordinates differently on the basis of whether the subordinate is an in-group or out-group member. Leaders are more dominant in conversations with followers with whom they have an out-group relationship (Fairhurst, Rogers, & Sarr, 1987). In the case of in-group relation-

Box 2.4

Assessing the Leadership Situation

Let's assume that Lee Williams, an employee at Termco, a national life insurance company, is an active member of the sales team for which you are the leader. Bob, a co-worker of Lee's, comes to you with this complaint: "I don't know what to tell you about Lee. Something's gotten into him. He's just so moody these days and he's becoming very absent-minded. I just don't know what to do. He's running so hot and cold. Sometimes, I say 'hello' to him and he just snaps at me like I'm interrupting him. Other times, he's very pleasant to work with. I would really like you to do something about it."

ASSIGNMENT 1

To help you decide what to do about Lee, write out the details of your approach to the situation.

ASSIGNMENT 2

You talk to a friend about how you plan to approach Lee. You like this particular friend because she often plays the devil's advocate and tends to scrutinize your ideas. As you talk with her, she asks a series of questions. Write your responses to the following questions:

1. Would you say that to Lee if he was from a different ethnic group?
2. How would you change what you would say if Lee was female?
3. Would you treat Lee differently if he had been with the company for a long time? If he was a newcomer?
4. How would you talk to Lee if he was physically handicapped?
5. If Lee was significantly older or younger than you, would you approach him differently?

ASSIGNMENT 3

Given your skill at leading the sales team, you have been asked to give a speech to the sales managers at Termco entitled "The Importance of Adapting to the Situation." In an outline of that speech, identify four situational factors that you think are important to consider when deciding how to lead people.

ships, however, leaders and followers exert mutual influence during conversations (Fairhurst & Chandler, 1989). Determining how in-group and out-group relationships are created through communication and how the type of role relationship influences communication is important. However, the majority of LMX research documents how in-group and out-group relationships are associated with personal and organizational outcomes. Several researchers report that in-group relationships are positively associated with increased employee satisfaction (Ferris, 1985; Graen & Ginsburgh, 1977) as well as employee performance (Liden & Graen, 1980; Tjosvold, 1984; Vecchio, 1982).

Leader substitutes theory. Underlying most leadership theories is the assumption that leadership behavior influences followers' motivation to work as well as their loyalty and commitment to the organization. Most, if not all, leadership theories seek to "clearly identify and best explain the supposedly powerful effects of . . . leadership upon the satisfaction, morale, and performance of subordinates" (Kerr, 1977, p. 136). Unfortunately, most theories and models of leadership have difficulty in clearly demonstrating leadership's supposed effects on organizational outcomes. Thus, some researchers argue that a leader's behavior may be irrelevant or redundant in some situations (House & Mitchell, 1974; Howell & Dorfman, 1981, 1986; Howell, Dorfman, & Kerr, 1986; Kerr, 1977; Kerr & Jermier, 1978; Kerr & Slocum, 1981; Pfeffer, 1978). They contend that situational factors that neutralize the influence of leadership behavior should be identified.

The leader substitutes theory recognizes that, in some instances, leadership behavior may directly influence subordinate behavior and performance. However, it also recognizes that numerous individual, organizational, and task characteristics may neutralize, enhance, or suppress leadership's ability to influence a work group. A subordinate's level of training, the repetitiveness of the task, or the formalization of the subordinate's work role may all substitute for the leader's behavior (Kerr, 1977). For example, assembly-line work may be a highly structured and regimented task that employees routinely perform or in which they are already well trained. In this case, because employees do not require further guidance from the leader, the level of training and repetitiveness replace and neutralize the leader's guidance.

Steve Kerr (1977) initially proposed a typology of subordinate, task, and organizational characteristics that may neutralize leadership behavior. Within these three broad conceptual categories, fourteen specific characteristics were identified:

Subordinate

1. Ability, experience, training, and knowledge
2. Need for independence
3. Professional orientation
4. Indifference toward organizational rewards

Task

1. Unambiguous and routine
2. Methodologically invariant
3. Provides its own feedback concerning accomplishment
4. Intrinsically satisfying

Organizational

1. Formalization (explicit plans, goals, areas of responsibility)
2. Inflexibility (rigid, unbending rules and procedures)

3. Highly specified and active advisory and staff functions
4. Closely knit, cohesive work groups
5. Organizational rewards not within the leader's control
6. Spatial distance between superior and subordinates

To provide effective leadership, according to Kerr (1977), leaders must be able to recognize how these factors may enhance or neutralize the impact of their behavior. The variables may act as *enhancers* by increasing the influence of a leader's behavior, or they may act as *substitutes* by replacing a leader's influence. Effective leaders recognize how the factors influence their behavior; in addition, they are able to create substitutes for overcoming ineffective leadership (whether their own or that of other leaders within the organization). Table 2.1 summarizes some of the potential substitutes and enhancers for leadership directiveness and supportiveness.

Transformational Theory

Interest in the study of the *transformational theory* of leadership surfaced in the 1980s. As organizations and businesses came to be viewed as possessing a corporate culture, explaining how corporate visionaries help construct organizational cultures took on added importance. In their book, *Corporate Cultures,* Terrance Deal and Allen Kennedy (1982) explain that heroes are particularly important in creating the myths, stories, rites, and rituals that characterize an organization's culture. Furthermore, Tom Peters and Nancy Austin (1985) characterize visionary transformational leadership behavior as including "passion, care, intensity, consistency, attention, drama of the implicit, and explicit use of symbols" (p. 312).

Although many theories of charismatic and transformational leadership have been offered, the most developed and researched version is that of Bernard Bass (1985). He bases his theory of transformational leadership on Burns's (1978) study of political leadership. Burns argues that leaders vary in how they use strategies and techniques to organize and coordinate followers' activities. He contends that two types of political leadership exist: transactional and transformational. *Transactional leadership* is based on a social exchange model, whereby leaders initially approach followers and gain their compliance by exchanging rewards for services rendered. Transactional leaders typically rely on their formal position within a corporate hierarchy to provide rewards and punishments and to motivate followers. In contrast, *transformational leadership* describes leaders who rely on their rhetorical skills to create a compelling vision of the future, which prompts shifts in follower beliefs, needs, and values. Transformational leaders do not depend on their ability to manipulate formal rewards and punishments; rather, they set an example for followers and use rhetorical skills to establish a common vision.

Bass and associates apply the theory of transformational leadership to organizational settings in an attempt to examine more fully its influences on employee satisfaction and performance (Bass, 1985; Bass, 1990b; Bass & Avolio, 1993;

TABLE 2.1 Creative Strategies for Improving Leadership Effectiveness

Creating Substitutes for Leader Directiveness and Supportiveness	Creating Enhancers for Leader Directiveness and Supportiveness
Develop collegial systems of guidance: • Peer appraisals to increase acceptability of feedback by subordinates • Quality circles to increase workers' control of production quality • Peer support networks and mentor systems	Increase subordinates' perceptions of the leader's influence and expertise: • Provide a visible champion of the leader • Give the leader important organizational responsibilities • Build the leader's image through in-house publications and other means
Improve performance-oriented organizational formalization: • Automatic organization reward system (such as commission or gain-sharing) • Group management-by-objectives (MBO) program • Company mission statements and codes of conduct	Build the organizational climate: • Reward small accomplishments to increase subordinates' confidence • Emphasize ceremony and myth to encourage team spirit • Develop subordinates' goals to encourage cohesiveness and create high-performance norms
Increase administrative staff availability: • Specialized training personnel • Troubleshooters for human relations problems • Technical advisers to assist production operators	Increase subordinates' dependence on the leader: • Create crises requiring immediate action • Increase the leader's centrality in providing information • Eliminate one-over-one approvals
Increased professionalism of subordinates: • Staffing based on employee professionalism • Develop plans to increase employees' abilities and experience • Encourage active participation in professional associations	Increase the leader's position power: • Change title to increase status • Increase reward power • Increase resource base
Redesign jobs to increase: • Performance feedback from the task • Ideological importance of jobs	Create cohesive work groups with high-performance norms: • Provide a physical setting that is conducive to team work • Encourage subordinates' participation in group problem solving • Increase the group's status • Create intergroup competition

(continued)

TABLE 2.1 *Continued*

Creating Substitutes for Leader Directiveness and Supportiveness	Creating Enhancers for Leader Directiveness and Supportiveness
Start team-building activities to develop group self-management skills, such as: • Solving work-related problems • Resolving interpersonal conflicts among members • Providing interpersonal support to members	

Source: Adapted from J. P. Howell, D. E. Bowen, P. W. Dorfman, S. Kerr, and P. M. Podsakoff (1990), Substitutes for leadership: Effective alternatives to ineffective leadership, *Organizational Dynamics, 19*(1), 31.

Bass, Avolio, & Goodheim, 1987; Bass, Waldman, Avolio, & Bebb, 1987). To test the theory, they developed the Multifactor Leadership Questionnaire (MLQ). It measures seven different aspects of transactional and transformational leadership behavior:

1. *Charismatic leadership* concerns the faith and respect shown by a leader to a follower as well as the inspiration offered by a leader.
2. *Inspiration,* a subfactor of charisma, refers to the ability of a leader to make emotional appeals to motivate followers and enhance their understanding of the desired goals.
3. *Individualized consideration* consists of considerate and supportive leadership directed toward each individual subordinate. For example, leaders may provide personal attention to followers who seem neglected.
4. *Intellectual stimulation* represents the degrees to which leaders promote new ways of viewing situations or problems and stimulate deeper analysis of job problems.
5. *Contingent reward* represents the degree to which rewards are given to followers when they perform well.
6. *Management-by-exception*, or *contingent aversive reinforcement,* refers to leaders' intervention when subordinates deviate from acceptable performance levels. The emphasis is on maintaining the status quo and intervening only when subordinate performance falls below minimal performance standards.
7. *Laissez-faire* is a nonleadership factor in that it indicates when leadership is absent. Laissez-faire leadership is neither transactional nor transformational.

Bass (1985) classifies factors 1–4 as transformational and factors 5–6 as transactional. As already noted, factor 7, laissez-faire, is viewed as a nonleadership factor. Box 2.5 describes the differences between transactional and transformational leaders in terms of these seven factors.

Preliminary support for transformational leadership theory is strong. Bass (1985) predicts that transformational factors will be found more strongly correlated than transactional factors to the extra effort expended by followers, the effectiveness of a leader, and followers' satisfaction with a leader's style and methods. In a summary of seventeen studies using the MLQ, Bass and Avolio (1990) report that transformational leadership scores are strongly correlated with extra effort by followers, employee satisfaction, and overall organizational effectiveness. Transformational leadership factors are also positively related to employees' satisfaction with performance appraisals (Waldman, Bass, & Einstein, 1987) as well as to group performance (Avolio, Waldman, & Einstein, 1988). Whether leaders exhibit transformational behaviors appears to be contingent on their level of cognitive development. Ted Zorn (1991), in an examination of whether individuals perceived as transformational have more sophisticated and complex cognitive systems, found that as the number and variety of elements in a leader's cognitive system increased, the leader tended to exhibit more charismatic leadership, inspiration, and individualized consideration. Taken as a

Box 2.5
Characteristics of Transformational and Transactional Leaders

THE TRANSFORMATIONAL LEADER

Charisma: Provides vision and a sense of mission; instills pride; gains respect and trust

Inspiration: Communicates high expectations; uses symbols to focus efforts; expresses important purposes in simple ways

Intellectual stimulation: Promotes intelligence, rationality, and careful problem solving

Individualized consideration: Gives personal attention; treats each employee individually; coaches and advises

THE TRANSACTIONAL LEADER

Contingent reward: Contracts exchange of rewards for effort; promises rewards for good performance; recognizes accomplishments

Management by exception (active): Watches and searches for deviations from rules and standards; takes corrective action

Management by exception (passive): Intervenes only when standards are not met

Laissez-Faire: Abdicates responsibilities; avoids making decisions

Source: B. M. Bass (1990), From transactional to transformational leadership: Learning to share the vision, *Organizational Dynamics, 18*(3), 22.

whole, the research indicates that transformational leadership is more capable than transactional leadership at empowering employees and at generating higher levels of employee commitment, satisfaction, and motivation.

COMMUNICATION AND LEADERSHIP

The variety and sheer number of leadership theories can be confusing. As Ralph Stogdill (1974) observes, the past four decades of leadership research "have produced a bewildering mass of findings . . . [but] the endless accumulation of empirical data has not produced an integrated understanding of leadership" (p. vii). This lack of an integrated view of leadership also means that the importance of communication varies according to each leadership theory. We need to clarify the role of communication and how the nature of the situation influences communication if we are to assess its importance in leadership. In doing so, three key questions must be addressed.

What Is the Role of Communication in Leadership?

The importance of communication varies greatly among leadership theories. In the universal trait and contingency trait theory, the role of communication in the leadership process is relatively minor. These two perspectives, which focus on the traits that characterize leadership, de-emphasize the types and quality of messages that characterize leadership. Gary Yukl (1989) found that trait research generally does not directly measure leadership behavior, even though it is clear that leader traits affect behavior. At best, communication is acknowledged indirectly as social traits, such as extraversion, interpersonal skills, sensitivity, sociability, talkativeness, verbal fluency, and tact. Communicative traits and abilities are only one aspect of the various physical and constitutional factors, technical skills, and personality characteristics that distinguish leadership.

Universal style theories, such as Blake and Mouton's managerial grid, and situational behavior theories, such as Hersey and Blanchard's (1982) life-cycle theory, tend to elevate the importance of communication. In both perspectives, individual messages combine to form the behavioral styles through which we explain leadership effectiveness. Leaders adopt certain behavioral styles to motivate others, coordinate actions, and accomplish goals. Behavioral style, from both perspectives, is defined according to the content and function or direction and intensity of communication. The former is best illustrated by the universal style and situational theories, which incorporate dimensions of task-oriented or people-oriented behavior in characterizing leadership. Leadership communication is designed to fulfill key task and relational functions. The latter is best illustrated by Lewin's (Lewin, Lippitt, & White, 1939) notion of democratic leadership and Vroom and Yetton's (1973) normative decision theory, which defines leadership according to decision-making style. In both cases, it is the direction and intensity of communication that distinguishes the various styles, which can range from intense two-way communication (democratic leadership) to intense one-way communication (autocratic leadership) to a lack of either type of communication (laissez-faire leadership).

Although the universal style and situational approaches emphasize the importance of communication, they tend to downplay its creative improvisational nature. Instead, communication is reduced to a technique. Both approaches contend that a small number of leadership styles can be mastered and that it is possible to specify a set of messages that reflects those styles. Universal style theory suggests that mastering the nuances of a given style can facilitate leadership effectiveness. Situational behavior theory requires leaders to master a variety of leadership styles and to understand how the situation dictates which style should be employed. However, the need to create new leadership styles not specified in the existing theory and to construct unique and innovative enactments of specific styles is diminished. Effective leadership is equated with the mastery of effective communication techniques.

The importance of communication is even more pronounced in transformational leadership theory. Here the combination of individualized attention and charismatic leadership emphasizes the creative function of communication. The transformational leader must assess the unique qualities of the situation and then select from a large repertoire of communication skills, rather than rely on a predetermined set of such techniques. Effective leaders model desired behavior and articulate a vision through their rhetorical and persuasive skills. The ability to compose a message that is not only clear but also visionary and inspiring requires a sophisticated use of communicative skills. Transformational leadership cannot be scripted; its success depends to a great extent on the leader's ability to create novel communication messages, especially crafted for particular individuals, at a particular place, and at a given time.

What is the appropriate level for examining leadership skill? Implicit within all leadership theories is the notion that leaders are most effective when they can dissect the demands and constraints of a situation and perform the required actions to take advantage of a situation's opportunities and overcome its constraints. Thus, leaders must be skilled in order to perform their role effectively.

In Chapter 1, *skill* is defined at three different levels: (1) molecular, (2) molar, and (3) process. Most leadership theories tend to approach leadership skill from a molar level. The universal trait and contingency trait theories view leadership skill at this level. Leaders may be characterized on the basis of global dimensions, including task and people orientation, extraversion and introversion, fluency and nonfluency, or sociability and unsociability. Traits provide a global label that allows us to classify a number of individual beliefs, attitudes, and values into a single dimension. The universal style, situational, and transformational theories of leadership also approach skill from a molar perspective. Although the importance of molecular behavior is recognized, such behaviors are reduced to global dimensions. For example, a number of molecular behaviors comprise the dimensions of instrumental and consideration behavior. Yet, in explaining leadership behavior—whether for Blake and Mouton's (1985) managerial grid or House's (1974) path-goal theory—the dimensions of instrumental and consideration behavior, rather than the individual behaviors comprising these dimensions, are used to account for leadership. In Bass's (1985) leadership theory, the various factors of transformational and transactional leadership are measured by way of the seventy-three-item Multifactor Leadership Questionnaire. Rather than explaining leadership according to the seventy-three items comprising the MLQ, however, Bass groups the items in terms of the seven factors identified earlier in the chapter. The result is an emphasis on the global styles of leadership and a de-emphasis of individual message strategies.

What is the appropriate relationship between communication and the situation? Richard Crable and Steven Vibbert (1986) define *corporate public relations* as the "art of adjusting organizations to environments and the environments to organizations" (p. 394). In other words, while consumers place certain constraints on an organization's behavior, the organization can actively change and alter those constraints through the effective use of public relations. This conveys two images of the relationship between an organization and its environment: One portrays the organization as a passive entity that is constrained by its environment; the other sees the organization as a proactive organism that can actively change its environment. The same relationship holds true for leadership theory. Theories differ in terms of whether they view a leader's communication as dictated by the situation or able to be changed to fit the situation.

The nature of the situation does not influence the relevant traits and styles required for effective leadership in the universal trait and universal style theories. What a leader must be or do to be effective is independent of the situation; that is, it is *context independent.* The communicative abilities required for effective leadership remain the same across situations. An opposite view is offered by situational behavior theories: that effective leaders adapt their communication according to the nature of the situation. Leaders may need to provide more instrumental behavior when subordinates are psychologically immature or when the nature of the task is ambiguous. In short, the situation constrains the type of communication that is appropriate and effective in respect to the accomplishment of goals. Here communication is *context dependent.* Transformational leadership is neither independent nor dependent of context or the existing situation. Rather, it is *context creating.* One of the key aspects of transformational leadership is its ability to create new definitions for situations by instilling compelling visions in followers. The obstacles and constraints of the old situation are stripped away as a new way of viewing the situation emerges. For example, transformational leaders may encourage followers to view a large task as a challenge rather than an impossible amount of work. They can change the nature of the situation by altering how followers view the task. The new vision empowers followers and stimulates higher levels of commitment and loyalty.

Leadership theories approach the importance of communication and its relationship to a situation in different ways. Table 2.2 summarizes the various approaches to leadership. At this point, you may be wondering how the communication skills approach outlined in Chapter 1 addresses these issues. First, the communication skills approach is an outgrowth of the behavioral style and transformational models of leadership. In both style and transformational leadership theory, the role of communication is critical. The composition of mes-

TABLE 2.2 Leadership Theories: An Overview

Leadership Theory	Necessity of Communication	Skill Level	Communication and Context
Universal trait theory	Low	Molar	Context-independent
Universal style theory	High	Molecular; molar	Context-independent
Contingency trait theory	Low	Molar	Context-dependent
Situational behavior theory	High	Molecular; molar	Context-dependent
Transformational theory	High	Molar	Context-creating
Communication skills model	High	Molecular; molar; process	Context-dependent Context-creating

sages, in the form of either a behavioral style or vision, is the medium through which leaders organize groups of people. Unlike these two perspectives, however, the communication skills approach focuses on the many levels of communication. It emphasizes not only the molar level of skills that comprise leadership, but also the message strategies that leaders use to activate molar skills and the cognitive and behavioral processes that lead up to their performance. The approach allows a small set of core skills to be identified at the molar level, yet retains the complexity of leadership by acknowledging that the skills performed at the molecular level, as well as the sequence of messages and processes, may all vary. Second, from a communication skills perspective, the communicative acts appropriate for leadership are partially constrained by the situation. The appropriateness and effectiveness of messages are constrained by the organizational culture. Yet, leadership is proactive and can generate messages that change or alter the rules governing appropriate and effective communication. Therefore, leadership is constrained by the situation but also has the ability to perform new kinds of behavior in order to change that situation.

SUMMARY

A variety of approaches to leadership have been developed over the past few decades. Despite the diversity of the approaches, two issues typically distinguish them from other leadership approaches: (1) whether leadership is a behavioral- or trait-based phenomenon and (2) whether the required traits or behaviors for effective leadership change according to the situation. These two issues provide a framework for classifying leadership theories into four categories.

Universal trait theory suggests that leadership is best characterized by a set of physical, cognitive, and social traits that do not change according to situation. Universal style theory assumes that one behavioral style for leadership can be developed and universally applied across all situations. Blake and Mouton's (1985) managerial grid theory, and Lewin, Lippitt, and White's (1939) theory of democratic leadership reflect this approach. Contingency trait theory contends that leaders possess particular traits that must be correctly matched to a situation in order to be effective. Fiedler's (1967) contingency theory best represents this perspective. Situational behavior theory holds that leadership behavior must adapt to the demands of the situation. Hersey and Blanchard's (1982) life-cycle theory and House's (1971) path-goal theory adopt this approach. In recent years, transformational leadership theory, developed by Bass and associates (1985), has gained popularity. It emphasizes the importance of rhetorical skills in motivating and inspiring employees. The transformational leadership approach does not fit neatly into any of the four traditional leadership perspectives.

The leadership theories discussed in this chapter vary in the degree of importance they attach to communication. For example, universal trait theory diminishes the role of communication, whereas transformational theory emphasizes the power of communication in creating new ways of thinking and organizing collective behavior. Universal and situational behavior theories recognize the importance of communication in leadership but view it as a means of responding to an existing situation. Communication is not considered proactive in the sense of being able to change the constraints of a situation.

QUESTIONS AND APPLICATIONS

1. Assume you are the head of college campus recruiting for Crawfish King, a southern-based restaurant chain that specializes in Cajun and creole food. You supervise a number of recruiters who perform on-campus interviews. The recruiters will screen applicants for three entry-level positions in restaurant management, accounting, and research and development. As part of the evaluation process, the recruiters will rate interviewees on a number of personal qualities, including leadership. They recently asked you to define the qualities of leadership. In a memo to be circulated to your recruiters, include a list of the traits you believe define an effective leader. Also consider whether your list of traits should remain the same for all three jobs.

2. How can you characterize your style of leadership? Do you use different styles of leadership? Under what conditions do you alter your style of leadership?

3. Some of the theories you have read about maintain that effective leadership involves adapting to the situation. How do you balance the need to adapt to the situation and the need to be consistent in your behavior? Can leaders be too flexible in their willingness to adapt to the demands of the situation?

4. Think of someone you perceive as a transformational leader. Also think of someone you believe is more of a transactional leader. Make a list of how each person communicates with other people. How do the lists compare? Using the following scales, which measure Norton's (1983) dimensions of communication style (7 = exhibits this quality a great deal; 1 = doesn't exhibit this quality at all), rate how the two people communicate. In what ways are they similar and different?

TRANSACTIONAL LEADER	TRANSFORMATIONAL LEADER	COMMUNICATION STYLE
________	________	Friendly
________	________	Leaves an impression
________	________	Relaxed
________	________	Contentious
________	________	Attentive
________	________	Precise
________	________	Animated
________	________	Dramatic
________	________	Open
________	________	Dominant

5. What are some of the problems that you commonly encounter when leading others? List those problems on one side of a piece of paper. Then, on the other side, list the skills that allow you to manage the problems.

Part II

COMMUNICATION SKILLS AND LEADERSHIP

Chapter 3

From Networks to Networking

> The first task of an executive, as Roosevelt saw it, was to guarantee . . . an effective flow of information and ideas. . . . Roosevelt's persistent effort, therefore, was to check and balance information acquired through official channels by information acquired through a myriad of private, informal, and unorthodox channels and espionage networks. At times, he seemed almost to pit his personal sources against his public sources.
>
> *(Deal & Kennedy, 1982, pp. 86–87)*

> Not long ago, there were two junior officers in the Dutch Navy who made a pact. They decided that when they were at the various navy social functions, they would go out of their way to tell people what a great guy the other guy was. They'd appear at cocktail parties or dances and say, "What an unbelievable person Charlie is. He's the best man in the Navy." Or, "Did you hear about the brilliant idea Dave had?"
>
> They revealed this pact to the public the day they were both made admirals—the two youngest admirals ever appointed in the Dutch Navy.
>
> *(Deal & Kennedy, 1982, p. 95)*

What do these two passages have in common? A cursory glance reveals more differences than similarities. The first passage focuses on a former president of the United States, and the second on two members of the military. The nationality of the people also differs—one is a citizen of the United States of America, whereas the others are citizens of Holland. Roosevelt used other people to acquire information; the Dutch navy officers used other people to enhance their personal power and reputation. Although the two narratives differ in several ways, they both illustrate how people utilize communication networks. Roosevelt cultivated a communication network of informants and spies to compare the quality of the information he received through formal and informal channels. The two Dutch officers created a communication network to accumulate and collect power within the Dutch navy. Their rapid rise in the organizational hierarchy was a tribute to the Dutch Admiral's Paradigm, which assumes that a small, tightly knit coalition can influence other organizational members' perceptions.

Organizations are comprised of people working together to accomplish a task. As people work collectively, they form links with readily identifiable clusters or groups, commonly called *networks.* The formation of networks occurs for a variety of reasons. Some networks are created by people on the basis of friendship. Others are constructed by organizational members based on the nature of a task. In this type of network, the members need to talk to one another and exchange needed technical information to accomplish their work. Still other networks may be formed on the basis of power. In this case, people seek to preserve their own interest and status. Regardless of the reasons people have for creating or participating in networks, however, they are an important thread in the fabric of organizational life. Without them, companies would not be able to organize themselves toward accomplishing goals because needed information, materials, goods, and services would not flow through organizations. Furthermore, people who are not firmly anchored to an organizational network may view their role as unimportant or meaningless. Those not involved in communication networks withhold information from others and are less satisfied with their jobs. They also avoid interpersonal interaction and, as a result, often have lower rank and tenure than those involved in networks (Monge & Eisenberg, 1987; Roberts & O'Reilly, 1978).

Information is the raw material that flows through communication networks. Many different types of messages—about such things as how to do a job, who has power in the organization, who is being promoted, the personal idiosyncrasies of employees, changes in the company—travel through various communication networks. Leadership cannot help individuals and groups within organizations make sense of their environment without gaining access to the systems of information within organizations. Access to that information is accomplished through the leader's involvement in communication networks. To understand more fully how leadership relates to communication networks, we need first to examine the basic structure and organization of such networks.

NETWORKS AND THE PROCESS OF ORGANIZING

Let's assume you have just been hired by Acme, Inc., a computer software firm, as associate director of the Human Resource Management Department. It is your first day on the job, and the director of the department, Kim Zook, welcomes you and gives you an orientation of the department. You are also given Acme's employee handbook, which contains an organizational chart for the department (see Figure 3.1).

Kim is briefing you about the department. "As you can see," she says, "the department is divided along functional lines. Bob Mackey is our training and development specialist. He does most of the planning for new employee orientation and assesses the need for training workshops. Laura Monroe is our com-

FIGURE 3.1 Organizational Chart for Acme, Inc.

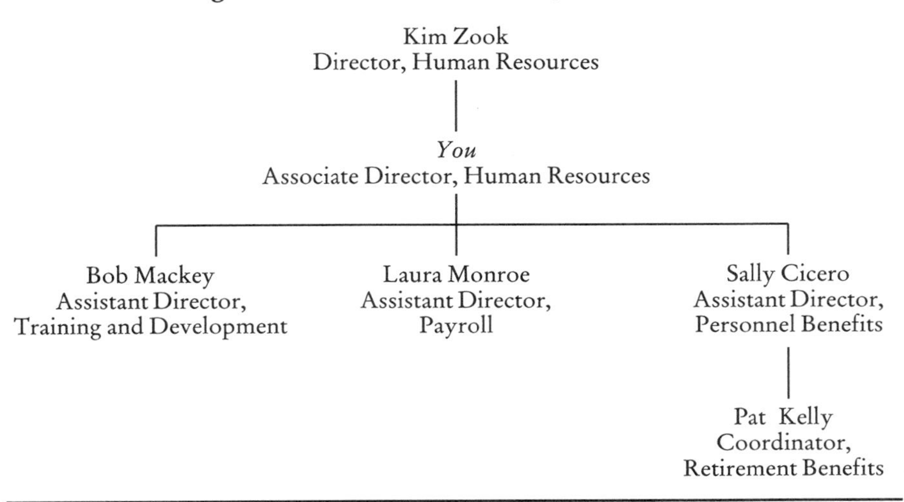

pensation expert. She keeps track of payroll and monitors new legislation regarding compensation. Sally Cicero is our benefits person; she keeps a tight reign on medical and dental insurance benefits. Her assistant, Pat Kelly, is in charge of retirement benefits. Each of these four people has two assistants who are barely able to keep up with the paperwork. You will help oversee these four people, and make sure they coordinate their efforts. You need to make me aware of any problems they are facing as well as the suggestions they make."

After your first few weeks at Acme, you are frustrated about your inability to access sufficient information about the Human Resource Management Department. With the exception of weekly department staff meetings, your interaction with other unit heads has been limited. Moreover, you note that the organization relies strongly on "management by walking around" (or MBWA). For example, Kim walks around the office talking to employees at their desks to find out where they are in their work and to offer encouragement. In this way, Kim monitors the flow of work in the office and, as she says, keeps her "finger on the pulse of the department." However, you feel that her MBWA method undercuts your position in the department, since she is acquiring on her own the information that you were hired to coordinate and relay back to her.

You decide to find out what is really going on in the department, discreetly asking your assistant for some information about the other unit heads. Your assistant has good access to departmental gossip—she and other support staff often spend lunchtime together in the company cafeteria. You find out that Sally Cicero is irritated with Bob Mackey and Pat Kelly because of their friendship and golf outings. In addition, Sally feels that Bob conveys more work-related information about upcoming changes and new programs to Pat than he does to her. You also discover that Kim takes Laura and Sally to lunch on Fridays to troubleshoot problems with their jobs. Furthermore, your assistant tells you that it is common knowledge within the department that Kim sees herself as a role model for other women in the organization. As a result, she devotes herself to making sure that women workers are given sufficient support to succeed. Shortly before you came to Acme, Kim and Bob had a major disagreement about purchasing a new interactive training program available on laserdisc—Bob wanted to purchase it but Kim felt its cost outweighed the potential training benefits. Bob went over Kim's head to higher-level management to obtain the funds to buy the program. Resentful of Bob's actions, Kim will only talk with him about work-related issues.

With your new insights into the networking at Acme, answer the following questions:

1. What kinds of networks exist within the department? Does a single network or a set of multiple networks exist?
2. What has contributed to the creation of these networks?
3. What roles do people play in the networks?

These questions are not only useful in developing a vocabulary to discuss communication networks, but they also highlight the three basic issues confronting network analysis and research.

What Kinds of Networks Exist?

Communication networks are differentiated on the basis of two criteria: (1) their adherence to an organization's formal hierarchy, and (2) their communicative function.

Networks that are categorized according to their adherence (or lack of adherence) to the formal organizational hierarchy include formal networks and informal networks. *Formal networks* reflect the organizational hierarchy, which specifies the responsibilities and duties of formal organizational positions, delineates reporting relationships, and sanctions the organizational chain of command. Organizational charts, such as the one for Acme, Inc. in Figure 3.1, and other organizational documents, such as position or job descriptions, are the artifacts of formal networks. *Informal networks* differ from formal networks in that they emerge from the personal interactions among employees and are characterized by links and connections not necessarily reflecting the organizational hierarchy. For example, Bob and Pat are friends and share both personal and work-related information, even though Pat's official reporting line is to Sally. Similarly, the assistants have cultivated an informal network through the time they spend together at lunchtime. The informal network, sometimes referred to as the "grapevine," is considered a more accurate and more reliable source of information than the formal network (Goldhaber, 1993).

Networks are also categorized according to the communicative function of the messages they transmit. Farace, Monge, and Russell (1977) point out that network research traditionally has focused on three types of message functions:

1. *Production:* The messages conveyed by the network focus on the performance of task activities (for example, the task activity that needs to be executed and how and when to perform it).
2. *Innovation:* The messages transmitted through the network relate to the implementation and introduction of new processes and procedures within the organization (for example, new ideas and suggestions for future changes).
3. *Maintenance:* The messages conveyed by the network concern the status of personal relationships and the needs of organizational members. Emphasis is placed on interpersonal relationships, emotional ties among members, and organizational climate.

The maintenance network is differentiated on the basis of whether its messages transmit information about the relative power status of organizational members or the assumptions and values inherent in the climate and culture of an organization. According to Noel Tichy (1981), the *political network* transmits messages about personal and group goals. It is concerned with exchanging influence and focuses on persuasive communication aimed at influencing individual and group goals. An analysis of the political network in an organization provides insights into who influences whom and which members have power status. The *cultural network* conveys messages regarding common values, meanings, and interpretations of organizational events. It also transmits the assumptions and meanings that organizational members use to make sense of their environment. Thus, the components of the maintenance network allow us to describe most organizations according to four types of communication networks: production, innovation, political, and cultural.

In our Acme, Inc. case study, various kinds of networks exist within the department (see Figure 3.2). A production network linking unit heads appears to be present given the weekly staff meetings about work performance. However, the innovation network appears to be limited to only Bob and Kim, as they primarily undertake discussions about new training technology. Distinct groups within the cultural network also appear to exist: the assistants share information about themselves and the company during lunchtime; Bob and Pat have established a friendship; and Kim, Sally, and Laura use weekly luncheons to discuss problems. You are isolated from these friendship cliques. The political network within the department is less clear. On the one hand, given Kim's position in the formal hierarchy and her informal relationships with other women in the department, she clearly has higher status than the other departmental members. On the other hand, Bob may have equal or greater status than Kim in light of his ability to forge ties with other organizational members, allowing him to circumvent Kim's decision not to purchase the new training technology.

Despite the convenience of characterizing groups along the lines just mentioned, it is important to remember that relationships among people create the complexity of organizational life; therefore, we cannot characterize people according to their involvement in a single network. Rather, relationships are usually a combination of a person's involvement in all four types of communication networks—the production, innovation, political, and cultural networks.

FIGURE 3.2 Network Structures for Acme, Inc.

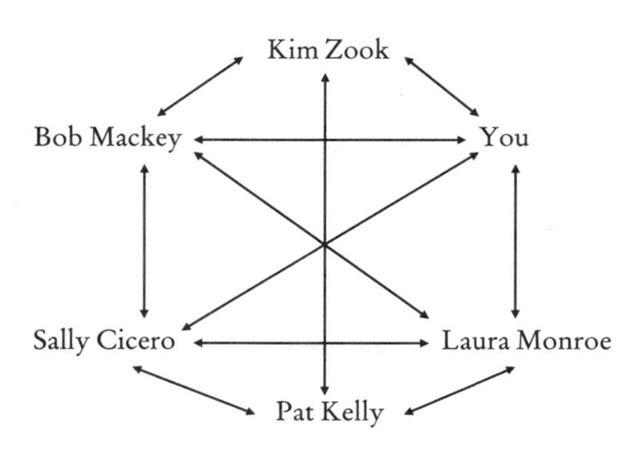

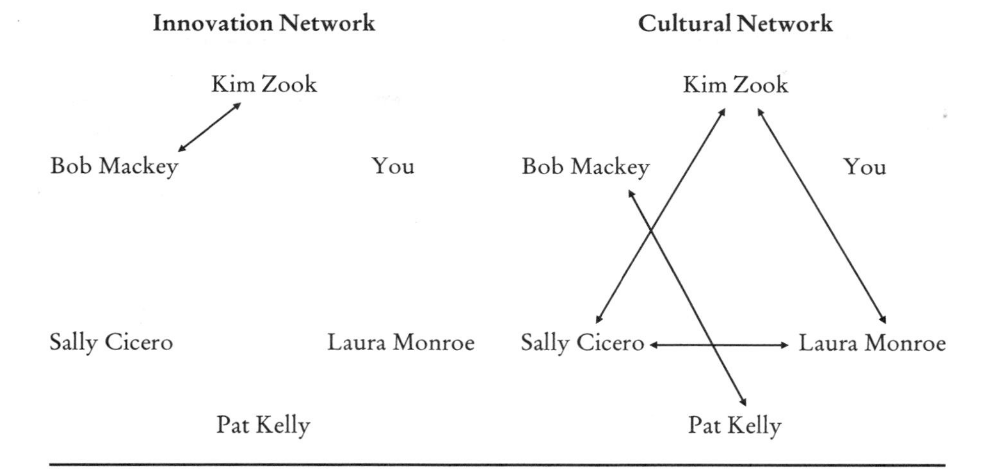

How Are Networks Created?

How you explain network emergence in organizations depends on one's perspective. Whether one views individuals as having the resources and capabilities for creating novel network structures or as being constrained by preexisting organizational rules and regulations influences the question's answer.

Early network research emphasized the importance of the formal organization's influence on the role relationships formed among people. Peter Monge and Eric Eisenberg (1987) refer to this perspective as the *positional view,* whereby "structure is a pattern of relations among positions in the social unit (the society, the organization, or the group). Attached to each position is a set of roles that the people occupying the positions are expected to perform" (p. 305).

This view is consistent with the structural perspective, which sees the organization as a configuration of roles and role relationships governed by rules and regulations. Furthermore, the role enacted by a particular individual within the organization sets the parameters for whom that person can talk to, what networks are available, and what topics are acceptable for discussion. Regardless of who occupies the role, the individual would be expected to talk with the same people about the same topics over the lifetime of that position within the organization. From this perspective, the existing communication network within Acme, Inc. is derived from the formal organizational chart, which specifies the needed roles and role relationships.

At the other extreme, some theorists argue that networks are not an entirely "top–down" phenomenon; rather, the existing network structure is more of a "bottom–up" phenomenon. In this view of organizational structure, which stems from the *relational tradition,* individuals collectively organize themselves and, through communication, create structures that help them make sense of the workplace, provide support, and stimulate work incentive. Existing organizational structures are not considered to influence developing networks greatly. Peter Blau (1982) points out that the relational tradition is most useful in describing how new networks form without preexisting formal structures. For example, Ben and Jerry's Ice Cream company began as a small ice cream shop in Vermont (Hubbard, 1990). In the early days of the organization, owners Ben Cohen and Jerry Greenfield performed many organizational functions and kept in constant contact with employees, suppliers, and customers. Their network consisted of daily contacts with people involved in their business. No preexisting organizational structure constrained contacts with business associates. However, as the company became larger and more successful, Cohen and Greenfield brought in specialists in computers and manufacturing to oversee daily operations. The specialists had clearly defined duties, which marked the transition of the organizational structure from a relational approach to a more positional approach.

The *cultural approach* to networking represents a middle-ground between the other two competing positions. It assumes that communication enables people to create and maintain organizational structures, such as networks, but that they are simultaneously constrained by the rules and norms of preexisting networks. This view is consistent with Anthony Giddens's (1979) theory of structuration, which recognizes that communication is not only influenced by preexisting systems but also has the power to maintain, alter, and modify existing structures as well as to create new ones. The cultural approach also differs from the relational and positional approaches in its emphasis on the importance of meaning and interpretation (Monge & Eisenberg, 1987). In other words, it is not information alone that passes through networks but also the meanings and interpretations attached to that information. The news that an individual has been fired from a company is one example of the information that may be transmitted through a network. Employees may be concerned about the event, but they are more likely to be concerned about what the event *means* in the context of the organization. Hypotheses and speculations would likely be generated to account for why the person was fired (such as the personal habits and work ethic of the individual or the overall financial condition of the company) in order to explain, justify, and legitimate the reasons for the event. Such interpretations flow through networks, helping employees make sense of the organization as a whole and of their standing in the organization.

In our case study, the informal support group formed by Kim, Laura, and Sally is an example of a cultural network. They meet for lunch each Friday to discuss obstacles and challenges in the workplace. The formal network and strict reporting relationships inherent in the organizational chart are adapted as a consequence of the mutual interests of Kim, Laura, and Sally. The formal network may minimize interaction between Laura and Sally because of the different positions they occupy and the functions they perform. However, their mutual concern about gender issues in the workplace transcends these restrictions, and they forge a relationship. It is highly likely during their meetings that Kim, as the senior member in the group, explains what certain organizational acts mean and helps the others place messages and actions into context. In this way, Kim is transmitting interpretations and meanings for certain organizational events and, as a result, is helping her employees make sense of the organizational culture. Thus, the network provides explanations and rationales for organizational actions.

What Roles Do People Play in Networks?

Networks are comprised of individuals whose participation in a network can range from high to minimal involvement. Groups are collections of individuals who talk to each other on a regular basis regarding a general topic. Several kinds of organizational groups exist, including work teams, special project groups, committees, task forces, and cliques. Organizational members participate in varying degrees in each of these groups, and their level of participation influences the role they play in the larger organizational network. In other words, people are members of a specific group within the network, are not involved with a network, or serve to link different groups together.

Peter Monge and Eric Eisenberg (1987) identify three roles that organizational members enact in networks: (1) isolates, (2) group members, or (3) group linkers (such as a bridge or liaison). *Isolates* are not involved with a network but function alone within the organization. When individuals are involved with a network, their membership status may change as a function of network density. *Network density* refers to the degree to which individuals are interconnected and linked to one another. An individual with high network density who also talks to many people within a group in the network may be termed a *group member.* An individual may be a member of two groups within the network. As a result, a person may serve as a *bridge* between groups and is the primary mechanism through which information can be transmitted. Individuals who are not members of any group but who link competing groups together are known as *linkers* or *liaisons.* In Figure 3.3, which illustrates the various network roles, the lines drawn between individuals illustrate how they are linked.

Network analysts typically use four characteristics to describe the qualities

FIGURE 3.3 Network Roles

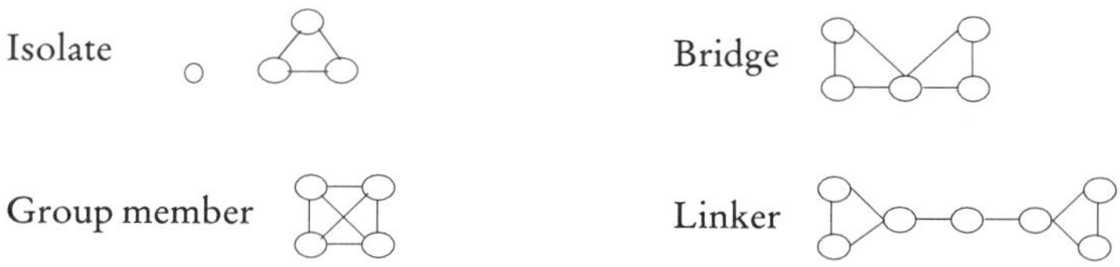

of links and role relationships present in communication networks. Using the preceding case study and the production network, we can demonstrate how the four basic characteristics of links are used to describe role relationships in the production network. First, the *intensity* of the linkage—the amount of information, goods, or services exchanged among individuals—centers on the amount of exchange in the link. A weak link may exist when little information is exchanged, such as when Bob provides task information to Sally only during weekly staff meetings. A strong link is indicated by a high level of exchange, as when Bob relays task information to Pat during staff meetings and while playing golf. Second, a *symmetrical* relationship exists when both individuals enact the same role. *Asymmetrical* links exist when individuals enact differing roles. For example, if Kim primarily gives advice and Laura primarily receives advice during staff meetings, the two have created an asymmetrical link. Third, the level of agreement or *reciprocity* delineates a different type of link. If Kim feels she has established a link with Laura regarding discussions about production and Laura agrees, the level of agreement is high. If Kim feels such a link exists and Laura does not, the level of agreement is low. Finally, individuals may be linked in a single network or may talk to one another regarding a variety of topics. *Multiplexity* refers to the number of different connections that two individuals may have with one another. A *uniplex link* exists when two individuals communicate with one another through only one network. A *multiplex link* exists when two individuals are involved with one another in multiple networks.

LEADERSHIP AND NETWORKS

Historically, research relating networks and leadership has focused on either how networks contribute to a leader's ability to form accurate impressions of the organizational environment or how they affect a leader's organizational power and influence. In recent years, the importance of leaders' networking to the existing organizational culture and of how leaders utilize networks to facilitate innovation have taken on added importance. In this section, we examine how communication networks aid leadership in acquiring accurate information, maintaining power and influence, making sense of an organization's culture, and facilitating innovation.

Networks and Information Accuracy

Within the computer science field, the acronym *GIGO* stands for "garbage in, garbage out," meaning that the output stemming from any given computer program or analysis is only as good as the original input. Similarly, to help groups and organizations adapt to their environment, leadership requires an accurate data base from which to draw inferences and make decisions. Leaders, therefore, have developed a variety of strategies to obtain accurate information, including promising information sources such rewards as favors, support, and recognition (Kaplan 1984). Information sources who are full-fledged members of the production network are particularly useful because they can provide leaders with valuable insights into the technical aspects of the organization (Tichy & Devanna, 1986). By gaining access to communication networks, leaders are able to collect the needed imprints of their information environment to make sound and effective decisions.

Why is access to communication networks critical for effective leadership? According to Hosking and Morley (1988), leaders become more skilled perceivers as they become networked into an organization. Leaders' ability to create accurate interpretations of situations is enhanced because their knowledge base regarding the nature and structure of the organization is strengthened through networking. By becoming more involved in the organization, leaders are more likely to identify problems successfully, recognize possible threats, and take advantage of opportunities by implementing certain solutions. Leaders who move about in the organization to obtain information are less likely to distort or misread organizational problems. Ultimately, knowledge of how "things are done" results in leaders being able to argue their own interests successfully. The importance of networking in acquiring accurate information is reflected in the popular management practice mentioned earlier—MBWA, or "management by walking around" (Peters & Austin, 1985). MBWA emphasizes keeping in touch with employees, taking the "pulse" of the organization, and most of all, listening to what employees have to say. By listening, leaders collect genuine impressions of what the organization is like and can subsequently plan and execute appropriate actions.

The importance of leadership's involvement with communication networks is underscored by the link between individual or group performance and network involvement and structure. At an individual level, several studies suggest that network involvement is correlated with personal performance (O'Reilly, 1977; O'Reilly & Roberts, 1977a, 1977b). When leaders are isolated from networks, their ability to gain insight into organizational problems and alternative solutions is minimized. At the group and organizational levels, particular kinds of network structures are required to help organizations adapt to their environment. Effective leadership must aid in the construction of appropriate networks to facilitate the flow of information between and among individuals and work groups. Lawrence and Lorsch (1967) observe that turbulent and fast-paced environments are successfully managed by organic and flexible organizational structures, whereas placid and stable environments are successfully managed through hierarchical and mechanistic structures. An organic organizational structure is characterized by densely interwoven and decentralized networks. A mechanistic organizational structure is more formalistic and hierarchical in nature, emphasizes highly centralized networks, and restricts whom organizational members can talk to and what they can talk about. In addition to the organization's environment, the nature of the task influences the required network structure. Centralized networks are effective when the problems faced by the group or organization are simple and do not require the cooperation of all group members. For problems that are complex and necessitate the cooperation of all group members, decentralized communication networks are required for successful resolution (Hirokawa, 1990; Roberts & O'Reilly, 1979).

Networks and Power

What allows leaders to exercise power and influence within a group or organization? One prominent explanation for leaders' power stems from involvement in communication networks. Leaders gain power and influence by being highly involved within a network. Position centrality has been correlated with power, and since leaders are typically the most centrally located individuals within a network, they usually possess a high amount of personal power. Their location within the network allows them to gain access to critical information as well as to regulate others' access to that information and other resources. Having access to critical information and control over its dissemination allows leaders to preserve their own interests and increase their status. That leadership influence is positively associated with leaders' level of involvement in the network and the number of ties they form within and outside of the organization has been confirmed in a variety of contexts. Within organizations, individuals' perceived influence is positively associated with their centrality in work flow, communication, and friendship networks (Brass, 1984). Between organizations, leaders' reputations and influence increase as they cultivate more linkages with influential people outside of the organization (Kaplan, 1984). At a community level, leaders who are able to influence community opinion regarding education and other public issues tend to be better linked to the media (newspapers and television) than those who do not have such influence (Heath & Bekker, 1986).

Two explanations account for why a leader's personal influence may be associated with his or her position of centrality in a network. First, because information is a strategic resource within organizations, leaders are able to gain and preserve their power because they control others' access to information. For example, a leader might influence how organizational members perceive a particular issue by withholding critical information. Some leaders may even withhold information about the nature of a problem or its potential solutions in order to preserve their own interests and goals. As Doris Graber (1992) points out, during the Environmental Protection Agency's (EPA) discussions about air pollution regulations in regard to power plant emissions, people on different sides of the issue deliberately withheld information from one another. By transmitting certain pieces of information and withholding others, EPA leaders attempted to influence how organizational members perceived the debate over air pollution regulations.

The other explanation for why network involvement may enhance a leader's personal power relates to the leader's ability to "see" accurately the organization's network structure. As individuals become socialized into an organization and gain experience, they are better able to discern the groups to which particular employees belong. Freeman and Romney (1987) contend that individuals who become more involved in an organization have a more accurate "mental picture" of its social structure. It is this cognitive representation of the organizational network, and not necessarily the actual involvement in the network, that allows leaders to exercise power. Understanding the network can serve as a base of power apart from network centrality. David Krackhardt (1990, p. 343) suggests that knowledge of an organization's social structure can be used by leaders in three different ways: (1) Central powerful figures within the network can be ascertained; (2) Coalitions within the organization can be identified; and (3) Weaknesses in coalitions or other political groups can be identified and weak support for specific positions isolated. Leaders can use their influence more effectively to obtain goals by knowing who talks to whom, knowing which constituencies must be enlisted to support their viewpoint, and knowing where weaknesses exist in a coalition's position.

Networks and Culture

Every organization has a culture—an underlying set of values, beliefs, and assumptions that helps members interpret actions within organizations and plan subsequent actions. Tichy and DeVanna (1986) suggest that it is through analysis of friendship networks that leaders gain insight into the culture of the organization. Others argue that friendship networks in the workplace are counterproductive and that organizational members should not mix business and pleasure. Yet, it is through the stories, jokes, and advice passed among friends within an organization that much information regarding how to act appropriately and perform a job is transmitted.

Consider the following passage about Tom Watson, former president of IBM:

> [A] twenty-two-year-old bride weighing ninety pounds whose husband had been sent overseas and who, in consequence, had been given a job until his return. . . . The young woman, Lucille Burger, was obliged to make certain that people entering security areas wore the correct clear identification.
>
> Surrounded by his usual entourage of white-shirted men, Watson approached the doorway to an area where she was on guard, wearing an orange badge acceptable elsewhere in the plant, but not a green badge, which alone permitted entrance at her door. "I was trembling in my uniform, which was far too big," she recalled. "It hid my shakes, but not

> my voice. 'I'm sorry,' I said to him. I knew who he was all right. 'You cannot enter. Your admittance is not recognized.' That's what we were supposed to say."
>
> The men accompanying Watson were stricken; the moment held unpredictable possibilities. "Don't you know who he is?" someone hissed. Watson raised his hand for silence, while one of the party strode off and returned with the appropriate badge. (Mumby, 1987, p. 121)

Although on one level the story may be seen as amusing "office gossip" with a humorous ending, it also transmits underlying assumptions about such things as who is in charge of the organization, how individuals are expected to perform their jobs, and what defines appropriate behavior (Mumby, 1987).

Some leadership theorists argue that leaders must tap into the cultural network to understand the basic attitudes and beliefs existing within an organization (Schein, 1988; Tichy & DeVanna, 1986). Without this understanding of an organization's culture, a leader may face difficulty implementing decisions and facilitating innovation and, as a result, problems may arise that could have been avoided. A case in point is Mary Cunningham's rapid advancement in the Bendix Corporation. Cunningham, a former executive at Bendix, was romantically involved with her mentor and the president of the company, William Agee. As she advanced in the corporation, colleagues attributed her rise to her romantic involvement, rather than to her skill and performance. As a result, Cunningham's credibility suffered and colleagues' respect for her seriously declined. In this instance, office gossip served to undercut her abilities and, ultimately, caused her to leave Bendix. If Agee and Cunningham had been more attuned to the cultural network at Bendix, they may have been better able to assess the effects of their behavior and to anticipate potential problems. In this sense, then, leaders' ability to adapt to the organizational culture influences their effectiveness in accomplishing a task.

Networks and Innovation

Bill Creech, a general in the U.S. Air Force Tactical Air Command (TAC), faced a problem in 1978: When he took over as head of the TAC, four hours were required to get an inoperable plane into the air. Moreover, the sortie rate—or the number of times planes are tested in battle conditions—had bottomed out over the last ten years. Creech launched a plan to innovate the TAC and to improve the sortie rate (that is, the time it took to make an inoperable plane airborne). He decentralized the maintenance department to facilitate the speedy acquisition of airplane replacement parts. He reinstituted competition among the various squadrons, provided statistics on how each squadron was performing, and allowed the squadrons to reintroduce their own pennants, flags, and markings. He pushed down responsibility from the top and empowered people at all levels of the organization to pursue excellence. He changed the facilities of the maintenance units by providing artwork and amenities so workers could take pride in their unit. In less than two years, the sortie rate had increased by

11.8 percent, and it took only eight minutes for a plane classified as inoperable to be readied for flight. Creech reinvigorated a $35 billion organization by forging new organizational structures.

One of the characteristics of an effective leader is the ability to help the organization transform itself to meet the challenges posed by its environment. An organization that does not encourage its members to be innovative is not likely to succeed. For an organization to be innovative, leadership must help it make the transition by creating new organizational ties. Leaders who are innovative and skilled at facilitating innovation in an organization are characterized by a high level of involvement in communication networks (Monge and Eisenberg, 1987).

Innovation carries with it uncertainty and risk. In order to address these concerns directly, individuals need to engage in open discussions of the potential benefits and risks associated with innovation. Unfortunately, open discussions are often hindered by people's insecurity about how others will view their proposals and ideas, particularly when it is felt that volunteering the information might be detrimental to one's career, and by people's lack of trust. Relationships characterized by such conditions are referred to as "weak ties." The weak ties hypothesis suggests that people shy away from discussing innovative ideas with one another when their level of uncertainty is high (Gramovetter, 1973). In contrast, when "strong ties" exist among individuals, innovative ideas are more likely to be discussed openly. Strong ties are characterized by individuals who discuss a broad array of topics and ideas (Albrecht & Ropp, 1984). When people talk about a variety of topics, they become linked in multiple ways and gain more information about one another. When we are relatively certain about a person's beliefs and can anticipate his or her potential reactions, we tend to be more open in discussion.

Strong ties are typically characterized as multiplex relationships. A uniplex relationship exists when an individual only talks about a single topic with another individual. If you only talk to a co-worker about the job, you would be characterized as having a uniplex relationship with that person. However, if you talked about work, family, and hobbies, you would have a multiplex relationship given the variety of topics. Multiplex relationships indicate that individuals are more socially integrated into the organizational system (Albrecht & Hall, 1991; Bach, 1989). Individuals involved in multiplex relationships also tend to be supportive of others' ideas, receptive to new ideas, and likely to view the individual proposing the ideas as trustworthy and credible (Albrecht & Hall, 1991).

For leaders to introduce innovation successfully into an organization, they must cultivate multiple linkages with various individuals and constituencies within the organization. Creech forged new ties within the TAC. By reorganizing the system, he encouraged squadron members to talk with one another about work. Pilots could relay information about the status of their planes to the actual mechanics who would repair them. Mechanics could talk directly with the parts people to facilitate the acquisition of spare parts. The task network was completely realigned. By enhancing team spirit through competition and the recognition of squadrons, Creech fostered an atmosphere in which team members were more likely to interact with another.

GAINING ENTRY TO COMMUNICATION NETWORKS

Although communication networks disseminate and provide valuable information to employees regarding the organization, and effective leaders must access them as valuable information sources, there are other types of information sources that are also important to a leader's knowledge of the organizational environment. The environment of an organization may be revealed by analyzing such written documents as the company's mission statement, internal memoranda, policy statements, employee handbook, stock reports, and newspaper and magazine articles. Yet, as we all know, not all relevant information is contained within written reports and documents. Coupling research of written materials with contacting others who have relevant information gives leaders access to multiple sources of information. The use of multiple information sources guards against the possibility that a single source may present biased information.

It is clear that leaders must be skilled at networking to gain entry to communication networks. But how the skill of networking translates into concrete message strategies is less clear. Networking is a skill that involves first establishing relationships with other people and then seeking information from those people.

Establishing Relationships

Leaders become "networked" within an organization by identifying existing communication networks and, on the basis of the information acquired, by establishing relationships that make them a part of that network. There are several strategies for identifying existing networks:

1. *Talking to the clerical and support staff.* While this may seem unimportant, clerical and support staff typically form a communication network and thus have an accurate understanding of the inner-workings of the organization (Deal & Kennedy, 1982). Assistants often observe a wide range of organizational activity and, therefore, may provide a more accurate interpretation of organizational events and activities than others in an organization.
2. *Requesting additional contacts from information sources.* When a leader acquires information from an individual, he or she may ask about other people informed of the particular problem or situation. In this way, the leader begins to form a map of the network, identifying the key constituencies and players within it.
3. *Systematically observing who talks with whom in the workplace.* Many times information about networks can be gained by observing individuals in their natural work setting. Who goes to lunch together? Who goes out for drinks after work? During work breaks, who tends to congregate in groups? The answers to those and similar questions allow a leader to begin mapping the communication networks within the organization.

4. *Looking for surprises and contradictions.* As leaders talk with and observe people, they may be surprised by what they find. Edgar Schein (1988), in *Organizational Culture and Leadership,* observes that by focusing on surprises, leaders can reexamine their assumptions about the organization's culture and structure. For example, two people who severely dislike one another are found to join forces to push a new project through the organization. Seek out informed counsel and try to make sense of this discovery.
5. *Observing mundane activity in the workplace.* Leaders should also pay attention to the common everyday activities that transpire in the workplace. In any organization or group, most behaviors are symbolic—they convey messages about status, appropriate behavior, and pressing problems. By taking note of who talks first at a meeting, who defers to whom when making a decision, who receives memoranda first, and who initiates discussion, for example, leaders can find clues to the network and the positions that members occupy within the network.

By observing organizational activity and cultivating contacts through the support staff, leaders begin to develop an understanding of the communication network. However, in order to become a part of that network, leaders need to establish relationships with other organizational and group members. Direct observation, walking around the office, asking questions, and requesting the names of potential contacts all provide glimpses of the existing communication networks. These experiences must then lead to establishing favorable relationships with other group and organizational members. Consider the case of Fred Hammer, an executive at Chase Manhattan Bank:

> Fred Hammer spent the first several months mapping out the networks at Chase Manhattan Bank. He did a great deal of management by walking around, visiting branches, talking to people. He also roamed the halls of Chase headquarters, getting to know key individuals, figuring out who needed to talk with whom to get things done. He then focused on the inside of his organization to develop credibility in the wider Chase political system. He looked for high leverage actions that could gain him credibility and political access outside his own section of the bank. (Tichy & Devanna, 1986, p. 205)

As this example suggests, once a leader begins to recognize some elements of the communication network, it is necessary to tap into that network by forging relationships with others. For Hammer, this meant looking for opportunities to enhance his credibility so that others would be more prone to listen to him.

Numerous strategies exist for creating favorable relationships. John Kotter (1979) outlines four strategies that may enhance an individual's ability to establish favorable relationships with other organizational members:

1. *Encourage identification.* People like other people who are similar to themselves. When we perceive others as possessing similar attitudes, be-

liefs, and ideas, we typically are more attracted to them. By highlighting similarities when interacting with others, leaders can decrease the amount of uncertainty that others have about leaders' beliefs, attitudes, and ideas. When others are confident about their knowledge about a leader and are able to predict or anticipate his or her reactions, they are more likely to disclose information to the leader.

2. *Create perceived dependence.* As individuals become more dependent on a leader, they are more likely to cooperate (Pfeffer, 1990). Creating such dependencies can be accomplished in one of two ways. First, leaders can attempt to control the resources that others need but do not have direct access to, thereby enhancing employee cooperation. Second, rather than controlling resources, leaders can create perceived dependencies by influencing others' perceptions of the leaders' actual influence. By cultivating the image that they possess needed resources—by talking only to high-status individuals within the organization, participating only in certain projects, or even arranging the office in a certain manner—leaders can influence how others perceive their power.
3. *Create a sense of obligation.* By performing favors for people, taking the unique characteristics of people into account, and providing personalized support, leaders can cultivate personal relationships. As the relationships become closer, the amount of obligation increases.
4. *Build a good professional reputation.* Most employees like to communicate with and be friends with those in high-status positions. A leader with a solid professional reputation is more likely to cultivate relationships with others in the organization. How a leader goes about building a professional reputation within an organization can vary. In academic organizations, it may mean publishing research reports and technical papers, whereas in a manufacturing organization, it may mean solving important manufacturing problems or successfully introducing new innovations. Because the events that lead toward building a professional reputation vary among organizations, leaders need first to determine the standards for their particular organization.

These strategies represent only a few of many that can be used to enhance the likelihood of forging relationships with other organizational members. For leaders to become skilled at networking, they must master strategies that not only give them insight into communication networks but also help them establish relationships with members of those networks. Some networking strategies raise ethical concerns, however. The types of strategies selected depend in part on the culture of the organization.

Mentoring: A Special Kind of Relationship

Establishing relationships is a prerequisite for gaining access to communication networks. One special type of relationship for gaining access to communication networks is the mentor-"mentee" relationship. Kram (1985) defines a *mentor* as an experienced, able, and productive upper-level manager who takes a special interest in assisting lower-level employees with personal development within the organization. The ultimate goals of a mentor are to improve the mentee's level of productivity and to increase organizational productivity and effectiveness by developing the mentee's personal skills and abilities. Mentors help explain organizational policies to their protégés and introduce them to communication networks.

Despite the positive benefits of mentoring, not all organizational members have equal opportunity to develop and maintain relationships with mentors. Women typically have more difficulty in developing mentoring relationships within organizations. Some researchers argue women often develop personal networks that mainly exist outside of the organization. The term *personal networks* refers to the total number of people with whom a person interacts. In studies examining the personal networks of men and women, researchers note that while men and women develop personal networks of about the same size (Fischer, 1982; Marsden, 1987), women's networks tend to have more relatives than nonrelatives and fewer co-workers than men's networks. In addition, men's networks typically include fewer neighbors and more co-workers, advisors, and friends than women's networks (Moore, 1990). As a result, it is argued that women tend to develop fewer organizational contacts, which decreases the number of potential mentors.

Why might women have difficulty in acquiring mentors? There are three credible explanations. First, women may not have access to potential mentors. A recent survey reveals roughly 5 percent of upper-level managers in U.S. corporations are female; thus, there may not be enough women in upper-level management positions to serve as mentors (Fisher, 1992). As a result, lower-level women managers may not gain access to a mentor. While male managers may serve as mentors to women, it is more likely that they will develop relationships with other men (Larwood & Blackmore, 1978). Second, women may be reluctant to seek out male mentors because of possible misconceptions by the organization and the male mentor. Cross-gender relationships are more complex than same-sex mentor relationships (Parker & Kram, 1993). For example, organizational members and the potential mentor may misconstrue the opening for establishing a mentor-mentee relationship as a sexual advance (Ragins & Cotton, 1991). Third, women may be excluded from mentorships because they are misperceived as not possessing the necessary technical competence and skills for successful management (Noe, 1988, p. 68). Women may negate this perception by acquiring the needed expertise and knowledge to cause other managers and co-workers to become dependent on them (Fairhurst & Snavely, 1983).

While gender differences may be attributable to the opportunities and constraints created by the organization's structure, the obstacles can be transcended. By utilizing some of the strategies discussed previously and developing new ones, women are able to develop mentoring relationships. Women may more easily acquire potential mentors by enhancing professional reputations, increasing expertise in a particular aspect of work, and developing control over critical resources.

Seeking Information

Individuals seek information when a high level of uncertainty exists and to make sense of an organization's culture, problems, challenges, and obstacles. There are many strategies from which leaders may draw in seeking information

TABLE 3.1 Information-Seeking Strategies

Strategy	Definition
Overt questions	The direct questioning of or soliciting of an information source. Includes use of open- and close-ended questions.
Indirect questions	Questions are veiled; phrased so as not to put either the employee or the information source on the spot. Tactics include asking around the information, hinting, and using noninterrogative questions.
Third parties	Involves the use of a secondary source (a co-worker) rather than a primary source (a supervisor) to acquire information. Provides a means of confirming the meaning, validity, and reliability of the primary source's messages.
Testing limits	Involves creating situations to which the information target must respond (such as violating a written policy to assess its relative importance). The information target's responses are then gauged by the employee to assess the target's feelings and attitudes toward the particular behavior or attitude.
Disguising conversations	Information-seeking attempts are disguised as natural parts of conversations. Information seekers typically put the target at ease and then subtly encourage the target to talk about a particular topic. May include joking, self-disclosure, prompting the target to elaborate on a comment, and commenting about objects within the environment as ways into the topic.
Observing	Information seekers unobtrusively watch how targets react and behave in salient situations. The goal is to assess information targets' specific attitudes or to see what job behaviors are desirable.
Surveillance	Rather than focusing on a specific situation, surveillance involves monitoring work activity with no specific information target in mind. Information seekers later evaluate behaviors and make inferences regarding particular instances.

Source: Adapted from Vernon Miller and Fred Jablin (1991), Information seeking during organizational entry: Influences, tactics, and a model of the process. *Academy of Management Review, 16* (1), pp. 102–113.

from co-workers, supervisors, assistants, and colleagues in their own and other organizations. Vernon Miller and Fred Jablin (1991) identify a number of the information-seeking strategies that individuals can employ (see Table 3.1 on page 83). Although their model is developed specifically for organizational newcomers, it also offers insight into how established organizational members can acquire and seek information.

The tactics that leaders select to acquire information depend on the costs associated with the information. Whenever we seek information, there are certain costs involved. An employee may be reluctant to seek information from an immediate supervisor, for example, for fear of seeming uninformed. In this case, the costs are quite high, and the employee may refrain from seeking the information from the supervisor. The social costs associated with acquiring information vary among individuals, ranging from the social approval of co-workers and the establishment of a good professional reputation to threatened friendships. Leaders need to assess the importance and the cost of the information before it is sought.

Miller and Jablin (1991) suggest that seeking information within a network involves several steps. *First, determine who is most likely to have the information.* As you become more involved in the network, you should obtain a clearer picture of the network's structure, enabling you to identify appropriate sources of information.

Second, evaluate the associated costs for acquiring the information. Your relationship with the information source may vary greatly. You may have direct and ample contact with the individual, as in the case of a mentor-mentee relationship, or you may not know the person at all. You may be on friendly terms or have an antagonistic relationship. It may be appropriate or inappropriate, in light of the organizational culture, to approach the target for information. The target may be a fellow co-worker or a member of the formal organizational hierarchy. The factors of access, closeness, cultural appropriateness, and status all influence the relative cost of the information.

Third, on the basis of your evaluation of the social costs, determine an appropriate information-seeking strategy. Certainly, any of the strategies identified in Table 3.1 can be utilized. Miller and Jablin (1991) suggest that the selection of a particular information-seeking strategy depends on the status of the information target as well as the social costs associated with the information. Their hypotheses can be summarized as follows:

1. Individuals who view information targets as having high status and limited access are:
   - less likely to use overt questions.
   - more likely to use indirect tactics.
   - more likely to use third-party tactics.
   - more likely to use disguised conversations.
   - more likely to use observing tactics.
   - less likely to use surveillance tactics.
2. When the social costs associated with acquiring the information are high, individuals are:
   - less likely to use overt questions.

- more likely to use indirect tactics.
- more likely to use third-party tactics.
- less likely to use testing limits.
- more likely to use disguised conversations.
- more likely to use observing tactics.

Whether an individual uses overt questions or disguised conversation to seek information in a particular situation depends on the personal qualities of the information seeker and the elements of the specific situation. On the basis of careful assessment of the situation and the information source, you need to draw on a repertoire of strategies to seek out the information.

SUMMARY

Historically, leadership has been tied to communication networks. On the basis of the existing research, four general conclusions can be drawn regarding the link between communication networks and leadership:

1. Network involvement is positively associated with the accuracy of the impressions generated by a leader.
2. Network involvement is positively correlated with the level of personal influence of a leader.
3. As the knowledge of the existing network increases, the level of personal influence of a leader is enhanced.
4. Leaders are better able to facilitate change and innovation within organizations when they are involved in multiple communication networks.

The key to effective leadership is involvement in communication networks. In helping organizations adapt to their environments, networking enables leaders to form accurate impressions of the problems that face organizations. Leaders must be aware that a variety of communication networks exist within organizations, including the production, innovation, political, and cultural networks. Leaders' ability to collect information depends on their level of involvement with communication networks. Yet forming accurate impressions and identifying problems are not sufficient for effective leadership; it is also important to be able to do something about those problems. Network involvement gives leaders an understanding of how others can be moved to action. As leaders become more involved with communication networks, they are more likely to understand the political and cultural aspects of the organization. This enables leaders to recognize obstacles within the environment as well as instigate change and innovation through their personal influence. They become able to identify the supporters and detractors of a particular position, to isolate the strengths and weaknesses of particular positions, and to formulate arguments based on their understanding of what is appropriate for a given organizational culture.

If organizations are to adapt to their environment, they must be innovative. Leadership that fosters successful innovation and adaptation is involved in the organization's communication networks. The ability of a leader to be a good object mediator depends directly on the individual's level of network involvement.

Networking involves two key processes: establishing relationships and seeking information. The keys to establishing relationships include encouraging commonality between the leader and a specific target and developing an image that conveys to other organizational members the leader's importance to the functioning of the organization. Building a repertoire of information-seeking strategies enables leaders to adapt their communication according to the social costs associated with acquiring the information as well as the status of the information target.

Gaining access to communication networks is an initial step toward understanding the organizational environment. However, leadership must successfully dissect the information and identify potential challenges, obstacles, and opportunities. How leadership can help organizations successfully analyze information is the focus of Chapter 4.

QUESTIONS AND APPLICATIONS

1. For a job that you held for a long period of time or a leadership position you had in a service or social organization, list the people inside and outside of the organization with whom you talked on a regular basis. Use the following table as a guide. For each person, check off the topics you typically talked about.

PERSON'S NAME	PERSONAL ISSUES AND TOPICS	WORK-RELATED ISSUES AND TOPICS	HISTORY AND CULTURE OF THE ORGANIZATION	NEW IDEAS AND INNOVATIONS IN THE ORGANIZATION
________	________	________	________	________
________	________	________	________	________

Now analyze your list of people. Did you talk more often with men or women? With people within the organization or outside of the organization? Were most of your discussions about a single topic or multiple topics? How can you describe the kind of network you had? How did the kinds of links you established with others influence your ability to access information within the organization?

2. Your friend and co-worker, Chris, is upset because a mutual acquaintance approached her and accused her of being "political" and of "snooping around to get the dirt in the organization." You know Chris is well connected and networked to a lot of people in the organization. What advice can you give Chris regarding the balance between being networked (using connections to gain information) and being viewed as "political"?

3. Your supervisor recently returned from a management seminar on mentorship programs and is enamored with the idea of creating one in your department. For the next departmental meeting, you have been asked to prepare a one-page sketch of the mentorship program and the potential problems associated with its implementation. In your report, identify those problems and how you would deal with them.

4. For each of the following scenarios, determine how you would go about seeking information.

> **a.** You are the leader of a project work team assigned to investigating new computer applications for monitoring and tracking clothing in dry cleaning companies. Dry cleaners across the country are beginning to use computerized systems to monitor the collection and processing of clothing items to enhance their record keeping. Your team needs to know how much money will be allocated for developing the new system. The only person who has access to this information is the new chief financial officer who joined the company a week ago. How would you obtain the information?
>
> **b.** In your work team, you have discovered that one of your co-workers has a drinking problem. Company policy is unclear about how to deal with employees with a drug or alcohol problem. In some instances, employees have been directly dismissed from employment without any explanation. In other cases, they have been given counseling and rehabilitation. You value the co-worker and want him or her to keep the job. You have a good friend in the human resources department, but you're not sure if you can use that friend for information. How would you obtain the information?

Now examine the strategies you selected. How are they similar? Different? What accounts for the similarities and differences?

Chapter 4
Making Sense of Information

"You want me to look for tracks? Is that it?"

"You're supposed to be good at it," Kennedy said. "That's what you always tell us."

"All right," Leaphorn said. "Show me where it is."

. . . He walked down the railroad embankment some twenty paces and started a circle through the sage, snakeweed, and chamisa. The soil here was typical of a sagebrush flat: loose, light, and with enough fine caliche particles to form a crust. An early autumn shower had moved over this area about a week ago, making tracking easy. Leaphorn circled back to the embankment without finding anything except the marks left by rodents, lizards, and snakes and confident there had been nothing to find. He walked another dozen yards down the track and started another, wider circle. Again, he found nothing that wasn't far too old or caused by an animal. Then he crisscrossed the sagebrush around the body, slowly, eyes down.

Behind him, far down the track, an ambulance had parked with a white sedan behind it—the car used by the pathologist from the Public Health Service hospital in Gallup. Leaphorn made a wry face. He shook his head.

"Nothing," he said. "If someone carried him in from this side, they carried him up from way down the tracks."

"Or down from way up the tracks," Baca said, grinning.

"What were you looking for?" Kennedy asked. "Besides tracks."

"Nothing in particular," Leaphorn said. "You're not really looking for anything in particular. If you do that, you don't see things you're not looking for."

(Hillerman, 1989, pp. 12, 16–17)

Joe Leaphorn, a Navajo tribal police officer, appears in many of Tony Hillerman's novels about life at Navajo reservations in the southwestern United States. Leaphorn's success at solving crimes directly depends on his ability to examine the crime scene dispassionately and objectively and to draw appropriate inferences. In the excerpt you have read from Hillerman's book, *Talking God* (1989), Leaphorn was called to the scene of a murder and was asked by local authorities to examine the crime scene for tracks and clues left by the murderer.

Leaphorn's examination of the crime scene is rigorous and exhaustive. He examines the entire area surrounding the murdered victim before concluding that there were no tracks. He also maintains an open mind by not looking for specific clues. Good detectives recognize that their own biases and preconceptions can color their approach to analyzing a crime scene. Good detectives suspend their biases and enter a crime scene totally focused on the clues present at the scene. Their power of observation is directed toward separately analyzing each bit of information without allowing a particular fact in the crime scene to color their judgment. This is important because a detective's bias may cause him or her to see things in a crime scene that are not there, or to miss clues that are present.

In many respects, leadership is like being a detective who looks for clues at the scene of a crime. Effective leadership also involves acquiring and examining clues—those present within an organization's environment. Information about organizational members, the institution, tasks and procedures, and the political landscape are just a few of the types of information within an organization's environment. As information is collected from within and outside of the organization, leadership helps the organization make sense of that information. However, as individuals, groups, and organizations collect and acquire information, they may be susceptible to certain biases that affect their judgment. Therefore, leadership also helps organizations interpret information. In order to interpret information correctly, leaders need first to understand how people perceive, organize, and structure information.

THE NATURE OF INFORMATION

Effective organizations and groups depend on having sufficient information to diagnose and assess a situation accurately. If the information that organizational members obtain is not sufficient to permit strong and valid inferences, the success of any future planned action is jeopardized. The ability of organizational members to create useful interpretations depends on two factors: (1) the nature of the information environment and (2) the quality of the information.

Types of Information Environments

Individuals, groups, and organizations function within an information environment and, consciously or unconsciously, participate in making sense of and understanding that environment. In addition, organizations create and function within different types of information environments.

Early research on information environments focused mainly on creating typologies. The classic example of this approach identifies four different types of information environments (Emery & Trist, 1965). *Placid-randomized environments* tend to be stable in that organizations confront similar levels of favorable and unfavorable conditions, and those conditions are randomly distributed within the environment. While *placid-clustered environments* are also stable, the dangers and obstacles associated with them are more tightly linked, such that the presence of one danger may be closely tied to the potential emergence of another danger in the future. Organizations operating in this type of information environment must identify dangers quickly in order to avoid them. A *disturbed-reactive environment* is characterized by instability, complexity, and nonroutine dangers. Here organizations compete with one another for needed resources to manage rapidly changing environmental dangers and obstacles. The information environment takes on added importance because it is the means through which organizations gain information about their relative standing among competitors. Finally, the *turbulent environment* is the most complex type of information environment. Although its instability and complexity are similar to that of the disturbed-reactive environment, the turbulent environment differs in that it often questions whether the current organizational form and purpose should be changed. Here organizations must assess whether their current organization and purpose are suitable for the environment.

Later research has extended Emery and Trist's (1965) pioneering work by focusing on identifying the dimensions of information environments (Aldrich, 1979; Dess & Beard, 1984; Sharfman & Dean, 1991; Tung, 1979). Numerous dimensions have been identified, but Huber and Daft (1987) summarize the five major dimensions that researchers traditionally use to describe information environments (see also Table 4.1).

1. *Quantity of information:* This dimension focuses on the amount of information that an organization receives. As the number of messages about an organization's or a group's standing within its environment increases, the quantity of information also increases.
2. *Clarity/Ambiguity:* This dimension focuses on the degree to which messages can be interpreted in multiple ways. Clear messages are easily interpreted because they have only one meaning or a few possible meanings. Message clarity decreases as the number of alternative meanings for a message increases.

TABLE 4.1 Characteristics of Information Environments

Characteristic	Degree of Complexity	
	Simple	*Complex*
1. Quantity of information	Low	High
2. Clarity/ambiguity	Clear	Unclear
3. Number of information sources	Low	High
4. Stability/instability	Stable	Unstable
5. Randomness	Predictable	Unpredictable

Source: Adapted from G. P. Huber and R. L. Daft (1987), in F. M. Jablin, L. L. Putnam, K. H. Roberts, & L. W. Porter (Eds.), *Handbook of organizational communication* (Beverly Hills: Sage), pp. 130–164.

3. *Number of information sources:* The amount of an organization's information sources is the focus here. Business competitors, government agencies, consumer groups, and suppliers may all provide information to an organization. Further, each source may provide a different type of information, such as the political, social, or business aspects of the environment.
4. *Stability/instability:* This dimension describes how frequently the organization's environment changes. Stable environments remain relatively constant over time, whereas unstable environments, such as those faced by high technology organizations, are subject to rapid change due to the business climate, consumer preferences, and technological breakthroughs.
5. *Randomness:* This dimension focuses on the degrees to which changes in the information environment and the direction of those changes can be predicted. In a nonrandom environment, the ability to anticipate and forecast changes increases.

As information environments become less clear, more unstable, and random, their complexity increases. Organizations operating in a rapidly changing information environment constantly evaluate information, not only to make sense of it but also to adapt to obstacles and challenges. Similarly, individuals and groups assess the organization's internal information environment to make sense of the problems they face within the organization.

Evaluating Information Quality

Information environments provide the raw materials—the messages and symbols—that help organizations determine appropriate actions for attaining desired goals. Without high-quality information, an organization's ability to overcome environmental obstacles is hindered. As Doris Graber (1992) observes, evaluating the quality of information is a highly subjective process. The same information may be viewed differently by people because of their differing personalities and preferences. For example, managers are sometimes asked to provide job references for former employees. They may face difficulty writing a recommendation for an employee whose performance was poor, but they are prevented from explicitly stating this in the recommendation because of legal restrictions. Managers sometimes resort to ambiguous statements in these cases. Called LIARs by Robert Thornton (1988), a professor at Lehigh University, for the lexicon of intentionally ambiguous responses, a manager might describe the qualifications of the former employee by writing, "I can enthusiastically recommend this employee with no qualifications whatsoever." If the receiver of this message has a low tolerance for ambiguity, the message will be viewed as containing poor information. If the receiver has a high tolerance for ambiguity, however, the message may be viewed as acceptable.

What distinguishes high-quality from low-quality information? Despite individuals' unique perceptions of information, six basic evaluative criteria for information quality can be identified (see also Table 4.2).

1. *Amount of information:* The amount of information is defined as the number of messages or symbols obtained by an individual during a set period of time.
2. *Clarity:* Message clarity is determined by how many plausible interpretations can be constructed for a particular message, or the degree to which a message is unambiguous. As the amount of information increases, clarity typically increases because the information provides a context for interpreting individual messages.
3. *Validity:* Valid information is characterized by the consistency of the facts being reported and the actual events. Validity refers to the truthfulness of the information.
4. *Reliability:* Reliability regards the consistency of information and the absence of contradictory messages. Reliable information can be confirmed by other information sources. Information may be valid but unreliable; for example, a leader concerned about employee morale and motivation may talk to organizational members and discover that they feel unmotivated by the organization. Yet, a recent company survey reveals that employee satisfaction and productivity are higher than ever before. Assuming that both information sources are valid, the contradictory nature of the information makes it unreliable.
5. *Timeliness:* Timeliness refers to whether the information received is current or outdated. Timely information is available at the moment it is needed.
6. *Depth:* Depth regards the level of the information received. Adequate depth of information includes a complete accounting of all relevant facts and the inclusion of a wide range of facts, options, and opinions.

High-quality information provides organizational members with sufficient depth to make sense of situations because it is clear, reliable, and timely. It is also

TABLE 4.2 The Quality of Information

Characteristic	Low-Quality Information	High-Quality Information
1. Amount of information	Low	High
2. Clarity	Ambiguous	Unambiguous
3. Validity	Inaccurate	Accurate
4. Reliability	Inconsistent	Consistent
5. Timeliness	Untimely	Timely
6. Depth	Inadequate	Adequate

Source: Adapted from G. Graber (1992), *Public sector communication: How organizations manage information.* Washington DC: Congressional Quarterly.

simpler for people to process and make sense of because it does not convey conflicting images or ideas and is not subject to multiple interpretations. However, organizational members encounter problems when little information is available or when the information is inaccurate, inconsistent, or untimely. As a result, organizational members lack the information they need or face situations that are ambiguous and contradictory. In such instances, the task of trying to make sense of the information becomes much more complex. Communication is especially important in helping members to distinguish between valid and invalid information, to discover why inconsistencies exist, and to create appropriate interpretations for ambiguous messages. High-quality information decreases the amount and types of communication needed for interpretation, whereas low-quality information requires more and varied types of communication to arrive at appropriate interpretations (Kreps, 1980; Weick, 1979).

Effective leadership helps an organization make sense of the complex information contained within the environment. It also helps organizational members distinguish between important and unimportant information inputs. Therefore, we need to examine how leadership facilitates organizational members in managing their information environment.

MANAGING THE COMPLEXITY OF THE INFORMATION ENVIRONMENT

When individuals and groups seek and receive information, they must ultimately interpret what it means and base their subsequent actions on those interpretations. Consider, for example, the following sequence of symbols. What four symbols follow and what do they represent?

What steps did you take to solve the puzzle? Did you visually compare the string of symbols to other symbols you had seen before? Did you apply a mathematical algorithm to predict the remaining sequence? Did you consider the possibility that the figures are random and not part of a sequence? How did the symbols influence your selection of the remaining four symbols? (The solution to the puzzle is given at the end of the chapter.)

The steps you took to solve the puzzle are similar to the processes leaders and organizational members use to make sense of information environments. They recognize the need to bracket or categorize the information they receive. The incoming information must be interpreted and placed into a meaningful context in order to choose appropriate subsequent actions. Leaders and organizational members typically rely on their past experience and a variety of devices to interpret information. To solve the puzzle, you may have compared the string of symbols to the pictograms utilized by foreign languages as a means of making sense of the symbols. Or, you may have adopted a rational mathematical view of the puzzle to determine which formula best fit the string of symbols. Leaders and organizational members also use decision-rules, analogies, and comparisons to make sense of and interpret information environments as well as to comprehend messages within the organization. Effective leaders and organizational members are able to break down the components of an information environment by using a number of cognitive devices.

Leadership and the Information Environment

Most researchers focus on how leadership helps an organization adapt to the constraints placed on it by the information environment. As noted in Chapter 1, Ashby's (1960) law of requisite variety states that leadership processes must be as complex as the information environment if they are to help an organization successfully achieve its goals. In other words, the complexity of the organization must match its environmental complexity. In describing how organizations manage the information environment, some theorists observe that organizations operating in stable environments tend to be hierarchical, to emphasize uniform organizational policies, and to structure work units in a similar manner (Emery & Trist, 1965; Lawrence & Lorsch, 1967). In contrast, organizations operating in complex and turbulent environments tend to be organic, to organize departments according to the unique relationships they have with the environment, and to place less emphasis on uniform policies.

In addition, organizational structures appear to be characterized by certain types of leadership practice. Organizations with a relatively stable information environment tend to use a directive style of leadership and centralized decision making (Emery & Trist, 1965; Lawrence & Lorsch, 1967). It is argued that the relative simplicity of stable information environments allows for directive leadership because leaders have sufficient time and resources to gather and analyze information effectively. Consultative leadership may be used by leaders to help consolidate and interpret information under turbulent and complex conditions. Since departments have unique relationships with their environments and are thereby organized differently, leaders rely on the insights and inputs of department members when making decisions. Consultative leadership is more complex than directive leadership in that it requires listening to and coordinating the views of followers. As the research demonstrates, organizations and leadership need to be complex in order to manage the information environment successfully.

In terms of individual leaders, a complex information environment demands that they exhibit variety in their behavior. Osborn, Hunt, and Bussom (1977) examined the relationships among environmental complexity, leadership complexity, and group performance. Their findings suggest that similar levels of environmental and leadership complexity promote increased group performance. The notion that leaders employ consultative decision making in complex environments also stresses the importance of matching leadership variety to environmental variety. Consultative decision making requires more skills and abilities than directive leadership.

Underlying the relationship between leadership and information environments is the assumption that effective leadership helps an organization adapt to its external environment. Thus, theorists focus on how leadership helps an organization perceive its external information environment. In addition, theorists emphasize the need for leaders to maintain complexity in their behavior because, with knowledge and expertise, they are more likely to perceive the environment accurately (Perrow, 1984). The key factor here is *accuracy*—it connotes a high degree of correspondence between one's interpretation of the environment and what actually characterizes it. Leaders' perceptions are accurate when they match the phenomenon that exists apart from them. Traditionally, the environment has been treated as an objective entity, separate from the interpretive actions of organizational members.

Recently, however, the assumption that leadership accurately interprets the external information environment has been challenged. Linda Smircich and Charles Stubbart (1985) label the traditional view of information environments the objectivist viewpoint, and contrast it with the subjectivist and enactment views. The traditional or *objectivist view* of the information environment treats it as an independent, external entity that directly influences the organization. From a systems view, the organization is a subsystem of the larger entity known as the environment. Similarly, groups are viewed as subsystems within an organization and dyads as subsystems within groups. Systems and subsystems may exchange information and resources. It is the larger system, however, that most directly influences the actions of the subsystem, whether it is an organization, a work team, a dyad, or an individual worker. The objective qualities of the information environment, not the interpretations of the individuals within a system, drive individual and collective action.

The objectivist view of information environments is strongly criticized by analysts who contend that organizational members' perceptions of the environment influence their decision making (Duncan, 1972; Lawrence & Lorsch, 1967). Hence, a *subjectivist view* of information environments has emerged. Assessing the information environment from this perspective means obtaining the perceptions of key decision makers within an organization and evaluating the environmental factors that they view as important to the decision-making process. The perceptions of key members may be used to predict the choices of other organizational members (Scott, 1981); however, they cannot be used apart from the objective view of the environment to predict outcomes, such as productivity and performance. Bourgeois (1985) notes that low economic performance may occur when top management's perceptions of environmental uncertainty differ from objective measures of environmental uncertainty.

The *enactment view* of the information environment suggests that individuals do not react to their environment; rather, organizations initially create the environment to which the organization then adapts (Weick, 1979). This view does not disregard the fact that real objects (such as machinery, buildings, computers, and people) exist in the workplace, but maintains that these "objects are inconsequential until they are acted upon and then incorporated retrospectively into events, situations, and explanations" (Weick, 1988, p. 306). The relative importance of a particular object depends on how one perceives an experience and subsequently acts toward the object on the basis of that preconception.

The power of the enactment view is highlighted by the experience of one of the author's students as a bank teller. At the bank where she worked, the manager noticed an increase in the number of customer complaints about bank tellers. If you were the bank manager, what would you consider the cause of the problem and how would you attempt to solve it? If your background was in human resource management, you might choose to characterize the information as a clue to a training problem. If your background was in sales and marketing, however, you might be more inclined to view the cause of the problem as a lack of motivation among the bank tellers. You would then attempt to increase their motivation to provide high-quality service. Although both perspectives view the problem as residing with the tellers, each adopts a different course of action: One sees training as the solution, whereas the other seeks to change the motivational system. However, the actual bank manager chose neither of these approaches. Instead, he placed mirrors behind the tellers' heads and the complaining stopped. Once customers saw how ugly they looked when they complained, the number of complaints dropped dramatically. The manager's view of the problem did not target the tellers but the unrealistic expectations of bank customers.

The subjectivist and enactment views of the information environment emphasize the importance of leadership in aiding organizational members in making sense of information. Being aware of information is not enough; it must be perceived, interpreted, and placed into a meaningful context for making subsequent decisions. Yet leadership is more than a means of helping organizational members deal with the information environment; it also frames others' perceptions of that environment and, in some cases, may even help to create it. An old joke in baseball circles about three umpires' approaches to calling balls and strikes is relevant here. The umpires are asked to describe how they call balls and strikes. The first umpire replies, "I call them as I see them." The second umpire replies, "I see them as I call them." The third umpire, shaking his head at the other two, says, "They ain't nothing till I call them!" Much like the last two umpires' approaches to calling balls and strikes, leadership either frames the information environment for organizational members or enacts the environment after realizing that it needs to be created.

The degrees to which an information environment, within or outside of the organization, is viewed as placid or turbulent depend on how leaders help frame the environment. Similarly, whether information is viewed as complete, valid, and reliable depends on how leadership helps frame that information. To make sense of the environment, leaders use a variety of cognitive devices to construct interpretations of information.

Leadership and Cognitive Schemata

The term *cognitive schemata* refers to the mental framework that people use to organize and process information. Cognitive schemata influence how we organize incoming messages and process and analyze information, for example. In leadership, schemata can affect a leader's general perception of the environment, the complexity of the environment, and the analysis and solution of problems. Researchers identify four basic types of cognitive schemata for leadership: (1)

decision-premises and rule systems, (2) analogies and metaphors, (3) prototypes, and (4) scripts.

Decision-premises and rule systems. The formal and informal guidelines that leaders and followers use when analyzing situations and making decisions are referred to as *decision-premises* or *rule systems.* They allow individuals to prioritize information and to identify what needs to be closely monitored. Decision-premises are often reflected in the slogans or mottos of an organization; for example, Ford Motor Company's "Quality is job one!" and Delta Airlines' "We love to fly, and it shows." Mottos serve to focus attention on certain aspects of the information environment and provide guidelines on identifying what is considered important within the organization. Ford's slogan may encourage employees to approach and interpret situations and problems in terms of product quality. Similarly, Delta's motto may help employees analyze and interpret information in terms of what it means for providing customer service.

Formal decision-premises and rule systems include the bureaucratic rules for generating interpretations and responses by organizational members and leaders. March and Simon (1958) contend that organizations cannot anticipate all contingencies or specify particular courses of action in all circumstances. Controlling employees and leaders, therefore, depends on instilling certain decision-premises and assumptions that employees can use when they face any decision-making situation. A bureaucratic form of control is emphasized here in that all employees are expected to share the same set of values.

In contrast, informal decision-premises and rule systems are forged among organizational members and are not specifically contained within an organization's formal policy manual or written procedures. Edgar Schein (1988) observes that when leaders create new organizations, they outline the rules and expectations that will be used to influence other organizational members' behavior. These initial expectations become embedded in the organization over time as they are transferred to new employees. Although the initial assumptions and premises may change over time, leaders continue to exert informally a high level of influence on followers' decision-premises. For example, a leader's problem-solving style may influence lower-level employees, resulting in their use of a similar approach for solving problems (Bass, Waldman, Avolio, & Bebb, 1987). Research on strategic decision making demonstrates that the cognitive schemata used by members of an organization often parallel those used by upper-level management (Hambrick & Mason, 1984; Schwenk, 1988).

Analogies and metaphors. A *metaphor* is a figure of speech that represents one phenomenon in the terms of another. Similarly, an *analogy* compares two unlike things that share some characteristics. Within organizational life, the organization has been compared to a machine, a living organism, even a prison (Morgan, 1986). In terms of viewing organizations, however, metaphors and analogies serve as a means for interpreting and analyzing information. Thus, leaders employ metaphors and analogies when dealing with the information environment. (See Box 4.1.)

Many leaders in top business and governmental organizations use metaphors

Box 4.1
Of Metaphors, Messes, and Markets

Diversified Food and Beverage, Inc., formed eighty years ago by Charlie McLaughlin, started out by selling high-caffeine, high-sugar carbonated beverages in the small working-class town of Granite, Indiana. The beverages became quite popular with night-shift workers, who enjoyed the rush of energy provided by the sugar and caffeine. The company was later expanded to include a consumer foods group, which currently manufactures chips, deep-fried pork rinds, pretzels, and other snack foods. In addition, a restaurant division was added ten years ago. At the present time, Diversified Food and Beverage consists of the following three divisions:

Beverage Division: Affectionately known as the "buzz" division, the beverage division specializes in carbonated beverages. It continues to sell "stimulating" soft drinks laden with caffeine and sugar and has recently branched into wine coolers.

Restaurant Division: Starting with the fast-food hamburger business, the restaurant division has moved into specialty foods, such as Leonardo's Italian Ristorante and Tommy's Tamale Stand, a Mexican restaurant. A year ago, a new chain, Pizza-Cal, emphasizing California-style cooking, was launched. Fresh wheat-dough pizzas made in woodburning stoves are the mainstay on its menu and numerous specialty salads are offered. The emphasis is on providing a healthy array of foods with high flavor.

Consumer Foods Group: The consumer foods group manufactures a number of snack items that are marketed in convenience stores and vending machines. Over the years, this has been a highly lucrative market for the company.

Each year at Diversified Food and Beverage, a top-level management group consisting of four regional managers reviews the preceding year's results and makes recommendations to the CEO about such things as expanding or downsizing particular markets and divisions. The following reply memo was recently sent to the management group from Michelle McLaughlin, the CEO and the original founder's granddaughter.

TO: Jack Gardner, Linda Carpenter, Maurice Childs, Jan Darwin

FROM: Michelle McLaughlin, CEO

RE: Company evaluation

I appreciate the time you took to evaluate the company. This past year has been somewhat mixed, as some of our divisions increased their market share and profitability while others did not. I have enclosed the following information for your consideration. Please let me know what your group thinks should be our strategy for the upcoming year.

Exhibit 1: Division Balance Sheet. Following are the revenues and costs (in $ millions) for each of the divisions.

Division	Gross Revenues ($ millions)		Fixed Costs ($ millions)		Variable Costs ($ millions)	
	Current Year	Preceding Year	Current Year	Preceding Year	Current Year	Preceding Year
Beverage Division	$37	$33	$10	$10	$20	$21
Restaurant Division	20	27	10	8	12	15
Consumer Foods Group	90	79	20	20	40	35
Total	$147	$139	$40	$38	$72	$71

Exhibit 2: Division Market Shares. A number of industry standards have been published that rank market shares for particular industries. Our positions in the market, as based on the share of market for the current and preceding years, are listed.

Division	Market Rank		Net Gain or Loss in Market Position
	Current Year	Preceding Year	
Beverage Division	5	5	−2
Restaurant Division	11	7	−4
Consumer Foods Group	2	3	+1

Exhibit 3: Reprint from Eat, Drink, and Be Merry *Magazine.* The following market report on Pizza-Cal by market analyst Leona Sharp appeared in the latest issue of the magazine:

> Pizza-Cal is an excellent idea whose time will come someday. I project it will lose money for at least three years until the word gets out to the public about the food. Our market analysis shows that people who have eaten at Pizza-Cal enjoy the pizza. Unfortunately, people who have only heard the advertising maintain a negative impression of the pizza chain because of the odd names given the pizzas and salads, such as Thai-style Tofu and Cilantro pizza. My projection is that Pizza-Cal will eventually succeed because of the current trend toward eating healthier foods.

Box continued

Exhibit 4: Report from Accounting Office. Our projections for the Pizza-Cal restaurant chain include the following. First, it will continue to drain resources and lose money for the next two years until the fixed costs associated with starting the chain decline. Second, profits after the two-year mark will rise steadily but will be moderate. Pizza-Cal will never reach the profit margins achieved by the beverage and consumer foods group divisions.

DESCRIPTIONS OF THE PLAYERS

The four upper-level regional managers will make the decisions regarding the attainment of goals for the upcoming year.

Jack Gardner, regional manager of the Northeast region, is an avid supporter of the organization and has been with the company for twenty-three years. He has witnessed the ups and downs of Diversified Food and Beverage over the years. Also an avid gardener, Jack views all organizational phenomena through the view of a gardener. His favorite saying is, "Any organization is like a garden. In order for the garden to grow, each spring you must prune back the dead vegetation to stimulate new growth."

Linda Carpenter, regional manager of the Northwest region, is relatively new to the organization, with only four years on the job. Her background is in strategic planning. Linda enjoys woodworking, and has been known to remain in her workshop for days creating furniture. Her love of woodworking has influenced her view of life. In fact, she carved her motto in a piece of mahogany and put it above the desk in her office: "Any organization is like a three-legged stool. If you take one leg away, then the stool is not balanced and it will fall."

Maurice Childs, regional manager of the Southwest region, has been with the company for only two years. Previously, he was president of a small beverage company, but had become so involved with that company that his marriage failed. He subsequently sought counseling and developed a new view toward life. After joining Diversified Food and Beverage, Maurice quickly became known as "Big Daddy" because of his efforts at cultivating a family feeling in his region. He describes his philosophy in this way: "I believe every organization is like a family. We have to stick together through thick and thin if we are to survive."

Jan Darwin, regional manager of the Southeast region, has been with the company for fifteen years. She has a thrill-seeking personality and enjoys mountain climbing and sky diving. Her involvement with these hobbies caused her to rethink her philosophy about people. She believes that some people can "cut it" and others cannot. As a result, she only takes mountain-climbing and sky-diving excursions with people who demonstrate enough skill to survive the toughest obstacles. Jan's philosophy also influences her approach to managing her region: "Like animals in a jungle, organizations are involved in the survival of the fittest. Only the strong survive."

ASSIGNMENT 1

Each regional manager uses a different metaphor for viewing Diversified Food and Beverage. Describe how you think each leader will respond to the CEO's memo and the exhibits it contains. Given how the leaders view the organization, what pieces of information will each one focus on in the exhibits? What kinds of recommendations will each manager make?

ASSIGNMENT 2

Each manager's metaphor for viewing the company has a different focus. Think of a metaphor or an analogy of your own that could link the four competing ones together. Explain your choice.

and analogies to interpret information because they provide simple, clear, and vivid representations of problems (Duhaime & Schwenk, 1985; Schwenk, 1984, 1988). The selection of a particular metaphor or analogy can be crucial because it places limitations on the information to be included in an analysis (Einhorn & Hogarth, 1982). In the 1950s, for instance, the metaphor "communism is a cancer" helped to shape U.S. government policy for dealing with certain segments of the population.

Prototypes. *Prototypes* are cognitive structures that facilitate categorization of a phenomenon by attempting to capture its essence. A prototype is the ideal example of something in any given category. Specific phenomena may reflect to varying degrees the characteristics specified in the prototype. Leaders use prototypes to categorize the elements of an information environment and to clarify the types of situations they confront. In many respects, Gibb's (1960) delineation of defensive and supportive climates illustrates the properties of a prototype. According to Gibb, defensive and supportive climates can be distinguished by the following types of behaviors:

Defensive Acts	*Supportive Acts*
1. Superiority	1. Equality
2. Certainty	2. Provisionalism
3. Neutrality	3. Empathy
4. Evaluation	4. Description
5. Strategy	5. Spontaneity
6. Control	6. Problem orientation

When leaders approach a situation, they will tend to view that situation as either defensive or supportive if they can classify the behaviors present as representative of a defensive or supportive climate. The criteria thus provide the means for leaders to categorize a specific event. Similarly, leaders may have a prototype for what they consider the ideal worker, a productive team meeting, or an organizational crisis.

Scripts. *Scripts* are guides that identify preferred courses of action. They allow us to anticipate what comes next and to plan appropriate action. For example, try organizing the following scrambled list of key decision-making steps:

Evaluating solutions
Analyzing the problem
Generating solutions
Orienting the group toward the problem
Implementing the solution
Selecting solutions

According to many normative decision-making theorists (for example, Dewey, 1910), effective decision making is sequential: It begins with the analysis of a problem, moves on to generating and evaluating solutions, and ends with determining and implementing the best solution. This is a script for decision making.

Decision-premises and rule systems, analogies and metaphors, prototypes, and scripts are types of cognitive schemata used by leaders and organizational members to help explain the information environment. Consciously or unconsciously, leaders employ cognitive schemata to interpret the messages conveyed by a situation. The degree to which leaders develop useful and effective interpretations depends on their ability to employ the various cognitive schemata successfully. Leaders need to recognize that gathering large amounts of information, cultivating multiple sources of information, avoiding hasty analyses, and knowing that information is valid are not enough to guarantee useful interpretations of the information environment and its messages. Leaders also need to be aware of the problems associated with using cognitive schemata.

Problems Associated with Cognitive Schemata

Since interpretations for situations and events form the basis for future action, it is important that interpretations be consistent with available information. Cognitive schemata serve as "rules of thumb," or *heuristics*, that help leaders make complex information and problems more manageable and identify key patterns and underlying assumptions. While heuristics serve a valuable information management function, they may also lead to poor information processing. As Tversky and Kahneman (1974) note, "heuristics are quite useful, but sometimes they lead to severe and systematic error" (p. 1125). Many times, leaders are not aware of the prototypes, decision-rules, or scripts they use when acquiring and interpreting information. Gioia and Poole (1984) suggest that when groups and organizations have "strong" scripts, they tend to neglect a thorough assessment of incoming information. A strong script emerges when a particular event occurs repeatedly and individuals develop standardized ways of dealing with it. Your daily drive or walk to work is an example of a strong script. The route taken becomes so routinized that you may not pay close attention to the cars and people you encounter on your way. In fact, you may not even recall turning at a particular corner or using your car's turn signal at a given intersection. Strong scripts cause us to gloss over the fine-grained details of a situation, rather than examining them with a critical eye.

Spyros Makridakis (Makridakis, 1990; Hogarth & Makridakis, 1981) identify several biases caused by heuristics that lead to problems with acquiring information (see Table 4.3). One such bias, *availability*, refers to the tendency of people to remember the details of events or situations that occur on a frequent basis and to consider them the norm. As a result, people tend to judge other events or situations on the basis of those that occur regularly and that can be drawn easily from memory. The availability heuristic may cause individuals to overestimate or underestimate the frequency of an event, as well as to set up a bias toward a particular direction for analyzing a problem.

Selective perception, another source of bias in information acquisition, refers to the tendency of an individual to form an impression of an event early on and to interpret new information in the context of that initial impression. Ellen Langer (1983) argues that people attempt to exercise control over their environment by forming hypotheses about it, seeking out information that confirms those hypotheses, and ignoring contradictory information. Yet people not only interpret problems on the basis of their own past experiences; once they have framed a problem, they tend to seek out information that confirms their own views and to disregard information that contradicts their views. Employment interviews are a good example of selective perception. Most job interviewers make a judgment regarding the qualifications of a job applicant during the first few minutes of the interview. Once this initial judgment is formed, interviewers typically seek information that confirms it (Swann & Snyder, 1979) and dismiss information that contradicts it. Similarly, as Randy Hirokawa (1988a) observes, decision-making groups tend to look more for the positive rather than the negative elements in a plan when attempting to select among competing plans. He argues that one of the primary reasons groups make poor decisions is their tendency to focus on positive information that confirms preferred alternatives and to neglect negative information that may be important to the decision-making process.

People also can be biased toward *concrete information*. When individuals are aware of their own personal experiences or the experiences of others regarding an event, they tend to pay more attention to that information than to other, more objective or quantitative information. Even though the quantitative information may be more reliable and valid, it has limited impact. The personal nature of the information provided by a friend or acquaintance often outweighs objective data.

In *illusory correlation*, two phenomena are associated with one another even

TABLE 4.3 Types of Bias and Their Effect on Information Acquisition

Bias	Description	Example
Availability	The ease with which specific events or situations can be recalled affects judgments of frequency.	The frequency of well-publicized events are overestimated (for example, deaths due to homicide or cancer). The frequency of other events are underestimated (for example, deaths due to asthma and diabetes).
	The chance availability of particular "cues" in the immediate environment affects judgment.	Problem solving can be hindered or facilitated by the cues perceived by chance in a particular setting (hints set up one's cognitive direction).
Selective perception	People structure problems on the basis of their own experience.	The same problem may be viewed by a marketing manager as a marketing problem, by a finance manager as a financial problem, and so on.
	The anticipations of what people expect to find affects what they actually see.	The identification of incongruent objects (for example, playing cards with red instead of black spades) is either inaccurately reported (for example, people think they see black spades) or causes discomfort.
	People seek out information that is consistent with their own views or hypotheses.	Interviewers seek information about a job candidate that is consistent with their first impression rather than information that could refute that impression.
	People downplay or disregard conflicting evidence.	When forming impressions, people tend to underestimate the value of information that does not yield to a consistent profile.
Concrete information	The cue used to judge the strength of a predictive relationship is observed frequency rather than observed relative frequency. Information on the "nonoccurrences" of an event is unavailable and ignored.	When purchasing a car, the positive or negative experience of a *single* known person (a friend) may weigh more heavily in the person's decision than other, more valid statistical information (for example, *Consumer Reports* ratings).
Illusory correlation	The assumption that two unrelated variables are connected in a cause-effect relationship. (Possibly related to the availability bias.)	Selection of an inappropriate variable to make a prediction.

TABLE 4.3 *Continued*

Bias	Description	Example
Data presentation	Order effects (primary/recency).	Occurs when the first or last item in a sequential presentation is given undue importance.
	Mode of presentation.	Sequential versus intact data displays can affect people's interpretation of the data (for example, complete unit-price shopping versus one's own sequential information search).
	A mix of information types (for example, qualitative and quantitative).	A concentration on quantitative data to the exclusion of qualitative data, or vice-versa.
	Logical data displays.	Seemingly complete and logical data displays can cause people to overlook critical omissions.
	Context affects perceived variability.	An assessment of variability—for example, of a series of numbers—is affected by the absolute size or mean level of the numbers.

Source: R. M. Hogarth and S. Makridakis (1981), Forecasting and planning: An evaluation, *Management Science,* 27(2), pp. 117–118.

though they are unrelated. This type of bias is particularly problematic when one variable is perceived as causing another. A good example of illusory correlation is provided by attribution theory, which holds that observers typically associate an employee's poor performance with low motivation or effort. Thus, it is assumed that low motivation causes poor performance. Although this relationship is possible, other factors, such as a lack of experience, knowledge, or resources, may also account for the employee's low performance. The bias of illusory correlation, however, causes individuals to accept the attributions as facts.

The manner in which data are presented can reflect another type of bias in information acquisition. Biases associated with *data presentation* include the tendencies to concentrate on quantitative rather than qualitative data and to give the first or last items in a sequential display of information more importance.

Leaders are subject to the various types of bias when they acquire information from the environment. Organizational members appear to manifest informational biases under three conditions:

1. *The frequent recurrence of similar problems or events within an organization.* As events frequently occur, standard patterns of handling them emerge. Organizational members then become accustomed to viewing and handling situations in certain ways. As Peterson and Sorenson

(1991) observe, heuristic biases tend to develop when situations occur frequently because they serve as a means of reducing the complexity of the situation. Organizations may, therefore, develop strong scripts that preclude a thorough analysis of information.

2. *The leader possesses a high level of power status within an organization.* One of the key problems confronting groups and organizations is the negative influence of leaders who misuse their power. Dennis Gouran (1986) argues that group decision making may suffer when a high-status individual makes faulty inferences. Given the leader's status within the group, the other group members may begin to exhibit similar behaviors, imitating the faulty inferences of the leader.
3. *The organization is highly cohesive.* Irving Janis (1972) uses the term *groupthink* to refer to bias caused by high levels of cohesiveness within an organization. Organizational members who tend to "think alike" share information-processing biases because of their high level of cohesion.

It is difficult to characterize the effects of heuristics on organizations as either positive or negative. On the one hand, heuristics serve a valuable function when they help individuals, groups, and organizations simplify a complex information environment. The importance of heuristics as a means of successfully analyzing problems is reflected in their incorporation into the manufacturing of expert systems (Stubbart, 1989). Expert systems take the heuristics that are employed by experts in a particular field and model them on the computer. This knowledge then can be used by comparative novices in the field to make decisions. For example, the knowledge possessed by doctors regarding illnesses and diagnoses has been modeled in an expert system known as the Apache III, which enables doctors to make diagnoses and adjust their treatments in matters of hours as opposed to days (Schwartz, 1992). On the other hand, heuristics can hinder the quality of inferences. Overreliance on heuristics can cause individuals, groups, and organizations to ignore competing definitions of situations and contradictory information. Successfully balancing the effects of heuristics partly involves mastering the skill of data splitting.

FACILITATING INFORMATION PROCESSING THROUGH DATA SPLITTING

Leaders can help organizational members avoid the various types of bias associated with information acquisition simply by making members aware of them. Information acquisition bias may also be avoided by sampling from a variety of sources, and comparing and contrasting the accuracy of the information. Another possibility involves structuring processes in a way that prevents members from accepting information without a thorough analysis.

According to Ian Mitroff (1978), a major reason leaders have difficulty in helping groups and organizations achieve goals is that they are prone to type III error. A type III error occurs when an individual solves the wrong problem. As a result, leaders may be working on problems that are not real problems because they misdiagnosed the actual problems. Mitroff contends that leaders must be able to "split" incoming information and analyze it thoroughly in order to avoid type III error. Initially, it is important to identify a problem correctly because this will determine the domain of future decision making. The skill of *data splitting* is thus a key to avoiding information acquisition biases. A leader may attribute poor organizational performance to inadequate internal processes and procedures without considering other possible explanations or environmental factors, such as a lack of necessary materials to complete the job. Through data splitting, the leader breaks down and analyzes other possible explanations for the problem.

In order to split incoming data effectively, the communication practices of the leader and group must be appropriately structured. Hogarth and Makridakis (1981) suggest that three such practices allow leaders to help organizational members avoid information acquisition biases: (1) role playing, (2) dialectical inquiry, and (3) the devil's advocate procedure. However, these are only a few of the many leadership strategies employed to split data. They should be used carefully and selectively, as their overuse can lead to the creation of a strong script and thereby hinder subsequent analysis.

Role Playing

Role playing provides opportunities to practice new behaviors and prepare for future situations. It also heightens participants' understanding of a situation. By actively playing a role, the person is forced to react in the simulated situation just as he or she would in the real situation. The role players thereby gain insight into the situational characteristics they consider important, the basic assumptions that guide their actions, and their biases toward the situation.

Structuring a particular role play typically involves the following three steps:

Step 1: The circumstances surrounding the situation are described. All events leading up to the situation and other relevant information are disclosed, including (a) the identification of individuals and groups involved in the current situation, (b) the background of the situation, (c) the scope and seriousness of the situation, and (d) the results of any previous analyses of the situation.

Step 2: The role players are each given a character to portray and are oriented toward the specific role. They should be given general information about how they are to behave as well as more specific information, such as the position occupied by each role player in the organizational hierarchy and the interests each one represents. The role play is then performed.

Step 3: After the role play is performed, the results are assessed. The role players are asked to describe their actions and motivation in the role as well as the insights they gained.

Role playing is especially valuable to leaders as a data-splitting tool. Its major advantage is that it encourages the participants to see others' viewpoints, leading to their enhanced understanding of a problem. Two types of role playing—counterattitudinal and reverse—are especially valuable in helping leaders examine the facets of a problem.

Counterattitudinal role playing requires participants to adopt a position that is counter to their initial approach to and evaluation of a problem. For example, a leader may attribute low productivity in an assembly line to a lack of effort among employees. A counterattitudinal role play would require the leader to act out the role of a member of the management team whose position on the problem is different. During the role play, the leader would not accept the premise that poor motivation is causing the low performance. Rather, by considering the counterposition, the leader is forced to explore other ways to characterize the problem, such as a lack of technology or raw materials, or poor coordination.

In *reverse role playing,* the participants act out roles that are the opposite of the ones they usually perform. In our preceding example, the leader in charge of the assembly line might role-play an assembly line worker. Similar to counterattitudinal role playing, reverse role playing would force the leader to adopt a perspective different from the one he or she typically employs. Both types of role plays serve to change participants' usual frame of reference about problem solving in order to generate new insights into the problems being addressed.

Dialectical Inquiry

In the strategic management literature, two primary approaches to formulating problems have been identified: dialectical inquiry and the devil's advocate procedure. *Dialectical inquiry* is based on the Hegelian notion of thesis, antithesis, and synthesis. A formulation for characterizing a problem is offered (thesis), a counterformulation is proposed (antithesis), and a debate comparing and contrasting the assumptions of the two positions is conducted until an integrated formulation is constructed (synthesis).

Dialectical inquiry involves the following five steps:

Step 1: The leader collects all available information regarding a specific problem or event.

Step 2: The leader develops an analysis of the problem, identifies a thesis, and provides an argument in support of the analysis and thesis. The support should include all relevant information, assumptions, and key facts. The analysis and argument should be presented in written form. The thesis can now be debated.

Step 3: Using the analysis and argument provided in step 2, the leader searches for arguments and positions that are counter to or negate the thesis. The leader also looks for counterrecommendations to those developed in step 2. The conditions under which the original analysis would be in error or open to question should be explored and identified. The analysis and accompanying arguments should be recorded in writing. The antithesis of the original analysis is thus identified.

Step 4: The leader compares the two lists constructed in steps 2 and 3 and engages in a systematic critique of the competing assumptions. The validity of both sets of assumptions is examined. Ultimately, a list of assumptions consistent with both analyses is identified. A synthesis of the two competing positions is developed.

Step 5: On the basis of the remaining assumptions, the leader can develop a set of recommendations.

Although the five steps of dialectical inquiry are described for use by a single leader, they can also be employed by a group. For example, working with a team, a leader might divide the team into two subgroups: one could be assigned to step 2 and the other to step 3. Both subgroups could participate in the debate in step 4 and in developing the recommendations in step 5.

Dialectical inquiry helps leaders and organizations avoid potential biases by forcing them to examine the assumptions underlying their original formulation of a problem and to consider its antithesis. By actively debating the assumptions underlying the interpretations of events, biases in information acquisition can be identified and prevented.

Devil's Advocate Procedure

The *devil's advocate procedure* differs from dialectical inquiry in that it relies on a simpler form of questioning for identifying assumptions and recommendations. Rather than structuring and debating two sets of conflicting ideas and assumptions, the devil's advocate procedure simply offers a critique of a proposed idea without necessarily comparing it to an opposing set of ideas (Schweiger, Sandberg, & Ragan, 1986). The purpose of the "devil's advocate" is to keep the group honest. Analysis is rigorous and acceptance of ideas without rigorous questioning is avoided.

Typically, the devil's advocate procedure involves the following four steps:

Step 1: All required information for analyzing a particular event or situation is collected.

Step 2: An analysis of the situation is developed and an argument in support of the analysis is provided. A written record of the analysis and argument should be prepared. The supporting argument should identify all relevant facts, assumptions, and premises used to substantiate the position.

Step 3: Using the analysis and recommendations developed, a formal critique of the position is undertaken. It might include addressing the following questions:

a. Does the analysis contain high-quality information?
b. Are the assumptions underlying the position valid?

c. What other alternatives exist?

Step 4: The analysis and position are revised according to the results of step 3. Any new information revealed by the critique is incorporated into the analysis, and the recommendations are made.

The devil's advocate procedure is useful to both individual leaders and work teams. In the latter case, the work team is divided into two subgroups. One subgroup performs step 2 and the other participates in the debate in step 3. In step 4, all group members help to revise the analysis and to develop a set of recommendations.

Whether role playing, dialectical inquiry, or the devil's advocate procedure is most effective is an issue that has received only limited attention in the research. One study found that the devil's advocate procedure and dialectical inquiry both generate high-quality decisions (Schweiger, Sandberg, & Ragan, 1986). Given the relative comparability of the procedures in producing high-quality decisions, leaders should examine the degree to which a given procedure is appropriate to the culture of the organization. Groups that are low in cohesiveness, have personality conflicts, and are under stress may opt for role playing rather than dialectical inquiry. Role playing is less threatening to those involved, whereas dialectical inquiry requires participants to debate competing ideas. In low cohesion groups, the pressure produced by dialectical inquiry may be counterproductive.

SUMMARY

Effective leadership depends on object mediation. Yet leaders must not only collect impressions of the information environment; they also must utilize those impressions to identify the obstacles and problems that face the group or organization. The information environment that an organization occupies may range from stable and simple to turbulent and complex. Similarly, the information that an organization acquires about its environment may vary from low to high quality. Leadership aims to help the organization interpret the information environment as well as other relevant data, including messages and symbols. When leaders construct appropriate interpretations of the challenges posed by the environment, they help the organization adapt to and overcome the challenges it faces.

Leaders evaluate and simplify the information environment through the use of cognitive schemata, such as decision-premises and rule systems, analogies and metaphors, prototypes, and scripts. Cognitive schemata are useful heuristics because they can help simplify a complex information environment. However, biases may negatively influence the pragmatic value of cognitive schemata. Availability, selective perception, concrete information, illusory correlation, and data presentation can introduce bias, causing leaders to formulate problems and obstacles in ways that do not benefit the organization. As a result, the organization may waste time and effort on the wrong problems.

Data splitting is one skill that leaders can employ to avoid the biases associated with acquiring information and formulating definitions of a problem. Data-splitting involves separating the component parts of the incoming information and analyzing each. This approach is intended to prevent leaders and other organizational members from confusing incoming information with how they *think* the information appears according to the cognitive schemata they utilize.

The biases associated with schemata can be avoided by employing strategies that encourage leaders and organizations to consider multiple ways of viewing the information environment. Role playing, dialectical inquiry, and the devil's advocate procedure serve this function. As a result, the power of preconceptions and biases is diminished and leadership is better able to create interpretations that will facilitate the organization's adaptation to the information environment.

QUESTIONS AND APPLICATIONS

1. The following chart lists several different types of industries. For each industry, identify the kind of information environment you associate with that industry and place a checkmark in the space provided. Then consider how you formed your impressions. In what ways should the leaders in each industry go about understanding and acquiring information?

	Type of Information Environment			
INDUSTRY TYPE	PLACID-RANDOMIZED	PLACID-CLUSTERED	DISTURBED-REACTIVE	TURBULENT
Federal government	______	______	______	______
Pharmaceutical	______	______	______	______
Insurance	______	______	______	______
Oil and gas	______	______	______	______
Automobile	______	______	______	______
Computer	______	______	______	______
Airline	______	______	______	______

2. Assume that you are on a committee that is charged with planning a new media room for the company. The media room will have the capacities to generate computer images onto a large screen in the front of the room and to display a large number of multimedia images, such as films, videos, and computer graphics. As you examine the competing systems, you find that the quantitative specifications on one machine far exceed those of the others. Yet, a committee member who tried that computer system states unequivocally, "That computer is so hard to use that it's impossible." How can you help the committee make sense of this inconsistent information? Which piece of information do you consider valid? Why?

3. For the biases associated with information acquisition (see Table 4.3), list on one side of a piece of paper a personal example of each type. Describe how the bias influenced your acquisition and view of the information. On the other side of the paper, describe a strategy you could have used to avoid each bias.

4. You are the leader of a hotel chain's special task force charged with determining why customer complaints about service have risen dramatically. Unfortunately, your task force is having problems. Not only do the members not like one another on a personal level, they also disagree on many professional issues. To help the group members understand the nature of the problem, would you ask them to use role playing, the devil's advocate procedure, or dialectical inquiry? Explain your choice.

Solution to the puzzle on page 93: The following four symbols in the sequence are: |‾_| | |‾_| ‾_|. These symbols are the bottom halves of the numbers *0* to *9* as they appear on a digital clock or calculator.

Chapter 5
Decision Making

> Sometimes a company can risk too much for the sake of change. When that happens, the best thing to do is to bite the bullet as quickly as possible and start over. Take Coca-Cola Co. Less than three months after the highly touted 1985 reformulation of the company's flagship brand—a change heralded by the firm as "the most significant soft-drink development in the company's 100-year history"—Coca-Cola responded to a considerable public backlash against the new product by reviving the old Coke. New Coke would remain on the market, but Coke officials conceded that they had gone too far when they tinkered with the 100-year-old company fountainhead. . . .
>
> But Coke officials believe that they may be able to turn the disaster around into a boon for the company. "What we have today is we have Coke and Coca-Cola Classic. Pepsi now finds itself sandwiched in the middle," says Coca-Cola Chairman Roberto Goizueta. "I like to quote an ancient Chinese proverb—which I made up—which is, 'He who gets sandwiched in gets eaten up.' . . . Assuming that our job and that of our bottlers is to sell more gallons of soft-drink syrup, and thus more gallons of soft drinks, we have never been in a better position to do that than we are today."
>
> *(Potts & Behr, 1987, pp. 140, 141).*

Did the top management team at Coca-Cola Company make a poor decision? At first glance, it may appear that the company miscalculated the market's potential reaction to the introduction of a new version of the popular soft drink. The results could have been disastrous, because as public opinion against Coke increased, the company lost considerable market share. Yet, by reintroducing original Coke and renaming it Coca-Cola Classic, the Coca-Cola Company reasserted its market dominance by meeting the needs of its customers—both those who preferred the old Coke and those who had drifted toward Pepsi-Cola.

Being aware that a problem exists is not enough to manage it effectively. Individuals, groups, and organizations need to make informed choices when they assess competing plans for addressing problems present within the information environment. Whether the problem is rooted in the relational aspects of organizational life (such as conflicts among work teams) or in the work that people must perform, making informed choices about competing solutions is critical for minimizing negative consequences and maximizing positive outcomes. Coca-

Cola's management team attempted to maintain this balance between negative and positive consequences by choosing to offer new products, rather than diversifying the organization as they had done in 1982 when purchasing Columbia Pictures. Although the alternative of diversifying the company was available, upper-level management chose to "shake-up" the soft-drink industry by introducing new products. This process of selecting from among differing plans, options, tactics, or strategies is at the heart of Weick's (1978) notion of action mediation discussed in Chapter 1.

Leaders can facilitate organizational members' decision making by helping work teams create a system for organizing their decision-making behavior. Decision making by organizations cannot be avoided; it is necessary in the daily routine as well as in times of crisis. Decisions may range from having minor personal and organizational consequences to having major implications for the continued survival of an organization. Leaders help organizations manage the inevitable process of making decisions by communicating in ways that help individuals and groups avoid decision-making pitfalls, such as failing to examine all relevant viewpoints or to reason through alternatives, and succumbing to the desires of powerholders within the organization. To understand how leaders may facilitate decision making, it is necessary to examine the relationship between leadership and decision making and to recognize the potential pitfalls associated with decision making.

THE RELATIONSHIP BETWEEN LEADERSHIP AND DECISION MAKING

Mumford (1986) contends that leadership *is* the process of making decisions. Whether leaders make the decisions or assist organizational groups in making the decisions, leaders play a prominent role in organizational decision making. When individuals lead organizations, they individually or as part of a larger group select among various alternatives, and in so doing reveal their preferences for particular values, interests, and beliefs. Making decisions involves providing resources to certain individuals and groups while denying resources to others.

One central issue regarding leadership and decision making is leaders' and followers' *level of involvement* in making decisions. As noted in Chapter 2, the Iowa Child Welfare studies and participative management theories are based in large part on the degree of involvement permitted by followers. Democratic and participative approaches to leadership allow followers to have equal standing with leaders and to share in the decision-making process. Participative management is viewed as a desirable means for solving organizational problems because theoretically its focus on involvement in decision making generates better decisions and increases worker commitment, loyalty, and productivity. Vroom and Yetton's (1973) normative decision-making model differs from participative management in that it argues the level of follower involvement depends on the situation, ranging from low involvement under conditions of autocratic leadership to high involvement under group leadership.

Another key issue regarding the relationship between leadership and decision making is the *quality of the contributions* that leaders and followers make. Whether decision making is viewed as best accomplished by a group or a leader, it always requires a rigorous examination of potential solutions, including their strengths and weaknesses. In a series of books examining policy groups and decision making, Irving Janis (1982, 1989; Janis & Mann, 1977) contends that the *process* of decision making is critical to making good decisions. When people make decisions, unavoidable errors—such as those caused by unavailable information—can lead to poor decision making. However, avoidable errors—such as the steps followed to make the decision—are within the control of the participants. Many decision-making pitfalls can be avoided by controlling avoidable errors. Steiner's (1972, p. 9) often-cited maxim, "actual productivity = potential productivity – faulty group process," reflects the underlying assumption of Janis's approach. If the decision-making process is structured appropriately and people make appropriate contributions, good decisions can be made.

What, then, are the appropriate kinds of contributions for making good decisions? According to Janis (1989; 1982; Janis & Mann, 1977), high-quality decisions are more likely to result when people communicate in ways that meet the following guidelines. The leader or group:

1. Surveys a wide range of objectives to be fulfilled, taking account of the multiplicity of values that are at stake;
2. Canvasses a wide range of alternative courses of action;
3. Intensively searches for new information relevant to evaluating the alternatives;
4. Correctly assimilates and takes account of new information or expert judgments to which one is exposed, even when the information or judgment does not support the course of action initially preferred;
5. Reconsiders the positive and negative consequences of alternatives originally regarded as unacceptable, before making a final choice;
6. Carefully examines the costs and risks of negative consequences, as well as positive consequences, that could flow from the alternative that is preferred;
7. Makes detailed provisions for implementing and monitoring the chosen course of action, with special attention given to contingency plans that might be required if various known risks were to materialize. (Janis, 1989, pp. 30–31)

From this perspective, decision-making quality is associated with the number of guidelines met by individuals and groups. Messages may either facilitate reaching the guidelines or frustrate their accomplishment (Gouran, 1986). According to Janis, the guidelines can be used by both individual leaders and groups when making decisions.

The importance of involving followers in decision making and of communicating in ways that exhaustively examine potential problems and solutions is, in large part, based on the view that the decisions facing organizational members are complex and necessarily involve choosing from multiple competing policies and plans. However, many different kinds of decisions are made in organizations. Leaders and followers make decisions about relatively simple issues, such as setting work schedules, as well as more complex issues, such as long-term strategic planning. Therefore, the relative importance of fulfilling the seven criteria, as well as determining leaders' and followers' respective levels of involvement in decision making, may depend on the type of decisions that must be made.

DECISION-MAKING TASKS AND COMMUNICATION

Organizational members make the decisions that allow organizations to adapt to their external environments and to survive in the marketplace. To survive within organizations, employees also make decisions, individually or as members of groups, that help them adapt to the constraints of the internal organizational environment. The content of these decisions varies greatly—from determining organizational goals and strategies, choosing to branch into new markets, selecting among competing technologies, and projecting work force needs to restructuring the existing organization and hiring new employees. Although the content of decisions varies, theorists attempt to identify the features of decision-making tasks commonly confronted by people in organizations as well as the kinds of communication required to manage those tasks successfully.

Decision-Making Tasks

Think of a recent decision you had to make. What was the decision about? What adjectives can you use to describe it? The English language is filled with adjectives that can be used to describe a particular decision, such as *simple, easy, difficult, challenging, sensitive, personal, stupid,* or *confusing.* Adjectives provide clues to how we frame our task. Similarly, theorists propose several typologies of decision-making tasks. Although interrelated, the typologies ask different questions about the task and reflect contrasting approaches. The following three approaches are typically used to describe decision-making tasks.

Approach 1: What is the focus of the decision? This method for defining decision-making tasks is based on the type of question that needs to be answered. In other words, it focuses on the issue about which the leader or organization needs to make a decision. The focus of the question thus dictates the direction and content of the discussion undertaken by leaders and followers. Traditionally, four basic questions—about facts, conjecture, value, and policy—are used to frame the purpose and focus of a decision-making discussion.

Questions of fact require answers that are either true or false. Such questions often involve phenomena that can be empirically verified, such as "How much is the budget for the marketing department?" or "Are there any legal restrictions regarding hiring policy?" It is important to recognize, however, that discussions centered on questions of fact are not always simple or noncontroversial. Within organizations, debates can emerge over what constitutes a fact. During the early 1980s, for example, the school lunch program faced considerable controversy after the federal government categorized tomato ketchup as a vegetable. This meant that schools could serve ketchup as a vegetable rather than such items as salad, peas and carrots, and broccoli. Although ketchup is a vegetable product, many individuals questioned whether it could be defined and used as a vegetable for school lunches.

Questions of conjecture require answers that make some claim about what is probable or improbable, usually in respect to future events. Such questions involve predicting what kinds of events or circumstances are likely to occur in the future. Predictions about the state of the economy, probable governmental regulations, hiring needs, training for employees, and consumer behavior are examples of the types of questions organizations face regarding their environments. Questions of conjecture force organizations and work groups to project future events; these projections affect other kinds of decisions regarding how the organization should conduct itself.

Questions of value involve choosing from among several alternatives the one that constitutes appropriate opinion, belief, attitude, or mode of behavior. Values represent what is considered good or bad, important or unimportant, desirable or undesirable, and attractive or unattractive within an organization. For example, when management theorists argue for a shift in U.S. business practices, from hierarchical authoritative forms of management to empowering management (Kouzes & Posner, 1990; Peters & Austin, 1985), they are addressing a question of value. Empowerment takes some responsibility and decision making away from the highest levels of management and redistributes it to different levels within the organization. At General Motors' Saturn plant in Spring Hill, Tennessee, assembly line workers have the power to stop the assembly line at any time they feel product quality is threatened or when they see a problem on the line. This represents a shift in the typical management style—from the line supervisor having the sole power to stop the assembly line to the distribution of responsibility for product quality to all members of the assembly line. The debate over whether to shift from authoritative to empowering means of managing an organization centers on a question of value—is it *important* or *desirable* for all workers to be able to make decisions regarding their job?

Questions of policy involve choosing courses of action aimed at achieving some desired state of affairs. Policies are the plans, tactics, and strategies organizations implement to accomplish their goals. Within organizations, questions of policy typically involve such issues as marketing strategy, company mission, employee compensation, and sexual and racial discrimination.

Approach 2: What levels of coordination and knowledge are required? Another way of defining decision-making tasks is based on two factors: the knowledge of group members and the level of coordination required among group members to complete the task (Hackman & Morris, 1975; Steiner, 1972). Rather than classifying a task according to the focus of the discussion, Hackman and Morris (1975) argue that tasks are better classified according to the manner in which group members combine individual contributions to produce a group outcome. This yields three types of tasks: additive, conjunctive, and disjunctive.

Additive tasks lead to outcomes that represent the contributions of all members of a group. At a team meeting, for instance, a leader may ask each member to generate a solution to a problem. After obtaining all team members' ideas, the leader may then record them on a flipchart to assess the various kinds of solutions the team generated. The team's productivity for generating solutions is the sum of each team member's unique contribution.

Conjunctive tasks are characterized by group members performing essentially the same task. Moreover, conjunctive tasks tend to be sequential, such that the overall productivity of the group is determined by the effectiveness of the least-proficient member. The assembly line is a good example of a conjunctive task. Workers at the end of the assembly line depend on those at the beginning of the line to do their job. If the workers at the beginning of the line fail to complete their portion of product assembly, this directly affects the ability of the workers at the end of the line to perform their part of the overall task. This is why productivity for a conjunctive task is typically defined in terms of speed. Other examples of conjunctive tasks involving sequential steps include producing a company newsletter and going through the process of hiring a new employee.

Disjunctive tasks require people to select a plan or solution from a set of two or more possible options. Such tasks often involve an "either/or" solution, requiring the selection of one option over another. Policy-making groups typically encounter disjunctive tasks when they set out to select from among a variety of policies the one that will best address a specific problem. Because each policy emphasizes different elements of a solution—many of which cannot be combined—choosing between competing policies is necessary. However, in order for a group to perform a disjunctive task well, at least one group member must possess enough knowledge and information about the problem and its optimum solution.

Approach 3: What dimensions best describe the task? Unlike the two preceding strategies for defining decision-making tasks, which classify a task on the basis of its purpose or according to group members' interdependence and knowledge, respectively, the third approach focuses on dimensions of task complexity or difficulty. In this perspective, tasks may differ in terms of several underlying dimensions. Because decision-making tasks are viewed as multidimensional and their dimensions as independent of one another, classifying a task into a single category is difficult.

The following six dimensions of decision-making tasks are identified by Shaw (1981):

1. *Difficulty:* The amount of physical and cognitive effort required to complete a task.

2. *Intrinsic interest:* The degree to which the task in and of itself is interesting, motivating, or attractive to group members.
3. *Solution multiplicity:* The number of possible solutions that may appropriately complete a task. Low solution multiplicity means that decision-making tasks have few alternative solutions from which to select, whereas high solution multiplicity means that a large number of possible solutions may be selected.
4. *Goal-path clarity:* The level of ambiguity characterizing the task and the manner in which to achieve the task most effectively.
5. *Cooperation requirement:* The degree to which the integrated action of group members is required to complete the task.
6. *Population familiarity:* The amount of experience members of the group have had with the task.

Although Shaw's dimensions are independent, they may be combined to create a variety of possible decision-making tasks.

Table 5.1 outlines the three approaches to defining decision-making tasks along a continuum of task complexity. Within each typology, certain types of tasks may be viewed as more complex than others. For example, questions of fact are relatively simple to answer, whereas questions of policy are more complex and require discussion about a number of issues. In addition, questions of policy tend to be more difficult in terms of the number of possible solutions than questions of fact. Table 5.1 demonstrates that all three typologies can be used simultaneously to describe a task.

Communication and the Decision-Making Task

Leadership mediates between the types of decisions that must be made and the group's final decisions. Leaders may facilitate discussion so that groups can better organize themselves to make effective decisions. The assumption is that communication by both leaders and followers is important in decision making. However, some theorists contend that communication has little effect on decision making under certain circumstances (Hewes, 1986; Hirokawa, 1990; Bottger & Yetton, 1988). In this view, the implications for leadership are clear: Leaders must know (1) under what circumstances communication—their own and followers'—may or may not influence decision making and (2) how the task influences the type of contributions that should be made. Thus, leaders are required to identify decision-making situations that neutralize the influence of communication as well as decision-making tasks that demand particular kinds of communication.

Simple tasks neutralize the importance of communication. The influence of communication on decision making may be neutralized in particular situations. *Neutralizers* are attributes of the task, people, or organization that diminish the ability of communication to influence the decision-making process. When com-

TABLE 5.1 Defining Task Complexity and the Importance of Communication

Typology	Factors Used to Define Decision-Making Tasks		
Approach 1: What is the focus of the decision?	Fact Conjecture	Value Policy	
Approach 2: What levels of knowledge and coordination are required?	Additive Conjunctive	Disjunctive	
Approach 3: What dimensions best describe the task?	Low task difficulty	High task difficulty	
	Low intrinsic interest	High intrinsic interest	
	Low solution multiplicity	High solution multiplicity	
	High goal-path clarity	Low goal-path clarity	
	Low cooperation requirement	High cooperation requirements	
	High population familiarity	Low population familiarity	
Task complexity	Low	Moderate	High
Communication complexity	Low	Moderate	High

munication loses much of its influential power, a host of other factors can affect the decision-making process and the final outcome.

Randy Hirokawa (1990) offers a model for identifying the conditions under which the effects of communication on decision making may be neutralized. When the communication process is neutralized, the ability of leaders to influence decision making is also limited. According to Hirokawa (1990), three basic task characteristics may limit communication influence. First, when the *task structure* is simple, the importance of communication decreases while the influence of inputs on the decision-making process increases. A simple task exists when the goal to be achieved is clear, the steps needed to achieve it are unambiguous and limited in number, and potential obstacles are few. Furthermore, when the task is simple, group performance is based on the knowledge, skills, and abilities of the group members as well as their level of motivation for achieving the task.

Therefore, simple tasks may neutralize communication because they may be associated with a higher level of consensus among decision makers than complex tasks. However, the level of consensus prior to making a decision may also neutralize the importance of communication in complex tasks. When people agree on a particular approach for solving a simple or complex problem prior to their formal discussion of it, the influence of communication may be neutralized. If every person in a group concurs regarding the relative rankings of possible solutions, the importance or necessity of the communicative process is diminished. Phillip Bottger and Phillip Yetton (1988) note that when a high degree of prediscussion consensus for a given course of action exists, it is the consensus rather than the interaction of the group that best predicts the final outcome. In contrast, when group members have a wide diversity of opinion on what actions are acceptable or appropriate, the communication process within the group becomes more important. Through communication, group members must share their ideas, articulate their reasons for supporting a particular view, and attempt to persuade others. Group consensus regarding a task may also neutralize a leader's behavior during discussion.

The second task characteristic that may limit the influence of communication has to do with the *information requirements* of a task. When information requirements are means-independent, the performance of the group is better predicted by decision-making inputs than by communication. *Means-independence* refers to the degree to which collaboration and coordination are required among organizational members to achieve a goal. Therefore, when a task is means-independent, group collaboration and coordination are not required; rather, the information needed to solve the task is equally distributed among group members, and the amount and complexity of the information required to solve the task are low.

The third characteristic is the *evaluation demand* of the task. As the evaluation demand becomes less ambiguous in regard to the task, the importance of communication decreases. The ambiguity of the task places an evaluation demand on the group. Communication processes take on added importance when the number of potential solutions increases, when the clarity of the criteria used to evaluate solutions is low, and when answers cannot be objectively determined as correct or acceptable. However, group members' inputs in the decision-making situation are more important than the communication process when a small number of solutions exist, when the evaluation criteria to be employed are clear, and when the solutions can be easily judged as correct or acceptable. According to Hirokawa, in such instances decision-making performance "is largely dependent on the ability of group members to search through possible choices, recognize the correct choice, and demonstrate its correctness using established evaluation criteria" (1990, p. 199). Therefore, successful performance is a function of the ability of individual members to evaluate information, not the group's ability to evaluate and analyze solutions. (See Box 5.1)

When the information-processing requirements of a decision task are low and organizational members share a high degree of consensus regarding possible solutions, decision making is relatively unaffected by communication. In addition, when the nature of the task is low in complexity, the importance of communication is diminished. However, as outlined in Table 5.1, the importance of communication increases with the complexity of the task situation, and the vari-

Box 5.1
The Case of the Emerson Foundation

James Emerson was born and raised in Artis, Tennessee, a moderately sized city of approximately 100,000 people. He founded the Emerson Motivation Institute, which specializes in publishing motivational and leadership materials. Emerson was raised according to the "Golden Rule": "Do unto others as you would have them do unto you." He strongly believes in returning to the community what the community gives to him. To help the local community, Emerson recently set up a foundation for the city of Artis. The goal of the Emerson Foundation is to provide funding for community projects that will enhance the quality of life in Artis.

You have been appointed to the board of directors for the Emerson Foundation because of your participation in community activities. You are widely recognized as a leader in the community and have a great deal of influence in community affairs. The board of directors has received its first funding requests for a variety of projects from community agencies and must decide which agencies will receive funding. The board is aware that because this is the first money that will be distributed by the foundation, the kinds of projects it funds will send a message to the community about the foundation's mission.

The foundation's executive director has sent you the following list of seven funding proposals and has asked you to rank them prior to the next foundation meeting. Due to limited funding, only a few of the projects will be funded.

Cooper Family Life Center: The Center is designed to meet the needs of low-income families in the Artis area and is located near federally funded low-income housing. It is requesting $150,000 to build an outdoor swimming pool for use by the entire community.

Artis Family Alliance: The Alliance's mission is to provide low-cost family counseling to the citizens of Artis. It services individuals, groups, and families with such problems as marital disputes and troubled children. It is requesting $30,000 to add one counselor to its staff.

Artis Chamber of Commerce: The Chamber of Commerce is attempting to boost tourism. The city has a number of attractions, including the second-largest public park in the United States and over a half-dozen museums. It is requesting $75,000 to manufacture signs that will direct tourists to the various museums. Currently, tourists often get lost as they travel among the museums. Any remaining money will be used to buy billboard space on the nearby interstate highway. Revenue from tourism doubled from the previous year due to modest advertising.

Citizens for Responsible Parenting (CRP): CRP is a newly formed agency designed to decrease the number of teenage pregnancies in Artis, which currently has the third-highest teenage pregnancy rate and the fifth-highest amount of sexually transmitted diseases among teenagers in the United States. The agency teaches an abstinence-based approach to sex education. It has requested $55,000 to purchase materials for distribution to the teenagers of Artis and to hire a consultant to train its members in conducting workshops and presentations.

Artis Arts Council: Although a national financial magazine recently rated Artis as one of twenty top places to live in the United States given the quality of its educational system, medical care, and housing prices, the article criticized the cultural opportunities available in the city. Last summer, the Artis Arts Council sponsored four free concerts in the public park that were each attended by approximately nine thousand people. The Artis Arts Council is requesting $15,000 to double the number of free concerts this summer.

Historic Homes Foundation: Within Artis there are a half-dozen historic homes that have been refurbished and opened to the public. The homes were rated as the primary tourist attraction last year. Visitors from a 200-mile radius of the city make the trip to tour the annual Christmas Parade of Homes, sponsored by the Historic Homes Foundation as a major fund-raiser for maintaining the historic sites. The foundation also decorates the homes and holds an annual arts and crafts show at the local fairgrounds. It has requested $7,500 to advertise the Christmas tours on local radio and television stations.

Shining Light Rehabilitation Center: Established as a center to provide group counseling to recovering drug abusers, Shining Light recently purchased a large old home to serve as a halfway house for its clients. The home needs a new air-conditioning system as well as plumbing and electrical repairs. Total remodeling costs are estimated at $125,000. The director of Shining Light has requested $75,000 to help defray the costs.

ASSIGNMENT 1

You have been requested by the executive director to provide a ranking of the seven funding requests. Rank each request in order of preference (1 = most preferred; 7 = least preferred). Explain your reasoning.

ASSIGNMENT 2

Working in a small group, rank the seven proposals from least to most preferred. The group must reach a consensus on the issue; that is, at least 80 percent of the group members must agree on the appropriate ranking. Hold a board meeting to discuss the issue.

ASSIGNMENT 3

Obtain an average of the rankings that each group member had before the board meeting. Then use the average for each funding proposal to construct a final ranking of the proposals. (For example, if the average

Box continued

ranking for Shining Light was 1.5 and the average ranking for the Artis Chamber of Commerce was 2.3, you would rank Shining Light first and the Chamber of Commerce second.) Compare your personal rankings to the group's rankings after discussion. How do the rankings compare to the averaged rankings? Are the average prediscussion rankings similar to the postdiscussion rankings? What does this suggest about the importance of communication in decision making?

ety and depth of communicative acts increase with task complexity. Yet the nature of the decision-making task may also influence the kinds of required leadership behavior.

Task complexity enlarges the number of issues and topics that must be examined. As the nature of the task becomes more complex, it encompasses a larger domain of discussion content. The depth and variety of discussion topics also increase as the discussion content moves toward questions of policy or tasks that have multiple solutions. Questions of policy always involve questions of fact, conjecture, and value. This occurs because questions of policy build on and use preceding questions.

Consider, for example, General Motors' decision to redesign the 1991 Chevrolet Caprice Classic LTZ sedan (Rimer, 1992, pp. 18–19). In the late 1980s, GM had decided to redesign the Chevrolet Caprice, one of its hottest sellers during the 1960s. Imagine you were one of the members of the top management team deciding in 1991 whether to redesign and reengineer the Caprice. What kinds of questions would you need to ask in relation to policy decisions? Remember, this kind of decision would be a policy decision in that the Willow Run Michigan plant, which would produce the car, would need restructuring, and two other plants, which manufactured the old Caprice, would close. Think about the questions you would ask.

Now consider some of the questions that GM likely addressed when making the decision to manufacture the new Caprice:

Questions of fact: Do we currently have any plants available to produce the new car line? Do we currently have sufficient engineers and design people to build the new car? Does our cash flow permit redesigning the Caprice? What are the sales of the current Caprice? What are the revenues generated by other car lines? Are other car lines increasing market share and profits? According to market research, what qualities are consumers currently looking for in a new car?

Questions of conjecture: Knowing that it will take two years to redesign, produce, and market a newly designed Caprice, will the consumer still want the car at that time? Will the consumer want a larger, luxury-type car in two years? Will the consumer be able to afford a luxury car? What are the projected sales of the new Caprice for 1992? How do we think retooling the Willow Run plant for producing the Caprice will influence our other factories? At what point do we project that we will break even?

Questions of value: Do we want to maintain our market share in the luxury car line? Is this important? Is it more desirable to design vehicles with high miles-per-gallon? Is maintaining tradition important? That is, since we have built some version of the Caprice for over twenty years, is it important to maintain the continuity by redesigning the Caprice?

As you can see, addressing the key policy issue of whether to redesign the Caprice requires that many other issues and topics be included. Leaders can facilitate decision making by identifying an exhaustive and thorough list of relevant topics and then carefully examining each item in the list.

Task complexity influences the number and complexity of communicative functions. The nature of the task not only influences the overall role of communication in the decision-making process but also influences the specific functions and roles that communication serves. As the task moves from questions of fact to questions of policy, and from additive tasks to conjunctive tasks, the number of functions that communication serves increases. Table 5.2 details how the complexity of the situation is associated with increases in the complexity of the communication. For example, let's examine situations 1, 5, and 8 in the table. In task situation 1, the role of leadership communication is neutralized. Given that the task structure is simple, the information requirements of the task are low, and the evaluation demands are low, all the leader must do to facilitate the group is to make sure that a group member announces the correct choice and that another confirms the choice. In contrast, task situation 5 is moderately complex because the task structure is complex; the group must engage in problem analysis and procedural orientation and planning. Yet, the task also has low information requirements, which means that the group does not need to exchange information or collectively process that information. The evaluation demands of situation 5 are low, which suggests that the group does not need to exert massive effort in generating and assessing solutions. This unique combination of characteristics suggests that the primary responsibility of leadership here is to help integrate group members' knowledge and to develop a decision-making strategy. Upon completing these orienting and planning functions, the leader must ensure that the solution is announced and confirmed.

Task situation 8 is the most complex situation detailed in Table 5.2. Here the group must analyze the problem in depth and structure appropriate procedures. The group must also spend time collecting, distributing, and processing information because the information requirements are high. Finally, the high evaluation demands necessitate that the group engage in much solution generation, criteria identification, and solution assessment. The complexity of task situation 8 demands that communication be highly complex, which is why the role of communication is much broader here than in situation 1. Communication must do much more than simply announce and confirm the correct choice; complex situations require that communication facilitate a variety of functions—centralizing important information, orienting the group toward an understanding of the

TABLE 5.2 Communicative Functions and Task Structure Complexity

	Degree of Task Complexity			
Task Situation	**Task Structure**	**Information Requirements**	**Evaluation Demands**	**Role of Communication**
1 (simple)	Simple	Low	Low	Announce correct choice; confirm correct choice
2	Simple	Low	High	Obtain insights, reasons, alternative choices, and consequences
3	Simple	High	Low	Centralize important information; announce correct choice; confirm correct choice
4	Simple	High	High	Centralize important information; obtain insights, reasons, alternative choices, and consequences
5 (moderately complex)	Complex	Low	Low	Integrate individual competencies; develop a decision-making strategy; announce and confirm correct choice
6	Complex	Low	High	Understand the problem; obtain insights, reasons, choices, and consequences
7	Complex	High	Low	Centralize important information; integrate individual competences; develop a decision-making strategy; announce and confirm correct choice
8 (highly complex)	Complex	High	High	Centralize important information; understand the problem; obtain insights, reasons, choices, and consequences

Source: Adapted from R. Y. Hirokawa (1988b), *The role of communication in group decision-making efficacy: A task-contingency perspective.* Paper presented at the annual meeting of the Central States Speech Association, Schaumburg, IL.

problem, collectively interpreting and analyzing information, identifying the reasons for group members' positions, generating alternative solutions, and, ultimately, assessing the consequences of solutions in order to select a final solution. Leadership in this situation must perform a wide variety of functions to help the group make an informed and appropriate decision.

The complexity of the decision-making task may effectively neutralize the influence of leaders' communicative behavior or it may enhance its overall importance. As the complexity of the task increases, the number of discussion topics and the overall function of leadership communication also increase. With increased complexity, however, comes the possibility of making errors. There are several potential problems associated with making complex decisions.

DECISION-MAKING CONSTRAINTS AND DEFICIENCIES

The messages produced by leaders and followers are not highly influential in decision making when the task is relatively simple. However, as task situations become more complex, the importance of communication and the influence of leadership behavior on decision outcomes both increase. Yet the increased importance of communication in making decisions also brings with it potential problems. The ability to meet Janis's (1989) seven guidelines (discussed earlier in the chapter) becomes more difficult as tasks become more complex. It requires decision makers to structure their communication in ways that facilitate *vigilant decision making*—surveying all available information, examining information rigorously, reexamining old information in light of new information, and assessing the positive and negative consequences of potential solutions. The ability of an individual or group to engage in vigilant decision making is challenged as the task becomes more complex. Time pressures may limit information searches, or the amount of relevant information that needs to be surveyed may be too great. The potential for conflicts among team members or between decision makers and other organizational powerholders may increase. The opportunity to pursue one's personal agenda may exist when several possible solutions are present.

Based on Alexander George's (1980) model of presidential decision making in foreign policy, Janis (1989) suggests that there are three major types of constraints or trade-offs that prevent individuals and groups from engaging in vigilant decision making. *Cognitive constraints* exist when an individual or a group cannot successfully manage information due to time pressures, limited expert knowledge, or overwhelming amounts of information. When people must make a quick decision or process an overwhelming amount of information, they tend to use other means of decision making rather than vigilant decision making. *Affiliative constraints* are associated with the social dimension of decision making. When people want to maintain membership within an organization, be accepted by an organization, or preserve group harmony, they may bypass some of the seven practices of vigilant decision making. Affiliative constraints cause individuals and groups to limit their information searches as well as their analysis of competing viewpoints. Finally, *egocentric constraints* concern the pursuit of personal agendas and goals. Individuals may purposefully bias the decision-making process to pursue personal goals (for example, to maintain or improve their status in the organization).

Each type of constraint is associated with particular rules, or ways of reasoning, in decision-making situations. Box 5.2 describes many of the rules associated with cognitive, affiliative, and egocentric constraints.

Cognitive Constraints

Cognitive constraints limit the amount and quality of thought that individuals can devote to a single issue due to the great number of decisions they must make. Allocating a disproportionate amount of time to a single decision prevents assigning appropriate levels of support and resources to other pressing issues. According to Janis (1989), decision makers use heuristics or "rules of thumb" to help them simplify the complexity of a task and manage it more efficiently. As discussed in Chapter 4, heuristics are the mental rules of thumb that individuals or groups use to reduce the amount of effort needed to process information. Cognitive constraints are associated with two types of decision-making deficiencies: informational and inferential.

Informational deficiencies. *Informational deficiencies* address whether individuals or groups have adequate and accurate information on which to base their decisions (Gouran, 1986). This type of decision-making deficiency results not from drawing wrong inferences from existing information but from the characteristics of the existing information. Many times, individuals and groups limit the information search to manage the complexity of a task. However, inadequate information searches may lead to several types of informational deficiencies.

Inadequate information base. When people do not have all the relevant information needed to make a decision (for example, key facts, figures, and opinions may be missing from the data base), they cannot effectively assess the information or achieve a reasonable decision. A common complaint associated with decisions made on the basis of inadequate information, "If I had only known that, I would have done something different," shows how access to all relevant information can dramatically improve information analysis and the final decision.

Faulty information. Groups working with inaccurate or invalid information are likely to make poor decisions. The quality of the information may be poor because it is flawed, outdated, distorted, or incorrect. Dennis Gouran (1982) argues that "whether deliberately or accidentally distorted, inaccurate information increases the probability that a group will make a poor or ineffective decision" (p. 92). Suppose, for example, that you are part of a team developing a new company product. You hear a rumor that top-level management is consid-

Box 5.2
The Rules Associated with Cognitive, Affiliative, and Egocentric Constraints

COGNITIVE CONSTRAINTS

Satisficing rule: If there is a standard operating procedure (SOP) that can be used to meet the minimum requirement for solving the problem, use it. If there is no SOP, think of an analogy, an adage, or some comparable example that fits the present situation and use it to determine what to do.

Nutshell briefing rule: When faced with a complicated policy problem, save time and effort by asking someone familiar with the issue to tell you what it is all about "in a nutshell," and then decide.

AFFILIATIVE CONSTRAINTS

Avoid punishment rule: Sometimes known as the CYA ("cover-your-ass") rule, this means doing enough work so that the decision reflects the supervisor's wishes. It also means that the blame for poor decisions is placed on leaders.

Follow-the-party-line rule: When caught between two competing factions in a group, find the one that offers the most protection and benefits, and then follow that party line.

Rigging rule: To guarantee consensus at meetings, decide what to do before a meeting and then "rig" it so no one can object. This might involve, for example, presenting information or briefings that support a particular position or scheduling meetings when opponents cannot attend.

Preserve group harmony rule: To ensure that the group operates smoothly and arrives at a consensus, accept without criticism anything the group agrees on.

EGOCENTRIC CONSTRAINTS

"What's in it for me?" rule: Always push for options that maximize your personal status, power, and standing within the organization.

Rely-on-gut-feelings rule: When emotionally distressed, do what your gut tells you.

Retaliate rule: When embarrassed or humiliated, do anything in your power to punish the responsible party.

"Can do" rule: When challenged or nervous about a decision, bolster your confidence by stating "I can do it!" You don't want to be perceived as being a chicken.

"Wow, grab it!" rule: When frustrated in your attempts to come up with a solution, grab the first one that meets some of your criteria.

Source: I. L. Janis (1989), *Crucial decisions: Leadership in policymaking and crisis management* (New York: Free Press), pp. 27–88.

ering terminating your team unless it manages to get the product to the marketplace within six months. As a result, the team spends more time on the project and, at the same time, overtime pay your team accumulates rises rapidly. An upper-level manager demands to know why you've "racked up so much overtime." After talking with the manager, you discover that the rumor was false—that top-level management had not intended to decrease the level of support for the team.

Faulty assumptions. Assumptions form the basis for people's judgments and evaluations. The reasons we give, the inferences we draw, and the conclusions we make may be based on invalid assumptions. For example, assume you have determined that an individual employee is performing poorly. In the past, you found that poor performers typically lacked motivation. As a result of your assumption, you plan a whole series of personal talks designed to motivate the employee. You base your decision on how to manage poor performance on the assumption that it stems from a lack of motivation. Yet other factors could be contributing to the problem, such as a lack of job knowledge, insufficient training, or unavailable resources.

Inferential deficiencies. Unlike informational deficiencies, *inferential deficiencies* occur when decision makers draw unwarranted assumptions or conclusions from the available data base. Many times, inferential deficiencies emerge as decision makers are forced to make trade-offs in search of high-quality decisions. Several heuristics, or rules, influence how inferences are drawn from data. For example, the rules in Box 5.2 may facilitate drawing inappropriate inferences from the information. The *satisficing rule* emphasizes adopting the first possible solution that meets the situation. Many times, people search out possible analogies or situations that can be applied to the current situation for making a decision. Tversky and Kahnenman (1974) contend that people make judgments on the basis of the degree to which they view current events as similar to past events. If true, this heuristic may cause an individual or group to assume incorrectly that a current situation may be managed like earlier ones.

The *nutshell briefing rule* is designed to simplify information by asking an expert to provide a summary of the relevant facts. It can be problematic, however, when the person preparing the report is unaware of what facts are relevant to the present situation. There is a fictional story of a military briefing officer, summoned to the Pentagon and asked to determine the best way to get enemy submarines off the ocean floor. Several weeks later, the briefing officer returned and announced that the best way to remove the enemy submarines from the ocean floor was to heat the ocean to boiling, causing the submarines to rise. Bewildered, the Pentagon officials looked at the briefing officer and inquired, "How do you propose we boil the ocean?" The briefing officer replied, "I don't know. I decided on the solution; you can work out the details." In this example, whether the briefing officer was inexperienced, naive, or unaware of the obvious, the solution proposed is not feasible. Leaders and work groups that receive a briefing must be careful not to accept without question its contents because the briefer may not possess relevant knowledge in the area being addressed or may ignore relevant information required to make the decision.

Dennis Gouran (1986) highlights several other rules or heuristics that decision makers use to limit their cognitive activity. Many times, for instance, people reduce their cognitive functions by using the *anchoring heuristic*—revising later projections and decisions on the basis of their earlier decisions. That is, earlier decisions provide an "anchor" for current or future ones. When groups make initial decisions, they tend to escalate their commitment to these decisions in future discussions rather than reexamining them (Bateman, 1986; Brockner, 1992). Groups typically do not radically depart from an initial decision but tend to confirm and increase their commitment to a particular course of action. An excellent example of the anchoring heuristic is the 1986 decision to launch the space shuttle *Challenger*. One of the reasons cited by administrators for launching the spacecraft was that in the preceding twenty-four launches the structural problems present in the O-rings—the gaskets that joined the booster rockets—had not compromised the safety of the shuttle (Gouran, Hirokawa, & Martz, 1986). Thus, the preceding twenty-four launches formed much of the context in which the administrators made their decision. They erroneously assumed that the O-rings would function as they had in previous flights.

Decision makers also lessen the amount of cognitive activity they give to a decision when they passively accept unusual, novel, or *atypical information* as fact. According to Nisbett and Ross (1980), individuals tend to pay attention to information that is novel and unanticipated, giving it more weight and presumed validity than ordinary information when making decisions. The novelty of the information heightens people's awareness of particular facts that otherwise occupy a salient position in their thoughts as they make decisions. For example, in the early 1990s, the National Endowment for the Arts (NEA) decided to review applications for funding according to the criteria of "artistic merit," developed because of controversial projects funded by the NEA. The funding of Robert Maplethorpe's exhibit, Serrano's depiction of a crucifix in a bottle of urine, and a performance artist's staging of an artistic event in the nude were viewed as major reasons for demanding greater accountability of the projects receiving public funds. Such projects, however, were atypical; the overwhelming amount of funds allocated went to more usual projects. However, the atypical nature of the other projects caused NEA decision makers to focus on them and to rewrite the criteria for allocating its funds.

In addition, *scripts* and *scenarios* in decision making can limit the amount of cognitive activity devoted to making a decision and may lead to inferential deficiencies. Scripts and scenarios are the plot lines that emerge during discussion. As a plot unfolds, it may take on a direction of its own; the unfolding narrative for the discussion emphasizes and associates certain concepts with one another and heightens their importance during discussion.

In the development of an alternative to roach sprays, plastic trays with roach killer (e.g., Roach Motels) were created. Decision makers used a scenario that assumed women homemakers did not like using roach sprays because they were messy (Alsop, 1988). Users had to spray the roach, watch it die, and then pick it up and discard it. Roach Motels were developed on the assumption that women homemakers would prefer a product that could be set out easily and disposed of neatly. The scenario depicted all women homemakers as helpless and squeamish about roaches. The design of the ultimate product fitting this scenario was a small box into which roaches crawled and died. After the Roach Motel was on the market, market researchers conducting focus groups consisting of women found that they actually enjoyed spraying roaches and watching them die! The faulty assumptions about women homemakers in the scenario led to the creation of a product that turned out to be of little interest to those at whom it was targeted.

Affiliative Constraints

The "melting pot," a metaphor for describing the intermingling of diverse ethnic groups and cultures in the United States, emphasized that people should blend into U.S. culture, including the norms, values, and beliefs deemed important to the nation. Affiliative constraints reflect the kinds of restrictions that emerge when people seek to "fit in" with an organization. For some people, the need to fit in and to share similar ideas is quite high. For others, the need may be low. One aspect of the need for affiliation with a group is manifested when individuals want to avoid being punished or criticized by other group members. Individuals who want to fit in with a group may use the *avoid punishment rule* or the *follow-the-party-line rule* (see Box 5.2). Rather than challenge the ideas of an influential member of the group or of the group as a whole, the decision maker abides by the viewpoints of those with the most power. Or, if an individual feels strongly about disagreeing, he or she may take steps to avoid punishment. The gist of these two rules is that when dealing with people of high status, there is an impetus to avoid doing things contrary to those persons' wishes and a tendency to maintain the present level of affiliation.

Adopting the views of people or groups with high status is understandable. Within all work groups, certain individuals possess higher status, and they tend to exert greater influence within the group. Furthermore, lower-status members tend to defer to higher-status members of a group. This process often results in decisions that reflect the desires and positions of the high-status individuals. However, when those of high status exhibit faulty reasoning, the work group may also adopt faulty reasoning patterns (Gouran, 1986).

Some people in high-status positions possess specialized knowledge. However, even an individual with specific task-related knowledge may make inaccurate statements. Those statements may go unchallenged by the work group, for it is assumed that the expert possesses a high level of knowledge. For example, suppose that a division manager calls a meeting of the unit you manage. During the unit meeting, the division manager says, "Of all the units under my supervision, your unit has the largest payroll. You really need to cut back on the payroll." Would you or any of your unit's members challenge the division head's assessment? Probably not, because the division manager has higher status in the division and is expected to have greater knowledge. The division head can access all relevant financial data to assess whether your unit's payroll is similar to other units' payrolls. But what if the division manager assessed only the total amount of payroll rather than the average employee salary? If you have a large unit, you may necessarily have a large payroll. Among all the units, yours might have the lowest average employee salaries. By deferring to the manager's claim without question because of status, the manager's statement is accepted by the group as fact.

Another rule associated with affiliative constraints concerns the need for harmony among group members. Some members avoid conflicts in order to preserve harmony in the group. The *preserve group harmony rule* emphasizes the need for the group to maintain its positive climate. Ideas are not challenged so as to avoid destroying the group's harmony. In some instances, this may require using the *rigging rule* to ensure agreement and stifle disagreement (see Box 5.2).

Egocentric Constraints

It is a part of human nature to possess an ego. Our concern with developing and protecting our ego manifests itself in many ways. We sometimes view interactions in terms of the *"What's in it for me?" rule.* We may satisfy our ego needs by collecting power and status within an organization. When making decisions, we may approach them from a selfish vantage point aimed at enhancing our own personal prestige. When we are attacked or lack confidence in our abilities, we may preserve our ego using a number of strategies.

The *retaliate rule* causes people who have been embarrassed or humiliated by others to punish those responsible. The object is revenge—to make sure that the transgressor regrets having caused the problem. When frustrated or challenged by a decision that must be made, people may employ the *"can do" rule* or the *"Wow, grab it!" rule.* The former aims to build a person's ego by articulating why a decision will work. Aubrey Fisher (1970) observes that once people have made a decision, they tend to offer reinforcement for the option they have selected. To avoid feeling frustrated by or not confident in the decision, people may talk themselves into believing that they can do it. Just like the childhood story of the little engine who kept saying, "I think I can," decision makers keep saying, "I think the decision is good," to convince themselves of the wisdom of their choice. The *"Wow, grab it!" rule* reflects the tendency of individuals and policy making groups to grab the first viable solution after a period of frustration. Regardless of the merits of the solution, frustration causes the individual or group to adopt the first solution that meets a few of the criteria. If neither of these rules works to resolve the problem, employing the *"rely-on-gut-feelings" rule* may be used: this entails simply giving yourself over to your emotions and allowing your intuition to guide your response.

Making decisions necessarily involves making mistakes. Leaders cannot always make appropriate decisions and their ability to make good decisions is hampered by a variety of constraints. For individuals desiring to be leaders and for organizations desiring to create effective leadership practices, certain kinds of communication practices can be employed to facilitate effective decision making. (See Box 5.3.)

Box 5.3
The Case of Education 2000

Kim Walker is sitting in her office on a sunny Friday afternoon wishing to be any place else than at Education 2000, a for-profit organization that specializes in creating training material for high school students in math and English. "If I weren't director of personnel," she thinks to herself, "I could be gardening in my backyard right now. I've still got to plant those Iris bulbs this weekend." Her thoughts are interrupted by a knock at the door.

"Kim, do you have a few minutes?" asks Dave Lamb. Dave is a new employee at Education 2000 and has been hired because of his knowledge of computer technology. High schools are beginning to use more interactive teaching techniques that involve classroom computers, and Dave will help Education 2000 integrate computer software and hardware as well as new audio-visual technologies into the training packages.

"Sure, Dave, come on in. Take a seat."

"Kim, I just got out of a strategic planning meeting," Dave explains, "and I guess I just need to get some things off my chest. You know the meeting I'm talking about. Linda Jones, Paul Palmer, Kathy English, John Cervantes, and I are all members of the task force charged with determining our goals for the year 2000. We were charged by the president of the company to determine whether we need to expand into other kinds of training. Our recommendations will be put into a report and sent to the president for approval."

"Yeah," Kim replies, "I remember when that committee was formed. I had hoped I wouldn't get put on the task force. I really have too many other things on my agenda to get involved in estimating future personnel needs. So what's the problem?"

"Look, I don't want to sound like a whiner," Dave says, "but I'm confused and, honestly, a bit angry about the way John is heading the task force. At our first meeting, he asked us what areas we felt most comfortable about developing a strategic plan to take us into the year 2000. Kathy and Paul decided to look at the issue of whether we need to expand from simply doing training programs aimed at high school students to adapting the programs to the work force. Linda and I decided that we would take a look at technology issues and determine what areas we could expand into for the future. The idea was that each group would research its ideas and develop them separately.

"It surprises me that John organized the group in this way," Kim replies. "I've heard his reputation is pretty much a hard-nosed, hands-on kind of a leader. I heard that when he was in charge of developing the training material for MathSpeak, he ran roughshod over the whole group. Don't get me wrong, John gets results and MathSpeak has been a big moneymaker. It's just that he doesn't let anyone get in his way.

"Well get this—today we presented our proposals. Linda and I spent a lot of time on the project and came up with some different kinds of ideas. Well, John ripped our report to shreds, and implied that we didn't do a good job." Kim replied, "Well, in fairness to John, his job as a leader is to provide an honest assessment of ideas and proposals."

"I *know* that!" Dave shot back. "Its just that after ripping our proposal apart, John then put some changes on it and proposed it as his own! I feel that John thinks no one can have a good idea except him. Look, I know every idea can be improved on, but he doesn't have to be nasty about it. I talked to the other task force members afterward and asked why they didn't help me out. They told me that when John headed the MathSpeak project a few years ago, he went to Linda and Paul and told them if they didn't support his proposals, he'd make their lives difficult at work. They are very intimidated by him."

"Well, how can I help?" asks Kim.

"If you could think about it over the weekend, I thought maybe I could check with you on Monday after I have a chance to cool off. I just want to know what you think."

After Dave leaves the office, Kim returns to her thoughts about gardening. Then John Cervantes enters.

"Kim, I need to talk to you," he says.

"Yes, John, how can I help," Kim replies.

"You know the new guy, Dave Lamb? He's a member of the task force I'm heading," John begins. "Well, I don't know what to do with him. He seems to be a whiner and he doesn't take criticism too well. We just finished up a meeting and he looked upset. I went over his ideas with a fine-toothed comb and redeveloped them into a better format. You would have thought I had defaced a work of art with the looks he shot me. He just doesn't get it. The whole purpose of these meetings is to pit differing ideas against one another and see who wins. Besides, no one else said anything to support him. I asked everybody what they thought and they just sat there. That just tells me they also see problems with his ideas and don't want to embarrass him."

"Well, John, what do you want me to do about it?" asks Kim.

"Nothing, really," John says. This is more of an FYI. If you hear anything through the grapevine, just set the record straight, okay?"

As John leaves the office, Kim thinks to herself, "If I left right now, I bet I could plant those Iris bulbs by evening."

DISCUSSION QUESTIONS

1. Kim is scheduled to meet with Dave on Monday to give him some feedback on his reactions to the meeting. To help her prepare, she asks you—a confidant in the firm—to help her make sense of the information. Write a short description of the constraints that you see operating in the task force.
2. What advice would you give Dave? What advice would you give John? Write a memo to each character detailing your recommendations for improving their relationship.

SKILL BUILDING: FACILITATING VIGILANCE IN DECISION MAKING

People tend to make better decisions when they actively seek all relevant information, engage in a thorough analysis of possible solutions, and critique, or second-guess, their decisions (Janis, 1982, 1989; Janis & Mann, 1977; Hirokawa & Scheerhorn, 1986; Hirokawa & Rost, 1992). Vigilant decision making entails meeting a majority of the seven guidelines discussed earlier in the chapter. The criteria apply to the decisions made by individuals and collectively by work teams and groups. How leadership can facilitate vigilant decision making depends in part on the ability of leaders to articulate messages that meet the seven guidelines and to create procedures that counteract cognitive, affiliative, and egocentric constraints.

It is clear that leaders may either facilitate or inhibit decision making in organizations. Leaders may create an open environment in which information is freely exchanged and people are encouraged to debate the merits of ideas and solutions. How communication functions to create such an environment or to inhibit decision making has been tied to two general behavioral areas (Gouran & Hirokawa, 1983, 1986; Hirokawa & Scheerhorn, 1986). *Facilitative behavior* positively contributes to making high-quality decisions, whereas *inhibitive behavior* leads to poor-quality decisions. The relationship between a leader's communication and contribution to making decisions is similar to the navigator who uses a map to give directions to some distant place. Decisions, like trips, proceed along a path toward an endpoint or destination. For any long trip, there are many paths one can take to reach the final destination; some paths are direct, others are more roundabout. In addition, the ability to reach that destination depends in large part on the skill of the navigator. Some navigators read maps well and can provide detailed directions that allow travelers to arrive at their destination in a timely manner. Others are not as skilled and may lead travelers off track into dead ends, meaningless side-trips, or even to the wrong destination. Decision making also follows a path. As people and groups travel the decision path, they typically establish operating procedures, define the nature of the problem, generate solutions, evaluate solutions, and select among options for implementing solutions. The facilitative function of communication keeps individuals and groups on the path toward making a decision that reflects a majority of the seven guidelines discussed earlier. However, when leaders use inhibitive forms of communication instead, work groups may take a path that leads to poor-quality decisions.

A wide variety of messages are associated with individuals and work groups that facilitate or inhibit quality decision making (Barge, 1990). Despite the bewildering variety of messages that can be used to assist quality decision making, the following four themes appear to characterize most message strategies.

Facilitative messages critically assess the positive and negative aspects of potential solutions. Hirokawa and Scheerhorn (1986) suggest that one factor in particular—improper assessment of positive and negative qualities of various solutions to a problem—contributes to poor decision making. Message strategies that solicit individual viewpoints, provide reasoned assessments of the qualities of particular solutions, and address the strong and weak points of solutions provide more thorough analyses of the positive and negative consequences of decisions.

Facilitative messages structure and encourage participation. Across the various decision-making functions, facilitative messages emphasize taking action toward accomplishing the task through such behaviors as soliciting input, offering suggestions, proposing definitions of the task, establishing an order for the discussion, and delegating responsibilities.

Facilitative messages motivate others by offering encouragement and showing respect for diverse viewpoints. Giving encouragement may take many forms, such as urging others to view the task at hand as a challenge, recognizing that external constituencies support the group, and emphasizing the value of the group's task. Facilitative messages also encourage others to speak. In addition to directly asking for input, leaders may encourage continued participation by effectively managing dissenting or disagreeing views. When negative criticism is offered in evaluating a solution, it can be done in a constructive manner—by either explaining how individuals arrived at their judgment or offering a balanced assessment of the solution. Offering criticism with explanation shows that the evaluator understands the idea and, after a careful assessment, has decided to disagree with the idea.

Facilitative messages alert group members to the importance of other organizational constituencies. Individuals and work groups are embedded within an organizational hierarchy. The need for leaders to manage the boundary between a work team and the organization is explained by Deborah Ancona (1987). She contends that a chief problem confronting leaders is that most of the knowledge and prescriptions associated with leadership have been produced in laboratory settings. Such laboratory research precludes the possibility that a work group's effectiveness "may be as much a function of how well [it] deal[s] with problems in the environment as of how well the group members deal with each other" (Ancona & Caldwell, 1988, p. 468). Leaders do more than simply manage the task and relational activities of group members; they also help the work group manage its relationship with the larger organizational environment. Thus, leaders serve an important boundary-spanning function, whereby they manage how much information from the external environment is introduced into the team's discussion and how much information about the team's activities is made available to external constituencies.

Leaders tend to use three basic strategies when managing their environment (Ancona, 1990). Leaders who use the strategy of *informing* are concerned with developing effective internal group processes; they intentionally hold back information to outside audiences until the team has developed a clear sense of its identity and goals. *Parading,* in contrast, balances the focus of the informing strategy by letting outside constituencies know of the group's primary concern and commitment. Finally, leaders who use *probing* attempt to collect from out-

Box 5.4
Strategies for Managing Decision-Making Constraints

Type of Constraint	Situation	Strategy
Cognitive constraints	The severity of the impending threat is so great that group members want to shorten the appraisal.	• Role-model the resolve to take adequate time to seek and evaluate information. • Encourage group members to take steps that will allow them additional time to manage the problem. • Highlight relevant resources that can be applied to solving the problem. • Obtain outside expert opinion.
	Group members are discouraged because they have not been successful despite high levels of effort.	• Subdivide the large problem into a series of smaller, more manageable problems.
Affiliative constraints	Group members feel that their recommendations will be opposed by influential organizational members.	• Encourage discussion among group members about how they can persuade the organization to adopt their decisions. • Be skeptical and downplay the level of opposition. • Invite former opponents to the decision to speak to the group.
	Group members try to avoid punishment by conforming to the organization's wishes.	• Avoid exerting any pressure that may indicate your preference for a particular solution. • Facilitate power struggles by helping the parties discuss their views. • Assess which group members or coalitions are attempting to influence the group toward conformity; then provide messages that emphasize the importance of each individual group member's participation in the discussion.
	Group members withhold and distort bad news to avoid being punished by people in power.	• Create and announce a policy of no punishment for bringing bad news or information to the attention of organizational members.

Type of Constraint	Situation	Strategy
Affiliative contraints (continued)		• Challenge the accuracy of information, and send the message that accurate information is always desired. • Reward members who reveal unwanted or unwelcome information.
	A group member wants to "rig" the group's discussion because of suspected opposition to his or her preferred plan.	• Avoid holding meetings when the major dissenters cannot attend. • Provide fair and balanced reports to all group members. • At meetings, allow all group members to participate and to present counterarguments. • Be open to others' views; do not cue group members to your preferred solutions.
	The group is so cohesive that groupthink may emerge.	• Assign a group member to play the devil's advocate role. • Run each meeting in an unbiased and impartial manner so as to stimulate inquiry. • Have group members report their progress to outside constituencies so as to receive feedback. • Divide large groups into two smaller groups that will work independently.
Egocentric constraints	The rewards for pursuing policies that are self-serving are high.	• Make group members aware of this possibility. • Highlight organizational and legal policies that are intended to minimize this risk and to prevent conflict of interest.
	During meetings, group members pursue options that are prompted by self-serving motives.	• Express disapproval for pursuing self-serving motives. • Confront group members privately and discuss your impressions of their pursuit of self-serving solutions.

Box continued

Type of Constraint	Situation	Strategy
Egocentric constraints (continued)	The group is moving rapidly toward a decision that will serve a personal motive or an emotional need of one group member.	• Bring in organizational powerholders who object to the self-serving motives and have them evaluate the group's deliberations. • Distribute a summary of the group's deliberations, including a list of the advantages and disadvantages of all viable solutions to organizational constituencies to which the group is responsible.

Source: I. L. Janis (1989), *Crucial decisions: Leadership in policymaking and crisis management* (New York: Free Press), pp. 231–264.

siders information that the group can use to make its decisions. Groups that depend on the external environment are more effective when they use probing, whereas isolated groups that emphasize the informing strategy are more likely to fail.

Although the various types of messages provide insight into some of the general facilitative functions of effective leaders, they do not provide strategic means of dealing with the constraints discussed earlier in the chapter. Box 5.4 describes the strategies that Janis (1989) recommends for facilitating vigilant decision making. Overall the general image of an effective leader is one who attempts to motivate group members, introduces skepticism and self-doubt, and is intent on arriving at a decision that meets the needs of the organization, not the personal self-interest of a few select individuals.

SUMMARY

To survive, organizations must make sense of and plan and execute actions that help them manage their environment. It is the process of adaptation that makes one of the primary tasks of leadership the facilitation of decision making. The degree to which leaders are able to facilitate an organization's decision making depends on the nature of the task. Simple decision-making tasks effectively neutralize the influence of a leader's communication. Tasks that deal with questions of fact, that are additive in nature, or that have low information requirements and evaluation demands diminish the influence of a leader's communication. More complex tasks, such as questions of policy, disjunctive tasks, or tasks with high information requirements and evaluation demands offer greater opportunity for leadership communication to influence the decision-making process.

As the complexity of a decision-making task increases, the likelihood that deficiencies in decision making will emerge also increases. Deficiencies in decision making may arise from cognitive, affiliative, or egocentric constraints. To counteract these constraints, leaders must be skilled in facilitating a group's discussion; that is, they must be able to help groups establish operating procedures, analyze the nature of the problem, and generate, evaluate, and implement solutions. Leaders may use a variety of message strategies to fulfill these needs. Messages that help the group evaluate positive and negative elements of solutions, encourage participation in the decision-making process, and offer encouragement to facilitate decision making are needed.

QUESTIONS AND APPLICATIONS

1. Make a list of some of the important decisions you have made in the past. Which ones were particularly difficult to make? Which were relatively simple to make? Describe three factors that make decisions difficult for you.

2. You have been charged with leading a task force to determine ways to increase awareness of gender issues in your organization. The group is to determine the kind of programming that needs to be adopted for promoting awareness of gender issues. To focus their discussion, the task force members have asked you to specify in a memo the issues that need to be addressed. Write the memo, making sure to highlight questions of fact, value, conjecture, and policy that need to be addressed by the task force.

3. In the space provided here, write three typical kinds of decisions that are made by a group. On a scale of 1 (low) to 7 (high), rate each decision in terms of its difficulty, intrinsic interest, solution multiplicity, goal-path clarity, and cooperation requirements.

	Degree of				
DECISION TYPE	DIFFICULTY	INTRINSIC INTEREST	SOLUTION MULTIPLICITY	GOAL-PATH CLARITY	COOPERATION REQUIREMENTS
________	________	________	________	________	________
________	________	________	________	________	________
________	________	________	________	________	________

For each decision, describe how the group can best organize itself. How well does the group conform to the predictions outlined in Table 5.3?

Chapter 6
Managing Organizational Relationships

> Culture shock occurs when members are involved in an organizational culture that has rules and practices different from their own. Shock sets in when workers do not know how to function successfully in that culture. They react with anxiety, fear, or withdrawal. . . . These [feelings] often create an immediate loss of productivity, prolonged frustration, disillusionment, and they can result in job termination.
>
> *(Coleman, 1990)*

Members of an organization typically try to carve out their own personal space or niche within the company in order to make sense of their work experiences and to learn the formal and informal rules that define the workplace. A variety of emotions and reactions may accompany this sense-making process: an unclear sense of the organization's purpose, satisfaction in fulfilling one's role in the organization, dissatisfaction with organizational procedures, irritation with non-motivated organizational members, comfort in the support of co-workers, and concern about personality conflicts or a lack of employee commitment to the organization. While that list is not comprehensive, there are numerous surprises, joys, obstacles, and roadblocks that influence the kind of relationship we cultivate with an organization and its members. At first glance, these reactions and emotions may appear to have little in common. However, they all stem from the way individuals negotiate their relationships with the larger organization and with other organizational members. Consider some of the typical questions that you might ask during your tenure with an organization: "What role should I play in the organization?" "Am I motivated to do my work?" "How committed am I to the organization?" "How do I manage conflicts?" These and other questions flow from the kind of relationships that people establish within the organization. Thus, the relational dimension of organizational life is captured in the interpersonal climate—that is, in the relationships formed by organizational members. As individuals interact with one another and form a collective system of organizing, the roles that individuals are to play emerge. Some individuals may not be enthusiastic about their relationships with organizational members and, therefore, must be motivated to involve themselves and to perform their job well. As people negotiate roles and make decisions about their role relationships with others, conflicts over status and other issues may occur. For individuals to become a collective group, a sense of identity and commitment to the organization must be fostered. *Relational management* involves defining roles, motivating followers, and managing conflict.

Can leadership alone influence how people find their place in an organization? Is leadership employees' primary motivational force? Can it manage conflict at all times for all people? The answer to all three questions is no. Several popular books on management emphasize that companies can develop highly committed employees by creating a high-performance culture, which provides a focus for employees regarding their work role, motivates employees through empowerment, and manages conflict quickly and efficiently (Peters & Waterman, 1982; Peters & Austin, 1985; Peters, 1987). Leaders can influence these processes at both the organizational and individual levels. When leaders initially create companies or radically restructure them, they also create or re-create an organizational culture. It, in turn, influences how workers approach the organization and their jobs. At the individual level, leaders forge relationships with employees and construct their roles and expectations. Leaders motivate people and are expected to resolve disputes among individuals and work groups. Although the overriding corporate culture exercises a major influence on these processes, leaders play an important influential role as well.

How leaders facilitate the processes of defining roles, motivating employees, and resolving disputes is best understood by way of example. W. L. Gore & Associates is an organization with an effective system of organizing that effectively carries out the processes of relational management.

RELATIONAL MANAGEMENT: W. L. GORE & ASSOCIATES

"Make money and have fun!"
—*Wilbert L. Gore*

Wilbert Gore's statement defines the overriding principle that guides W. L. Gore & Associates, a manufacturing firm that produces medical, camping, textile, and electronic products. W. L. Gore & Associates grew from three thousand employees at nineteen manufacturing sites in 1983 to over five thousand employees at thirty-five manufacturing plants in 1991 (Wilbert L. Gore, 1983; Wegner, 1991). The founder of the company, Wilbert L. Gore, initially worked for Du Pont (1945–1957), researching applications for a polymer called PTFE, more commonly known as Teflon. Gore became convinced that PTFE would be a good insulator for electrical wires. In his basement laboratory at home, he began attacking the problem of coating electrical wires with PTFE. Despite repeated efforts, he failed in this task until he talked with his son, Bob. According to Bob Gore, his father

> explained that he had tried various ways to make a PTFE coating but had failed. He held up an aborted section of ribbon cable and pointed

> out where his attempts had broken down. "Then I noticed some sealant tape made by the 3M company," Bob says. "Dad has said it was ram-extruded PTFE so I asked him: 'Why don't you try this tape?' Dad said that would mean laminating the wires between two sections of tape and everybody knew you couldn't bond PTFE to itself. I went to bed.
>
> As near as Bob can recall, it was around 4 A.M. when his father shook him awake. "I really didn't grasp what he was talking about," Bob says, "except I knew my father was very excited. I was sitting on the edge of my bed blinking at him, and he was waving this small piece of cable around saying: 'It works. It works.' " (quoted in Rhodes, 1982, p. 37)

Wilbert Gore presented this breakthrough discovery to his supervisors at Du Pont, but they were not interested because they viewed their business as providing the raw material for manufacturing products rather than the products themselves. At that point, Gore decided to leave his job at Du Pont to start up his own company. On New Year's Day in 1958, Bill and Vieve Gore formed Gore & Associates. Since 1958, the company has created products ranging from vascular grafts and artificial organs to sealants. The product most known to consumers is Gore-Tex fabric, which repels water but also "breathes" and is used in a variety of camping and recreational products, such as tents, backpacks, and parkas. Product innovation and development allowed Gore & Associates to emerge as a Fortune 500 company. What led to the phenomenal growth and success of Gore & Associates? If you asked Bill Gore, he would attribute his success to (1) lattice work organization and (2) four operating principles.

Lattice Work Organization

When Gore was working at Du Pont developing applications for PTFE, he was impressed with the amount of work and fun that could be accomplished by a group. As he put it, "the task was exciting, challenging, and loads of fun. Besides, we worked like Trojans. I began to wonder why entire companies couldn't be run the same way" (quoted in Rhodes, 1982, p. 36). Gore thus initiated a management structure at his company known as the *lattice* framework. The lattice work organization views all people as equals. In fact, all employees at Gore & Associates are called "Associates" (with a capital "A") and, with the exception of the legal titles of president, vice-president, chairperson, and treasurersecretary, no other titles exist at the company. The concept is that all people should have direct access to one another in order to get their work done efficiently.

The Four Operating Principles

The lattice work organization is held together by four basic operating principles:

1. *Fairness:* All Associates should strive to be fair with each other, with suppliers and customers, and with anyone else they deal with.
2. *Freedom:* All Associates should facilitate each other's growth in knowledge, skills, and abilities. They should be encouraged to try new things and learn.
3. *Commitment:* All Associates should make and honor their commitments to other Gore Associates and outside constituencies.
4. *Waterline:* If a boat gets a hole in it above the waterline, it can survive; if it gets a hole below the waterline, it takes on water and may sink. Similarly, there are decisions that may also sink a company. The principle of waterline emphasizes that if a decision to be made may severely injure the financial health of the company, hurt its reputation, or adversely affect its survival, the Associates should consult with each other before taking any action.

The four operating principles reinforce the lattice work organization by prescribing the kinds of behaviors that are expected by employees. Gore & Associates applies them in its approaches to defining roles, motivating employees, and managing conflict.

DEFINING ROLES

> On July 26, 1976, Jack Dougherty, a newly minted MBA from the College of William and Mary, became an associate. Bursting with resolve and dressed in a dark blue suit, he presented himself to Bill Gore, shook hands firmly, looked him in the eye, and said he was ready for anything.
>
> What happened next was the one thing for which Jack was not ready. "That's fine, Jack, fine," Gore replied. "Why don't you look around and find something you'd like to do." Three frustrating weeks later, Jack found that something. Now dressed in jeans, he loaded fabric into the maw of a machine that laminates Gore-Tex membrane to other fabrics. And, by 1982, he had become responsible for all advertising and marketing in the fabrics group. (Shipper & Manz, 1992, pp. 56–57)

When individuals join an organization, they go through a series of surprises and shocks as they adjust (Louis, 1980). Part of that adjustment process is accompanied by newcomers trying to make sense of the roles they are to play. Newcomers are in a transitional phase—moving from a previous set of expectations developed in another organization to a new set of roles appropriate to the present organization. A *role* is made up of a set of prescribed behaviors that individuals are expected to perform. Using an improvisational theater metaphor, people are provided with general descriptions of the character they are to perform, of the general motivations for that character, and of the plot line. In improvisational theater, actors have great latitude in producing a number of different lines. However, failure to perform consistently the general character or plot lines in a scene leads to the disintegration of the play, for the form and structure of the general plot are destroyed. Similarly, organizations specify a general role structure with character descriptions and plot lines that help the organization complete its work effectively and efficiently. However, organizations need to develop a role structure that is sufficiently flexible to adapt to the needs of the environment.

Organizational Roles

People may play a variety of roles within organizations. One classic typology of group roles is offered by Benne and Sheats (1948). It is based on the type of behavioral function performed by the individuals playing the role. Three general classes of roles are identified:

Task roles. These roles function to help the group achieve its task or objective. They include behaviors that orient the group to the task at hand, manage the exchange of ideas and opinions, and encourage the group to complete the task.

Relational roles. These roles include behaviors that function to maintain the interpersonal climate within the group. They provide harmony to the group, create openness for sharing information, convey the feelings of group members, and help manage the relational environment of the organization.

Ego-centered roles. These roles emphasize the individual's personality and thereby favor the needs of the individual over the group. Such roles are typically viewed as destructive to a group because they hinder the organization's ability to achieve a task.

Table 6.1 details a variety of individual roles within each major category.

In addition to task, relational, and egocentric roles, people may assume formal or informal organizational roles. The *formal organizational role* is rooted in the organizational hierarchy; it specifies the formal duties, responsibilities, and behaviors that the organization requires of its employees. The *informal organizational role* is formed through interaction in the informal network. The individual's and group's expectations form the basis for the informal role. The kinds of informal roles that people assume may maintain the organization's culture or attempt to alter it. Some people create custodial roles within an organization, through which they maintain the organizational status quo. Others adopt more innovative role orientations and are open to and facilitate change (Jones, 1986).

It is important to remember that roles are not taken; rather, they are created in conjunction with other members of the organization. Roles are worked out through interaction and negotiation, and feedback from leaders and other organizational members influences the types of roles individuals assume. Earnest Bormann (1975) argues that the feedback provided by other group members

TABLE 6.1 Group Role Functions

Role	Function
Task Roles	
Initiator	Provides direction and guidance to a group. Proposes definitions of problems, suggests solutions, gives ideas, and suggests operating procedures.
Information seeker	Recognizes the need for additional information. Requests clarification of ideas and relevant facts about the group's task.
Information giver	Provides relevant facts about the group's task.
Opinion seeker	Solicits people's feelings and views about any aspect of the group's task. Tests for the group opinion.
Opinion giver	Offers personal views and evaluation of the group's work. May comment on the value of certain group procedures, the solutions under consideration, or the nature of the group's task.
Clarifier	Eliminates confusion by identifying points of agreement or restating ideas or viewpoints.
Elaborator/coordinator	Extends information and clarifies relations among various viewpoints, ideas, and solutions within the group.
Problem identifier	Proposes definitions of a problem and its related causes or antecedents.
Procedure developer	Proposes and identifies the procedures a group should use when making a decision; includes setting and proposing an agenda.
Orienter-summarizer	Focuses the group on the task and summarizes its discussion by reviewing the relationships among solutions, facts, and opinions.
Information recorder	Records group discussion.
Tester of agreement	Checks to see how close the group is to reaching an agreement.
Energizer	Motivates the group and prods it toward action.
Relational Roles	
Supporter	Recognizes others' contributions and encourages them to participate.
Harmonizer	Attempts to balance and manage conflicts within the group. Serves to maintain and restore a positive interpersonal climate. Includes helping the group express its feelings to relieve tension.
Tension reliever	Through joking and humor, attempts to relieve group stress.
Compromiser	Seeks to maintain group cohesion by compromising his or her own ideas that are in conflict with the group's. Admits error to the group.

(continued)

TABLE 6.1 *Continued*

Role	Function
Gatekeeper	Manages and directs the flow of communication and participation within the group.
Feeling expresser	Highlights for the group its feelings, emotions, and attitudes. Shares feelings with other group members.
Standard setter	Articulates the standards the group must achieve. Refers to these standards when evaluating the group's progress.
Follower	Accepts the ideas and views of other group members without question.
Self-Centered Roles	
Blocker	Inhibits group discussion by refusing to cooperate. Rejects other group members' ideas.
Aggressor	Tries to gain power within the group by criticizing other group members' ideas and competence.
Deserter	Withdraws from group participation.
Dominator	Monopolizes group discussions.
Recognition seeker	Seeks personal recognition and praise from other group members by boasting about past accomplishments.
Confessor	Distracts the group from its task by using the group as a means of solving personal problems.
Playboy	Uses cynicism, humor, and horseplay to distract the group from its task.
Special interest pleader	Pursues a personal agenda or the agenda of an outside group.

Source: Adapted from K. D. Benne and P. Sheats (1948), *Journal of Social Issues, 4,* 41–49.

frames the types of roles that an individual can legitimately assume within a group. Bormann's model, as extended to organizational settings, is summarized as follows:

1. If organizational members give *ambiguous feedback* to an individual about role performance, the individual will continue to display the behavior until clear approval or disapproval is received.
2. If organizational members give *positive feedback* or *approval* to an individual about role performance, the individual will integrate the behavior into his or her role repertoire.
3. If organizational members give *negative feedback* or *disapproval* to an individual about role performance, the person will begin to avoid the behavior.

Feedback is the mechanism that provides information to individuals about the types of relationships they will form with others in the organization.

As newcomers become socialized in an organization, numerous sources provide feedback about the appropriateness and effectiveness of their developing role. One key source of feedback is the formal and informal leader (Jablin, 1987). As leaders cultivate relationships with other organizational members, they provide feedback and negotiate duties and obligations. George Graen and Terri Scandura (1987) suggest that this process of role development occurs in three stages (see Figure 6.1). In the first stage, *role taking,* the leader assesses the task

FIGURE 6.1 A Dyadic Model of Role Making

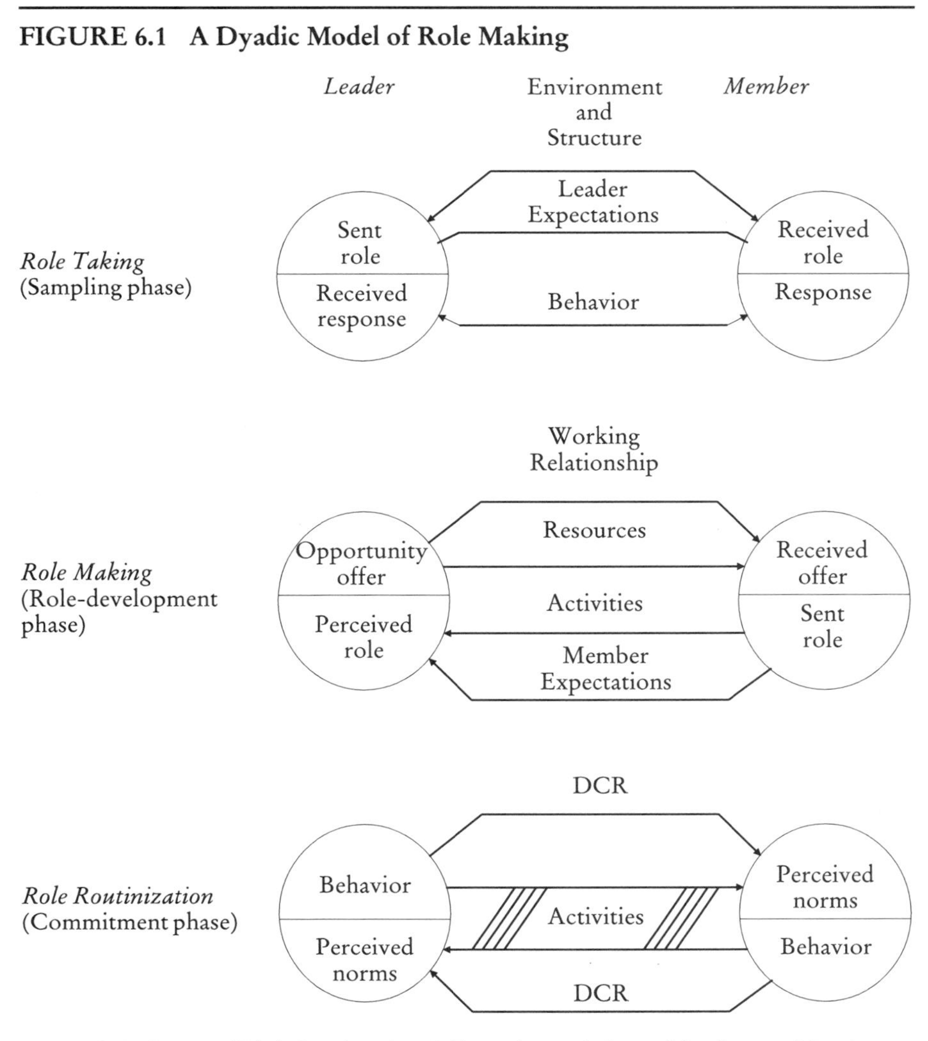

Source: G. B. Graen and T. A. Scandura (1987), Toward a psychology of dyadic organizing, in L. L. Cummings and B. M. Staw (eds.), *Research in organizational behavior,* vol. 9 (New York: JAI Press), p. 180.

skills and abilities as well as the relational qualities of the member. Leaders may test employees' limitations by assigning them to a variety of tasks and evaluating their success at completing each one. The employee receives information about the type of role the leader is suggesting be performed. The employee's behavior tells the leader whether the role has been accepted or rejected. The leader may then decide whether to introduce another test role. Through this process, which may last from a few hours to several months, the leader can assess employees' abilities.

The second phase of role development, called *role making,* occurs over the course of several months. In it leaders and employees begin to develop standard ways of approaching tasks and to define the kinds of roles they assume when problems emerge. By working together, an unspoken agreement emerges as they develop problem-solving patterns for certain kinds of problems. In the role-making phase, either the leader or the employee can initiate the creation of this pattern. In Figure 6.1, for example, the leader is seen as initiating the sequence. The leader offers some type of opportunity for the employee to participate in the typical role-making process. This opportunity may include the leader sharing valued information with the employee or providing task opportunities for the employee to develop. The employee may accept or reject the offer or even make a counter-offer. The leader is then aware of the employee's perceived role and may choose to accept or reject it. Over time, a working relationship emerges.

Role routinization is the third phase of role development. By closely collaborating on a number of tasks, leaders and employees develop an understanding of their work relationship. They also develop standardized ways of interacting and performing tasks.

Leaders are a valuable source of feedback and information to employees who are in the process of developing their roles in an organization. Although there are other sources of feedback, such as co-workers, clients, and suppliers, leaders are one of the most influential sources of role-development information.

Roles at Gore & Associates

Gore & Associates provides an excellent example of the mutual role-negotiation process that occurs between individuals and leaders. The "Associates" are encouraged to carve out and develop new roles within the organization. In *The 100 Best Companies to Work For,* Levering, Moskowitz, and Katz (1984) warn:

> If you apply to work here, you may receive a letter that gives you fair warning of what to expect: "If you are a person who needs to be told what to do and how to do it, Dr. Gore says, you will have trouble adjusting. . . . An associate has to find his [or her] own place to a high degree. There's no job descriptions, no slot to fit yourself into. You have to learn what you can do." (p. 128)

Newcomers at Gore & Associates are encouraged to experiment with their organizational roles. However, they are not able to assume any role they desire.

Two organizational processes prevent the development of roles counterproductive to the organization. First, mentors known as *sponsors* provide feedback about employee performance. In essence, they are informal leaders charged with facilitating Associates' growth and helping them get started in the job. This includes providing feedback during the role-taking, role-making, and routinization stages of role development. Second, a *compensation* system is driven by the input from one's co-workers. Pay levels are assessed by evaluating each Associate's contribution to the success of the company. After input from sponsors, fellow team members, and peers is collected, the individual's contribution to the organization is ranked with other Associates' contributions. Gore & Associates thus provides feedback to its employees about the appropriateness of the roles they have created within the organization.

MOTIVATING FOLLOWERS

> The most striking memory about Gore that I have kept with me is a conversation that I overheard in one of the Gore lunchrooms between two associates—one the plant receptionist and the other the plant maintenance and security associate. Both were talking about why they liked working at Gore, and I doubt that they knew or cared that I was listening in. "I am thankful," said the one, "to be working in a place where I'm doing maintenance and security and anything else I want to tackle. It's not boring, but you know, it's more than that; it's that I feel I can honestly make a difference."
>
> And the other replied, "And that's the way it is for me, too. And I'll keep working here as long as it stays fun and I feel I can make a difference." (Pacanowsky, 1988, p. 371)

Gore & Associates employs the lattice work organization and its four operating principles as a means of motivating employees to high levels of performance. If gross revenue and the development of new products serve as indicators of success, then the employees at Gore & Associates are highly motivated. What accounts for this high level of motivation? To answer this question, we need first to examine the traditional perspectives of what accounts for motivation.

The Nature of Motivation

The importance of motivation in work settings has long interested organizational researchers. Beginning with the scientific management approach, which used a "carrot and stick" method of motivating workers, and the human relations movement of the 1960s, which equated the motivated employee with the satisfied employee, the issue of how to motivate employees at work remains an important issue today. Robert Baron (1991) defines *motivation* as "the internal processes that activate, guide, and maintain behavior (especially goal-directed behavior)" (p. 1). We see people as motivated when they exhibit behaviors that we view indicative of motivation. We attribute motivation to salespersons who exceed their sales quota and to individuals who consistently perform their jobs well over time. But is all behavior motivated? Landy and Becker (1987) suggest that behavior may range from automatic and reflexive (e.g., knee-jerk reactions), to a conscious awareness of selecting among alternative actions, to overlearned automatic behaviors that are performed out of habit. Motivation is typically indicated by behaviors that are directed at accomplishing some task, that require an exertion of effort on the part of an individual, and that persist over time.

What is the relationship between leaders and employee motivation? Raymond A. Katzell and Donna E. Thompson (1990) point out that a leader can influence an individual's level of motivation through exogenous methods. The means are exogenous or external to the employee who is the target of the motivation attempt. Although several exogenous motivation theories exist, the following four distinct themes characterize the past and contemporary views of motivation. The themes provided here are not exhaustive, but are illustrative of some of the general trends in motivation theory. (More general reviews of motivation can be found in Pinder, 1984; Landy, 1985; and Landy & Becker, 1987.)

Workers are motivated to meet and fulfill their needs. The underlying premise of human needs theory is that individuals within organizations are motivated to work in order to accomplish needs. Needs are basic wants, desires, and necessities; they may include elements necessary for our survival, such as food and water, as well as unnecessary but desirable elements, such as warmth and the affection of others. Human needs theories explain why people initiate certain kinds of behaviors by identifying the motives that prompt their actions. Policymakers and leaders within organizations attempt to meet the employees' needs and influence their perceptions of needs through orientation, socialization, and training programs, and by providing them with realistic previews of job responsibilities (Katzell & Thompson, 1990).

There are a variety of needs that individuals attempt to fulfill in their personal and work life. Abraham Maslow (1970) and C. P. Alderfer (1972) each developed a hierarchy of human needs (see Table 6.2). Both theorists view human needs as ranging from basic or simple needs to higher-level or complex needs. For Maslow (1970), needs range from a very low level—such as the needs for food and water—to a high level—the need for self-actualization. Alderfer (1972) adapts a slightly different arrangement; he views people as wanting to achieve needs of existence, relatedness, or growth. Furthermore, Maslow contends that once people achieve the low-level needs, they move to the next higher level of needs. However, most empirical research fails to confirm the existence of all five needs or the assumption that individuals progress through levels of needs (Lawler & Suttle, 1972; Hall & Nougaim, 1968; Raushenberger, Schmitt, & Hunter, 1980; Veroff, Reuman, & Feld, 1984). Alderfer (1972) argues that people may actually regress to low-level needs. Higher-level needs are more complex, abstract, and ambiguous and, as a result, more frustrating. When individuals become frustrated in their effort to achieve a particular goal in the hierarchy, they may move back to a lower-level need that is more concrete, easier to achieve, and less frustrating.

TABLE 6.2 A Comparison of Maslow's (1970) and Alderfer's (1972) Human Needs Theories

Underlying Common Assumption

All human beings are motivated to fulfill their needs.

Maslow	*Alderfer*
KEY CONCEPTS	
Self-actualization: The desire to develop one's self to the fullest potential. *Esteem needs:* Achieving self-respect through attaining recognition from others.	*Growth needs:* The need to develop oneself personally and to become self-actualizing.
Affiliation needs: The desire to be loved by others and to be a part of a group. *Safety needs:* The importance of creating an environment that is secure and that allows protection from environmental dangers.	*Relatedness needs:* One's desire for affiliation and to belong to a group.
Physiological needs: The basic elements required for human survival, such as food, water, air, and rest.	*Existence needs:* Material existence needs, such as food and water.

KEY DIFFERENCES

- Maslow argues that people continually progress to higher-level needs, whereas Alderfer argues that people may regress to lower-level needs.
- Maslow arranges needs from high-level (self-actualization) needs to low-level needs (physiological), whereas Alderfer arranges needs along a continuum of abstraction levels ranging from concrete needs (existence) to abstract needs (growth).

People are motivated when they receive positive consequences for their work. One of the most important lessons that children learn as they are growing up is the "pleasure principle"—that people seek pleasure and avoid pain. Similarly, leaders develop sophisticated incentive and reward, compensation, and feedback systems to provide the necessary rewards and punishments to move people in directions consistent with organizational goals. The pleasure principle is the basis for both the reinforcement and expectancy theories.

Reinforcement theories of motivation are primarily concerned with influencing the direction and persistence of a person's behavior. They seek to control the individual's persistence to perform a behavior through reinforcement and punishment. Reinforcement theories of motivation are based on the behaviorist theory of B. F. Skinner (1969), who argued that people learn through operant conditioning. Operants are behaviors that can be altered or modified. They may be reinforced to enhance the likelihood that individuals will continue to perform the behaviors. For example, if a leader wanted to try reinforcement to encourage an employee to come to work on time, two forms of reinforcement could be attempted:

1. *Positive reinforcement* is the administration of a desirable outcome. (When the employee shows up to work on time, the leader would offer praise or a compliment.)
2. *Negative reinforcement* is the removal of a negative outcome as a means to reward the individual. (Some employees who are always late to work are teased when they finally show up on time. A leader using negative reinforcement might refrain from teasing the employee and take steps to prevent co-workers from making snide comments.)

Punishment may also be used to control behavior. A leader using punishment may administer some type of negative consequence for not performing a desired behavior. Punishment may take two forms:

1. *Punishment by application* is the administration of negative outcomes. (A leader might reprimand or warn the employee of the negative consequences if the employee continues to be late.)
2. *Punishment by removal* is the removal of positive reinforcers or the taking away of privileges. (A leader may decrease the tardy employee's privileges by not allowing the employee to choose a certain lunch time or by not giving the employee desirable work assignments.)

The goal of motivation theory, from a reinforcement perspective, is for leaders to motivate employees to higher performance by reinforcing desirable behaviors and eliminating undesirable behaviors. Positive and negative types of reinforcement are assumed to enhance learning, motivation, and performance to a greater degree than punishment.

The notion that people seek to maximize their pleasure is also present in *expectancy theory*. People do not react passively to their environment; rather, they calculate the relative payoffs of accomplishing certain goals (Vroom, 1964; Garland, 1984; Locke, Motowidlo, & Bobko, 1986). Deciding whether to perform a particular behavior depends on three calculations. First, people calculate their *expectancy*—the amount of confidence that certain behaviors will be followed by a particular outcome. High expectancy is associated with the high probability that the outcome will follow. For example, a salesperson who believes that by making ten extra sales calls increased sales and commissions will result would classify the behavior-outcome link as high in expectancy. Second, individuals also calculate *valence*, or their view of whether the outcome is desirable. Valence ranges from positive to negative and may vary in its intensity. Using the preceding example, if a salesperson viewed the end result as extremely desirable, we could say that the outcome is positively valenced. Finally, individuals assess *instrumentality*—the belief that if they exercise effort, the outcome will come about. The salesperson may believe that exerting the effort of making the ten extra sales calls will bring about the goal of increased commissions. The likelihood that the salesperson will be motivated to perform a particular goal is a function of expectancy, valence, and instrumentality. Expectancy theory is a choice-making process in which people pursue goals viewed as realistic, attainable, and desirable.

Although expectancy theory explains how people go about making choices to maximize gains, it does not completely account for people's behavior. When the number of possible outcomes people can select and choose from grows too large, it becomes difficult to calculate all the expectancies associated with the outcomes (Leon, 1979). Our cognitive ability to calculate the number of expectancies is taxed when numerous outcomes exist. Thus, people do not always calculate their level of motivation as intended by expectancy theory. They may avoid pursuing an outcome with negative consequences whether the valence is small or large (Leon, 1981). When people view an outcome as more positively valenced, they tend to pursue the outcome that has the highest probability of being achieved. When outcomes are negatively valenced, individuals tend to avoid them.

People are motivated by goals. The underlying assumption of goal theory is that performance is directly related to goals (Locke & Latham, 1984, 1990a). According to Edward Locke (1991), the central premise of goal theory is "that conscious goals regulate much human action and specifically performance on work tasks" (p. 18). Goals are the objectives or endpoints that people want to achieve. Individuals perform better when goals are specific, challenging, and clear rather than vague, easy, and ambiguous. Over four hundred studies have been conducted on goal theory, and four basic findings have emerged (see Locke & Latham, 1990a, for a detailed summary):

1. *Goal setting is better than no goal setting.* By structuring goals, individuals are given a direction to pursue and exert effort to attain those goals.
2. *Specific versus vague goals are better.* When individuals are given specific goals to attain, they perform at higher levels than individuals who are given either no goals or "do your best" goals.
3. *Difficult goals are better than easy goals.* Setting challenging goals and expectations yields higher performance results than less challenging goals. However, it is important to keep in mind the task difficulty. Setting difficult goals for simple tasks are associated with larger effects than setting difficult goals for complex tasks (Wood, Mento, & Locke, 1987). Since simple tasks have relatively easy and identifiable pathways to achieve the task, difficult goals make more of a difference. Complex tasks have more varied and complex pathways—any number of strategies may be pursued. The strategy a person selects to achieve a task is then a better predictor of success than the difficulty of the goal (Wood & Bandura, 1989).
4. *Participative goal setting is equal to assigned goals.* Whether an individual participates in setting performance goals or is assigned a goal, having a goal increases effort and motivation (Latham & Lee, 1986; Locke & Latham, 1990a). At first, this finding appears counterintuitive. After all, many of the participative management approaches reported in Chapter

2 emphasize that participative goal setting leads to increased commitment to the organization. When a rationale is provided with the assigned goal, participatively set goals demonstrate no significant advantage over assigned goals (Latham, Erez, & Locke, 1988). Locke and Latham (1990b) suggest several reasons assigned goals are equally effective as participatively set goals: people who assign goals may be viewed as having more authority, power, and expertise and are viewed as having the legitimate right to assign the goal; by assigning a goal, the person displays confidence in the subordinate's ability to complete the goal; and assigned goals may be more challenging and thereby stimulate higher levels of performance.

The use of goal-setting theory can be seen in any number of activities structured by organizational policymakers and leaders, such as management by objectives, quality circles, and participative management techniques.

Goal-setting theory has recently been incorporated as part of the high-performance cycle (Locke & Latham, 1990a; 1990b). Although the theory is not designed to explain leadership's role in motivation, Locke and Latham (1990b) observe that leaders may play an important role in maintaining and creating the high-performance cycle. As shown in Figure 6.2, the high-performance cycle incorporates elements of expectancy theory and reinforcement theory. Goals, expectancies for success, self-efficacy, and confidence all contribute to high performance. These elements are mediated by such mechanisms as effort and knowledge. If high performance is rewarded, employees will be satisfied and increase their commitment to the organization. With increased commitment comes the feeling that they need to structure even higher goals and that they are even more confident in their ability. Once set in motion, the high-performance cycle spirals to higher levels of performance. As Locke and Latham (1990b) point out, leaders play important roles in articulating the goals of the organization to members and in administering rewards and punishments to employees.

People are motivated when they are empowered by the organization. In contemporary organizations, people are using such phrases as "being empowered" or "having a voice" to refer to the importance of their participation in decision making. Employees are more likely to feel empowered and to be committed to an organization when they are involved in making decisions. They are also more likely to achieve high levels of motivation. Commitment moderates empowerment and motivation. Organizational commitment is typically viewed as "the relative strength of an individual's identification with and involvement in a particular organization as well as the willingness to exert effort and remain in the organization" (Ferris & Aranya, 1983, p. 87). Commitment to an organization is critical, because of the impact it can have on important organizational outcomes, and is positively associated with job satisfaction (Cook & Wall, 1980). Committed employees make decisions that reflect the interests, needs, and goals of the organization (Cheney, 1983). Moreover, organizational commitment has been negatively correlated to job turnover (Mowday, Steers, & Porter, 1979) and the tendency of employees to seek other jobs (Cheney, 1983).

FIGURE 6.2 The High-Performance Cycle

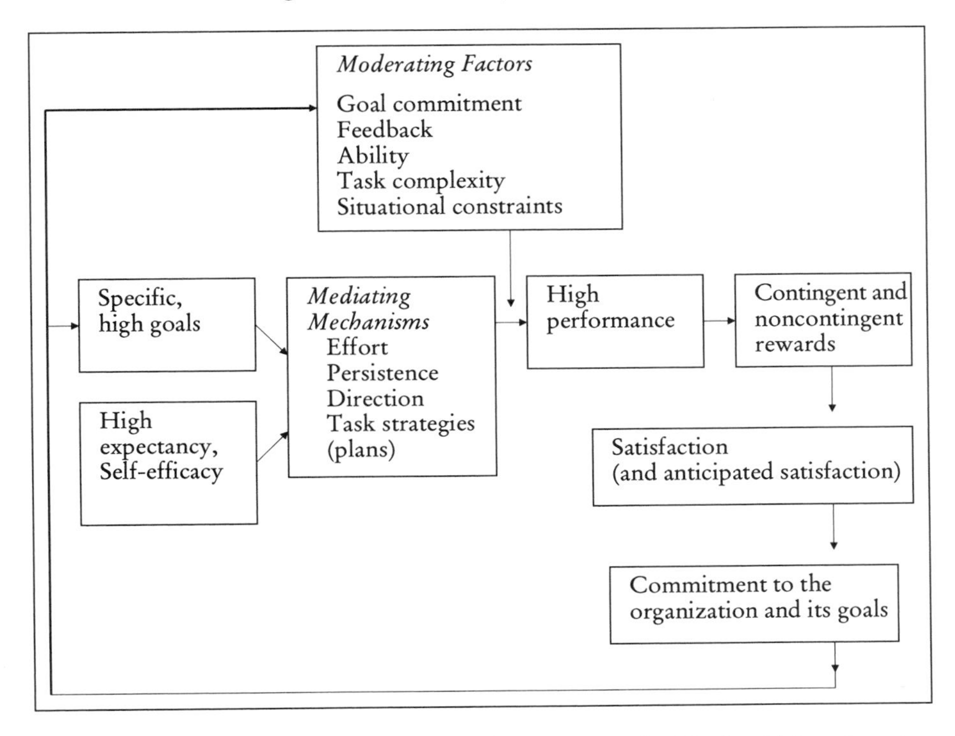

Source: E. A. Locke and G. P. Latham (1990), Work motivation and satisfaction: Light at the end of the tunnel, *Psychological Science, 1*(4), p. 244

Empowerment is defined in numerous ways, ranging from employee participation and delegation to a type of motivational construct. Jay Conger and Rabinda Kanungo (1988) argue that empowerment is best described as a motivational construct because it provides employees with a sense of opportunity and enables them to take action. Delegating behavior and involving employees in decision making do not guarantee that the employee will be empowered; rather, employees must have a heightened sense of self-efficacy—of powerfulness, self-determination, and confidence in their ability to perform a task. *Empowerment,* then, is a process whereby feelings of self-efficacy are produced by removing the formal and informal organizational practices that lead to feelings of powerlessness.

According to Conger and Kanungo (1988), a variety of conditions may lead to feelings of powerlessness and low self-efficacy among employees (see Box 6.1). *Organizational variables* are those that characterize the entire organization. When organizations are initially formed or face transitional events (for example, hostile takeovers or competitive markets), employees may feel powerless as forces beyond their control lead to reductions in force or a high turnover. Simi-

Box 6.1

Factors Leading to Low Self-Efficacy Among Employees

ORGANIZATIONAL VARIABLES

Significant organizational changes or transitions
Start-up ventures
Competitive pressures
Impersonal bureaucratic climate
Poor communications and networking systems
Highly centralized organizational resources

SUPERVISORY STYLE

Authoritarian (high control)
Negativism (emphasis on failure)
Lack of reason for actions and consequences

REWARD SYSTEMS

Noncontingency (arbitrary reward allocations)
Low incentive value of rewards
Lack of competence-based rewards
Lack of innovation-based rewards

JOB DESIGN

Lack of role clarity
Lack of training and technical support
Unrealistic goals
Lack of appropriate authority or discretion
Limited task variety
Limited participation in programs, meetings, and decisions that impact job performance
Lack of appropriate or necessary resources
Limited networking opportunities
Highly established work routines
High rule structure
Limited advancement opportunities
Lack of meaningful goals or tasks
Limited contact with senior management

Source: J. A. Conger & R. N. Kanungo (1988) The empowerment process: Integrating theory and practice. *Academy of Management Review, 13* (3), 471–482.

larly, in a highly bureaucratic organization that does not allow the free exchange of information, employees may feel unable to affect change in the workplace. A *supervisory style* may also cause individuals to have low efficacy. Supervisors employing autocratic methods deny employees a voice in decision making. An individual's self-esteem may suffer when a supervisor emphasizes the negative elements of the employee's performance. Even *reward systems* can disempower employees. As noted in Chapter 2, Phillips Podsakoff and associates (e.g., Podsakoff & Todor, 1985) demonstrate the importance of administering contingent rewards to increasing employee motivation and performance. When such systems do not reward appropriate performance, by administering rewards on bases other than a merit basis or by reinforcing the status quo and diminishing innovation, employees are less likely to be motivated. Finally, the *job design* can lower feelings of self-efficacy. Jobs that are unclear, lack set goals or adequate resources, or provide little opportunity for advancement decrease employees' level of self-efficacy.

Leaders play an important role in empowering employees. According to Charles Manz and Henry Sims (1989) in *Superleadership: Leading Others to Lead*, empowerment requires leaders to develop employees' own ability for self-management so that they can learn to lead themselves. "Superleadership" uses empowerment as the means by which leaders can lead others to lead themselves. Teaching employees to make their own decisions not only facilitates their growth and development but, by maximizing the potential of all employees, it also helps the organization provide good products and services to its customers.

There are several techniques that Manz and Sims (1989) suggest Superleaders can use to empower followers:

- **Model self-leadership.** People who are self-starters or "go-getters" tend to be exciting and stimulating. Excitement is contagious in that it tends to spread to others. Leaders should model the self-initiative and motivation they expect in employees.
- **Reward self-leadership behaviors in employees.** The public recognition of an employee's initiative and high performance provides a signal to others that the leader is serious about employee development and growth. A leader's failure to reward employees is one of the largest obstacles to empowering them.
- **Encourage employees to set personal goals.** For employees to be self-leading and motivated, they must be able to set their own goals. As employees learn how to set goals, the leader may need to provide assistance by asking such questions as "What do you think needs to be done?" and "Is that enough time to reach your goal?" Over time, employees develop their own systems for setting goals.
- **Create positive thought patterns.** Half the battle in accomplishing any goal is thinking that you can. By expressing confidence in employees' ability and helping them believe in themselves, leaders can create a climate for self-leadership.
- **Reward and constructively reprimand performance.** People tend to perform particular behaviors when they are rewarded and to avoid other behaviors when they are reprimanded. When it is necessary to reprimand

an employee's behavior, leaders should strive to use a constructive reprimand, one that clearly identifies the poor performance and explains why it needs to be eliminated or changed.

The preceding techniques are consistent with those suggested by Conger and Kanungo (1988), who identify enactive attainment—giving employees a complex task and allowing them to succeed—as one empowerment strategy. Other such strategies include modeling the desired behavior, providing encouraging feedback, and giving emotional support to offset the apprehension associated with new tasks.

Motivation: Gore & Associates

Which of the four preceding principles of motivation—human needs theory, reinforcement theory, goal theory, or empowerment theory—best describes how Gore & Associates attempts to motivate its employees? Although some elements of all four principles are present at the company, it is best characterized as an empowering organization. Founder and leader Bill Gore developed the principles that guide employee behavior, including the sponsors' task of facilitating Associates' motivation.

Gore & Associates provides an environment for individuals to become self-actualized and grow. Sally Gore, responsible for professional recruiting at Gore & Associates, emphasizes the company's self-actualizing environment: "We do not feel we need to be the highest paid. We never try to steal people away from other companies with salary. We want them to come here because of the opportunities for growth and the unique work environment" (quoted in Levering, Moskowitz, & Katz, 1984, p. 130). Gore & Associates seeks and retains employees who want to grow and self-actualize.

Individual merit and behavior are recognized through the use of sponsors and the compensation system. According to reinforcement theory, people are motivated when they receive reinforcement that appropriately directs their behavior. Sponsorship and the compensation system together work to achieve that type of reinforcement at Gore & Associates. There are no supervisors at the company; instead, the sponsors advise other Associates, offering guidance and providing feedback to maximize employees' strengths and to minimize their weaknesses. New employees at Gore & Associates may request any Associate to serve as their sponsor or mentor. The sponsor's role is that of chief advocate for the Associate and includes providing constructive feedback so the Associate can develop an appropriate role within the organization. Similarly, by gaining performance information from numerous sources and comparing Associates' performance, the compensation system is designed to maintain equity among employees at Gore & Associates.

Gore & Associates gives employees the responsibility to set their own goals. Individual initiative is encouraged at Gore & Associates. The principles of freedom, commitment, and waterline discussed earlier in the chapter allow employees to grow. Employee initiative is directed toward helping the organization maintain commitment, set goals, and take actions that are in the corporation's best interests. Furthermore, employees are responsible for their own actions. It is this sense of accountability that appears to be the strongest motivational force for employees at the company:

> It is hard to find someone at Gore who doesn't like the job. "I love it," says H. Edward Smith, 24, who took a $3-an-hour pay cut to come to Gore. Says Frances Hughart, an inspector with 22 years of service: "We manage ourselves here. If you waste time, you're only wasting your own money." (Hoerr, 1985, p. 98)

Associates retain control over the design of their jobs. Associates are responsible for clarifying unclear job roles because they defined them initially. This philosophy of self-determination applied to job design is reflected in the following story related by Anita McBride, an Associate at Gore:

> Before I came to Gore I had worked for a structured organization. . . . I came here, and for the first month it was fairly structured because I was going through training . . . "this is what we do, and this is how Gore is" and all of that, and I went to Flagstaff for that training. After a month I came down to Phoenix and my sponsor said, "Well, here's your office"—it's a wonderful office—and "here's your desk" and walked away. And I thought *now what do I do,* you know? I was waiting for a memo or something, or a job description. Finally, after a month I was so frustrated, I felt *what have I gotten myself into?* I went to my sponsor and I said "What the heck do you want from me? I need something from you," and he said, "If you don't know what you're supposed to do, examine your commitments and opportunities." (quoted in Shipper & Manz, 1992, p. 57)

By giving its employees the opportunity to define their roles in the organization, allowing them to create meaning in their work, supporting them through sponsors and team members, and facilitating their access to other organizational members through the lattice structure, Gore & Associates has created an environment in which Associates can design their own jobs in ways that empower them.

MANAGING CONFLICT

> What the Gore culture does is increase the possibility that those who see problems, mistakes, oversights, and conflicts can do something about them. The issue is less "Who will take care of the problem?" and more "What energy, skill, influence, and wisdom do *you* have to con-

tribute to the solution?" Sometimes we act, sometimes we must be patient, and sometimes—no doubt unfortunately—we must accept the reality that we live in an imperfect world and we lack the energy, skill, influence, and wisdom to solve some of the problems that confront us. (Pacanowsky, 1988, p. 371)

Michael Pacanowsky, a professor at the University of Colorado, made the preceding statement after an eight-month study in which he actively participated in Gore & Associates. His observations suggest that Gore & Associates recognizes when individuals join together to solve a common set of issues, challenges and problems will arise from the group's dynamics. Personality conflicts, differences of opinion, and disagreements about solutions to problems are inevitable aspects of group and organizational life. As Dian Hosking (1988) observes, part of a leader's role is to help organize the group toward collective action. As part of this organizing process, leaders manage conflicts through bargaining and other techniques. Moreover, as Dean Tjosvold (1991) argues in *The Conflict-Positive Organization*, contemporary leaders must encourage risk taking and innovation among employees. Leaders play an important role in creating conflict management systems that allow for honest examinations of problems and possible solutions. To work collectively with others, leaders need to master skills that allow them to anticipate conflicts and to manage conflicts arising from collective interaction. The central issue, then, is determining the best way to manage conflicts successfully. At Gore & Associates, conflict appears to be directly confronted by each employee and, in accordance with the principle of fairness, to be resolved in a manner that is equitable for all parties. Therefore, conflict management at Gore & Associates necessarily involves (1) initially defining the nature of the conflict and (2) identifying how the conflict may be managed.

The Nature of Conflict

What is conflict? Is it the same as a disagreement or an argument? Typically, conflict is characterized according to three elements: (1) interdependence, (2) interaction, and (3) incompatible goals. In a comprehensive review of organizational conflict and negotiation, Linda Putnam and Marshall Scott Poole (1987) define *conflict* as "the interaction of interdependent people who perceive opposition of goals, aims, and values, and who see the other party as potentially interfering with the realization of these goals" (p. 352). Conflict is a social phenomenon that is woven into the fabric of human relationships; therefore, it can only be expressed and manifested through communication. We can only come into conflict with people with whom we are interdependent; that is, only when we become dependent on one another to meet our needs does conflict emerge.

Organizational conflicts are differentiated in a number of ways. One method of distinguishing among conflict situations is based on the context in which the conflict occurs. Traditionally organizational conflict is viewed as occurring in the following three contexts:

1. *Interpersonal conflict* exists between two individuals within a group or organization.
2. *Intergroup conflict* is any struggle that occurs between two groups within a larger social system.
3. *Interorganizational conflict* is any dispute that occurs between two organizations.

Another strategy for defining conflict is based on its content—the issues about which conflicts emerge. Two primary types of conflict are identified. First, *substantive* or *ideational conflict* is related to the issues, ideas, and positions of a conflict. Its primary focus is the ideas that organizational members discuss. Substantive conflict may be reflected, for example, in discussions about the merits of adopting one type of computer system over another, of expanding into a new market, or of implementing a new manufacturing process. Second, *affective conflict* is concerned with the interpersonal relationships among organizational members. Such conflicts may emerge due to status, power, role development, or personality issues. The domain of affective conflict includes power struggles for control of a group and concern about the attitude a certain individual brings to the group.

Conflict Management

Although conflict is generally viewed in a negative way and as something to avoid, when appropriately managed it can generate many beneficial results. For example, through conflict creative ideas can be explored, feelings can be ventilated, and employees' diverse interests and backgrounds can be used effectively (Putnam, 1986; Tjosvold, 1991). However, conflict management theorists distinguish between constructive and destructive conflict (Putnam & Poole, 1987). *Constructive conflict* is functional because it facilitates organizational members in accomplishing goals and in generating new insights into old problems. In contrast, *destructive conflict* is dysfunctional because it negatively affects organizational members by disrupting their activity. Following is a list of the characteristics that distinguish constructive from destructive conflict:

Constructive Conflict

1. Allows constructive change and growth to occur within a system.
2. Provides the opportunity for resolving problems associated with diversity of opinion.
3. Provides a forum for unifying the group.

(*continued*)

Destructive Conflict

1. Lack of common agreement leads to negativism.
2. Respective positions are hardened and the likelihood of a resolution is diminished.
3. The group divides into camps, each supporting a different position.
4. Group productivity, satisfaction, and commitment decrease.

Constructive Conflict (cont.)

4. Enhances group productivity.
5. Enhances group commitment.

Given the complexity of conflict, many times elements of both constructive and destructive conflict enter into the process. Whether conflict is viewed as constructive or destructive, however, depends on how well it is managed.

Researchers have long focused on handling conflict through certain conflict management styles (Blake, Shephard, & Mouton, 1964; Filley, 1975; Kilmann & Thomas, 1978). Paralleling the leadership style based on Blake and Mouton's (1985) managerial grid theory, five basic conflict management styles are identified in the research:

1. *Withdrawal:* This style of conflict management is characterized by avoidance. A limited concern for accomplishing the task or maintaining the relational climate allows the individual to cope with conflict by avoiding it.
2. *Smoothing:* The emphasis of this style is on maintaining positive interpersonal relationships. Differences of opinion and disagreements on substantive issues are minimized in order to maintain a positive interpersonal climate.
3. *Compromise:* A compromising style is characterized by moderate levels of concern for both the task and the relationship. Rather than aiming for an ideal solution to a conflict, compromise is characterized by both parties making concessions to reach a solution.
4. *Forcing:* This style resolves conflict by accomplishing task goals with little concern for the interpersonal relationships of the conflicting parties. It is aimed at breaking down the opposing forces in order to achieve goals.
5. *Problem solving:* This is a collaborative style of conflict management in which both parties attempt to achieve the best solution to the conflict. Both task and relational goals are emphasized, as the chief concern is to accomplish the task in the best way possible while simultaneously maintaining a positive interpersonal climate.

Most conflict management theorists agree that the problem-solving style is the most effective because it manages conflict constructively by encouraging the two parties to share their ideas about the conflict. When people mutually participate in resolving a conflict, a common ground can be identified and a mutually satisfying resolution can be created—one that heightens their commitment to and satisfaction with each other.

The use of conflict management styles varies according to the situation. Rahim, Garrett, and Buntzman (1992) observe that such situational factors as issue complexity may influence the selection of a conflict management style. Complex issues are typically characterized by differing parties possessing unique information. To share the unique information possessed by both parties, mutual effort and evaluation of options are necessary. This dictates selecting a problem-solving style. However, when people perceive their position on a particular issue as incorrect, they may use a compromising style. Particularly when the person desires something from the other person at a later time, compromise is useful for achieving that future goal. Leaders dealing with minor issues or who need to take an unpopular stand on an important issue may find forcing an appropriate strategy. Finally, the relative power of the two parties in conflict may influence style selection. When both parties are high or equal in power, the compromising style may work best because each party has the ability to block the other from achieving goals. These factors represent only a few of the many that can influence the selection and use of conflict management styles.

The five styles of conflict management are criticized by Monroe, Borzi, and DiSalvo (1989), who argue that they are based on ideal situations in which conflict is represented as relatively easy to manage. They propose that, in order to understand the full range of behaviors characterizing conflict management, it is necessary to investigate situations in which managing conflict is difficult due to complex relational and personal variables. One such variable is dysfunctional or difficult employees. Francine Hall (1991) contends that as contemporary organizations continue to emphasize employee assistance programs, they will have to deal with the difficult behaviors of employees from dysfunctional families. According to Hall, employees who were raised in dysfunctional families tend to have difficulty with managing conflict in the workplace because of certain personal characteristics, including their fear of losing control, their reactive rather than proactive stance, their trouble with maintaining personal relationships, and their tendency to avoid rather than confront conflict when possible.

Monroe, Borzi, and DiSalvo (1989) examined how difficult employees manage conflict within the workplace. They found that difficult employees, like dysfunctional employees, tend to have low self-esteem, to lack interpersonal skills, and to approach relational problems in predictable ways. In addition, employees with difficult personalities tend to use different conflict management strategies. Four such strategies seem to characterize conflict management by difficult employees. Some may manage conflict passively through *apparent compliance.* It occurs when the employee agrees to the supervisor's suggestions, promises to make the changes, and then reverts back to the initial behavior. Difficult employees may also cope with conflict through *avoidance.* They avoid either the person or the situation from which the conflict arises. Others may employ *relational leverage,* playing an adversarial role in the conflict management process by refusing to accept any advice or feedback from the superior. Similarly, the use of *alibis* is aimed at making excuses and shifting the blame to a situational factor or another person.

An alternative means for managing conflict is the message-based strategy of *negotiation.* Whereas the five traditional conflict management styles focus on generalized patterns of behavior, negotiation focuses on the proposals and counterproposals that each side makes when attempting to resolve a conflict. Communication thereby facilitates reaching an agreement. Leaders can employ the negotiation strategy to organizational situations in which two opposing sides or sets of ideas must be brought to agreement. Ideational and affective conflicts, as well as conflicts over how to define roles or motivate individuals, may be resolved through negotiation.

Two distinct types of bargaining characterize negotiation. *Integrative bargaining* is a cooperative venture in which both sides attempt to reach an agreement that allows the other to achieve its goals. It is similar to the conflict management style of problem solving. *Distributive bargaining* is a win-or-lose situation in which one side attempts to maximize its gain at the expense of the other side. Similar to the forcing style of conflict management, distributive bargaining encourages a winner-take-all attitude. Putnam and Poole (1987, pp. 566–567) identify the following communicative strategies that characterize integrative and distributive bargaining situations:

Integrative Bargaining

1. Information is shared in order to discover the facts of the situation.
2. Bargainers attempt to elicit more reactions from the other bargainers.
3. Multiple alternatives for resolving the conflict are offered.
4. Soft rather than hard tactics are used. Confrontation, hard demands, and a lack of making concessions are exhibited infrequently.
5. Bargainers use statements that accept the other's view, support the other's view through arguments, and explore different resolutions.

Distributive Bargaining

1. Bargainers withhold and screen information from each other.
2. Bargainers exaggerate and misrepresent their bargaining position.
3. Direct disclosures are intended to distort the intentions and objectives of the bargainer.
4. Bargainers manipulate information to generate false inferences by the other bargainer.
5. Contradictory messages, bluffing, exaggeration, and threats are used to confuse the opposing bargainer.
6. Threats, put-downs, demands, and charges of blame are common.

Integrative bargaining tends to be characterized by communication that shares information to reach equitable solutions. Distributive bargaining, in contrast, emphasizes withholding information, disguising information, and holding firm during negotiations in order to tilt the final agreement in one's favor.

Should leaders use integrative or distributive bargaining communication strategies? In some ways, this is a false question because all negotiations are mixed in terms of motives and require cooperation to achieve agreement; at the same time, however, competition is needed to protect one's self-interest (Putnam, 1985). Steven Wilson and Linda Putnam (1990) contend that a negotiation is primarily integrative or distributive depending on the goals being pursued. Therefore, the goals leaders seek to accomplish through the negotiation process dictate whether integrative or distributive bargaining behavior is more or less displayed. If the leader's goal is to empower employees, an integrative approach to negotiation would be useful. A heightened sense of ownership by employees could be instilled due to the cooperative relationship created through open, mutually supportive dialog. Individuals can become empowered only when their sense of self-efficacy is increased; integrative bargaining contributes to perceptions of self-efficacy. However, as situational leadership theories, such as Hersey and Blanchard's (1982) life-cycle theory, point out, individuals may not be emotionally mature enough to manage a cooperative exchange. In such instances, a more telling or distributive style may need to be adopted. Similarly, the expectations of the other bargainer may constrain the type of bargaining that can be employed. Deal and Kennedy (1982) tell a story about a manufacturer who went into a negotiating session with a labor union and decided to be honest about the company's financial situation. The manufacturer gave the union its best offer the first time. The union did not trust the offer, and made a counteroffer that was significantly higher. While honesty may be the best policy, in this case the expectations surrounding the bargaining situation prevented the manufacturer from using an integrative bargaining strategy. Therefore, when deciding between integrative and distributive bargaining strategies, leaders must take into account the maturity level of the other bargainers as well as the expectations inherent in the bargaining situation.

Conflict Management at Gore & Associates

At Gore & Associates, employees face typical interpersonal and interorganizational conflicts over substantive and relational issues. Unlike most other organizations, however, Gore & Associates emphasizes collaborative or problem-solving conflict management. For example, Ralph G. Bateman, a Gore Associate, says that leaders "solve problems rather than bark orders. People work harder in this type of atmosphere than when somebody stands over [them] with a club" (quoted in Hoerr, 1985, p. 98). The mutual collaboration of all concerned parties is required to generate mutually desirable and acceptable solutions to problems. Moreover, dealing with problems and conflicts must be handled quickly. For example, consider how a potential crisis was managed in 1975 involving vascular grafts made of Gore-Tex. During an experimental period of graft testing, Dr. Charles Campbell at the University of Pittsburgh discovered a graft he had used in a patient who had developed an aneurysm. This was a very serious matter because if the aneurysm burst, the patient would die. As Lucien Rhodes chronicles:

> Only days after his call, Dr. Campbell flew to Newark to present his finding to Bill and Bob Gore and several other Associates drawn from production and research. The meeting adjourned after two hours of discussion and the Associates went their separate ways to consider solutions. But one of the Associates, Dan Hubis, already had an idea he thought might work. If he could wrap another layer of Gore-Tex around a section of graft, he reasoned, he might be able to increase the rupture tolerance of the entire section. He tried various wrapping techniques, and after each try he forced compressed air through the specimen section to see if it would hold. On his twelfth try, after three hours

> of work, he found the right method. Hubis had resolved a potentially serious setback in only one afternoon. (1982, p. 42)

The principles of commitment and fairness necessitated resolving the problem in a collaborative way. Shifting blame and defensiveness could not be a part of resolving this conflict. The Gore culture, with its emphases on open communication and fairness, appears to favor win-win solutions to conflict management over win-lose strategies such as forcing. Our Gore example is not intended to equate problem solving with conflict management, for managing conflicts includes a host of other issues and phenomena. However, the example demonstrates the emphasis placed on achieving tasks at high levels of proficiency while maintaining good interpersonal relationships among team members. Similarly, the goal achieved is an example of the win-win orientation of Gore & Associates, which the company likely uses to manage other types of conflict as well.

LEADERSHIP STYLES: GORE & ASSOCIATES VERSUS THE TYPICAL HOSPITAL

W. L. Gore & Associates is a unique organization. As you were reading the case study in this chapter, you may have felt that the company is unlike any of the organizations for which you or others have worked. Although organizations adopt many different kinds of systems of organizing, each with its own set of organizing principles, rules, and norms, most are not as radical as Gore's. The leadership at most companies is not likely to stand back and say to new employees, "Just find something you'd like to do, and when you do, let us know what it is." Indeed, Gore & Associates represents a dramatic departure from the classically oriented organization, and it is in the process of pioneering new ways of organizing that future organizations may adopt.

Still, many contemporary organizations continue to use bureaucratic leadership, which has several implications for the kind of organizing system a company selects (Morgan, 1986). Bureaucratic organizations, for example, are organized on the basis of a hierarchy. The chain of command dictates that people in low-level positions report directly to those in high-level positions. In addition, departments and positions within the organization are clearly specified and their duties and responsibilities are defined in written descriptions. New employees are given a job description that specifies their responsibilities, and they are expected to perform those activities only. The bureaucratic organization operates on the principle of *division of labor*—each individual has a particular job to do and an area of specialty for which he or she is responsible.

Hospitals often use the classic bureaucratic model of organizing that emphasizes a formal hierarchy. In contrast to Gore & Associates, the typical hospital uses a different approach to help its employees define their roles within the organization, to motivate its employees, and to manage conflicts. (The following comments about hospitals are meant to be illustrative, not exhaustive. The organizing systems used by individual hospitals differ just as they do for other types of companies. Some hospitals emphasize empowering forms of organizing, such as teamwork, particularly in surgical teams; however, many times, other areas of the hospital remain bureaucratically organized [Larson & LaFasto, 1989].) Most hospitals define the roles that employees perform. People are hired on the basis of their education and training for a specific position within the general area of nursing, custodial work, medical technician, or some other area. Written job descriptions are provided and employees are expected to adhere to the activities that define the job. Formal leadership is typical in hospitals; members of the managerial hierarchy are expected to perform certain leadership roles. Formal leadership serves to supplement the role-definition process by providing employee counseling and clarification of duties. Personal leader-employee relationships are often discouraged. When leaders are expected to reinforce the hierarchy of roles, the only type of leader-employee relationship that can be formed is a formal role relationship.

The typical hospital motivates its employees through monetary compensation and the administration of rewards and punishments. With the exception of physicians, most hospital workers are paid an hourly rate. Employees who perform tasks inappropriately may be punished by being "written up"—that is, the incident is recorded and placed in the employee's file. Further disciplinary action may include temporary suspension or termination. Formal leadership depends on the power given it by the organizational hierarchy to administer rewards and punishments. Other types of punishments may include decreasing an employee's hours or changing the employee's work schedule. Rewards may include providing employees public recognition for high performance. Leaders depend greatly on their formal position within the hierarchy to motivate employees. Because the hospital sets the standards and expectations for job performance, leaders typically are not empowering.

Although leaders in many hospitals and other bureaucratic organizations may opt for any number of different conflict management styles, they may emphasize forcing. Given their position in the hierarchy, they are able to choose this style exclusively. Power in the classic bureaucratic organization flows from the top levels of the hierarchy downward to the lower levels. Employees may have some voice in managing conflict, such as through established grievance systems, but the formal authority allows leaders to emphasize forcing and distributive strategies of conflict management.

FEEDBACK: THE KEY TO MANAGING ORGANIZATIONAL RELATIONSHIPS

W. L. Gore & Associates works hard to unleash the potential of its employees. Yet the problems and obstacles it faces when organizing the collective activity of its employees are shared by other companies as well. Leaders in all organizations must face the relational obstacles associated with helping employees find their place within the organization, encouraging high levels of group performance, managing conflicts among organizational members, and building a strong sense of commitment to the organization. How does leadership accomplish these multiple tasks? Although leadership skills relating to role definition, empowerment, motivation, and conflict management are crucial, an important skill that cuts across the differing processes is feedback. The skillful use of feedback is critical to leaders' successful management of relational obstacles.

Feedback—the process of giving individuals and groups information about their level of performance—is important to many aspects of leadership. It is important in defining roles because it provides information about the appropriateness of a role that an individual is creating. Feedback is important in motivating employees in that it furnishes information about an individual's goal achievement and standing in the organization. Feedback is important in managing conflict because it makes people more aware of others' perceptions of the conflict. Finally, feedback is important in empowering employees because it can provide encouragement and support of an individual's performance.

Constructive Feedback

There are several rules that leaders should consider when providing constructive feedback.

When giving negative feedback, maximize the level of information while minimizing the evaluation. Positive feedback promotes a greater sense of confidence and competence than negative feedback (Nadler, 1979) or neutral feedback (Cusella, 1984). However, negative feedback is necessary because employee performance is not always excellent. In these instances, leaders should maximize the amount of information given in the feedback by providing concrete examples of the problem and of what needs to be changed. Feedback that focuses on employee behaviors tends to be viewed as more credible than feedback that is more abstract or emotional (Jacobs, Jacobs, Feldman, & Cavior, 1973). For example, feedback aimed at decreasing an employee's aggressiveness in a group situation may be more effective when it focuses on specific behaviors ("When you say things like, 'I just don't see how anyone could oppose that idea,' people tend to see you as being too aggressive") than when it focuses on vague emotional reactions ("I just think you're awfully aggressive").

Phrase feedback in terms of "more or less" rather than "either/or." Messages that reflect certainty or superiority are associated with increased levels of defensiveness among employees (Gibb, 1961). Similarly, feedback that reflects the certainty of the leader's convictions allows no room for dialog or negotiation. Feedback messages such as "This is the only way . . . " or "You definitely need to . . . " can generate feelings of defensiveness. In contrast, feedback that emphasizes the equality of the relationship and communicates the expectation of dialog between the leader and employee is more likely to be accepted ("One possible problem I see caused by your behavior is. . . . How do you see it?").

Focus the feedback on the idea, not the person. In conflict situations, people tend to personalize the conflict rather than focus on the issue at hand (Fisher & Ury, 1981). If the feedback is also personalized, it is likely to be counterproductive. Leaders giving feedback should thus focus on the critical issues and positions that need to be resolved, not on the employee's personality.

Focus the feedback on the task performance, not the performer's personal qualities. It is also important to focus feedback on the employee's task performance, rather than personal factors, in order to influence subsequent motivation and performance (Cusella, 1980, 1982, 1984). Such comments as "You're not demonstrating enough initiative" or "You need to work harder to fit into the organization" do not focus on the employee's specific behaviors. Leaders should use examples to illustrate the point of the feedback. ("I feel you need to demonstrate more initiative because, when we get behind on a project, everyone else pitches in while you sit in your office.")

Feedback should be timely. Feedback should be given soon after the inappropriate behavior is observed. Maximum learning will not occur if the feedback is given too long after the event (Downs, Johnson, & Barge, 1984).

When preparing to give feedback, carefully assess the cause of the performance. For feedback to be helpful, it must focus on the employee's performance. According to several research studies, leaders tend to make two fundamental attribution errors when giving feedback. First, they may attribute the cause of poor performance to something within the employee's control rather than to an environmental cause (Green & Mitchell, 1979; Brown & Mitchell, 1986). Second, leaders may attribute poor performance to a lack of effort rather than to a lack of true ability (Fisher, 1979; Ilgen & Knowlton, 1980). In both cases, the feedback will be ineffective. Leaders must recognize that instances exist where feedback will not be useful for improving productivity. In such instances, leaders may need to concern themselves with retraining employees to equip them with the knowledge and skills to do the job, or focus on removing obstacles that prevent good employee performance.

SUMMARY

Leaders confront a variety of problems concerning the relationships employees have with an organization. As groups and organizations develop over time, relational problems may include defining roles, motivating followers, and managing conflict. Such problems can be overcome by leadership that recognizes them and takes appropriate action to resolve them. At Gore & Associates, the founder resolved these problems by structuring a special type of organization. The company's lattice work system of organizing, its four operating principles, and its use of sponsors provide the means for organizing collective action in order to achieve high levels of employee motivation, performance, and commitment. All organizations cannot be like Gore & Associates, but all leaders can facilitate resolving relational issues through conflict management, bargaining, and feedback. Leadership effectiveness is enhanced by providing constructive feedback, by using communication strategies associated with particular conflict management styles, and by combining both integrative and distributive bargaining techniques.

QUESTIONS AND APPLICATIONS

1. The communication department for your organization has asked you to write a brief article on conflict management for the in-house company newsletter. In a two-paragraph article, describe what you consider the most effective way to manage conflict within the organization. Remember to give your article a title and to give readers advice on how to implement the strategy.

2. Choose an organization you worked for in the past. Using the criteria presented in Box 6.1, determine the company practices that encouraged or discouraged employee empowerment. For the practices that discouraged feelings of empowerment, what could the company's leaders have done to change them?

3. For this phrase—"I believe you can motivate people by . . . "—write as many answers as possible. Then indicate which answers reflect the following assumptions: (a) people are motivated to fulfill their needs, (b) people are motivated when they receive positive consequences for their work, (c) people are motivated by goals, and (d) people are motivated by power. Finally, determine your dominant means for motivating people.

4. People tend to soften their feedback when it is given in a face-to-face situation or to someone with whom they share a personal relationship. What suggestions can you give leaders about providing feedback in these two situations?

Chapter 7
Exercising Social Influence

> It was a short sequence of a child, weakened by hunger, trying and trying and trying again to stand up on his little matchstick legs. They had edited [the Canadian Broadcasting Company video] over a record. It was the Cars' "Drive." The juxtaposition was bizarre. The child's pitiful courage turned the poignancy of the song into a profound sadness. "Who's gonna pick you up when you fall down? We can't go on saying nothing's wrong. Who's going to drive you home tonight?" My eyes filled with tears and my voice caught in my throat. "We've got to have this, lads, for the day." . . . Back at . . . [the] office, the room went silent as a church when I showed it. Phone calls ended prematurely. People stopped what they were doing and just watched. [David] Bowie was in tears. He had been allocated five songs in the tight schedule. "I want to give up one of my spots to show this. I'd like to introduce it," he said. . . . [The day of the concert] the telephone system broke down completely when the CBC video was shown. . . . Billy Connolly and Pamela Stephanson were supposed to be doing an appeal after that video. When the camera came back on to them they were both in tears and couldn't speak. Later that night they showed it again on BBC2 and when the camera came back to the presenter, he was devastated, tears pouring down his face. He began to shuffle his papers and looked away. In the end he turned to the cameraman and said, "I don't think we need to keep the camera on me." The effect of the film was traumatic in everyone who saw it, but it also put the concern in perspective.
>
> *(Geldof, 1986, pp. 369, 384)*

That leaders must find a "voice" to persuade others was clearly demonstrated by Live Aid, an organization headed by Bob Geldof that provided famine relief to Ethiopia during the 1980s. Geldof organized the global broadcast of a Live Aid concert, July 13, 1985, featuring performances by recording artists in New York and London. In order to solicit contributions for the relief effort, the Live Aid concert organizers needed to construct a message that would compel viewers to contribute to the cause. As part of this process, Geldof decided to show the powerful music video clip described above.

The impact on the audience of the message contained in the music video was strong. The plight and problems associated with the famine victims in Ethiopia were clearly demonstrated to the mass audience through the video. Although the basic function and content of the message could have been conveyed in a speech, Geldof chose a more potent means of articulating the message. As a result, viewers could better understand and relate to the problems in Ethiopia.

Inevitably, a leader needs to articulate persuasive messages aimed at influencing workers' thoughts and actions and organizing them toward achieving goals. But persuasive messages need to be articulated in meaningful and understandable ways. Articulation in this case refers to the ability to structure and phrase persuasive messages that are both coherent and motivational. Leaders thus search for appropriate ways to phrase messages. The failure to create interesting, inspiring, and clear messages inhibits a leader's ability to motivate workers toward accomplishing organizational goals for several reasons. Employees do not understand the importance of poorly phrased messages, do not establish an emotional connection to the message, do not comprehend the reasons for the message, and are not persuaded to comply with the directions. The importance of articulating messages in meaningful ways is summed up by the old cliché, "It's not what you say, but how you say it."

Effective leaders, then, are articulate. They express themselves in ways that allow employees to understand the challenges and obstacles facing an organization and that stimulate workers toward removing those obstacles. Leaders need to articulate persuasive messages in ways that enhance employee compliance with the requests or directives contained in the messages. The ability to persuade others is related to the concept of organizational power. Leaders manifest, use, and exercise power in numerous ways. To understand the relationship between leadership and power, it is necessary to examine the many different faces of organizational power.

THE FACES OF ORGANIZATIONAL POWER

Imagine that you head the marketing department at a local community hospital. At a meeting of department heads, the hospital CEO announces that at least 10 percent of the overall budget must be cut. The personnel department head notes that marketing was the last department to receive a large budget increase, so it should be the first to have its budget cut. Another department head asks the CEO, "What do you think?" Here is a list of the CEO's possible responses:

> I think there's a strong possibility we should cut marketing's budget.
> Well, I do think we need to consider all options regarding where we make our cuts.
> I haven't given this much thought, but it would seem that this could be one area we should give serious consideration to cutting.
> Well . . . huh . . . that's an interesting idea.

As you consider the possible responses, think about the following questions: Which of the responses is most clear? Which allows you, as head of marketing, to argue against the budget cut? Where do you think the CEO stands on the issue? Which response states the CEO's position most directly? Although all of the responses suggest that cutting the marketing budget is one potential solution, the phrasing of each message varies in its clarity, its directness, and its potential for flexibility. How leaders phrase messages makes a profound difference on the way individuals participate in discussion. The way a message is phrased can increase or decrease employee commitment to a decision or a set of actions as well as employee participation in discussion.

When we think of organizational power and influence, we imagine one person exerting control over others in dialog. Power is manifested in interactions as well as in the decision-making process, whereby people select particular persuasive strategies to influence one another. From this perspective, *power* is defined in terms of the amount of force or effort that one person can exert to control another person. Power is also typically viewed as a resource, whereby person A has power over person B when B is dependent on A for acquiring certain desirable resources (Emerson, 1962). A number of researchers have explored the resources that serve as the bases for power. French and Raven (1959), for example, identify the following power bases that organizational members may use to influence others:

Referent power. A leader has referent power when the employee identifies with or likes the leader; thus, the relationship formed between leader and employee creates the power base.

Legitimate power. Sometimes referred to as *position power*, legitimate power emanates from one's formal position within the organization and, therefore, is based on the rights and privileges attributed to that position.

Reward power. The leader who provides desirable outcomes (for example, money, status, praise) for good performance is said to have reward power.

Coercive power. Leaders who punish employees by making their work experience difficult or unpleasant possess coercive power.

Expert power. Leaders who have expert power also have specialized knowledge and abilities in a particular area.

Leaders may employ one or more of these power bases when attempting to persuade employees. The hospital CEO, for example, might use legitimate power to persuade the management team that the marketing budget must be cut. Or, if the CEO has cultivated close personal relationships with other department heads, referent power might be used to gain the compliance of the management team.

Peter Frost (1987) labels the process of social influence *power in action.* It includes overt compliance-gaining attempts aimed at getting others to endorse a particular belief or action. When a leader attempts to persuade employees to arrive at work on time, to work hard, or to hold certain beliefs and reject others, the primary goal is to gain the compliance of others. Power in action is aimed at getting people to do a certain thing at a certain time or place and in a certain way.

Peter Bachrach and Morton Baratz (1962), arguing that power can be observed in situations other than those involving decision making and the influence of others, note that a covert type of power exists in nondecision situations. For example, Crenson (1971) studied Gary, Indiana, where some of the worst air pollution in the nation was left unquestioned by the city council and other government agencies. Health-related implications also were not addressed. According to Crenson, the issue was avoided because the townspeople realized it would impact on their financial well-being—the city's large industrial plants were the source of the pollution. Crenson thus contends that limiting power to an analysis of what people say during discussion is inadequate, as it was in Gary. The city's manufacturing plants exercised a great deal of "hidden," covert power, as reflected in their ability to influence how government officials handled the air pollution problem. This aspect of power, then, is rooted in one's ability to control the topics that are discussed and addressed by an organization.

Through covert power, a leader attempts to mold people's perceptions of other people, situations, or organizations by withholding information. The focus is not on gaining compliance to a specific decision or negotiation; rather, the focus is on constructing a message or a series of messages that will cause others to view organizational phenomena in certain ways and to act in desired ways. Frost (1987) relates this hidden face of power to *power in conception.* It depends on utilizing or modifying the existing organizational myths, cultural rules, and assumptions to create visions of organizational roles. Similarly, Dennis Mumby (1987) argues that covert power is best understood in terms of people's adherence to and belief in a rule system. When people orient their activity around a particular set of rules and norms, those rules cause them to view certain issues as open to discussion and other issues as taboo and not open to discussion. To the outside observer, this kind of control is unobtrusive. As noted in Chapter 4, decision-premises are a device for managing information. They are the underlying assumptions that organizational members use when making decisions and selecting among competing courses of action. As such, decision-premises are a valuable source of organizational control, for employees tend to act in ways that are consistent with the organization's formal and informal sets of decision-premises (Tompkins & Cheney, 1985).

Leadership researchers generally agree that power in organizations may be aimed at gaining compliance or may be targeted at shaping people's perceptions. The concept of power in action is similar to Bass's (1985) definitions of the transactional leader. Such leaders adopt an exchange perspective toward leadership, whereby they recognize the needs of employees and administer rewards and punishments in exchange for increased employee motivation and effort. The images associated with the transactional leader include that of task-master, negotiator, disciplinarian, and autocrat. However, the transformational leader uses power in conception to motivate and guide employees by shaping their view of the organization's mission and future. In this perspective, leadership is a rhetorical process, whereby the transformational leader articulates a vision about future organizational goals that is both utopian and realistic. The vision appeals to organizational members to pull together to make the vision a reality. Words such as *charismatic, visionary,* and *farsighted* are often used to describe the transformational leader.

Communication plays a role in how leaders use power in action and power in conception. Understanding its role requires an examination of the concepts of gaining compliance and creating visions.

POWER IN ACTION: GAINING COMPLIANCE

Sociologists, psychologists, and communication experts have long studied the issue of gaining the compliance of others. Beginning with Marwell and Schmitt's (1967) work, compliance-gaining researchers attempt to identify the persuasive strategies that people employ to secure others' compliance with an action or idea. Compliance-gaining attempts are a relevant aspect of leadership, for leaders construct messages aimed at encouraging employees to undertake certain activities and to avoid other activities. This requires leaders to select among persuasive message strategies and to phrase messages in ways that enhance the likelihood of compliance.

The study of compliance-gaining strategies initially focused on the idea that people are most easily persuaded when the rewards associated with compliance outweigh the costs of noncompliance. That is, people tend to comply with a directive when they view the action as producing a profitable ratio of costs and rewards. Therefore, much compliance-gaining research focuses on the types of inducements individuals can offer one another to gain compliance, including rewards, punishments, altruism, and rationale. *Rewards* are inducements or desirable resources that are offered in exchange for performing a particular action. *Punishments* include any strategy that withholds rewards from a person as a means to gain compliance or that warns of undesirable consequences for failing to comply. *Altruism* involves appeals made on the basis of commitment to other people or organizations. *Rationale-based strategies* include those that employ logical reasoning to persuade an employee. Box 7.1 gives detailed examples of the types of strategies that leaders can use to gain employee compliance (Hirokawa & Harper, 1988; Schlueter, Barge, & Blankenship, 1990).

The preceding typology of compliance-gaining strategies is primarily intended for use in interpersonal or one-on-one situations. It is based on the experiences of college students and the kinds of tasks involving power that they typically encounter (for example, persuading a roommate to lower the volume on a loud stereo). David Kipnis and associates propose an alternative scheme that is based on the experience of organizational managers (Kipnis & Schmidt, 1988; Kipnis, Schmidt, & Wilkinsin, 1980; Vecchio & Sussmann, 1991). They identify the following compliance-gaining strategies:

Reasoning: providing explanations for requests and using logic to persuade employees.

Friendliness: demonstrating support and respect through praise, being polite, and making the employee feel important.

Assertiveness: telling the employee what to do repeatedly.

Bargaining: exchanging resources desired by the employee.

Box 7.1
Compliance-Gaining Leadership Strategies

REWARD-BASED STRATEGIES

Ingratiation: A leader offers compliments or praise before requesting compliance.
Example: "I really appreciated your working overtime last week. It helped out the whole team. Could you spare a few hours this week to help us again?"

Promise: A leader promises goods or services in exchange for employee compliance.
Example: "Don't hesitate to come to me with suggestions, because we always reward good suggestions."

Debt: A leader refers to past obligations or debts as a way of inducing compliance.
Example: "I have been a good and responsive manager to you, and I hope you will respond in the same way by coming to me with your suggestions."

Positive self-esteem: The leader says that there will be a psychological benefit to compliance, such as increases in self-worth and competence.
Example: "You need to project a more positive work attitude, since fellow employees look to you as a role model."

Positive moral appeal: The leader explains that compliance is the ethical or right thing to do.
Example: "It is appropriate to come to work on time."

Allurement: The leader explains that through compliance the employee will be noticed by others in the organization and possibly rewarded.
Example: "Important people, other than myself, will take notice of your contributions to the organization."

PUNISHMENT-BASED STRATEGIES

Threat: The leader tells the employee that negative consequences may result from noncompliance.
Example: "If you don't start reporting to work on time, disciplinary action will have to be taken against you."

Aversive stimulation: The leader tells the employee that punishment will continue until there is compliance.
Example: "Over the next thirty days we will be keeping track of your tardiness."

Negative self-esteem: By informing the employee that co-workers are aggravated by his or her noncompliance, the leader uses psychological harm and the loss of social approval to secure compliance.
Example: "Other employees will become annoyed with you because you are inconveniencing them with your tardiness. They won't like you."

Negative moral appeal: The leader explains that the employee's behavior is wrong, inappropriate, or unfair.
Example: "It is not fair to others that you are late to work every day."

Ultimatum: The leader explains that failure to comply will result in termination or some other severe punishment.
Example: "Either show up for work on time, or find yourself another job."

Warning: The leader explains that noncompliance may result in punishments from other people in the workplace.
Example: "I must warn you that others in the organization are also concerned about your tardiness."

ALTRUISM-BASED STRATEGIES

Counsel: The leader offers to help or work with the employee in order to gain compliance.
Example: "What can I do to help you overcome the problems that are preventing you from coming to work on time?"

Favor: The leader requests the employee's compliance as a personal favor.
Example: "As a favor to me, I would appreciate it if you would share your ideas with me."

Duty: The leader explains that the employee is obligated to comply.
Example: "I expect you, as an employee with this company, to come to work on time."

Altruism: The leader explains that the employee's compliance is necessary to the well-being of the organization.
Example: "For the sake of the company, please share your ideas and suggestions with me."

RATIONALE-BASED STRATEGIES

Direct request: The leader asks or directs the employee to comply.
Example: "I ask that you come to work on time."

Disguised request: The leader uses hints and indirect attempts to influence the employee's compliance.
Example: (Laughingly) "Well, you've shown up to work on time three days in a row! You might want to consider making it a habit!"

Explanation: The leader presents logical reasons to persuade the employee to comply.
Example: "There are many important reasons why you should come to work on time."

Source: Adapted from D. W. Schlueter, J. K. Barge, and D. Blankenship (1990). A comparative analysis of influence strategies by upper- and lower-level male and female managers. *Western Journal of Speech Communication, 54* (1), 42–65.

Higher authority: gaining the formal or informal support of higher-level supervisors.
Coalition: acquiring the support of co-workers and subordinates.

Although both compliance-gaining typologies emphasize similar kinds of strategies, one key difference is the use of coalitions in Kipnis's version. His work is grounded in the workplace, and one aspect of exercising power in organizations is based on the support of influential third parties.

Leaders use different methods for influencing others in various situations. Gaining compliance, like leadership, is a complex process involving several individual, situational, and organizational variables that can influence the selection of a particular strategy. Some of these variables are documented empirically, whereas others are hypothesized to account for differences in gaining compliance.

Task Complexity

As tasks become more complex and serious, leaders tend to employ more assertive, coercive, and rationale appeals. When leaders confront a complex task such as trying to get a worker to improve performance or to adapt to change, they use more reasoning and assertiveness than with relatively simple tasks (Kipnis et al., 1980). Moreover, as the nature of the task becomes more serious, more authority-based and coercive appeals are used to gain compliance (Cody & McLaughlin, 1985; Seibold, Cantrill, & Meyers, 1985; Ricillo & Trenholm, 1983).

Hierarchical Position

The hierarchical relationship between the persuader and the target of persuasion also influences strategy selection. Hierarchical leaders tend to be more assertive and to use more sanction-oriented messages with people in low-level positions than with those in high-level positions (Rim & Erez, 1980; Erez & Rim, 1982; Kipnis, Schmidt, & Wilkinson, 1980). This finding may in part be due to the fact that people high in the hierarchy may perceive that they have the right to persuade and, therefore, to use more assertive and less supportive strategies (Vecchio & Sussmann, 1991).

Gender Differences

According to Harper and Hirokawa (1988), women managers tend to use more altruism-based strategies to influence subordinates, whereas men rely on punishment-based strategies. Conrad (1985) contends that women tend to use strategies formed by linguistic devices, including tag questions and disclaimers, and men tend to use strategies marked by logical reasoning and evidence. In addition, it has been suggested that women prefer need-based strategies, whereas men rely more on threats and promises and use less rational strategies (DeTurck & Miller, 1982; Falbo, 1977; Baxter, 1984).

Cognitive Complexity

The cognitive complexity variable, although more speculative than conclusive, attempts to link the complexity of a leader's cognitive system with his or her behavior. Kuhnert and Lewis (1987) contend that cognitive complexity influences the ability of a leader to be transformational. One of the few studies to test this assumption was conducted by Ted Zorn (1991). He argues that, as people develop more complex cognitive systems, they not only become more transformational but also use more person-centered messages. Because transformational leaders are highly attuned to the needs of the employee, increased cognitive complexity enhances their sensitivity to those needs. Although the results of Zorn's study have not been investigated further, transformational leadership is likely associated with increased cognitive complexity and somewhat related to the increased use of person-centered strategies. (See Box 7.2.)

POWER IN CONCEPTION: VISIONARY LEADERSHIP

Leadership becomes more relevant and important to people in times of perceived crisis and turmoil (Kouzes & Posner, 1990). In the late 1980s and early 1990s, several national and international developments signaled a clear need for leadership in the United States. An educational crisis, concern about the environment, the recognition that the United States was not competing well in the global marketplace, and the disintegration of the Soviet Union all emphasized the need for decisive and clear leadership. Several critics maintained that individuals were not assuming leadership roles within organizations. A prime example is the failure of leaders in the federal government to encourage employees to perform their primary function—to aid the citizens of the United States. According to one government employee:

> The unequivocal message throughout the federal bureaucracy is that nothing is to be accomplished by this government except the creating of good feelings and the illusion of action. . . . [T]he best and the brightest at my agency and others dutifully exercise caution in substantive matters, avoid action and continually seek another clearance, another authorization, until someone just finally says no. . . . Matters afflicting the current and future well-being of Americans are seen only as nettlesome disruptions that must be calmed, rather than problems that must be

Box 7.2 The Use of Compliance-Gaining Strategies

When researchers study the kinds of strategies that leaders use to influence others, they typically examine them in certain situations. They first look at the situation and then determine the appropriate strategy. The strategies are then classified according to some typology, such as the one shown in Box 7.1.

The two situations that follow are typically used by compliance-gaining researchers (Hirokawa & Miyahara, 1986; Harper & Hirokawa, 1988; Schlueter, Barge, & Blankenship, 1990). For each situation, describe in a few sentences the strategy you would use to gain the employee's compliance.

SITUATION 1

One of your subordinates has been reporting to work late several times a week for a long period of time. In most cases, the employee is about fifteen minutes late. Moreover, the employee's continued tardiness is beginning to annoy other people in the office. What will you say to persuade the employee to report to work on time?

SITUATION 2

It has recently come to your attention that one of your subordinates has some good ideas for improving productivity and efficiency in your company but is reluctant to communicate those ideas to you. What will you say to persuade the employee to share his or her suggestions and ideas with you?

QUESTIONS

1. What compliance-gaining strategy did you use for each situation? How can you classify the strategies according to the information provided in Box 7.1?
2. Did the strategies you selected differ? Why or why not? What does this tell you about the relationship between the nature of a situation and the selection of a compliance-gaining strategy? Explain.

solved or responsibilities that must be faced. (Bennis, quoted in Nanus, 1992)

In response to these perceived crises, leadership researchers called for bold, risk-taking, and innovative leaders who could articulate a direction and a vision for successfully managing the educational, environmental, economic, and foreign policy issues. Some contended that charismatic, transformational, and visionary leaders were required to manage these obstacles (Conger, 1989; Kouzes & Posner, 1990; Nanus, 1992; Peters, 1987; Tichy & DeVanna, 1986). Although the labels used to identify the type of leadership differed, it was generally agreed that a key component of effective leadership was creating a vision to direct the organization.

What Is a Vision?

A *vision* is a roadmap for organizational members to follow; it spells out the organization's final destination. Burt Nanus (1992) describes a vision as a mental model that highlights some preferred future existence, one that is more desirable than the current state of affairs. Visions differ from mission statements in that they provide a sense of direction—a sense of where the organization is going rather than of what the organization is. Visions are like roadmaps because they point people toward certain general directions. However, visions do not specify the strategy or route by which the final goal or destination can be reached. A vision might spotlight how an organization will contribute to society, fit into the future marketplace, or allocate resources to people. Ultimately, it serves as an organizing paradigm for helping organizational members understand where the company is headed, how they can help the organization move in that direction, and why certain actions and behaviors will be of value in the future (Tichy & DeVanna, 1986).

Visions are clearly related to power in conception in that they promote a sense of common purpose. They also detail the decision-premises that people use when making decisions. Steve Jobs of Apple Computer, for instance, had a vision—to create a technologically innovative company without the rigid structure of large bureaucratic organizations such as IBM. During the 1984 Super Bowl football game, Apple aired a one-time commercial to introduce its new Macintosh computer. Patterned after George Orwell's novel *1984,* the commercial went like this: An auditorium is filled with people mindlessly watching as Big Brother talks on an oversized movie screen. A female athlete runs into the auditorium and throws a hammer into the screen, shattering it and causing the people to react. The commercial represented IBM as Big Brother; when the screen was shattered, people could emerge as individuals. Similarly, in a subsequent address given to the Boston Computer Society, Jobs again used the *1984* theme, projecting on a back wall an oversized image of himself as he spoke (Conger, 1989). In both instances, the message was intended to persuade others to break away from the conformity and tradition associated with bureaucracies. Apple, designed to counter this tradition, seeks to breed innovativeness. Its employees are encouraged to emphasize innovation, change, and creativity when approaching any situation, decision, or action.

What, then, are the qualities of a good vision? Because a vision can have great influence on people's actions, it is important to recognize the qualities that make a vision powerful or weak. Although it appears that certain qualities tend to characterize good visions, it should be noted that theorists are not in agreement.

A vision highlights the future direction of the organization. Visions provide organizational members with a template that makes sense of their activity and that establishes a high set of standards for the organization. Tom Peters (1987), a noted management consultant, argues that a vision should be challenging and should articulate a standard for excellence that is partly idealistic and partly realistic.

A vision connects with people at an emotional level. A good vision energizes people to action and increases their commitment to the organization. People become committed to the organization in part because the vision helps to create meaning in their jobs. At the emotional level, a vision connects with the attitudes, values, and beliefs of employees and thereby inspires them to reach high levels of commitment and motivation.

A vision serves to bridge the past and the future. Although a vision is designed to position the organization for future success in the marketplace, it also must respect the company's past history and organizational members so as not to alienate employees. Therefore, a good vision helps prepare for the future and reinforces the importance of the past. For example, 3M (the Minnesota, Mining, and Manufacturing Company) manufactures a variety of adhesive, bonding, and coating materials that are used by other companies to produce such products as computer disks and tapes, audiotapes, sandpaper, tape, and Post-It notes. The typical 3M product is flat and two-dimensional. The company's culture informally emphasizes that when individuals want to produce a new product, they must be able to demonstrate how it will reflect the emphasis on adhesives as well as the "flat" nature of 3M products. When David Davies, a physical chemist, wanted to produce a new line of laser disks that did not fit with the initial vision of 3M, he realized that he would have a tough time selling his new technology to his supervisors (*In Search of Excellence,* PBS production). As a result, Davies geared his presentation and phrased his messages to emphasize that the product utilized adhesives to bond the laser. When he displayed the new product, he made sure to hold the disk horizontally so that it would look flat; he knew this would help his supervisors understand that the new product was in line with existing 3M products. Davies made a conscious decision to phrase his messages in ways that would present the new laser disks as mainstream 3M products. His vision of what the future held in laser disks had to be based in the history of the company (in its emphasis on producing products that are flat). Failure to connect his vision with the past would have led to the rejection of his product.

How Is a Vision Communicated?

Visions need to be communicated to other organizational members. Nanus summarizes the relationship between communication and a vision as follows: "vision + communication = shared purpose" (1992, p. 13). Visions create a sense of identity, unity, and purpose within the organization. They also provide a sense of direction to organizational members. Yet, the shared purpose of a vision cannot come about if it is not communicated to an audience. Leaders perform the function of communicating a vision. They do so by way of a variety of devices, including public speeches, informal discussion, and in-house publications such as newsletters or memoranda. In addition, leaders communicate a vision by using a variety of linguistic strategies.

Leaders may communicate a vision through analogies, metaphors, and organizational stories. According to Conger (1989), such rhetorical devices as analogies, metaphors, and organizational stories tap into people's emotions and attitudes and elicit the emotional response needed for attaining a vision. For example, Disneyland uses the dual metaphors of the family and showbusiness to describe its organization (Smith & Eisenberg, 1987). As a result, organizational members at Disneyland strive to treat fellow employees and guests with courtesy and hospitality, just as they would a family member. In fact, the employees are "performers" and the Disney park is the stage on which the live drama of entertaining guests is carried out. In Chapter 3, the story about IBM president Tom Watson's encounter with twenty-two-year-old security officer Lucille Burger (see pages 76–77) represents another way that leaders may communicate a vision. As Dennis Mumby (1987) points out, at one level the story reinforces the idea that all people at IBM are created equally. The vision of what the organization is to be is idealized by the stories told by leaders and other organizational members.

Leaders may communicate a vision through personification. Leaders who use personification live and breath the vision. They *are* the vision, as demonstrated by their commitment to the organization. Jay Conger (1989) describes the president of SAS airlines, a Scandinavian airline, who created a vision of an airline that views its consumer as the primary concern. The president personified the vision every time he traveled on SAS, by not seating himself before other passengers and by not taking any magazines until all other passengers had chosen theirs. SAS employees realized that the president had meant what he had said about the customer always coming first. Leaders personify visions by way of their behavior in the organization—who they talk to or devote attention to, what they say to others informally, the kinds of commitments they make, and whether they honor those commitments.

Leaders may provide frames for viewing a vision. Conger (1989) suggests that leaders use frames to help workers interpret a vision. Framing involves placing the vision in a larger context so to emphasize its importance or significance. Steven Jobs used frames to create a vision for NeXT, his new computer company. In a speech to NeXT staff, Jobs notes that he wants

> "to start a company that ha[s] a lot to do with education and, in particular, higher education, colleges and universities. So our vision is that there is a revolution in software going on now on college and university campuses. And it has to do with providing two types of breakthrough software. One is called simulated learning environments. You can't give a student in biology a five-million-dollar recombinant DNA laboratory. But you can simulate those things, you can simulate them on a

very powerful computer. It is not possible for students to afford these things. It isn't possible for most faculty members to afford these things. So if we can take what we do best, which is to find really great technology and pull it down to a price point that's affordable to people, if we can do the same thing for this type of computer that we did for personal computers, then I think we can make a real difference in the way the learning experience happens in the next five years. And that's what we're trying to do . . . [and] one of my largest wishes is that we build NeXT from the heart. And the people that are thinking about coming to work for us, or buying our products, or who want to sell us things, feel that we're doing this because we have a passion about it. We're doing this because we really care about the higher educational process, not because we want to make a buck, not because, you know, we just want to do it." (quoted in Conger, 1991, pp. 32–33)

Jobs frames the mission of NeXT in this speech. He emphasizes the value of the people within the company. A *value* is a state of existence or a way of acting that is desirable. One common value in the United States is helping and protecting children. The NeXT computer is aimed at helping students to learn. Jobs also uses employees' beliefs—those factors that encourage actions to be taken to achieve values—to frame the importance of his vision. Conger (1989) maintains that beliefs may include the importance of the mission, the needs for the mission, villains who may foil the mission, and determination to complete the mission. In the NeXT example, the importance of the mission—to revolutionize the education industry—is specified. (See Box 7.3.)

How Does Credibility Influence the Acceptance of a Vision?

The acceptance of a vision is greatly dependent on the validity and credibility of the leader. Individuals are viewed as more influential when they are perceived as legitimate and credible sources. Over two thousand years ago, Aristotle argued that *ethos,* or source credibility, is a critical component for successful persuasion. The credibility of the source exercises considerable influence on the perceived persuasiveness of a message. As a result, leaders and those who study leadership are concerned with issues of credibility. John Baird (1980) suggests that leaders are concerned with establishing credibility with their employees. He points out that the success of organizing hinges on a leader's credibility; if employees do not view a leader as credible, they are less likely to believe the leader, trust the leader's directions, or respond to the leader's attempts at motivation. Klauss and Bass (1982) confirm that there is a strong relationship between subordinate perceptions of a manager's credibility and managerial success.

Communication researchers are particularly interested in the dimensions of source credibility. In a summary of the source credibility literature, Michael Burgoon and Michael Miller (1990, p. 239) argue that individuals make five judgments when assessing a person's credibility. These are:

Box 7.3
A Visionary Speech

The following speech by Chuck Lamar, vice president of strategy development for U.S. West Communications, was delivered at the National Communications Forum in Chicago on October 2, 1991.

CURRENT TELCO MANAGEMENT: VISIONS AND STRATEGIES FOR SURVIVAL

Good Morning. My name is Chuck Lamar. I'm vice president of strategy development for U.S. West Communications. Thanks for sticking around for our closing session. I certainly hope we've saved the best for last.

In his famous novel about the French Revolution, *A Tale of Two Cities,* Charles Dickens opens with the observation that: "It was the best of times, it was the worst of times. . . . " If Dickens were alive today and writing about our industry, he might very well open with the observation that: It is the best of times, it is the worst of times. . . . We have both the good fortune—and certainly for some, the misfortune—to be part of an industry in the throes of a revolution. A revolution every bit as profound as the political revolutions of the late eighteenth century, including the one that Dickens wrote about, that reshaped the face of western Europe and gave rise to that upstart young country known as the United States of America. And every bit as profound as the Industrial Revolution that swept Western Europe and the United States during the eighteenth and nineteenth centuries.

Imagine for a moment that it's Tuesday, October 2, 2001—ten years from today. It's time to go to work. You don't have to check the morning traffic report. You work at home. You telecommute. Headquarters is halfway across the continent. Some of your colleagues still have offices there. But many others—like you—are scattered around the world, living where they choose.

While enjoying your first cup of coffee, you flip on the wall-sized monitor beside your desk and join the weekly staff meeting for your group. Because the images are lifesize and very high quality, you hardly notice that the people in the room with you are, in fact, scattered in a dozen cities, on several continents. Two meetings scheduled for the same time? No problem. Because you'll be able to use your remote control to flip back and forth between meetings—as easily as my kids flip between TV shows today.

The meetings are done; it's time to get down to work. First a trip to the library. Thanks to the magic of high-speed digital communications, you can browse through publications in libraries throughout the world, more easily and more rapidly than you could today even if all the mate-

Box continued

rial were sitting on your desk. Once you find what you're looking for, downloading it to your computer takes just a few seconds. Next, you prepare a sales report and transmit it instantly to a thousand salespeople in the field, tailoring the information, if you choose, so individual recipients receive information suited to their specific needs.

As the workday ends, you and your family check the movie listings. There are several new hits you haven't seen yet. You make your choice, press a couple of buttons on the remote control for your home entertainment center, and within a few seconds the movie is loaded into your system for you to watch at your convenience. You can even pick a separate movie for the kids, if you like. You'll have to supply your own popcorn, but the life-size high-definition screen and digital sound are every bit as good as the best movie theaters of 1991. And, of course, you'll be able to put the movie on hold if you need to take a break. Some things won't change, even in the twenty-first century. Or maybe you'll curl up instead with a good book or a magazine, delivered electronically, complete with advertising targeted specifically to your income level and personal interest.

My crystal ball is beginning to fade. But what I've described to you is not just science fantasy, it's a fairly realistic portrayal of what the world could look like ten years—or less—from now. And I've described only a few of the changes technology is likely to bring in the next decade.

My point is that the world will be even more dependent on telecommunications a decade from now than it is today. And that translates into incredible opportunity for our industry—opportunity almost beyond our ability to comprehend.

It is the best of times. But the competitive sands are shifting under our feet, and it will be a while before the changing contours of our industry settle into any semblance of a stable landscape. A decade from now my company, U.S. West Communications, almost certainly will not be the local phone company in most of the markets it serves, but one of several local phone companies. We expect competition in the local-exchange business from radio-based personal communications networks, from cable TV operators, and others. Continued advances in technology will continue to change the landscape of the communications business for all of us—local-exchange companies, long-distance companies, equipment suppliers, and others.

Regardless of whether you work for an established company like mine, faced with the prospect of competitive inroads into what was once a monopoly market, or a company just entering—or trying to enter—the telecommunications business, all of us face the very real challenge of investing billions of dollars—that's billions with a "B"—just to prepare ourselves to compete to serve a marketplace that does not yet know what it wants, or from whom.

There will be competitive casualties. Some of our jobs will go away. Some of our companies will go away. And, in fact, entire segments of our industry almost certainly will fall by the wayside over the next decade. As a result, some of us in this room today will not be at this conference a year from now. Fewer yet will be here five or ten years from now. On January 1, 1984, U.S. West had more than 70,000 telephone-company employees. Today, we have about 55,000. We expect another 5,000 to 6,000 telephone-company jobs to disappear within the next four or five years. And we are not unique. For many, it is the worst of times.

It is the best of times, it is the worst of times—because we are in the throes of a revolution. Let's take a look at some of the forces shaping that revolution and changing our industry. First, some market trends. One is the rise of the post–mass-market era. In the consumer market, for example, diversity of means and diversity of needs, in terms of lifestyle, age, and ethnic viewpoint, are fragmenting the market. We also see increasing customer expectations. Some competitors are achieving remarkable increases in quality, raising the standard for everyone else. And new competitors will put pressure on prices and margins, while raising customer expectations even more. Finally, consumers continue to lead more hectic lifestyles, which places increasing value on time. In short, the only thing any of us can count on in the marketplace is change and uncertainty.

Some other trends:

- International growth will outpace domestic growth within our industry, and we will increasingly see global suppliers, not national or regional suppliers.
- Data communication is growing 30 to 40 percent a year, while voice is growing 8 to 10 percent a year, and this trend will continue.
- Work-at-home will become more and more commonplace because of employee needs for flexibility in their day, and because high-speed digital voice-data communication will allow more and more people to give up their offices away from home without sacrificing their ability to compete effectively in the job market.
- Large companies will continue to downsize, which means most job growth will come from small businesses.
- The window of opportunity for new products will be short. There will be no generational products. The pace of the market means you will have to seize opportunities quickly as they emerge, or others will.
- We will continue to see a proliferation of networks, and they'll be far more interconnected than today, which has profound implications for everyone in this room.
- Changing technology—radio technology, computer technology, and laser technology—will continue to open up more and more choices for our customers, and make our job of competing for their business more and more challenging.
- The tremendous opportunity within our industry will attract more and more competitors, which will increase that challenge even more.
- Ironically, as competition increases, we will also see more strategic alliances, because no one company will be able to do it all.

We've already seen some interesting ones. The recently announced alliance between Apple and IBM is one example. My company has teamed up with AT&T and Tele-Communications, Inc. of Denver— the world's largest cable TV company—to test something we call viewer-controlled

Box continued

TV. Using a special cable box attached to their TVs, participants in the trial can order up movies and other entertainment programs, on demand, from a library that includes hundreds of titles. It's like having a video store in their homes. Here we are a phone company and a cable company involved in the market trial—in the suburbs of Denver, where both of us are headquartered. That's kind of like the Hatfields and McCoys going into business together. But it's happening. In fact, U.S. West also is a partner with several American cable companies in cable TV ventures overseas.

As competition and the formation of strategic alliances continue to grow so will something I call disintermediation. That's a fancy way of saying the boundaries are blurring. Taking a middle person out of business transactions is a good example—moving to electronic brokerage versus having your personal broker, desktop publishing versus the print shop, direct mail versus the retailer. Increasingly, it will also mean telepresence versus traveling to meetings or even to visit family. Yet more opportunity and yet more challenge for all of us in this room.

It is the best of times, it is the worst of times. But none of us will be bored. We'll be too busy fighting for survival. So, let me offer six strategies for survival. First, focus on customers. Technology is driving the changes within our industry. But technology is a commodity—available to all of us and to all of our competitors. To succeed in our increasingly competitive marketplace, you must focus on customers—providing products and services they want, when, where, and how they want them.

Survival strategy number two: People—your employees—are the key to your success. Again, technology is a commodity. And your employees will treat your customers the way you treat them. You cannot delight your customers if you ignore or abuse your employees. And your employees are the source of innovation—and plain old hard work—required to compete successfully.

Strategy number three: Change your cost structure. For years, Wall Street has graded the seven Baby Bells, including U.S. West, by how we compare to one another. Some of those comparisons are valid and useful. But many of our potential competitors have much different cost structures than any of the Baby Bells. To compete, we have to meet or beat them, too. Every competitive company, including yours, faces the challenge of investing limited resources wisely. For many, the idea of reducing costs means eliminating jobs. My company, and probably most of yours, have eliminated jobs in the recent past. More job reductions lie ahead. But this is not just a jobs issue. The real challenge is to eliminate costs that do not directly impact people by changing the way we do business and eliminating those things that do not serve our customers. And please note I said *change* your cost structure, not just reduce it. We have to free up resources being allocated to things that do not serve our customers, and invest them in things that will make a difference. We have to use our resources—people and money—much more wisely. And we face the very real challenge of doing this without alienating our employees, because they are the key to our success.

No one said it would be easy.

Survival strategy number four: Know your core competencies and build on them. The core competency of my company is operating large networks, voice networks. To remain successful into the twenty-first century, we will have to add data and image communications to our core skills. The specifics may differ for your company. But it's important to know your core skills and build on them.

Survival strategy number five: Develop new products that will give you a competitive edge and replace revenues lost to competition. All the Baby Bells—my company included—face massive revenue losses from competition during the coming decade. We've already experienced significant competitive erosion in some areas. So we have to bring new products to the marketplace—and they have to be big hitters—just to stay even. And we hope to do better than just stay even. And the rising expectations of customers will bring added pressure on all of us to develop new products to meet their demands.

Survival strategy number six: We must develop a new paradigm for regulation. Traditional rate-of-return regulation is designed to maintain affordable prices for basic phone service by limiting the profits of monopoly companies. But it is anticompetitive. It inhibits the kind of investment, innovation, and risk taking required for a competitive marketplace. We must shift the focus of regulation away from price and profit levels and refocus it on things like quality and customer service. We must make it pro-competitive, not anticompetitive. And, quite frankly, we have to make sure it's fair to all competitors—new and old.

That's a challenging agenda. Some people think our industry has a wonderful past, but a questionable future. I believe we have an excellent future. Certainly, the opportunities are there, because the world will be far more dependent on what we do a decade from now. But it won't be easy.

It is the best of times. And it is the worst of times. Revolutions are like that.

ASSIGNMENT

You are a reporter for a local newspaper assigned to a story on the importance of visions as they relate to leadership. Write an article in which you identify the qualities of a good vision and the rhetorical devices used to transmit the vision. Draw examples from the speech.

Source: C. Lamar (1991). Current Telco Management: Visions and strategies for survival. *Vital Speeches of the Day, 58* (5), 146–149.

1. *Competence:* the individual's level of knowledge and expertise for a particular topic.
2. *Character:* the degree to which an individual is viewed as honest and trustworthy.
3. *Composure:* the ability to remain calm within stressful situations.
4. *Sociability:* the basic degree to which an individual is liked by another.
5. *Extroversion:* whether the individual is perceived as outgoing and active in the dialog.

Sources of messages that possess these characteristics tend to be viewed as more credible. Moreover, leaders may influence their level of credibility through communication. Kouzes and Posner (1988) note that empowering forms of communication, such as challenging the process, enabling others to act, modeling the way to act, and providing emotional support, are moderately associated with the credibility dimensions of trustworthiness, competence, and extroversion. Jay Conger (1989) also suggests that workers are more likely to accept a vision when they view its source as possessing experience, insight or wisdom into the problem, and similar values.

ACQUISITION AND DEVELOPMENT OF POWER: THE CASE OF GENDER

There is little question that leaders are better able to influence how workers organize themselves when they are credible sources and able to tap into bases of power. Power and source credibility, then, affect a leader's ability to influence the direction of an organization. Gender may also influence leadership. In contemporary organizations, there are a disproportionate number of men in positions of leadership. While the number of female managers increased to 41 percent of all managers by 1991, as compared to 32 percent in 1983, only 4.8 percent of upper-level managers were women ("When Will Women Get to the Top?" 1992). This finding suggests that gender also influences leadership within organizations. One possible reason for the gender discrepancy in leadership may be due to power differences between men and women (Kanter, 1977). Women appear to be given lesser amounts of power than men, which, in turn, directly influences their opportunity to create and maintain leadership positions. Moreover, since power is correlated to personal success in organizations, women become disadvantaged in the workplace. What accounts for this power differential?

While several explanations have been offered to explain similarities and differences between male and female leadership behavior (Eagly & Johnson, 1990), two popular perspectives connect gender to organizational power. The structuralist perspective holds that power is embedded in the organization and constrains the range of influence strategies available to individuals (Kanter, 1979, 1977, 1976). It attempts to explain how women are segregated into low power positions, how this affects organizational life for women, and how it limits their selection of influence options. Conversely, the socialization perspective contends that women are acculturated into a lower power position within society. This difference spills over into the workplace, causing patterns of communication and influence to vary between men and women (Henning & Jardim, 1977; Johnson, 1976).

Structuralist Position

Although a variety of power bases exist within organizations, structuralists argue that position in the organizational hierarchy is the most important source of power. They contend that organizational structure is the basis for power differences between men and women and assume that outcomes, such as productivity and career success, are primarily rooted in the organizational hierarchy. According to Kanter (1976), position is a "shorthand symbol for potential or actual power" (p. 424) that determines the influence strategies available to organizational members. According to this perspective, because women occupy more lower-level positions than men, women and men have different levels of power and use different influence strategies.

According to structuralists, women tend to be channeled into positions lower in power, information, and organizational support upon entering the workplace and, as a result, are unable to keep pace with men starting out in positions of status and influence (Bartol, 1978; Huerta & Lane, 1983; Kanter, 1977, 1976; Stewart & Gudykunst, 1982; Terborg, 1977). Consequently, women generally are given control of fewer valued resources, are made less visible in the organization, and are given limited opportunities for success, influence, and upward mobility. Women may not be afforded the opportunity to be leaders owing to their segregation into formalized, low power positions. For example, since upward influence is a valued managerial resource (Jablin, 1980; Trempe, Rigny, & Haccoun, 1985), a manager's inability to influence the organization for the benefit of his or her subordinates may lead to decreased perceptions of managerial competence and ability. Being relegated to low power positions possibly leads not only to decreased success but also to lower motivation, optimism, and satisfaction. In a survey of males and females in lower-level positions, Mottaz (1986) found that women tend to perceive fewer intrinsic rewards from their jobs and fewer opportunities for upward movement in the organization than men.

Apart from hierarchical position, informal organizational practices may also serve to disadvantage women and empower men. Women face difficulty in being accepted as key figures in important communication networks (Brass, 1985; Rosen, Templeton, & Kichline, 1981). Many may be excluded from key information that could help them interpret and adapt to organizational practices. This further limits the opportunity of women to increase their power and maximize their success in the workplace. While mentoring is one strategy that can be used to compensate for this problem, many women are not given access to mentors (Berry, 1983; Shockley & Stanley, 1980). Consequently, the limited channels made available to women may lower their opportunities for power and influence in the workplace.

Socialization Position

Those who advocate that socialization is the basis for power and influence differences assume that sex-role socialization prescribes varying sets of appropriate expectations and behaviors for men and women. It is argued that these differences subsequently spill over into the workplace, and not only may influence male and female leaders' behavior, but also our evaluations of their behavior (Eagly, Makhijani, & Klonsky, 1992; Corcoran & Courant, 1987; Eccles & Hoffman, 1984; Marini & Brinton, 1984). Through socialization, it is argued, men learn to be task-oriented (confident, competitive, and independent) and women learn to be relationship-oriented (supportive, noncompetitive, and dependent). Furthermore, the predispositions associated with female gender roles may contradict the expectations associated with leadership roles in the workplace (Ragins & Sundstrom, 1989).

These socially learned expectations and behaviors may leave women unprepared to manage subordinates and may dissuade women from seeking positions of accountability and influence. Wong, Kettlewell, and Sproule (1985) found that women who internalize such role expectations as nurturance and eagerness to soothe hurt feelings have decreased levels of career achievement and women who internalize role expectations such as assertiveness and independence possess higher levels of career achievement. Instone, Major, and Bunker (1983) argue that differences in confidence, as opposed to differences in gender, explain how supervisors influence subordinates. While women and men have the same kinds of power needs, the sources of power and influence tend to differ (Chusmir, 1986, 1985; Winter, 1988). Johnson (1976) contends that men and women use power and influence that conform to their cultural expectations.

Resolving the Structural versus Socialization Debate

One possible reason for the apparent differences between men and women in organizational leadership positions may be because traditional views of leadership and power are male-centered. Male-centered views of organization privilege competitive over cooperative behavior, separate task over relational behavior, and emphasize rationality over emotionality (Mumby & Putnam, 1992; Wyatt, 1993). In a study of leadership, Wyatt (1993) contends that male-dominated conceptions of leadership emphasize active aggressive performance of task functions and neglect the possibility that narratives are also a means of getting the task done. Most leadership theories classify storytelling as a relational function.

When trying to account for the apparent differences between men and women in the workplace, it is important to recognize that our conceptions of what we view as power may be biased. With that in mind, one explanation for the power differences between men and women combines aspects of the two competing models. Schlueter, Barge, & Blankenship (1990) contend that this combination best explains the power and communication differences between men and women in the workplace. In lower-level management positions, men and women tend to communicate in different ways, whereas upper-level male and female managers tend to communicate in similar ways. They suggest that a socialization perspective may account for the differences in persuasive communication at lower levels. Even though men and women may hold similar work values (Chusmir & Parker, 1991), they may rely on cultural stereotypes or understandings when persuading others at lower levels. As men and women enter higher levels in the organization, they increase their level of power and use similar strategies as they are socialized into the organization's culture (Eagly & Johnson, 1990). The structural model appears to operate at high levels. Ragins (1989) adds partial support for this view, as she found that when males and females used similar power bases and amounts of power, they were rated similarly. The implication is clear. Women need to be given more opportunity to develop networking skills, including mentoring (see Chapter 3), so to develop their influence strategies and power bases. When organizations limit women's opportunity to network into the cultural system, women are prevented from reaching their potential for leadership.

THE POWER OF LINGUISTICS

Both power in action and power in conception suggest a variety of techniques and strategies that can be used to gain an employee's compliance or frame an employee's viewpoint. Linguistics is a key component in phrasing persuasive messages. Some argue that it is very important to examine the linguistic elements of speech as they relate to gaining compliance. Compliance-gaining typologies are primarily based on the type of inducement one individual offers another for compliance. However, the phrasing of messages as well as the type of inducement offered may influence their acceptance. Consider the following two sentences aimed at getting an employee to work extra hours:

> I promise you, that if you work these extra hours, you will get paid overtime.
> "Well, I guess . . . you know . . . I could somehow find a way to pay you overtime for working these extra hours. It shouldn't be any problem unless. . . . "

While both sentences employ the strategy of promise to get the employee to work extra hours, the first one is more persuasive because it states the message clearly. While the form of the strategy and the inducement are the same, the phrasing of the messages changes the persuasiveness. Similarly, it is argued that visionary leaders are strategic and devise appropriate language strategies for particular audiences by using such linguistic cues as repetition and rhythm (Conger, 1989). Using words that are powerful and dynamic helps convey messages that contain an inspiring vision.

Bruce Drake and Dennis Moberg (1986) suggest that leaders must look beyond inducements when attempting to persuade others to the linguistic phrasing of their messages. The type of language that is used can make a particular strategy more or less appealing to an employee. Moreover, it is suggested that persuasion attempts can employ two different styles of language: sedative or palliative. Although designed to complement theories of gaining compliance, sedative and palliative speech may also be employed when creating visions.

Sedative Language

During influence attempts, employees calculate the benefits of the inducements offered by the leader and weigh them against the costs associated with compliance. When workers view the benefits as exceeding the costs, they usually comply. When they view the costs as exceeding the benefits, they may refuse to comply. *Sedative language* diminishes an individual's tendency to compare the rewards and costs of compliance. The intent is to short-circuit the process of comparing rewards and benefits and to generate compliance without the individual consciously evaluating the equity of costs and rewards. Sedative language is analogous to taking a sleeping pill or tranquilizer. When people take tranquilizers, their mental abilities are slowed and they lack the motivation, desire, or energy to engage in focused analysis. People under sedation may agree to things that they would otherwise refuse.

According to Drake and Moberg (1986), leaders can phrase their messages in ways that sedate, slow down, and discourage the employee's weighing of costs and benefits. Two basic linguistic strategies characterize sedative language. First, leaders can employ *semantic indirectness,* which disguises the intent of the persuader. Rather than directly seeking compliance, it is sought indirectly through hints, prompts, and teases. Statements such as, "Oh, you really didn't want to do that" said laughingly, indirectly indicate what the leader wants. Leaders may also use sequences of messages to obtain compliance. For example, leaders may "set up" followers by asking a general question or by requesting something minor to gain compliance with something more important later on. Consider this example:

Leader: "What are you up to?"
Employee: "Nothing."
Leader: "Would you mind helping me for a few minutes?"

If the employee responds instead that he or she is involved with something, the leader may move on and drop the compliance-gaining attempt at that point. By "setting up" the person, a leader may sedate the employee and circumvent the cost versus reward calculations.

The other strategy used with sedative language involves triggering certain cognitive scripts within individuals. As noted in Chapter 4, people use a variety of cognitive structures, including prototypes, rules, and scripts, to make sense of a situation. When cognitive scripts become routine, they may be performed out of habit. Leaders can phrase messages that tap into cognitive scripts in order to get people to do something without really thinking about it. A classic example comes from the former television series *M*A*S*H.* When the character Radar wanted his commanding officer to authorize an action that under normal circumstances the commander would reject, Radar would slip the authorization form into a stack of papers that required the commander's signature. While mindlessly signing the other forms, the commander also signed the form authorizing Radar's request. Radar tapped into a script that the commanding officer performed routinely, using it to his advantage to get the activity authorized. Similarly, as leaders try to persuade people to follow a particular vision, they may tap into some widely accepted organizational rule. The earlier description of how Davies presented his new laser disks to 3M is another example.

Palliative Language

When leaders suspect that employees will view a request as having high costs and low rewards, messages that alter the perception of costs and rewards can be constructed. Leaders create ways of making an unfavorable cost-reward ratio appear less severe and more desirable. The form of the request may serve as the inducement. Unlike sedative language, *palliative language* encourages the target of the persuasion to think through the various costs and rewards associated with compliance. However, it is aimed at reframing the perceptions of the costs and rewards so that the inducements appear more palatable. A variety of linguistic strategies may help leaders make the inducement appear more attractive.

Leaders may use either powerful or powerless forms of speech to gain compliance or create a vision. The concepts of powerful speech and powerless speech were coined by O'Barr (1982) during a study of courtroom communication. He attempted to identify the linguistic characteristics of speakers that create powerful and powerless images. Powerless speech is typically characterized by the use of the following:

Hedges: noncommittal and ambiguous statements ("I kind of remember . . . "; "It's important to sort of . . . "; "Maybe we could . . . ").
Intensifiers: strongly phrased words that increase the force of the statement ("I really think so . . . "; "I genuinely believe . . . ").
Hesitations: pauses or breaks in the message flow ("uh", "er", "oh").
Polite language: words that demonstrate concern for others or courtesy ("Excuse me"; "Thank you"; "Sir, I wonder . . . ").
Tag questions: questions that accompany or follow a statement ("I think we should do this project. Don't you?").

Powerful speech is absent any of these features. Overall, individuals using powerful speech tend to be viewed as more competent than those who use powerless speech (Bradac, Hemphill, & Tardy, 1981; Lind & O'Barr, 1979; Bradac & Mulac, 1984; Wright & Hosman, 1983).

Using powerful or powerless speech can be palliative in one of two ways. Leaders may flatter employees by using powerless speech that signals they have power in the relationship. If employees want to increase their level of power, they may be inclined to comply even if the costs outweigh the rewards. Conversely, if employees have a high need for direction and control, leaders may be able to use powerful forms of communication as a persuasive strategy. Even though the costs may exceed the rewards, the employee is open to the forceful direction provided by the leader. Particularly when framing a vision, leaders may utilize powerful forms of speech to create the vision (Conger, 1989).

Leaders may vary the formality of the request. Framing a request formally or informally can provide an inducement for compliance. For example, assume you view your relationship with your supervisor as distant and cold. Your supervisor approaches you and says, "I just wanted to come down and tell you personally how much I appreciate what you've been doing. You've done such a great job, and I wonder if you could do me a personal favor." You are surprised by the supervisor's warmth and informality. But the informality of the comments may serve as an inducement to comply with the request by facilitating the shift toward a personal relationship. If you value your privacy, you may be offended by the informality and refuse to comply. Adapting language style in this way, whether toward formality or informality, can help to create visions (Conger, 1989). Particularly when interacting informally with others in the organization, visionary leaders adapt the formality of their speech to build alliances.

Leaders may use disclaimers. When leaders recognize that a request may upset the employee, they may try to distance themselves from the request and lessen the severity of the reaction by using disclaimers—communicative acts that manage the potentially negative reactions to requests. According to Hewitt and Stokes (1975), five forms of disclaimers exist:

1. *Hedging:* Hedges express a minimal level of commitment to a line of reasoning, a viewpoint, or an opinion. They include such statements as, "Well, I don't really know a lot about this, but I think . . . " or "Now, I'm no expert in this area, but. . . . "
2. *Credentialing:* When aware that a message may be viewed negatively, leaders use credentialing to justify the negative statement. Statements such as "A lot of the time I just ignore this, but . . . " or "I know you're not going to like to hear this coming from me, but a lot of my best friends are. . . . "
3. *Sin licensing:* When leaders expect a message to be viewed negatively but are not concerned about the consequence, they may use sin licensing to indicate the conditions under which a rule may be broken. For example, "It's our usual policy to do X, but. . . . "

4. *Cognitive disclaimers:* Comments such as "Now, I haven't lost my mind, but . . . " and "I know this may sound strange but . . . " are examples of cognitive disclaimers—messages that are intended to let other people know the request is reasonable and that the person making the request is aware of the facts associated with the situation.
5. *Appeal to suspend judgment:* Such appeals are made when individuals make statements they fear will be responded to negatively. The appeal is to "hear me out" until you have heard the entire message.

Disclaimers attempt to reframe employees' perceptions of the balance of costs and rewards by legitimating the request. They can also lessen the negative reaction to a statement or request and thereby increase compliance.

Leaders may use accounts to gain compliance or create visions. Accounts, or explanations for behavior, may include excuses ("I just haven't been able to do it yet because . . . ") and rational justifications ("The reason I can't do X is because . . . "). In organizations, people develop explanations for behaviors that are viewed as inappropriate by other organizational members. For example, stock excuses such as "I'm tired" and "I haven't been feeling well" may be used to account for why a leader made the request. Accounts can soften the negative reaction expected from an employee. When leaders create visions, accounts may be useful in providing a framework for employees to follow as well as explanations of the visions.

SUMMARY

Effective leaders articulate messages that employees can understand and that motivate employees to perform actions that help the company organize itself. Leaders exercise power in two significant ways. First, they use power in action when they attempt to gain the compliance of an employee regarding a specific action or thought. Compliance-gaining strategies range from administering rewards and punishments to using coalitions and bargaining. The selection of a strategy may depend on the nature of the task, the leader's formal position in the company, and the leader's level of cognitive complexity. Second, leaders exercise power in conception through the creation of visions. By providing a theme around which employees orient their value and belief systems, visions serve as a means for controlling behavior. They also highlight the future direction of an organization. Good visions are personified or communicated in ways that are inspiring.

Phrasing persuasive messages in meaningful ways is critical. The linguistic elements of a message often determine whether compliance is gained or visions are created. *Sedative language* disguises the intent of the leader and short-circuits the employee's assessment of costs and rewards. *Palliative language* tries to lessen the severity of the request and to cause the employee to view the cost–reward calculation more favorably. In order to use language effectively, leaders must be versatile in their choice of linguistic style.

An implicit assumption regarding effective compliance-gaining and vision-making strategies is to assess the goals desired in terms of employees' needs. There should be agreement between the leader's and employees' goals and needs. However, many times the wants and needs of leaders differ from those of employees. How leadership phrases messages to manage these opposing desires and, in a larger sense, how it helps organizational members manage competing demands are the focus of Chapter 8.

QUESTIONS AND APPLICATIONS

1. Write a list of the persuasive situations that occur in organizations (for example, trying to get employees to work on time). For each situation, describe the strategy you would use to persuade the employee to perform the desired action. What similarities and differences exist among the strategies you selected? What situational factors influenced your selection of strategies?

2. Choose an organization of which you were a member at one time. Imagine that you are five years into the future. Write a brief article describing the expected accomplishments of the company during those five years. What is your vision for the organization?

3. Interview a leader in some organization of your choice. Ask the person to describe the stories, myths, and rules that characterize the organization and to explain how they help guide employees' work.

4. Select a topic to debate with someone that pertains to a situation requiring persuasion (such as the situations listed in Box 7.2). Tape-record the debate. After listening to the tape, determine whether you tend to emphasize powerful or powerless speech in your conversation.

Part III

MANAGING THE COMPLEXITIES OF LEADERSHIP

Chapter 8

Leadership and Paradox

The next planet was inhibited by a tippler. This was a very short visit, but it plunged the little prince into deep dejection.

"What are you doing here?" he said to the tippler, whom he found settled down in silence before a collection of empty bottles and also a collection of full bottles.

"I am drinking," replied the tippler, with a lugubrious air.

"Why are you drinking?" demanded the little prince.

"So that I may forget," replied the tippler.

"Forget what?" inquired the little prince, who already was sorry for him.

"Forget that I am ashamed," the tippler confessed, hanging his head.

"Ashamed of what?" insisted the little prince, who wanted to help him.

"Ashamed of drinking!" The tippler brought his speech to an end, and shut himself up in an impregnable silence.

And the little prince went away, puzzled.

"The grown-ups are certainly very, very odd," he said to himself, as he continued his journey.

(Saint-Exupéry, 1943, pp. 42–43)

Human beings are inherently inconsistent in their behavior. It is not unusual to say one thing and do or mean something else. It is not unusual to say things that are contradictory and confusing. In fact, contradictions serve as the basis for much of the humor in television situation comedies. In addition to humor, contradictions provide a lens for exploring the deeper side of the human condition. In the preceding passage from Antoine De Saint-Exupery's (1943) classic book, *The Little Prince,* we find the prince on a long journey, visiting many planets and people within the galaxy to search for meaning in his life. During his meeting with the tippler, negative aspects of contradiction are demonstrated.

In the passage, the tippler is involved in a fundamental contradiction. He does not want to drink and is ashamed of drinking. Yet, the only way that the tippler can escape from the past is to drink to forget. Yet, by drinking to forget, the tippler is engaging in the very activity that he wants to avoid. The tippler is stuck in a contradiction from which there appears no escape.

Part of the human experience is the ability to recognize contradiction in our own and others' behaviors. Part of our ability to manage life's pressures successfully is premised on our need to manage the contradictions we encounter. Similarly, leaders are confronted with contradictions in the workplace that require their attention. Effective leadership requires that individuals not only recognize the existence of paradoxes within organizations but also manage them effectively. Tom Peters (1987) contends:

> Today's successful business leaders will be those who are most flexible of mind. An ability to embrace new ideas, routinely challenge old ones, and live with paradox will be the effective leader's premier trait. Further, the challenge is for a lifetime. New truths will not emerge easily. Leaders will have to guide the ship while simultaneously putting everything up for grabs, which is itself a fundamental paradox. (p. 391)

The necessity for leaders to manage paradox increases with the complexity of the environment. Organizational environments today are more chaotic than ever before because of increased globalization, dramatic decreases in the speed of delivering products to market, increased interconnectedness among organizations as more services are being subcontracted, and a flattening of the organizational hierarchy. Leaders must learn to cope with the ambiguity that is inherent within these fundamental changes. As the complexity of the environment increases, the number and variety of possible paradoxes that leadership must manage also increase.

If the successful leader is one who can handle paradox and manage contradiction and ambiguity, several questions merit discussion: What is paradox? What types of paradoxes do organizational members face? What paradoxes must leadership manage? What strategies may leaders employ to manage paradoxes? To answer these questions, it is necessary to examine a fundamental shift in the ways we view organizations and the role leaders play in them.

THE SHIFT TO A CULTURAL PERSPECTIVE

During the early to mid-nineteenth century, the "organization as machine" metaphor dominated most conceptions of the organization. Underlying such organizational perspectives as scientific management and Weber's theory of bureaucracy, the *mechanistic approach* views people as cogs and wheels in the organizational machinery that must operate smoothly for the organization to run efficiently. Any machine has a set number of interrelated parts that perform particular functions, and there is a logical connection between the parts. Similarly, mechanistic organizations have a certain number of parts—individuals, divisions, and departments—that are rationally linked to one another. Gareth Morgan's (1986) list of the principles of classical management provide a glimpse at how organizations operate using a mechanistic metaphor (see Box 8.1). There is emphasis on establishing clear relationships among individuals and departments within the organization. Work is highly specialized with a strict division

Box 8.1
Principles of Classical Management Theory

Unity of command: An employee receives orders from only one superior.

Scalar chain: The line of authority from superior to subordinate, resulting from the unity-of-command principle and used as a channel for communication and decision making.

Span of control: The number of people reporting to one superior must be limited to avoid problems of communication and coordination.

Staff and line: Staff personnel can provide valuable advisory services, but must be careful not to violate line authority.

Initiative: Encouraged at all levels of the organization.

Division of work: Management should aim to achieve a degree of specialization designed to achieve the goal of the organization in an efficient manner.

Authority and responsibility: Attention should be paid to the right to give orders and to exact obedience; an appropriate balance between authority and responsibility should be achieved. It is meaningless to make people responsible for work if they are not given appropriate authority to execute that responsibility.

Centralization (of authority): Always present in some degree, this must vary to optimize the use of faculties of personnel.

Discipline: Obedience, application, energy, behavior, and outward marks of respect in accordance with agreed rules and customs.

Subordination of individual interest to general interest: Attained through firmness, examples, fair agreements, and constant supervision.

Equity: Based on kindness and justice, encourages personnel in their duties; fair remuneration encourages morale but does not lead to overpayment.

Stability of tenure of personnel: Facilitates the development of abilities.

Esprit de corps: Facilitates harmony as a basis of strength.

Source: G. Morgan (1986), *Images of organizations* (Beverly Hills, CA: Sage), p. 26.

of responsibilities. Each person has his or her place in the organization and is expected to abide closely to the job description. Clear chains of command highlight the authority structure. All employees are expected to be in their proper places at the proper times, reporting to the proper people.

Leaders in a mechanistic organization are viewed as the naysayers, disciplinERS, judges, and evaluators of the organization. They are expected to maintain the organizational order and the clarity of the organizational structure. They do so by administering rewards and punishments and by providing directions that keep people in their place within the existing organizational structure. Effective communication in the mechanistic organization is clear and unambiguous communication. Message fidelity—the degree to which a message received is the same as the message sent—is the standard by which communication effectiveness is judged (Krone, Jablin, & Putnam, 1987). Communication is what holds the organization together; it oils the parts of the machine so they move smoothly. There is no place for ambiguity, contradiction, or paradox within a mechanistic organization because it would confuse the well-ordered structure. The clarity and unity of the organizational structure make ambiguity or contradiction unlikely. Paradox also should not exist within the organization; if it emerges, it should be eliminated as quickly as possible to maintain the clarity of the organizational structure.

It is hard to avoid incorporating mechanistic elements into our view of the contemporary organization. After all, most organizations today are hierarchically organized, and most attempt to divide duties and responsibilities among their employees. However, contemporary theorists recognize that there is a connection between the communication practices of an organization and organizational structure. Anthony Giddens (1979) argues that organizational structures are produced and reproduced through communication. Organizations have a *deep structure* as reflected in the knowledge and the resources that make up the organizations. For example, many organizations have informal rules that regulate how employees should greet one another. Giddens calls the overt discourse *surface structure.* A mutual relationship exists between the deep and surface structures. The deep structure influences the kinds of communication choices made and produced; the surface structure influences the rules and resources that make up the deep structure. If the deep structure is comprised of a set of rules emphasizing formal greetings but people choose instead to greet each other informally, over time the surface structure will alter the rules to reflect the more relaxed approach to greeting.

This *cultural view* of organizations represents a significant departure from the mechanistic approach. Classified under the general rubric of organizational culture, communication is viewed as the key mechanism through which structure is created. Communication not only allows the parts of the organization to run smoothly, it also is the force that creates, maintains, and sustains the organization.

This view of the relationship between communication and organizations alters the role of the leader—from that of an accountant who keeps track of the technical aspects of the organization to one of an evangelist who articulates a vision (Weick, 1980).

> The charismatic leaders relate the work and mission of their group to strongly held values, ideals, and aspirations shared in common by their organization's culture. In organizational settings, they paint for their subordinate an attractive vision of what the outcomes of their efforts could be. This provides subordinates with more meaning for their work. It arouses enthusiasm, excitement, emotional involvement, and commitment to group objectives. (Bass, 1985, p. 40)

Leaders provide "explanations, rationalizations, and legitimation for the activities undertaken in the organization" (Pfeffer, 1981). Louis Pondy (1978) concurs with this expanded role of leadership by noting that leaders help others within the organization make their role and work meaningful.

What does the new cultural view of leadership and organizations have to say about the role of communication? Message fidelity is no longer the only standard for judging the effectiveness and appropriateness of communication. The organization's culture helps specify the standards for appropriate and effective communication (see Chapter 9). As a result, the possibility exists for appropriate and effective communication to be ambiguous, contradictory, and paradoxical. In a series of provocative articles, Eric Eisenberg and others (1984, 1990; Eisenberg & Goodall, 1993; Eisenberg & Witten, 1987) argue that the model of organizational communicators as clear and open speakers ignores the strategic use of communication. People may pursue multiple goals when they interact with others, such as managing an ongoing relationship, protecting one's ego, and trying to persuade the other person. Clarity and openness in communication represent only two of the many goals that may be pursued during interaction.

Ambiguous speech can have several advantages. Eisenberg (1984) suggests that ambiguous language may have three main benefits. First, ambiguity can facilitate organizational change. Organizations are driven by goal statements and metaphors. For example, for many years Disneyland used the metaphor of "family" to guide its business decisions and its treatment of employees (Smith & Eisenberg, 1987). What "family" means, however, is subject to interpretation. Families may emphasize parental domination, egalitarian relationships among parents and children, or patriarchal or matriarchal emphasis. It is this ambiguity in the metaphor that allows organizations and individuals to alter their behaviors and perform novel actions. Second, ambiguity allows people to maintain their position. Eisenberg (1984) observes that one of the biggest risks that people with high credibility can take is to speak clearly and unequivocally. By being open, clear, and unambiguous, leaders may give the receiver potentially damaging information that can be used against them. Moreover, those who make unambiguous statements lose the opportunity to deny the plausibility or validity of another individual's interpretation of an event. Leaders become unable to take back what they have said and claim they have been misunderstood when they speak clearly. Third, ambiguity promotes unified diversity. In organizations, there may be multiple viewpoints regarding a particular issue. If individuals are clear about how their viewpoints differ, their dissensus could prevent them from completing a task. The role of leadership is to build consensus at some level so that organizational members can do their work. Eisenberg (1984) notes that the process of doing so involves less of arriving at a consensus and more of using language strategically to express values at an abstract level so that agreement can occur.

It is this last benefit of strategic ambiguity that is particularly important. From a mechanistic viewpoint, disagreements, contradictions, and a lack of consensus are avoided at all costs to retain the clarity and specialization of the organizational hierarchy. From an organizational culture viewpoint, however, ambiguity, contradictions, and paradoxes are viewed as inevitable components of organizational life. Giddens (1979) notes that, as deep structures develop, contradiction is a part of the process. Unlike the mechanistic view of organizations, the cultural view emphasizes the management of contradiction, ambiguity, and paradox. One of the roles of leadership, then, is to help manage these phenomena. As Peters (1987) points out, the ability of leaders to manage paradox is critical to organizational effectiveness.

THE NATURE OF PARADOX

Paradox has long been a focus of attention, beginning with formal philosophy. Going back over two thousand years, when Epimenides of Crete uttered the immortal words "All Cretans are liars," philosophers interested in the study of human language have examined the characteristics and consequences of paradox. In its simplest of terms, paradox deals with contradiction or conflicting ideas. A *paradox* is defined as a contradiction that follows correct deduction from consistent premises (Watzlawick, Beavin, & Jackson, 1967). Traditionally, three characteristics serve to define paradox: (1) paradoxes are self-referential, (2) paradoxes are contradictory, and (3) paradoxes are circular or vicious circles. *Self-referential* means the statement comments about itself. Paradoxes are *contradictory* because, although they begin with a common set of premises, a logical analysis leads to two opposing conclusions. Finally, paradoxes trigger *circularity* or *vicious circles*—a system of reasoning from which there is apparently no escape. Once drawn into a paradox, one must step outside the paradox to analyze it and to choose a desired outcome or conclusion.

To understand the nature of paradoxes, consider the following two examples. Try to identify in them the elements of self-reference, contradiction, and circularity.

Example 1

All statements in this box are false.

Example 2

The next sentence is true. The immediately preceding sentence is false.

First, both examples are self-referential. In example 1, the statement in the box—"All statements in this box are false"— comments about itself. Example 2 is slightly more complicated because it has two messages that form the paradox: The first message comments about the second and the second comments about the first. In addition, both examples produce contradictory conclusions. For example 1, consider the following two lines of reasoning:

1. If it is true that all statements in the box are false, since the statement acknowledges that it is false, it must then be true.

2. If it is false that all statements in the box are true, then the statement must be false.

Both conclusions are logically valid, yet they are opposite. The same kind of logic applies to example 2:

1. If the first sentence is true, then the second statement must be false.
2. If the second sentence is true, then the first statement must be false.

Again, the conclusions are logically valid but they contradict one another.

Finally, both examples are caught in a circular pattern of reasoning. Imagine you are reasoning through example 2, talking through it out loud. Your spoken musing might sound something like this:

> Now, let me see. If the first sentence is true, then the second statement must be false. But, if the second sentence is true, then the first statement must be false. But, if it is true that the first statement is false, then the second sentence must be true. But. . . .

The reasoning is circular because it does not lead to a final conclusion.

Most philosophers agree that paradoxes are defined according to the characteristics of self-reference, contradiction, and circularity. However, can organizational and group theorists apply the same definition to paradox? While most organizational theorists agree that paradox involves some type of clashing of ideas, Kim Cameron and Robert Quinn (1988) point out that in the everyday language of organizations and organizational theorists, paradoxes are equated "with concepts such as dilemma, irony, inconsistency, or dialectic" (p. 3). Paradoxes are thus organizational phenomena that present conflicting elements. Tension exists between the two elements that form the paradox. For our purpose in this chapter, then, a *paradox* represents the fundamental opposition of two elements, which can be defined only in terms of each other (self-referential).

How do these criteria manifest themselves in organizational paradoxes? Let's take as an example the paradox of creativity, which is identified as occurring within both groups (Smith & Berg, 1987) and organizations (Cameron & Quinn, 1988). The *paradox of creativity* reasons that to create something new, something must be simultaneously destroyed. Every creative act is premised on destroying the existing status quo. To create change, individuals must simultaneously destroy the status quo and change the preexisting patterns of communication, values, and beliefs within the group. The paradox of creativity exemplifies all three characteristics of paradox:

Fundamental concepts in opposition. The two concepts involved are "change" and "not change." Each is the bipolar opposite of the other.

Self-reference. To define what "change" is, one must be able to define "not change," but in order to define "*not* change," one must rely on how one defines "change." Thus, defining "change" is self-referential.

Contradiction. To create something new means to create something new for the future; but creating something new involves destroying something old. For example, one of the major challenges facing organizational leadership occurs when the founder of an organization dies. When new leaders take over, they may want to forge new directions and create new opportunities for the company. Yet, the creative act of forging a new direction simultaneously destroys the existing company. It is common at that point for organizational members to voice their concern.

Paradoxes are associated with tension and discomfort. Leaders within organizations must be aware of the pathologies that paradoxes can trigger. For example, they may trigger opposite types of behavior that, when taken to an extreme, can be dysfunctional. Effective leaders are able to manage the variety of paradoxes they confront.

PARADOXES OF ORGANIZING

Leadership helps people construct a system of organizing. That system, in turn, helps interpret events within the organization, allowing people to take collective action toward removing obstacles and achieving company goals. During the process of helping people organize themselves, leadership must manage a variety of paradoxes. Like the challenges associated with networking, decision making, and dealing with difficult personalities, *paradoxes of organizing* also challenge leadership's ability to create an effective system of organizing.

Paradoxes within groups and organizations cannot be avoided. Certainly, one can ignore the paradoxical nature of organizations, but the paradoxes nevertheless remain. Moreover, while paradoxes pose problems for leaders, they also present opportunities. They can encourage leaders to adopt new perspectives toward situations, and to create innovative, perhaps more effective ways of thinking and acting. Consider, for example, how Einstein used paradox to create his theory of relativity:

> Einstein's conception of the theory of relativity emerged from what he described as the "happiest thought of my life." He conceived of a man jumping off a tall building, and on the way down, taking from his pocket a wallet, placing it in front of himself, and letting go. It occurred to Einstein that relative to the man, the wallet would remain stationary in the air. At that instant, therefore, the wallet (and the man) was simultaneously moving and at rest. That is, two conditions that seem to be mutually exclusive were present at the same time. Einstein's paradox led to a complete revolution in the accepted law of physics. (Cameron & Quinn, 1988, p. 5)

Leaders can thus use paradoxes to break rigid patterns of thinking and acting and to unlock innovation.

The inherent presence of paradox within organizational life and the recognition that organizations need to address the tensions present in paradox are the bases for Kenwyn Smith and David Berg's (1987) book, *Paradoxes of Group Life.* The authors contend that all groups and organizations face paradoxes, but only successful groups recognize the existence of paradoxes and manage them effectively. Leaders help groups and individuals manage the competing demands associated with belonging to a group, participating in a group, and exercising influence in a group.

Table 8.1 lists the various paradoxes proposed by Smith and Berg (1987). Three major categories of paradox are identified: (1) paradoxes of belonging, (2) paradoxes of engaging, and (3) paradoxes of speaking. Within each major category, several related types of paradoxes are listed. Smith and Berg's typology of paradoxes is used to isolate the paradoxes that leadership must manage. It represents one of the most extensive approaches to studying paradox, as it provides a useful framework for explaining the paradoxes associated with organizing collective action.

Table 8.2 details another category of paradoxes—risk-taking paradoxes. These are associated with breaking old behavioral patterns and creating new ones.

Paradoxes of Belonging

One basic relational function leaders perform is helping to establish the role expectations for organizational members. Leaders establish a role structure by framing the form and function of an employee's membership in an organization. During the role-defining process, expectations are created about the employee's contributions to the organization, the employee's connection to the larger organization, and the employee's manner of expression. Smith and Berg (1987) contend that the tensions associated with organizational membership constitute the realm of *paradoxes of belonging.* As people establish membership within an organization, they experience emotional conflict as they wrestle with and attempt to manage the tensions associated with belonging to that organization. The paradoxes of belonging include (1) the paradox of identity, (2) the paradox of involvement, (3) the paradox of individuality, and (4) the paradox of boundary (see Table 8.1).

Identity. One common question you might encounter during job interviews is, "Can you tell me about yourself?" The interviewer is asking you to provide a concise description of your qualities, interests, and special characteristics. The question is aimed at obtaining your view of your own *personal identity.* Similarly, when group members work collectively, a *group identity* is created. Both the personal identity and the group identity possess a definable set of characteristics, values, and beliefs that set them apart from other individuals or groups. Groups' identities can differ in many ways; for example, in terms of the goals they are attempting to achieve, whether they are ongoing or temporary groups, or whether they are comprised of different cliques.

TABLE 8.1 Smith and Berg's (1987) Typology of Paradoxes

Type of Paradox	Opposing Concepts	Contradiction
Paradoxes of Belonging		
Identity	Individual versus group	To identify with a group means I give up my individual identity. But I can't really give up my personal identity because part of my personal identity is belonging to the group.
Involvement	Involved versus detached	To be active in the discussion I must reflect on the discussion. But to have the raw material to reflect on, I must be actively involved.
Individuality	Isolation versus solidarity	I can only be an individual by being strongly connected to the organization.
Boundary	Freedom versus constraint	Defining the role boundary opens up possibilities for behaviors but forecloses others.
Paradoxes of Engaging		
Disclosure	Open versus closed	To disclose information I must trust the person I am disclosing it to. But to create trust, I must self-disclose information.
Trust	Reliable versus unreliable	To build trusting relationships I have to disclose highly personal information, but I am willing to divulge that information only if I trust the person already.
Intimacy	Self-acceptance versus others' acceptance	I want to be accepted and feel comfortable in the organization, which means that I must accept others. I need to accept myself, which depends directly on others accepting me.
Regression	Past versus future	To move forward, I must rely on my past experiences. But to rely on my past experience means I am living in the past and not progressing to the future.
Paradoxes of Speaking		
Authority	Gaining power versus giving power	To gain power, I must give power away.
Control	Independence versus dependence	To be independent, I must be simultaneously dependent.
Courage	Certainty versus uncertainty	To be courageous, I act as if I am certain of what will happen. But courage also means that I act when I am unclear of what will happen.
Creativity	Change versus not change	To create something, I must simultaneously destroy something.

Source: K. Smith and D. Berg (1987), *Paradoxes of group life* (San Francisco: Jossey-Bass), pp. 89–151.

TABLE 8.2 Paradoxes of Risk Taking

Type of Paradox	Opposing Concepts	Contradiction
Competence	Competence versus incompetence	By being overly competent, I may become incompetent.
Success	Success versus failure	To succeed I must fail.

The *paradox of identity* emerges in the tension created by the dichotomy of individual versus group identity. From the individual's perspective, the tension is played out in the dilemma of how much personal identity to retain and how much group identity to adopt. From the group's perspective, the tension is manifested in concern about how the group can maintain its collective identity while also embracing the various personal identities that members bring to the group. The paradox of identity is viewed in "either/or" terms from both perspectives: You either maintain your personal identity *or* you become a full-fledged member of the group. Both sides fail to recognize the paradoxical nature of identity. To have a personal identity, individuals must belong to a group, for their membership in the group provides part of their personal identity. At the same time, however, groups are groups because of the unique collection of individual identities they contain. The individual identities of group members form the group identity and, simultaneously, the group identity defines members' personal identities. Most individuals and groups tend to manage the paradox of identity, however, by emphasizing one of the two extremes.

When leaders confront debates over whether the organization has the right to impose certain restrictions (for example, dress codes) on its employees, underlying the struggles are the paradox of identity. Messages that vocalize members' concern over the group's identity taking precedent over the individual's identity, or concern that a person is acting in ways that violate the group's norms and rules, may signal a struggle with the paradox of identity. For example, consider the following messages:

> "I just can't seem to relate to the group. . . . "
> "The group seems so overpowering."
> "I wish Joe would quit bringing up these random thoughts. We don't do that here."
> "Since you're new, its okay. But you need to know that we usually don't tolerate that kind of behavior in the group."

These kinds of messages indicate to leaders that employees are struggling to maintain their personal identities or that they are concerned about deviant behavior within the group. In the former case, individual identity takes priority over group identity. In the latter situation, the group identity attempts to lessen the individual identity of group members.

Involvement. Think of some adjectives that describe an involved group member and others that describe an uninvolved group member. Did you use any of the following adjectives?

Involved Person	*Uninvolved Person*
active	reflective
doer	thinker
concerned	unconcerned
risk taking	risk avoiding

It is not uncommon to view involved and uninvolved group members in completely opposite ways (Smith & Berg, 1987, p. 99). We tend to classify these two types of people according to their behaviors. Involvement and detachment are the fundamental opposing concepts of the *paradox of involvement.*

Leaders encounter problems when certain members of a group are criticized as being uninvolved, or as "not pulling their own weight." However, this classification of a person as either involved or uninvolved with the work team is arbitrary. The paradox of involvement asserts that it is overly simplistic to assume a person is either involved with a group or uninvolved with a group. Rather, the individual is caught in a delicate balancing act between the two extremes of being involved with the group or being detached. The paradox is as follows: A person must possess the capacity to be detached from the group to be involved with the group. To obtain the needed information to reflect on the group's activity, that person has to gain insight into the group. The only way to collect that information is by active involvement with the group. Thus, a person becomes detached from and reflective about the group only after having participated actively in the group. However, the person can only be involved with the group through detachment and reflection, as this is how the person learns how to become involved with the group.

Through such comments as, "I'd better be quiet, until I know the group better," and "Let's slow down our decision making and think about this some more," people are expressing the tensions associated with the paradox of involvement. By being quiet and uninvolved, a person will never become involved with a group; involvement requires group interaction. However, by becoming involved at too quick a pace, without taking the time to reflect on the group's activities, poor decision making may occur. Leaders help groups manage the conflicting demands of involvement versus detachment created by the need to be both active and reflective.

Individuality. Although in American culture individuality is emphasized, the actual message is "Be an individual just like the rest of us in the United States." The same message is found in U.S. organizations; employees are told to be innovative but to act in ways that reflect the existing organizational culture. How can one be an individual and yet be like everyone else? This is the *paradox of individuality.* Its opposing concepts, isolation versus solidarity, pose problems for leaders.

Individuality can only be gained through a total immersion into the group so that a strong sense of connection with the group can develop. But a group is comprised of people who bring to it their individuality. People thus gain their individuality by being members of groups, and groups are made up of people who express their individuality. The more people become part of a group, the more they can express their individuality. Therefore, while a group requires a solid sense of connection, cohesion, and identity among members, it also requires people to retain their individuality in order for the group to learn and grow. Unlike the paradox of identity, which focuses on how people define their personal identity, the paradox of individuality focuses on the contradictions associated with developing one's individuality through connection with a group. The former asks the question, "Who am I?" whereas the latter asks, "How am I distinct?"

Organizational disputes over how employees may retain their uniqueness, personalize their job, and do things their own way are underscored by the paradox of individuality. Leaders may sense tensions associated with this paradox when employees voice concern about the dilemma of being themselves but also fitting into the group. Employees may be reacting to the tensions of the paradox of individuality when making comments like the following:

> "I can't really be myself."
> "It's frustrating because I feel like I'm so much a part of this organization, but I've left some of my personal beliefs and values behind."
> "I'd better cool it. I need to fit into the group."

Such messages reflect the tension individuals experience as they struggle to balance their needs to retain their individuality and to be a member of the group. In order to become full-fledged members of the group, employees must be involved and develop a set of connections with other group members. In so doing, they can gain confidence in expressing their individuality.

Boundary. People form relationships with one another in groups, and groups create relationships and ties with other groups. Developing a relationship requires that two distinct entities be involved. By setting the boundaries for a group, it is decided who is and who is not a part of the group. Setting boundaries also defines who people are and who they are not. Organizational members may form subgroups based on the boundary of age, gender, social status or interests. Individuals may also identify themselves according to their age, gender, social status, or interests. In both instances, people set the boundaries defining who they are and who they are not. When employees argue over the responsibilities of particular jobs, leaders may be confronting problems related to the paradox of boundary.

The opposing concepts of the *paradox of boundary* are freedom versus constraint. The paradox is summarized as follows: setting boundaries defines and enables action but also simultaneously constrains the kinds of actions people can take. By defining who people are, boundaries allow for the possibility of performing certain kinds of behavior. However, by defining who people are not, boundaries also constrain the number of appropriate behaviors that can be performed. One common boundary in organizations exists between management and labor. The boundary of manager, for example, defines the behaviors that managers can perform, such as creating work assignments, dealing with employee problems, and providing feedback on performance. However, the boundary of manager also defines the behaviors that managers should not perform, such as humiliating employees and getting involved in employees' personal problems. Therefore, being a manager opens up certain avenues for behavior but also limits other behaviors. How managers define themselves and set themselves apart from others also limits how they may interact with a group. Possibilities and constraints are created by the paradox of boundary. When an employee makes a comment such as "I'd really like to suggest that we do . . . , but it's not my place," the manager may be facing a problem related to the paradox of boundary.

The challenge for leaders: managing the paradoxes of belonging. When an individual joins an organization, he or she begins assimilating into the organization (Jablin, 1987). Part of this assimilation process involves the successful balancing of two socialization factors: (1) becoming a full-fledged member and adopting the organizational identity and (2) personalizing the job to maintain a sense of individuality. The former, in its most extreme cases, may cause organizational members to focus on maintaining the status quo of the organization. Rigid observance of role boundaries and of the existing organizational identity characterizes individuals who are heavily socialized into the organization. They may adopt a custodial role and become fixated on maintaining the existing organizational structure and culture (Jones, 1986). In contrast, employees who overemphasize individuality may lack cohesion because there are no common ties to bind them together.

As contemporary organizations face challenges associated with unions, temporary employees, flextime, and increased numbers of women and minorities in the work force, and so on, leaders must take steps that serve both to integrate employees into the organization and to allow employees to maintain their individuality (see Box 8.2). Organizations must work to cultivate a sense of unity among their employees as well as set boundaries that define individuals' behavior and activity. At the same time, leaders must strive to balance the negative impact of full-fledged employee membership with the organization with employees' potential to be innovative and creative. One model that attempts to meet these challenges is used at W. L. Gore & Associates (see Chapter 6). At Gore, leaders instill common principles to tie people together and to provide them with a sense of personal identity. At the same time, Gore allows its employees to personalize their roles.

Paradoxes of Engaging

Many contemporary organizations are turning to leadership styles that emphasize employee and group participation in shared decision making. One of the chief reasons for this shift is the recognition that individuals are limited in the knowledge, skills, and abilities they can use to analyze and solve particular prob-

Box 8.2
The Paradoxes of Belonging at Mona's Clothiers

Mona Santee is the owner of Mona's Clothiers, a small clothing factory that employs seventy-five people and manufactures specialty T-shirts and casual shorts. The company recently expanded into manufacturing wildly colored patterned bandanas or "do-rags" that are worn on the head. Since its opening three years ago, the company's sales have almost tripled.

Mona recently attended a workshop for small businessowners on how to increase employees' sense of belonging to an organization. As part of this workshop, each businessowner was encouraged to distribute a survey to employees to assess their commitment to the organization. Following the advice given at the workshop, Mona administered the survey to her employees. She was shocked to discover that most employees do not feel a sense of belonging or commitment to the company.

Concerned about this finding, Mona hires you—a communication consultant—to assess the problem. As part of the evaluation process, you interview several employees at Mona's Clothiers. You ask the interviewees to describe how the company does or does not make its employees feel like they belong. Following are some of the employees' comments.

Mona Santee (owner). "I'm not sure what the problem is. Our business is booming so much that I've hardly had time to think about it. I guess what I've tried most to do in this company is to make it very efficient. We sometimes get big orders at the last minute, so I've tried to divide up the work into specialty areas. Some workers cut the fabric, others sew, and still others press the finished product. I feel that the employees need to be trained in their respective jobs so they can get the product out quickly. This is a small company, so I must hire people for specific positions. Then workers in each area train the new employees. It's an efficient way of hiring and training because the new employees are trained by those who know the job best."

Charlie Mouser (line supervisor). "Well, I'd like to see people involved with more aspects of the company. We've got a lot of employees who come here and just want to do their own thing. They view their job as something that has to be done to put meals on the table and that's about it. Everybody does their own job. Even during breaks, people tend to talk only with the people they work with—cutters with other cutters, pressers with other pressers, and so on. The only time they get together as a group is during the annual company picnic. Also, when we make up a display of all the products manufactured during the year. It's always interesting because a lot of the employees don't see the finished product beforehand. They only see the part they work on."

Larry Beshear (line worker). "I didn't know there was a problem. Look, we just come to work and do our jobs and leave. We do what Mona tells us. If she wants an order of a hundred do-rags by noon, we do it. Don't get me wrong, I like Mona and so do most of the workers. But we all realize that this is *her* company. Since she's got the brains to put this factory together, she's got the right to

Box continued

tell us what to do. The only negative thing I've heard is that some people are frustrated because they have ideas for improving the efficiency of the assembly line but they don't think it's their place to say anything. They're grumbling, but they know who's the boss. I mean, hey, that's life."

ASSIGNMENT 1

Mona has asked you to write a report detailing your impressions of the company's employees. In the first part of your report, highlight how the company fosters or does not foster among its employees a sense of belonging to the organization.

ASSIGNMENT 2

In the second part of your report, suggest some solutions to the problems you see in the company and among its employees.

lems. Groups, in contrast, tend to make better decisions because the weak skills of some group members may be compensated by the strengths of other group members. Groups can bring more knowledge, insight, and effort to the decision-making process than can a single individual. Moreover, because groups encourage their members to respect others' ideas and opinions, people are more likely to generate novel ideas as part of a group than individually.

The task for leadership, then, is to create an environment in which individual members can freely express their ideas as well as their strengths and weaknesses. The leader helps organizational members become aware of their limitations and of the kind of participation required to manage those limitations. *Paradoxes of engaging* emerge from the tensions associated with determining how much to contribute to and become involved with the issues confronting an organization, as well as how much to engage oneself with other organizational members. Paradoxes of engaging include (1) the paradox of self-disclosure, (2) the paradox of trust, (3) the paradox of intimacy, and (4) the paradox of regression (see Table 8.1).

Disclosure. One common prescription for building trust in personal relationships is to engage in the norm of reciprocal disclosure. The norm maintains that mutual trusting relationships are developed as both parties disclose equal amounts of personal information. Moreover, as individuals work collectively as a team to solve problems, they become aware of the personalities and characteristics of other team members which, in turn, allows them to coordinate their actions successfully. People know each other well when they comment, for instance, "I know you so well, I knew you were going to do that." This level of knowledge decreases the uncertainty within the team to a reasonable level so work can be accomplished. In order to gain knowledge of others, individuals must disclose information about themselves to one another. The *paradox of disclosure* is as follows: To disclose information about yourself to others, you must first know something about those to whom you are disclosing information. However, to know something about them, you must first disclose information about yourself.

Inherent in the paradox of self-disclosure is the individual's concern about acceptance or rejection. When self-disclosing information, people risk others' rejection. If the risk is perceived as too great, the information may not be disclosed. The paradox of self-disclosure is particularly important when individuals make decisions, for they may be reluctant to disclose their views on issues because they fear rejection. The paradox also may prevent employees from taking the first step toward creating relationships with others in the workplace. When leaders find themselves censoring their own speech or hear workers privately voicing concern over disclosing certain kinds of information, problems related to the paradox of self-disclosure may be present.

Trust. The *paradox of trust* builds on the paradox of self-disclosure. Within an organization, people must inevitably trust other people. An employee may need to divulge a personal weakness to a supervisor in order to gain assistance. When mistakes are made, employees need to confide in someone and ask for help. The paradox of trust is related to the complex process of developing relationships with others in a group. Simply stated, trusting relationships are built on the disclosure of personal information, such as one's fears, problems, and concerns. However, to disclose personal information to others requires that a relationship of trust already exists.

Leaders must be sensitive to the paradox of trust, for trust is a key element of effective teamwork (Larson & LaFasto, 1989). In a work environment that does not encourage trust, employees may be uneasy about coordinating their actions with others and voicing their honest opinions. As a result, a lack of trust may prevent the open flow of information needed to make quality decisions. Leaders may note problems associated with the paradox of trust when employees make such comments as "I'm not sure I should say this, but . . . ," "Now, don't get me wrong . . . ," and "Certainly, that's one way of looking at it, but if I could suggest maybe another way. . . . " In each case, the speaker is partially discounting the validity of his or her own idea or argument. Through this disqualifying, the speaker is prepared to offer an idea or comment that may be rejected. That is, the person is protected against rejection by partially rejecting his or her own idea first.

Intimacy. Noted Oklahoma humorist Will Rogers used to say that he could never be a member of a group that would have him for a member. His statement has paradoxical implications. On the one hand, Rogers said he has difficulty accepting who he is because he feels joining any group that would have him as a member is one with problems. On the other hand, Rogers's refusal to join the group indicates that he is not willing to compromise his integrity by joining the group. This statement reflects how our acceptance of ourselves influences our acceptance of the group.

Generally, we tend to become more engaged with others when we feel closer to them. Our acceptance by others is directly related to how close or intimate we feel with those people. As Berg and Smith (1987) observe, the more we feel accepted by a group, the more likely we will divulge our thoughts, feelings, and views to others in the group. To be a part of the group and to feel comfortable enough to participate, we must first be accepted by the other group members. The *paradox of intimacy* is as follows: To accept ourselves and feel comfortable within a group, we must accept others. But to accept others within the group, we must first accept ourselves. Therefore, the acceptance of self depends on the acceptance of others and vice versa.

Regression. A common issue in organizations is whether the company is too dependent on its past. Disputes center on whether organizations need to make dramatic shifts in their direction and pursue new innovations. When leaders attempt to manage the balance between an organization's past history and future direction, they are encountering the *paradox of regression:* In order to function in the present and project the future, one must use past experiences; however, past experiences are simultaneously viewed through the lens of the present. For example, in the early 1980s Federal Express attempted to market Zap mail, which was designed to allow consumers to send mail immediately via fax machines (Conger, 1989). Its strongest supporter, Fred Smith, compared the obstacles confronting Zap mail to those faced by Federal Express when it pioneered overnight mail. To understand the current situation and place it into a meaningful context, Smith used previous experiences to interpret current events. Unfortunately, however, the past events did not apply to Zap mail, as it failed after a three-year effort.

In particular, leaders may encounter the paradox of regression in decision-making situations. Successful group and organizational decision making depends on a thorough analysis of available information. A rational approach to making decisions involves grappling with the information in order to arrive at a solid understanding of the problem. Failing to understand and assess a problem accurately generates a faulty basis from which no meaningful action can be planned. The strategies and techniques for analyzing information are often formulated on the basis of successful experiences from the past. However, using heuristics and analogies to guide decision making may result in too much reliance on past events for managing current ones.

Leaders may face problems with the paradox of regression when they hear comments that reflect the tension between the present and the past; for example, "In previous groups we . . . ," "In the past, our group has . . . ," and "The history of this problem. . . . " At times, leaders may need to persuade the group to rely less on past history. At other times, leaders may need to emphasize past experiences to ensure continuity between present and past actions. Leaders should help employees balance the importance of the past with the potential for the future.

The challenge for leaders: managing the paradoxes of engaging. Human relations approaches to organizations commonly stress the need to cultivate open personal relationships among workers. Recent approaches to teamwork emphasize maintaining the free flow of information among employees to solve work-related problems (Blake & Mouton, 1987; Larson & LaFasto, 1989). As leaders try to coordinate the actions of others, they facilitate the flow of information. Issues related to the paradoxes of self-disclosure, trust, intimacy, and regression all influence a leader's ability to get the group to share information. Leaders attempt to help workers engage in dialog and provide personal information, rather than holding back information and opinions because of possible rejection.

The key to managing the paradoxes of engaging involves eliminating the threat to the self-esteem and integrity of the person disclosing the information. But is the disclosure of personal information needed for effective work performance? On one level, it is needed. As employees learn more about each other, such as how they manage tasks, their uncertainty decreases and they become more open with each other. At the same time, personal information is not needed to coordinate actions. Eric Eisenberg (1990) refers to "jamming," or the coordination of action without the coordination of beliefs. Based on a jazz metaphor, the notion of jamming conveys the image of musicians from diverse backgrounds, and unknown to each other, working together to create and play a musical piece. In organizations, work groups and teams can "jam" in a similar way—by doing their work well even though they lack personal information about each other. However, jamming is dependent on the skills of the participants. Musicians often spend much time on finding the right combination of people to create the band and the sound they want. Moreover, when musicians jam, they are able to anticipate one another's moves even though they do not know one another personally. Leaders may be able to transcend the paradoxes of engaging through jamming. However, to do so, they need to enhance the knowledge, skills, and abilities of the participants. (See Box 8.3.)

Paradoxes of Speaking

All companies create their own organizing system; it helps them understand the obstacles they face and plan actions needed to remove the obstacles. Creating an organizing system requires that individuals exert enough influence within the organization to create a system that meets the demands of the environment. *Paradoxes of speaking* are associated with influence in organizations. They focus on the degrees to which opinions are voiced, changes are advocated, and actions are taken independently in an organization. Since individuals and organizations have a mutual influence relationship, either may influence the other. According to Smith and Berg (1987), the paradoxes of speaking include (1) the paradox of authority, (2) the paradox of control, (3) the paradox of courage and (4) the paradox of creativity (see Table 8.1).

Authority. The collective action of a group is characterized by tension as the centralized power of one group member is spread to the other group members. Traditionally, leaders and managers thought that by giving away power they would decrease their influence in a group or organization. More recently, however, many theorists suggest that the opposite is true (Peters, 1987; Smith & Berg, 1987). The *paradox of authority* states that by giving away power, leaders

Box 8.3
The Case of the Nervous Salespeople

You are the head of the marketing division for Packaging, Inc., which manufactures custom machines for packaging a variety of food and medical products. The company sells a series of machines that package such food products as hot dogs, potato chips, and other snack foods. It also has a line of machines that packages disposable medical supplies, such as syringes and needles. Salespeople make calls to different companies in order to sell the machines. They are expected to sell only twelve machines a year because they are quite expensive. Even so, the market is tight, and the salespeople have to work hard to meet the quota.

Recently, you promoted Kathy Lancer to the position of director of sales for the Northwest region. Kathy was a salesperson in the southern region before recently relocating to Seattle. She is a top-notch salesperson with a reputation for being straightforward and honest. She doesn't hold back her viewpoints and actively solicits others' views when solving problems. You just received the following letter from Kathy in the mail:

Dear _____________,

I just wanted to drop you a line and thank you for the promotion. I feel like I'm adjusting pretty well to the new region and am getting to know the salespeople fairly well. I've just held my first monthly sales meeting for the Northwest region. Overall, as you know, we are having difficulty reaching our quota, so I focused the agenda on what we could do to increase our sales. It was not a particularly good meeting and I'm at a loss at what to do. I'm writing this letter because I'm frustrated with my salespeople. Since I'm new at this, I thought you might give me some advice.

At the meeting, I initially asked the salespeople to describe the problems they face as a group in meeting the regional goals. I then asked them to convey the personal problems or challenges they face while on the road. I got no response at all; they just sat there and stared at me. I then asked them what we could do differently to increase sales. They all began talking at once about the sales campaigns and pricing schemes that worked well a couple of years ago. The ideas seem reasonable, but I just don't know if they will work in the current economic climate. When I mentioned some of the techniques I had used successfully in the southern region to boost sales, they again said nothing.

I wouldn't have written this letter if I hadn't overheard a conversation between two salespeople as they were leaving the meeting. The gist of the conversation was this: They were nervous about the meeting, choosing to sit back and listen to what I had to say. They were also uncomfortable about my questioning of their individual job performance. Finally, they didn't understand why I was reluctant about recycling some of the old sales strategies that were used previously.

This is not the way I want my meetings to continue. Since I'm new at my job, I'm hoping you can help me identify the problems and how to overcome them. I want to do a good job, but I'm not sure how to go about it. I look forward to your reply.

Cordially,

Kathy Lancer

Kathy Lancer

ASSIGNMENT

Write a letter responding to Kathy's request. Describe what you perceive as the problems and offer suggestions managing them.

can actually increase their power over a group. Employees who are actively involved in the decision-making process are more likely to be controlled by leaders in positive ways. Leaders establish a vision for the organization and set the kinds of assumptions and values that employees should use when making decisions, thereby enhancing their power and control.

The paradox of authority is manifested when leaders convey messages that simultaneously signal the desire to share power and demonstrate the need for control. Leaders are caught in the contradiction of the paradox of authority when they make such comments as, "You are running the show, however . . . ," "You make the decision, but clear it with . . . ," and "That's an interesting idea, but be careful. . . . " Chris Argyris (1988) suggests that such messages contain the mixed message of "We want you to have heightened control, but we really don't" (p. 258). Leaders may contribute to the paradox by producing mixed messages. Similarly, when employees make a comment like "I have control over this so long as I do what my boss wants," the underlying cause may be the paradox of authority.

Control. The *paradox of control* involves independence versus dependence: To act independently from a group, one must simultaneously be dependent on the group. The act of being independent means one moves away from patterns of dependency created earlier. For example, consider the rebellious teenager in the infamous "independence" stage. Becoming independent as a teenager means several things. Teenagers no longer want to be driven by their parents to school events; they want to drive themselves. They no longer want to spend time around the family; they want to be with their friends. They no longer want to talk to their family members because they "just don't understand." All of these acts of independence are premised on an earlier dependence on the family. A teenager cannot become independent unless a system of interdependency already exists within the family. Smith and Berg (1987) state that to be "independent but not connected is nothing more than isolation. To be dependent with no sense of autonomy is . . . enslavement (pp. 142–143).

As leaders attempt to manage levels of dependence and independence among workers, they seek to avoid the negative consequences of either extreme. The tensions associated with being dependent on a group and still desiring independence are manifested in several ways. Leaders need to be aware of the pathologies present in the following messages and to consider their implications for understanding dependence and independence:

1. "I can do whatever I want. I don't need the group." This extreme statement of independence can lead to isolation because the individual is not connected to the group in any meaningful way. Such a position can pose problems when people who desire independence find themselves needing resources that can only be provided by the group.
2. "Can I really depend on the group? I'm not sure that I agree with what the members are doing." At some point in your experience with a group, one or more of its members may do something that is disagreeable to you. While you may be dependent on the group to do something you would not be able to do alone, the group's act of doing things that contradict your personal beliefs heightens the tension between independence and dependence. Do you voice your independent views and risk hurting the group, or do you sit quietly and begin to view the group as undependable?
3. "I know I've acted this way before, but I completely changed my mind." Exhibiting independent behaviors and ways of thinking can upset the stability of the group. Dependency is based on predictable ways of acting. People are predictable if they act in similar ways in the same situation. Acting differently can cause turmoil in the group. The independent actions thereby undermine the dependency relationships within the group.

Leaders face a difficult challenge in managing the dependence versus independence issue of the paradox of control. They must be able to create a sense of interdependence among group members in order for collective action to take place. At the same time, leaders must find ways to foster independence so that new ideas and views can be generated.

Courage. To face the increasing complexity of the work environment, leaders and employees need to exhibit courage. When we think of courageous people, we typically conjure up an image of the confident, self-assured, dynamic, and successful person. Courageous people take chances in the face of difficult odds, and yet they usually succeed. They just seem to "know" when something will or will not work. This image of courageous people may lead us to equate courage with confidence and certainty. However, certainty versus uncertainty characterizes the *paradox of courage:* Courage can only be demonstrated in the face of severe doubt, despair, and uncertainty; but one can only act courageously when there is uncertainty about what one's actions will bring. To act courageously, then, one must also feel a lack of courage.

Exercising courage requires that leaders and employees confront many problems and challenges in working with a group. It is easy to adopt a negative attitude toward working with the group. Yet, it is only in the context of this despair that people are able to manifest courage. Courage involves taking a risk despite the likelihood of failure. When a leader or an employee says, "I'm not sure this will work, but we need to take a stand on this issue," the comment reflects the paradox of courage. The person wants to take a stand even though there is no certainty of success.

Creativity. When people create new ideas, products, and structures, they alter old ways of thinking, transform raw materials, and replace existing hierarchies. As noted earlier in this chapter (see page 209), the paradox of creativity means that change destroys the status quo.

The challenge for leaders: managing the paradoxes of speaking. Leaders are caught between the dilemma of trying to maintain their authority with the group and relinquishing some control. The paradoxes of speaking focus on who has influence within an organization. One strategy for managing the paradoxes of speaking is empowerment. By empowering employees, leaders may increase their own power. Empowerment means sharing with employees the responsibilities and decision making of the organization (see Chapter 6). When empowering employees, leaders provide a general sense of the goals of and aspirations of the company. These decision-premises simultaneously constrain the kinds of decisions employees make and allow them some latitude in selecting or determining decision areas.

Empowerment may also occur through visions. Leaders may manage paradox by articulating a vision, giving employees a general sense of direction and allowing them to retain their individuality in reaching goals. Visions allow people to be both dependent on the organization (in their commitment to the vision) and independent (in the way they pursue a goal). In addition, visions involve courage because there is no guarantee that they will succeed.

Paradoxes of Risk Taking

The typology of paradoxes offered by Smith and Berg (1987) evolves around the themes of belonging, engaging, and speaking. Another set of paradoxes of organizing focuses on taking risks. As mentioned throughout the text, the primary task of any organization is to manage the information inputs from its environment. This entails interpreting information (and breaking it down into an interpretable form), and analyzing information in order to make decisions about further action. *Paradoxes of risk taking* involve the problems that groups and organizations face when they attempt to break away from old patterns of behavior and try new ways of adapting to the information environment. There are two paradoxes of risk taking: (1) the paradox of competence and (2) the paradox of success (see Table 8.2).

Competence. As systems for analyzing information are developed, people typically develop routines that help them make sense of incoming information and make decisions based on that information. For example, the decision-making schemes of the devil's advocate procedure and dialectical inquiry (highlighted in Chapter 4) may be routinely used by organizations to analyze problems. Although it may seem to make sense that groups would be more competent when they follow a set of structured procedures, routines may actually decrease their competence. As Irving Janis (1989) points out, when groups develop a high consensus on ways of analyzing problems, the procedures may cause the groups to overlook key aspects of information. Using a different line of analysis, Chris Argyris (1986) argues that routines may actually lead to skilled incompetence. In this perspective, individuals and groups may develop procedures that actually disguise a person's true intent or meaning in order to avoid embarrassment or threat. Argyris calls those routines "defensive routines" because they protect people from situations that might expose them to threats or embarrassment. Such routines prevent groups from fully analyzing information and from growing and learning. It is termed "skilled incompetence" because individuals become highly skilled at masking their true opinions and feelings. For example, how do you react when someone says something that you don't appreciate? You might find it inappropriate so say anything in return. Or, you may have a stock phrase or comment that you use in such situations. This is a defensive routine because you avoid the embarrassing event of contradicting someone's attitude.

A good example of skilled incompetence is provided by Jerry B. Harvey (1988) in a story of when he and his wife visited her parent's home in Coleman, Texas. While they were spending a Sunday afternoon relaxing and playing dominoes, Harvey's father-in-law suggested that they go out for dinner in Abilene, which is about 53 miles from Coleman. Although Harvey thought that driving to Abilene in 100-degree-plus temperatures in a car without air conditioning was a little odd, he said nothing. Since everybody else appeared to want to go, he agreed, though he insisted that his mother-in-law express her desire to go and she did. They got into an old 1958 Buick and set off for Abilene. According to Harvey, the trip was miserable and the dinner unenjoyable. After returning home, they discovered that no one had wanted to go. Harvey's father-in-law had proposed the trip because he thought his daughter and son-in-law would be bored by sitting around the house. Harvey and his wife had agreed because they didn't want to go against the wishes of the entire group. Harvey's mother-in-law had agreed because she felt pressured by everyone else. The question quickly emerged as to how everyone ended up going to Abilene if no one wanted to go in the first place. Harvey termed this phenomenon as the "Abilene paradox."

The Abilene paradox is actually a defensive routine. From an early age, we are taught the importance of understanding and agreeing with one another. We are also taught that disagreements are negative and that we should avoid them at all costs. In this example, all parties involved developed strategies for disguising their true feelings and were skilled at performing them. While each person decided privately against taking the trip, in interaction they failed to communicate their true desires in order to avoid offending one another. As a result, defensive routines caused the group to make a decision based on faulty information.

The *paradox of competence* is as follows: To be competent in an analysis of information, one must also be incompetent. When people become too comfortable with routines, they tend to overlook important information or to be reluctant to voice contrasting opinions because they fear hurting someone's feelings. Routines and procedures can help people analyze information and make decisions, but they can also hinder these processes when they lead to poor information management. This is why it is important for members of groups to ask varied questions.

Success. According to Tom Peters (1987), organizations cannot successfully adapt their systems of organizing to meet the challenges of their information environment if they do not foster innovation and creativity. However, to increase their success rate at constructing new products and management innovations, organizations must simultaneously increase their failure rate. This is the *paradox of success.* It is only in an environment that facilitates the creativity of its employees that significant breakthroughs can occur. Students, for example, often find themselves caught in the midst of the paradox of success. When instructors give writing assignments, they tell the student to be creative, but if the student's writing differs too much from the instructor's expectations, the student may receive a poor grade. In this paradox of success, students are encouraged to take risks but are punished for risk taking. Similarly, leaders may encourage employees to take risks and penalize them when they fail.

An organization may be caught in the paradox of success when the underlying logic of leaders' messages are guided by the following rules:

1. Leaders openly proclaim their support for risk taking within the organization and encourage others to take risks.
2. Leaders qualify their support for "unbridled" risk taking, which occurs in two primary ways.
   a. Leaders proclaim their view that risk taking is important for the organization but they also qualify their support by conveying the importance of being careful and thoughtful with regard to the kinds of risks taken.
   b. After leaders support of risk taking is made clear, they later penalize people for taking failed risks.

Using the logic just described, what messages from your work experience parallel this logic? Are they similar to any of the following messages?

Leader's initial comments. "Herb, I want to stress to you that I will support you in any action you take. We can't grow as an organization unless we take risks. At the same time, we need to be careful about the kinds of risks we take. Let's make sure the risks we take have a good chance of success."

Leader's comments several months later. "I want to encourage you Herb to take on new projects and to think of new ways to help the organization."

An employee's comments, two months later. "Did you hear about Herb? He got started on that new project, but it didn't quite work out. His boss has now stuck him with a 'make work' project."

If you are familiar with these kinds of messages, you may have encountered the paradox of success.

The challenge for leaders: managing the paradoxes of risk taking. The underlying theme of the paradoxes of risk taking is the need for order. People develop routines for managing behaviors because they prefer stability and order. They may not want to experiment with new behaviors or take risks because they are uncertain about outcomes. However, by maintaining the status quo, people may disadvantage themselves in preparing for the future. In fact, a genuine act of leadership may be fixing something when it is not broken (Nanus, 1992; Conger, 1989). Having the foresight to prepare for the future may prevent decreases in performance later on.

Leaders can help manage the challenges of risk taking. At one level, simple awareness of the paradox provides some insight into its management. However, leaders may also need to introduce uncertainty into their daily routines. Karl Weick (1979) advocates that people should doubt what they know to be true and accept what they know to be false. By introducing skepticism into the daily routine and second-guessing, one can avoid being skilled at incompetence. Another strategy for managing the paradox of risk taking involves engaging in orderly assessments of the risks associated with proposed actions. If an organization is to succeed, it must fail. But because failure may lead to the disintegration of the company, this risk is especially important to assess. Although leaders need to be willing to take risks, they also need to be aware of the kinds of risks that may endanger the well-being of the company.

MANAGING PARADOX

As groups and organizations develop, they encounter a variety of obstacles within the information environment. Paradoxical tensions, such as those described in this chapter, are among the most difficult obstacles in group and organizational life. Leaders must recognize that paradoxes are an ongoing part of organizational history and that successfully navigating the organization through them will indicate a leader's effectiveness. To assist groups in managing the tensions created by paradox, leaders must be skilled at creating a sense of awareness among group members of the problems, challenges, and opportunities presented by paradox. As Smith and Berg put it:

> The role of leader in a group is one that facilitates the exploration of the full range of paradoxical tensions that arise. . . . The leadership role must seek to understand the relationship or link between seemingly opposite positions and to use this understanding to suggest actions that examine the patterns of stuckness that groups develop. (1987, p. 222)

Four communication strategies can be used by leaders to help groups become aware of and manage paradox: (1) explaining, (2) reframing, (3) escalating, and (4) redirecting.

Groups are better able to manage the tensions associated with paradox when they are aware of its existence (Peters, 1987; Smith & Berg, 1987). For many people, the concept of paradox is unfamiliar. The group experience is not generally viewed as consisting of paradoxes and contradictions. One communication strategy that may help organizational members handle paradox is *explaining.* Leaders can help group members become aware of the paradox they are facing by defining the problem in terms of the paradox. People cannot deal successfully with a problem unless they are aware of it. When the paradoxical nature of the situation is explained, people are better able to handle the problem. The conflicting and opposing elements within the paradox must be identified and their relationship to each other defined. Leadership can help group members understand that paradox is an inherent element of group life that can be used to unleash their potential. At the same time, leaders should avoid minimizing the negative consequences of paradox. It is not uncommon for groups, once aware of paradox, to attempt to eliminate the contradictions. Part of competent leadership involves explaining to the group that paradox cannot be removed.

Paradoxes emerge because the framework people use to make sense of a situation leads them to contradictory ideas and opposite conclusions. One solution for dealing with this aspect of paradox is *reframing* or casting the paradox into a different framework (Bogadan, 1982; Fisher, Anderson, & Jones, 1981). Reframing a paradox involves searching for a common denominator between the two conflicting elements and then viewing those elements not in terms of "either/or" but "both/and." Consider the paradox of boundary, in which groups may divide themselves into smaller groups, which causes them to distinguish between appropriate and inappropriate behaviors given their roles. A good example of this is the labor-management boundary present within organizations. It can be detrimental to the larger organization if each group refuses to cooperate with the other. While it is useful to define oneself in terms of the group, boundaries may inhibit the collective action of labor and management. Effective leadership may try to reframe the split between labor and management through a baseball team metaphor, for instance. Teams have individual players who try to maximize their individual talents and abilities. Yet, to play the actual ballgame, the players must coordinate their individual talents for the greater good of the team. They then become team players. Similarly, labor and management represent two important "players" in the organization; they must work together as a team for the organization to achieve its goals.

Leadership may find it necessary to escalate a paradoxical situation in order to get the group to take responsibility for managing it. In therapeutic situations *escalating* means to aggravate a particular symptom that the patient perceives as beyond his or her control. By escalating the symptom of the problem, it is anticipated that the patient will tire of the symptom and will stop performing it. Further, the problem confronted by the patient will dissipate because he or she is now unconsciously aware that the problem can be controlled (Fisher, Anderson, & Jones, 1981). Similarly, leadership can use escalation as a means of dealing with the symptoms of paradox within a group. For example, a work team may complain about the level of dependence that the various team members have on one another. They may feel that they cannot act independently because they need the approval of other group members. A leader may escalate the situation by proclaiming that "all decisions must be made at meetings of the entire group." By requiring formal team meetings to make all decisions, eventually the team members will tire of this process and begin to act independently in order to avoid the team meeting. Escalation allows the team members to take control of the degrees of dependence and independence they desire from the group.

Redirecting calls for the group or individual to perform the undesired behavior at particular times. Unlike escalation, which requires group members to perform much undesirable behavior, redirection only asks group members to exhibit the behaviors under specified conditions (Fisher, Anderson, & Jones, 1981). Escalation and redirection are similar in the sense that they both bring the undesirable behavior that the group wants to eliminate under its voluntary control. Consider, for example, a group that is stuck in the paradox of regression. The leader discovers that group members seem to want to focus on past successes during group meetings. They also lament that they do not seem to have a future, yearning to return to the "good old days." Using redirection, the leader can ask the group to reserve talk about the past for the last ten minutes of the meetings and to avoid it at all other times. Here the leader is facilitating group members' recognition that regressing to the past is acceptable, but only for limited times. In addition, by redirecting the group's focus to the present, the leader encourages members to concentrate on current activities and problems.

The four techniques for managing paradox discussed here—explaining, reframing, escalating, and redirecting—are aimed at helping groups and workers recognize the paradox present in a situation. The techniques are not intended to avoid or eliminate paradox. Rather, groups need to be aware of paradox so that they can exercise control over competing demands.

SUMMARY

Effective leadership involves managing the contradictions inherent within group and organizational life. The paradoxes that exist within groups pit conflicting ideas and viewpoints against one another. Leaders must manage four broad classes of paradox: (1) paradoxes of belonging, (2) paradoxes of engaging, (3) paradoxes of speaking, and (4) paradoxes of risk taking. Balancing the competing demands associated with belonging to and participating in a group is another challenge that leaders must help groups manage. Leadership may employ communication strategies, such as explaining, reframing, escalating, and redirecting, to manage paradox.

However, is it appropriate for a leader to make the group aware of the potential paradoxes it may face? Will this help the group be more effective? Or will it disrupt the group? These questions are related to the appropriateness and effectiveness of leaders' communication. Standards of communication competence are our focus in Chapter 9.

QUESTIONS AND APPLICATIONS

1. For a group or organization of which you were once a member, list the kinds of obstacles and problems you encountered. Then, referring to the paradoxes discussed in this chapter, explain why each problem occurred.

2. You have been placed in charge of the employee orientation program for new faculty at a university. You've been asked to develop a program that will orient and socialize new faculty members into the university. What kind of program would you develop that balances the need to socialize faculty members into the university and the need to foster creativity?

3. To avoid unpleasant situations, we all develop stock phrases or methods for making the other person feel defensive or for relieving the tension in situations. For example, rather than directly telling someone that he or she performed poorly, we might suggest some changes in performance. This is called skilled incompetence. Make a list of the situations in which you tend to use stock routines or phrases in these ways.

4. During a recent meeting, you noted that several employees do not want to take risks. You tried explaining to them that the only way to guarantee success is to fail sometimes, but they did not accept your explanation. How can you use the strategies of reframing, redirecting, and escalating to manage the paradox?

Chapter 9
Competent Leadership Communication

> In this highly materialistic nation, the prevailing ethic is at best, pragmatic, and at worst, downright dishonest. It's every man for himself, and never mind God, country or anything else. There seems to be no such thing as the common good or the public interest. Only self-interest. That old entrepreneurial spirit . . . is running amuck and the country is coming unstuck. . . .
>
> It is time, then, to face this ethical deficit or America will end in shambles. Ethics and conscience aren't optional. They are the glue that binds society together—the quality in us that separates us from cannibals. Without conscience and ethics, talent and power amount to nothing.
>
> *(Bennis, 1993, p. 163)*

Most professions have a code of ethics or a set of standards that defines appropriate conduct. In the medical community, for example, the Hippocratic Oath sets the standards that physicians are expected to follow when treating patients. Similarly, the Model Rules of Professional Conduct structured by the American Bar Association define the standards for attorneys' behavior, and the American Institute of CPA's (AICPA) Code of Professional Ethics is geared toward accountants' behavior (Backof & Martin, 1991). The business community also sets it own expectations for appropriate conduct, through such organizations as the Better Business Bureau and Federal Trade Commission. Codes of ethics are structured not only to meet minimal legal standards but also to set higher standards of appropriate conduct for individuals and organizations. Professional organizations structure their own standards for appropriate conduct by examining ethical standards, professional codes of conduct, and legal requirements.

There is no one set of principles that defines appropriate leadership communication. Although certain laws, such as the American Disabilities Act and the Civil Rights Act, constrain much of what leaders can say to employees, no clear set of principles is consistently employed to assess the appropriate nature of leadership communication. Moreover, identifying a single set of principles is difficult because the line between appropriate and inappropriate leadership practices is grey due to situational circumstances. As Bernard Bass (1990b) points out, flagrant acts such as lying, cheating, and stealing are easily identified as inappropriate. However, "telling white lies," cutting corners on standards, or using company property for personal gain may be viewed as appropriate or inappropriate under different circumstances.

This book has identified the types of skills that leaders need to possess and perform in order to help organize the collective activity of people. As leaders communicate, others assess the competence of their communication. In this closing chapter we explore the standards that people employ to judge the competence of leadership communication. Our premise is as follows: Competent leadership communication may be evaluated by two criteria: its appropriateness and its effectiveness. Therefore, this chapter explores the relationship between leadership and communication competence, identifies standards of communication appropriateness, and isolates criteria for communication effectiveness.

THE RELATIONSHIP OF COMMUNICATION COMPETENCE AND LEADERSHIP

Leadership competence is defined in a variety of ways, ranging from the possession of cognitive abilities needed to complete a task (Fiedler & Garcia, 1987) to the degree of personal drive or motivation possessed (Boyatzis, 1982). Similarly, various definitions are offered for *communication competence.* Competent communicators within organizations are skilled at the encoding and decoding of messages (Monge, Bachman, Dillard, & Eisenberg, 1982), appropriately follow existing organizational rules and norms, (Wellmon, 1989), and successfully coordinate actions to achieve desired goals (Barge, Downs, & Johnson, 1989). However, definitions of what constitutes *competent leadership communication* are less clear. To define competent leadership communication clearly, we must first examine the general area of communication competence.

Although communication competence is a widely researched topic, there is no consensus on what constitutes competent communication. According to Gerry Phillips (1984), defining communication competence is like "trying to climb a greased pole" (p. 24). Despite widely differing opinions regarding communication competence, Brian Spitzberg (1983) identifies three basic positions that are used to define communication competence—as knowledge, performance, and impression.

Competence as Knowledge

James McCroskey (1982) argues that communication competence can be defined as a base of *knowledge* that individuals use to structure their communicative actions. Individuals are viewed as competent communicators if they possess the relevant knowledge, skills, and abilities to perform a particular task. Competence is defined as "the ability of an individual to demonstrate knowledge of" the behavior that is dictated by a given situation (McCroskey, 1982, p. 5). For example, a leader of a work team would be viewed as competent if he or she possessed the necessary skills to structure work team meetings and discussions. Competence is an inherently psychological construct, not a behavioral one. Leaders do not need to perform a particular behavior in order to be viewed as competent, because they could have performed the behavior but opted not to demonstrate their knowledge. The performance of a communicative behavior is not viewed as either a necessary or sufficient condition for the presence of competence.

Consider, for instance, the knowledge, skills, and abilities associated with forging leader-member relationships. According to leader-member exchange theory (see Chapter 2), leaders may create close, personal, in-group relationships with employees. A knowledge-based perspective of communication competence holds that leaders who possess appropriate relational skills (such as self-disclosure) for building in-group relationships are competent. If a leader chooses not to build an in-group relationship with an employee, the leader will not manifest the relevant knowledge through behavior. This does not mean the leader is incompetent because the leader could display the skills if desired. Therefore, behavioral performance of a skill is not required for an individual to be classified as a competent communicator.

Competence as Performance

Another view of communication competence focuses on *performance.* It maintains that competent individuals perform situationally appropriate behavior. The underlying assumption is that particular behaviors can be identified as either competent or incompetent. Using the preceding example, leaders are viewed as competent at building relationships when they perform behaviors aimed at building in-group relationships. The performance of behaviors that function to praise employee productivity and effort or that offer encouragement indicate that the communication is competent because it is aimed at building relationships. In this viewpoint, leaders are competent communicators when they perform a behavior that is considered an indicator of competent behavior—that is, one intended to build relationships. However, a leader is viewed as competent only if he or she overtly performs the appropriate behavior. Knowledge of the appropriate behavior without its performance does not constitute competent communication. The assessment of competence must be grounded in the interaction of the participants, not in their level of knowledge about or their motivation to participate in a situation. From a behavioral perspective, it cannot be assumed that a leader can perform the behavior even if the leader is highly motivated. This is why performance becomes a critical component of assessing communicative competence.

Competence as Impression

Finally, communication competence is viewed as an *impression.* Viewing competence as an impression represents a significant departure from viewing competence as either knowledge or behavior.

According to Brian Spitzberg and William Cupach (1989), competence is not grounded in the behavior or knowledge of the interactants. Although these are important components in the assessment of an individual's competence, the key to competence is rooted in the perceptions of the participants within the relational context they have constructed. Labeled as the *relational approach* to competence, it is based on the following assumptions (Spitzberg, 1983, pp. 324–326):

1. *Competence is situationally based.* What may be viewed as competent communication within one situation may be viewed as incompetent in another.
2. *Competence is evaluated by the standards of appropriateness and effectiveness.* Both standards are highly interrelated and necessary for evaluating competence. Intuitively, it makes sense that behavior that is both appropriate and effective would be viewed as competent. Behavior that is appropriate but ineffective may be viewed as polite and does not allow individuals to achieve personal and organizational goals. Behavior that is effective but inappropriate may be negatively sanctioned and ultimately lead to lowered effectiveness. Achieving personal or organizational goals in an appropriate manner is considered competent communication.
3. *Competence ranges along a continuum of appropriateness and effectiveness and is not an "either/or" phenomenon.* Given the complexity of situations, individuals, and organizations, it is difficult to classify a behavior or a sequence of behaviors as either competent or incompetent behavior. The inherent complexity of human interaction suggests that it is difficult to know before a situation exactly what set of behaviors will be competent or incompetent. Rather, it is more realistic and pragmatic to recognize that behaviors may be "more or less" competent depending on the idiosyncratic nature of the situation.
4. *Competent communication is functional.* The purpose of communication is to achieve some purpose or goal. Given the functional nature of communication, the standards of effectiveness and appropriateness take on added importance. Functional behavior must be effective (achieves the goal) and appropriate (acceptable according to the relationship).
5. *Communication competence is an impression formed by others.* Competence does not reside in the behavior performed by others; rather, it lies in the evaluation of that behavior by other people. Competence is an attribution people make based on the standards of appropriateness and effectiveness.

Communication competence is an attribution made by observers. As Spitzberg and Hecht (1984) note, perceptions of competence may be summed up in the following formula:

$$\text{Competence} = F\,(\text{motivation} \times \text{knowledge} \times \text{skill level})$$

Communication competence is a function of the motivation, knowledge, and skill of the participants. It cannot be reduced to any one of these individual com-

Box 9.1
Perceiving Communication Competence on a Situational Basis

When communication competence is viewed as an impression, the perceptions of competence are embedded in the situation. Given different people, work situations, and organizations, the same message may be viewed as competent in one context but as incompetent in another. Following are some messages with negative connotations that a leader within an organization might use. For each message, think of a situation in which it would be viewed as competent and another situation in which it would be viewed as incompetent.

lying
withholding relevant information from decision makers
giving ambiguous instructions
publicly opposing someone with higher power status
praising someone for poor performance
advising someone to cut corners when doing a job
refusing to apologize for mistakes
supporting ideas that are known to be false
provoking heated discussions
spreading gossip
maneuvering around a superior for personal gain
supporting the company line even though it is ineffective
dealing with company members in selfish ways

ASSIGNMENT 1

Describe the kinds of communication behavior that you view as inappropriate and ineffective in all contexts.

ASSIGNMENT 2

What key situational factors strongly influence perceptions of communication appropriateness and effectiveness? Explain your choices.

ponents. Rather, it is a complex phenomenon that involves all three components simultaneously. As a result, effective leaders must be simultaneously motivated, knowledgeable, and skilled. For example, if a leader is knowledgeable about managing conflict between workers, is skilled at manifesting behaviors that promote a win-win solution, but is not motivated to perform the behaviors, the leader is likely to be viewed as an incompetent communicator. Similarly, if a leader is highly motivated to establish a close personal relationship with an employee but lacks the requisite knowledge and skill to do so, the leader's efforts may be viewed as incompetent communication. The complexity of competence, like leadership, cannot be reduced. (See Box 9.1).

Spitzberg (1983) takes issue with the preceding views based on knowledge and performance. He questions judging someone as competent without examining whether the person *knows* what is competent, *wants* to do what is competent, and *performs* in a competent manner. If individuals are competent, they must have first successfully fulfilled each of these requirements. Knowing how to do something is different than being able to do it. Similarly, it is possible to perform a set of appropriate behaviors without knowing how to do so. For example, in the novel and movie *Being There,* written by Jerzy Kosinski, Chauncey Gardner is a simple man who loves gardening and watching television. He genuinely does not understand how the world operates and mimics phrases and lines from television shows. Through an accident, he befriends a wealthy industrialist, Ben Rand. During a meeting with the president of the United States, Ben and Chauncey are asked their opinions on whether short-term incentives should be used to stimulate a weakened economy:

President:	Mr. Gardner . . . do you think we can stimulate growth through temporary incentives?
Gardner:	As long as the roots are not severed, all is well. And all will be well in the garden.
President:	In the garden?
Gardner:	Yes (*pause*). In the garden, growth has its season. First comes spring and summer. But then we have fall and winter. And then we hit spring and summer again.
President:	Spring and summer?
Gardner:	Yes.
President:	(*Clearing his voice*) Fall and winter?
Gardner:	Yes.
Rand:	I think what our insightful young friend is saying is that we welcome the inevitable seasons of nature. But we're upset by the seasons of our economy.
Gardner:	Yes. There will be growth in the spring.
President:	Hmmm. . . . Well, Mr. Gardner, I must admit, that is one of the most refreshing and optimistic statements I've heard in a very long time. (*Being There,* 1980)

In this movie dialog, Chauncey (played by Peter Sellers) does not understand the nature of economic incentives and is relaying information about gardening. The others interpret his comments as a metaphor and attribute great insight to them. From Spitzberg's (1983) perspective, Chauncey is not a competent communicator because he doesn't know what he's doing.

Spitzberg (1983) also questions viewing competence as knowledge or performance because of the difficulty in establishing consistent evaluative criteria for competent behavior. For example, the phrase "I really love your work" appears at face value to be a competent behavior aimed at praising an employee's work. However, given the history of the interactants, the nature of the situation, or the organizational culture, the behavior may function instead as an insult or meaningless small talk, making it incompetent. Therefore, to specify what constitutes competent behavior, the perceptions of the interactants must be taken into account.

For leaders to be viewed as competent they must perform messages and sequences of messages that are both appropriate and effective. The standards for judging appropriate and effective behavior are rooted in the organizational culture.

CULTURE AND COMMUNICATION COMPETENCE

Many contemporary organizational theorists adopt the metaphor of *organization as culture* for analyzing organizational life (Smircich, 1983; Smircich & Calas, 1987; Deal & Kennedy, 1982; Frost, Moore, Louis, Lundberg, & Martin, 1991). The cultural perspective allows researchers to examine the stories (Brown, 1985), metaphors (Krefting & Frost, 1985), and narratives (Pacanowsky & O'Donnell-Trujillo, 1983) of organizations in order to gain insight into the ways they organize collective action. The underlying assumption of cultural researchers is that organizations are rule-using entities. Rules provide guidelines for interpreting interaction and particular events (Searle, 1969) as well as for structuring subsequent actions (Pearce & Cronen, 1980). Weick's (1979) model of organizing employs the concept of assembly rules, which help people know the type, frequency, and desirability of communication sequences that must be performed to organize a group.

The view of organizations as cultures guided by rules provides a standard for judging a leader's communication competence. Cultures are value systems that adhere to certain beliefs, attitudes, and assumptions. Therefore, *competent leadership communication* upholds and "fits into" the existing cultural value system or transcends that system by articulating an alternative value system. This view of competence is important for two reasons. First, it emphasizes the relationship between individual action and the larger social system or organization. Because individual action is embedded within the larger organizational system, it is necessary to assess an individual's communication competence in relationship to that larger system (Harris, 1979). Further, because organizations have unique value systems, an individual's communication competence must be assessed in relation to the organization of which he or she is a member. What is considered competent communication by one organization may be viewed as incompetent by another organization. Second, this definition of competence emphasizes the role of leadership in helping organizations adapt to new and changing environmental situations. If the existing culture is poorly equipped to meet the changing demands of the environment, competent leadership communication can help the organization create a new way of organizing to overcome environmental constraints. In this situation, communication that reinforces the existing culture would be viewed as incompetent.

Competence as "Fitting In"

It is human nature to want to "fit in" with a culture. Our preoccupation with the clothes we wear and the cars we drive reflects our tendencies to compare ourselves to others and to try to meet the expectations of the social groups to which we belong. Similarly, a leader attempts to "fit into" the existing cultural system of the organization by performing actions that are acceptable, appropriate, and effective for particular contexts. This view of competence as *"fitting in"* emphasizes the *normative influence* of rules. As organizations develop strong cultures (Deal & Kennedy, 1982), they develop a fixed set of rules that organizational members are expected to follow. These rules are normative in nature in that they specify what organizational members should and should not do. Violating normative rules may be negatively sanctioned. By violating rules, organizational members may be viewed as challenging accepted time-honored traditions and, as a result, raise the level of uncertainty within the organization about what constitutes acceptable behavior. When people are uncertain about their social situation, they tend to view other people in that situation less positively (Sunnafrank, 1986).

The importance of leaders fitting in can be seen in a variety of organizations, including bureaucratic organizations. With their emphasis on formal written rules and well-defined organizational roles, bureaucracies are highly structured organizations. Individuals occupying roles in the bureaucratic organization are governed by rules that dictate who they may talk to, what they may talk about, and the appropriate manner for initiating contact with others. These rules are important in a bureaucratic organization because they allow it to maintain control over its employees (Tompkins & Cheney, 1985). Violating organizational rules is a serious offense. Whistle blowing, for example, occurs when an organizational member reveals an unethical organizational practice to outsiders. Whistleblowers are usually negatively sanctioned or punished by organizational members for violating the cultural norm of remaining silent (Glazer & Glazer, 1986). Even in a nonbureaucratic organization with a strong culture, there may be constraints placed on the kinds of relationships that leaders may form with workers, on the ways in which leaders may motivate employees, and on the methods leaders may use to make decisions. Leaders are instead expected to fit into the existing organizational culture.

Competence as Transcendence

Linda Harris (1979) argues that communication competence is more than simply fitting into an existing cultural system; it also *transcends* the cultural system by changing the rules and norms that guide collective action. *Optimal communication competence* means the individual is able to transcend or "move through" the existing system. At this level of competence, individuals are able to redefine the parameters and definitions of the existing system. For example, one key skill negotiators use to facilitate negotiation is reframing—the process of redefining what certain issues, events, or actions mean. Negotiations are viewed as a competitive game involving two parties, each motivated to maximize the advantage for its side. The nature of the existing system formed by the negotiators is competitive, and each side views the other as making choices that are rational, informed, and consistent with prior agreements. In Linda Putnam, Shirley Van Hoeven, and Connie Bullis's (1991) investigation of the bargaining between a teachers' union and a school district's negotiation team, it was found that the school district thought the teachers had reneged on a previous agreement and viewed this "breach of good faith" as a severe threat requiring forceful action. Such action could have led to a breakdown in the negotiation process. Since the relationship formed between the teachers' union and the school district assumed that each party was rational and fully informed of the importance of upholding prior agreements, such forceful action would be viewed as appropriate. The school district's chief negotiator, however, reframed the teachers' act as an unintentional one and suggested that the teachers' lack of experience in negotiation caused the apparent reversal of position. This allowed the school district to return to the negotiating table and ask for clarification of the teachers' position, rather than confronting the teachers with forceful action. It was discovered that the change had indeed been an oversight on the part of the teachers. Thus, the district's chief negotiator was able to transcend the parameters of the existing relationship (that the teachers were fully informed and experienced in negotiation) in order to articulate a new view of the relationship (that the teachers were uninformed and inexperienced in negotiation), thereby facilitating the clarification.

The importance of leadership competence is underscored by the necessity for organizations to change and adapt to the environment. Organizations need to be innovative to survive. Leaders must be able to articulate the need for change and to facilitate the introduction of new ways of organizing. This requires that leaders go beyond just "fitting into" the existing status quo of the organization.

DEFINING THE STANDARDS OF COMMUNICATION APPROPRIATENESS AND EFFECTIVENESS

Competent communication has the qualities of *appropriateness* and *effectiveness.* Judging a leader's communication competence must be done in the context of the organization of which the leader is a member. It also requires an understanding of the organization's definitions of appropriateness and effectiveness. In this section, a framework for identifying organizational standards of appropriateness and effectiveness is discussed. It is then applied to how certain cultures define competent communication.

Organizations and Appropriate Behavior

How can one determine what constitutes appropriate behavior within organizations? From a cultural viewpoint, it can be argued that standards of appropriate behavior are determined by the value system of each particular culture. Moreover, no particular set of standards is inherently superior to another. If a corporate culture values cut-throat competition, it may be considered appropriate to engage in activities that diminish the worth or value of workers. If a corporate culture instead emphasizes respect and cooperation, appropriate behaviors would build up the self-worth and esteem of workers. Although the cultural perspective sees both cultures as equally valid, most people would prefer to work for the latter company.

When determining standards of appropriateness, there is the question of whether the standards are culturally relative or universal. Anne Nicotera and Donald Cushman's (1992) analysis of organizational culture, national culture, and ethical standards provides a basis for understanding appropriate behavior. A *relativistic philosophy* toward ethics assumes that great diversity exists among cultures and that cultures are unique, self-regulating entities. Since no particular cultural system is inherently superior to another, then the standards applied to analyze an individual's ethical behavior must be based on the internal logic of the system. That is, the values adopted by a culture structure the rules for appropriate behavior, and adherence to those rules indicates ethical behavior. In direct opposition, a *monistic philosophy* assumes that organizational members and cultures share a common base—one that provides a superordinate set of standards for evaluating personal conduct. From this perspective, absolute moral standards and imperatives serve as the basis for evaluating the moral actions of individuals and organizations. For example, Froelich and Kottke (1991) propose that ethical practices within organizations can be characterized in two ways: (1) as exhibiting support for the company when it is falsifying information or engaging in unethical practices, and (2) as lying to protect the company. These two practices are monistic in nature because they assume that all types of companies, corporations, and industries view such practices as unethical.

Nicotera and Cushman (1992) argue in favor of a position in the middle of these two extreme philosophies. They call it *pluralistic philosophy.* It is a "within-organization" view of assessing ethical behavior in that it uses the organization's internal logic or value system as the primary means of isolating ethical behavior. However, organizations are embedded in a larger societal context. While the organization's value system can be used as the primary standard for evaluating ethical behavior, it "must be [used] in concert with the larger value system in which the organization exists" (Nicotera & Cushman, 1992, p. 442). The larger value system is the national culture to which the organization belongs. From the pluralistic perspective, then, ethical communication is behavior that upholds both the organizational and the national value systems.

While ethical and appropriate behavior are not synonymous, Nicotera and Cushman's (1992) analysis is useful for identifying appropriate behavior in organizations. The pluralistic view of organizational behavior has two important implications for assessing appropriate communication. First, it becomes critical to identify the *cultural value system of the nation.* Some of the kinds of communicative behaviors that are positively sanctioned within a nation are identified by John Gardner (1990), the founder of Common Cause and author of the book *Leadership.* Gardner (pp. 72–90) argues that the following qualities characterize the value system that links leaders and employees within U.S. culture:

1. *The release of human possibilities.* Human potential is great, and leaders must strive to tap into it. Moral values require that leaders facilitate the

release of human potential and foster the development of the individual's talents.

2. *Individual and group needs.* Effective leaders are able to blend the needs of the individual with the needs of the group. Individuals and groups are mutually dependent, and effective leadership recognizes the importance of balancing these two entities. It also recognizes the needs to foster individual initiative and communicate the expectation that "a certain amount of that initiative [is] to be expended on shared purposes" (Gardner, 1990, p. 75).
3. *Law, custom, and belief.* Effective leadership is aimed at maintaining the fundamental values of American society: "commitment to freedom, to justice, to equality of opportunity, to the dignity and worth of the individual, and to the sanctity of our private religious beliefs" (Gardner, 1990, p. 77). This does not mean dissent should not be tolerated; rather, dissent should be recognized as a right of human beings. At the same time, dissenters should recognize that they have the obligations to convey the moral purpose of their dissent and to pursue their objectives within the legal system.
4. *Individual initiative and responsibility.* Leadership has a responsibility to empower others by involving them in the process of obtaining organizational objectives. Moral leaders actively involve employees in making decisions and make workers accountable for their actions.

In Gardner's (1990) view, these are the dominant values of American society; and they imply that leaders must communicate in ways that empower people, highlight the connections between individual autonomy and responsibility to the organization, and uphold the fundamental values of society. In addition, leaders must communicate in ways that facilitate the involvement and decision-making powers of employees.

The other implication of the pluralistic approach is the recognition that *societal standards* of appropriate behavior *supersede the organizational code.* However, within organizations, there may be times when the organizational culture mandates behavior that is inappropriate according to societal standards. Whistleblowing is a good example of the conflict existing between the organizational culture and societal standards of appropriateness. In society, blatant corruption, lying, and stealing are not tolerated under any circumstances. However, in organizations members may at times be encouraged to conceal such behaviors from the public. The whistleblower instead reveals the acts of waste and fraud to constituencies outside of the organization. How can leaders balance the conflicting demands posed by an organization's culture and society? According to Kathy Laubach, the spouse of a whistleblower, one cannot balance the two: "A corrupt system can happen only if the individuals who make up that system are corrupt. You are either going to be part of the corruption or part of the forces working against it. There isn't a third choice. Someone, someday, has to take a stand; if you don't, maybe no one will. And that is wrong" (quoted in Glazer & Glazer, 1986, p. 38). Appropriate communication, then, may be aimed at helping organizations adapt to society's expectations.

Organizations and Effective Behavior

Organizational members frequently pose the question, "What's the bottom line?" At the root of this question is an inquiry into the effectiveness of a particular process, person, or product in aiding the organization to accomplish its objectives. For communication to be functional, it must facilitate accomplishing goals. Within organizations, this means that leaders' communication is effective when it facilitates accomplishing desired organizational goals. To assess an employee's contribution to achieving goals, most organizations structure performance evaluation standards. Barry Staw (1983) suggests that at least two basic issues need to be addressed by any performance evaluation system: (1) Should the individual or group serve as the unit of analysis for evaluating effectiveness? and (2) Should procedural or outcome variables serve as the basis for evaluating effectiveness? How these questions are answered depends on the organizational culture.

Individual versus group effectiveness. Each corporate culture forms its own assumption about who will be held accountable for performance. Organizations evaluate members in terms of their individual performance and actions. Although group and organizational goals may serve as reference points for evaluating an individual's performance, ultimately the actions of the individual, not of the group as a whole, influence the evaluation of effectiveness. The underlying assumption here is that personal effectiveness is correlated with organizational effectiveness. This may lead to situations in which one group member is viewed as highly effective even though the group as a whole is ineffective. However, the evaluation of effectiveness may also depend on the overall effectiveness of the group's collective actions. Particularly when tasks are highly interdependent, a group can only be successful if its members work well together. In such circumstances, it is difficult to evaluate only the individual's effectiveness, rather than as part of the group's effectiveness. Unless the individual actively participates, the group cannot succeed. Using the group's effectiveness as the basis for evaluating an individual's effectiveness means that (1) individual performance is measured in terms of the degree to which the individual contributes to the group or (2) the individual is only as effective as the group. The first assessment of effectiveness suggests that if an individual perspective is employed, leaders' communication is viewed as effective to the degree that it enhances the personal status and well-being of the individual. Conversely, if the second perspective is employed in the analysis, leaders' communication is viewed as effective to the degree that it helps the overall group accomplish its goals.

Unfortunately, organizations may view the perspectives of individual and group effectiveness as in conflict. Charles Kelly (1987) highlights the tension in achieving individual versus group goals in an examination of organizational ethics and power. He identifies five roles that individuals may adopt within an organization:

1. *Leader:* Ethical managers who utilize their charisma to help the organization achieve long-term goals.

2. *Builder:* Ethical managers without charisma who use their abilities to help the organization achieve long-term objectives.
3. *Destructive achiever.* An individual manager who is charismatic but lacks the values of a leader and who negatively influences the long-term health of the organization.
4. *Mechanics:* People who maintain the status quo of the organization.
5. *Innovators:* Individuals who push for creativity and lead organizations to new breakthroughs.

Although successful organizations require all five types of people, Kelly notes that destructive achievers tend to occupy prevalent positions within organizations. Given their charisma, they are able to manipulate situations for personal gain and are often rewarded for their performance through promotions and organizational advancement. However, destructive achievers may decimate organizational departments on their way to the top by driving off good employees and wasting resources to achieve short-term gains. Destructive achievers represent the tension between personal and organizational effectiveness.

Product versus procedural effectiveness. Another issue raised by evaluations of effectiveness is whether outcome or procedural variables should be used as standards for assessing communication effectiveness. Intuitively, most of us would use a set of outcomes as an indicator for assessing an individual's or organization's communication effectiveness. Effectiveness is an outcome or a *product-based judgment* that compares the actual product outcome to the initial goals. At the organizational level, a variety of indicators may be used—from return on investment and productivity to product deficiency and efficiency. The communication effectiveness of an individual can be assessed using a variety of criteria, including the individual's ability to provide support to others, to motivate them toward higher levels of performance, to show empathy for others, to encourage meaningful discussion at team meetings, and to improve the quality of ideas generated by groups.

The use of outcome variables as a primary means of assessing effectiveness has been challenged, however. For this approach to serve as a viable means of assessing effectiveness, three conditions must be met: (1) it must be possible to specify a specific level of performance that can be achieved, (2) no external obstacles can prohibit accomplishing goals, and (3) it must be clearly demonstrated that individuals' actions caused the outcomes (Gouran, 1990). These conditions may at times be difficult to satisfy. For instance, a leader may be unable to specify with accuracy the goals that must be accomplished, or unanticipated environmental obstacles may frustrate accomplishing goals. Sometimes goals are achieved by pure luck, rather than by the actions of a leader or an employee. These factors have led some theorists toward a different model for assessing effectiveness—the *procedural-based model.* In this perspective, individuals and organizations are viewed as effective when they follow a set of prescribed procedures. Effectiveness is measured by the correspondence between actual behavior and the behavior specified by the procedure. For example, when leaders handle difficult situations, such as charges of sexual discrimination or harassment, it is critical to follow the organizational procedures for dealing with the problems. Given that the final outcome is unlikely to satisfy all organizational members, it is important to adhere to the procedures in order to ensure an impartial airing of the grievance. The outcome does not serve as the basis for assessing effectiveness; rather, the correspondence of actual and prescribed behavior is the assessment's basis.

Organizational Cultures and Behavior

Whether an organization uses a product- or procedural-based model for assessing a leader's behavior depends on its existing organizational culture. By examining some distinct cultures and the various standards they employ, we can better understand how culture influences the standards that organizations use for assessing effectiveness and appropriateness.

The organizational culture structures expectations regarding what constitutes appropriate and effective leadership communication. Cultures emerge within organizations through the interlacing of the communication of workers. Culture is not a monolithic creation that encompasses the entire organization; rather, it includes the subcultures that work teams create on their own. Through the telling of stories, myths, and jokes, as well as through rites and ceremonies, organizational cultures are created, perpetuated, and modified. Although subgroups create their own unique cultures, they are still a part of the larger organizational culture.

During the early 1980s, Terrence Deal and Allen Kennedy's *Corporate Cultures* (1982) became a popular best-seller and a "must-read" for managers. The book has had much influence on how people in the field view corporate culture. It describes four basic cultures that the authors encountered while working with organizations and their implications for competent leader communication (see Table 9.1). In addition, a more contemporary form of organizational culture—the total quality management culture—has been identified by researchers.

Deal and Kennedy's four corporate cultures. The *tough-guy macho culture* is inhabited by individualists who strive to make decisions quickly. The decisions are often "tough" and feedback is provided rapidly. The culture is "macho" in the sense that it is characterized by competitiveness; all interactions within it take place on a battleground, and participants fight one another for respect. A "star system" is promoted that recognizes and provides resources to high performers. As Deal and Kennedy (1982) explain, this type of organizational culture is useful for environments that are high in risk and that provide quick returns.

In contrast, the *work hard, play hard culture* does not encourage risk taking; rather, it emphasizes activity geared toward meeting customer's needs. High service-oriented companies often have a work hard, play hard culture. Communication is aimed at motivating and inspiring employees. In return, employees are expected to be friendly and supportive. The culture emphasizes teamwork because it views the team, not the individual, as crucial to an organization's performance. Activities such as contests, special promotions, and recognition cere-

TABLE 9.1 Five Corporate Cultures and Their Standards for Communication Competence

	Dimensions of Appropriateness				Dimensions of Effectiveness	
Corporate Culture	*Releases human potential?*	*Blends needs of individual and group?*	*Emphasizes law, custom, and belief?*	*Involves followers?*	*Emphasizes individual or group effectiveness?*	*Adopts procedural- or product-based model?*
Tough-guy macho culture	Yes	Emphasizes individual	No	No	Individual	Product
Work hard, play hard culture	Yes	Blends both	Yes	Yes	Group	Product
Bet-your-company culture	Yes	Emphasizes company	Yes	Yes	Group	Both
Process culture	No	Emphasizes company	Yes	Yes	Group	Procedural
Total quality management culture	Yes	Blends both	No	Yes	Both	Both

monies are designed to help employees "play" at work and to motivate the entire organizational team to work together.

The *bet-your-company culture* is often found in high-risk organizations, where the ultimate success or failure of decisions may not be known for years. Such companies often place millions of dollars in investments for the future. Unlike the tough-guy macho culture, in which the individual places his or her reputation or career on the line, in the bet-your-company culture the company's health and future are placed at risk. This requires that new ideas for the future be encouraged and put into action at the same time they are discussed and critiqued at business meetings. The culture requires its participants to share ideas and views openly in order to develop interpersonal relationships. It operates best in such industries as oil development and exploration, the nuclear industry, and the space and aeronautical industry, which emphasize developing high-quality products and scientific breakthroughs.

Finally, the *process culture* is characterized by low amounts of risk and feedback. Bureaucratic organizations, such as government agencies, insurance companies, and banks, often have this type of organizational culture. The emphasis is on how things are done within the organization rather than what is done or with what effect. An attention to detail and a strict following of rules and procedures also characterize the process culture. Individuals who uphold the values and procedures of the culture are viewed as effective.

Each of the corporate cultures described by Deal and Kennedy (1982) holds a different assumption about what constitutes appropriate and effective communication (see Table 9.1). For example, the tough-guy macho culture emphasizes communication aimed at elevating the leader's status. Given the competitive environment of the culture, this type of communication is viewed as appropriate. Moreover, appropriate communication in this context may even undermine traditions within the organization as long as it results in the achievement of desired goals. Leaders' communication, in the tough-guy macho culture, is viewed as effective when it facilitates their advancement in the organization and produces desirable outcomes.

The communication standards for the leader in a work hard, play hard culture are quite different. Here competent communication is aimed at building teamwork and helping people fulfill their potential within the context of the team. This means that effective communication recognizes the importance of the individual team member but is aimed at coordinating behaviors within the larger team framework. As a result, competent communication encourages individual responsibility as it relates to the overarching organizational goals. Ultimately, the effectiveness of communication in the work hard, play hard culture is judged in terms of how the team achieves organizational outcomes.

Similarly, the bet-your-company culture is concerned with the contribution of communication to a company's overall goals. However, effective communication not only results in a quality product; it also reflects the accepted procedures and practices of the organization. Given the long-term nature of the products created by such cultures, it is important to consider the processes organizational members follow when making decisions. Appropriate communication stresses the importance of following tradition and maintaining organizational beliefs, while also emphasizing the company's needs over the individual's. This means that leaders may diminish the importance of individuals' viewpoints for the greater good of the company.

The process culture judges leadership behavior by the degree to which it conforms to company policy. Working through channels, following procedures, and conforming to policies are viewed as appropriate ways of communicating. Communication that recognizes the rights of the individual over the company is inappropriate. The company serves as the basis on which all individual behavior is evaluated. Therefore, communication that reflects and upholds the company's value system is viewed as competent.

Total quality management culture. In the late 1970s and 1980s, members of U.S. industries and management consultants lamented the lack of quality present in services and products. *Total quality management (TQM)* emerged as service-related, industrial, and educational organizations sought to develop a system for improving the quality of their services and products. The principles of TQM are exhibited by many of the companies that have received the government's Malcolm Baldridge National Quality Award, which is awarded on the basis of a company's quality planning and assurance as well as its ability to satisfy customers (Schonberger, 1992). Currently, TQM is a popular approach to improving organizational quality and is likely to grow in use throughout the 1990s.

TQM is based on a small set of assumptions and processes (Bowen & Lawler, 1992; Zabel & Avery, 1992). At the center of this set of assumptions is a focus on customer needs and desires. *Customers* are the individuals or groups that receive an organization's products or services. Customers may be *external* to the organization (for example, Maytag delivers home appliances to its retail associates) or *internal* (for example, several manufacturers often depend on each other to provide the needed parts and resources for a finished product). Regardless of whether the customer is external or internal, TQM emphasizes identifying and meeting customer needs.

Quality improvement is achieved through the continuous enhancement of organizational processes. TQM is not intended as a short-term solution to improving quality; rather, its quest for quality improvement is more a way of life. TQM creates an organizational culture in which employees are always looking for new ways to improve organizational processes. Underlying TQM is the assumption that the traditional ways of accomplishing organizational work are what lead to low-quality products and services. Thus, organizations attempt to identify good organizational processes and then to monitor them closely. In a manufacturing setting, for instance, TQM may emphasize that one process needs to be monitored, such as the response time for repairing damaged machinery. A company might monitor the time required to repair the machines and to return them to operation. Such organizations often post charts summarizing the various indicators numerically, making employees aware of the current level of quality and enabling them to monitor improvement.

In TQM organizations, employees are highly involved in decision making and other organizational processes. Work teams are a preferred means for instituting change in organizations, and employees are empowered to make changes. Employees are encouraged to work together as a team and to introduce innovations. They are granted the responsibility and the autonomy to make decisions. Their participation in the decision-making process is intended to foster a high level of employee commitment and dedication to the organization.

Competent leadership communication is viewed differently by TQM culture than by Deal and Kennedy's (1982) corporate cultures. As Thomas Patten, Jr. (1991/1992) points out, the status quo of organizational politics can endanger the successful implementation of TQM:

> The experienced managerial politician who has survived and succeeded by manipulative skill, guile, ingratiation, coat-tail riding, or simply by being a "yes" [person] is particularly dangerous [to TQM]. Such an individual usually is not open to change and knows how to appear to change by dissembling and going along with the prevailing drift of the day in organizational management. These people are very dangerous to the success of installing TQM as a way of life because they believe TQM is antithetical to *their* way of life. (p. 9)

Competent leadership communication upholds the set of assumptions about TQM. To a greater degree than the other cultures, TQM culture emphasizes employee potential and strives to involve workers in the leadership process. As a result, leaders are required to create messages that liberate rather than constrain employee development and that reduce workers' fear of failure. For employees that are not well trained to do a job, the leader may need to empower them by providing a strategy that will allow them to meet the job. When an employee does know how to do the job, the leader may also need to provide support and encouragement to increase the worker's confidence in the job.

In addition, TQM culture blends the needs of the individual with those of the organization. It recognizes that the "bottom line" of any organization is to produce a product or service in order to make a profit. Without products or profits, most organizations would not survive. At the same time, however, TQM culture recognizes that the keys to generating products and profits are the skills and abilities of workers. If employees are not able to perform their jobs well, the company will fail. Therefore, leaders must communicate in ways that allow employees to achieve both personal goals and organizational goals. Unlike the work hard, play hard culture, in which employee needs are met outside of the workplace through recreational and other social activities, TQM culture requires leaders to balance individual and organizational needs in the workplace by developing teams, modeling desired behaviors, and setting goals. Finally, TQM culture recognizes that the company is only as solid as its organizational processes. This means that leaders' communication needs to be aimed primarily at coordinating the collective action of the work team to achieve goals. However, TQM simultaneously recognizes that the personal confidence and effectiveness of employees must be increased if they are to contribute positively to the larger organization.

WORKING THROUGH COMMUNICATION DILEMMAS

Communication competence involves constructing messages that are viewed as appropriate and effective by other organizational members. It sounds simple, but in many instances it is not. Consider the following statements from Kristina Froelich and Janet Kottke's (1991, p. 380) survey on beliefs about organizational ethics:

1. It is okay for a supervisor to ask an employee to support someone else's incorrect viewpoint.
2. An employee should overlook someone else's wrongdoing if it is in the best interest of the company.
3. There is nothing wrong with a supervisor asking an employee to falsify a document.
4. An employee may need to lie to a co-worker to protect the company.
5. An employee may need to lie to a supervisor or manager to protect the company.

Which statements are examples of competent communication? All of them? None of them? Under what circumstances is it appropriate to lie? To enlist someone's aid in doing something that goes against company policy?

Most leaders want to be competent communicators. They know that if they communicate in a competent manner they will be more likely to facilitate the group in accomplishing its goals. Corporate cultures may have clear-cut rules for appropriate and effective communication in certain areas but ambiguous and contradictory prescriptions for communication in other areas. When the standards for appropriateness and effectiveness are contradictory, ambiguous, or absent, leaders may analyze the value systems relevant to the situation and determine how those systems view competent communication. When confronted with such communication dilemmas, leaders should consider the following questions.

What Value Systems Must Be Considered?

Communication competence is a relational concept. To determine whether one is communicating in a competent manner or whether one's communication will be viewed as competent, the communication must be assessed in the context of a value system. Two value systems—the organization's corporate culture and the national culture—are often considered when assessing communication competence. However, other value systems may need to be considered as well. According to Gatewood and Carroll (1991), *federal, state, and local laws* may influence what constitutes appropriate behavior. Sexual harassment, for example, is prohibited under the Civil Rights Act, and in financial institutions giving insider information is prohibited by the Securities and Exchange Commission. One's

Box 9.2
Finding Your "Plumb Line" for Communication Competence

When builders construct a house, they sometimes use a plumb line to make sure that the house is level and its beams straight. The plumb line is a guide for constructing the house according to acceptable standards. Similarly, people use their personal identity as a plumb line to judge the appropriateness and effectiveness of their communication.

Your personal standards for competent communication behaviors are among many other types of standards used to assess communication competence. The organizational culture and the nature of the profession, for example, offer guidelines as well. However, to decide whether you are acting in competent ways, you must at some level rely on what feels right for you.

ASSIGNMENT

To help develop your own personal "plumb line" for communication competence, describe your view of the issue in one or two paragraphs. In support of your view, describe the kinds of communication behaviors that you consider incompetent or competent in all situations, the factors influencing your perception of communication, and your model of ideal leadership communication.

professional identity may dictate what is considered competent communication. The legal, medical, accounting, and other professions structure standards for appropriate conduct within their respective fields. Finally, one's *personal identity* can influence perceptions of competent communication. Each organizational member has a unique set of values and attitudes that serves to define competent communication. (See Box 9.2.)

Do the Value Systems Conflict in What They View as Competent Communication?

Value systems can differ in terms of their views on competent communication. For example, consider the leader who feels that a worker needs encouragement and motivation. The leader may be caught between two competing sets of values—one personal, the other organizational. If the leader belongs to a tough-guy macho corporate culture, which believes in the survival of the fittest, communicating support to the employee would be not only considered inappropriate but possibly a sign of weakness as well. Furthermore, if on a personal level the leader is concerned and caring, communicating support would be viewed as a competent act. It is important to identify the various perspectives of competent communication in order to determine a possible consensus. If consensus can be reached, a clear definition of what constitutes competent communication in a particular situation is possible. However, when the value systems are contradictory and prohibit consensus, the leader must select the value system to be used in assessing communication competence.

Which Value Systems Hold a "Higher" Standard for Competent Communication?

When Abraham Lincoln was asked to speak about the ethics of the legal profession, he wrote the following comments in his notes:

> Resolve to be honest at all events; and if in your own judgment you cannot be an honest lawyer, resolve to be honest without being a lawyer. Choose some other occupation, rather than one in the choosing of which you do, in advance, consent to be a knave. (Quoted in Kunhardt, Kunhardt, & Kunhardt, 1992, p. 77)

Lincoln, aware of the conflicting value systems present in a person's professional and personal identities, provides a method for resolving the contradiction. He suggests that honesty is a higher principle to which people should aspire. Even though a profession such as law may carry with it certain benefits, sacrificing one's principles is not worth the social and material benefits. Similarly, organizational members may encounter competing views of what it means to be a competent communicator. An organizational culture may consider it appropriate for a leader to lie to team members in order to protect the company, but the leader may find this personally offensive. Although there is no clear way to resolve such competing views, Lincoln realized long ago what many contemporary theorists on ethics conclude today: Leaders should make decisions based on the highest principle (Barry, 1986). If the value systems suggest using two different communicative strategies, the leader should select the strategy that reflects the highest ideals of appropriateness and effectiveness.

While competent communication may at times be achieved by following the rules of a culture, there will be other times when those rules will not apply. Effective leaders assess the value systems' relevance to a situation, identify each system's implications for competent communication, and then select the message or sequence of messages that honors the highest possible ideal.

SUMMARY

In this book we have explored the various communication skills that competent leaders require. Leadership is a process that involves helping people organize themselves, make sense of their environment, and take actions geared toward overcoming obstacles and achieving goals. Leadership is a behavioral process in that it is aimed at coordinating the group's collective activity. All behaviors have consequences, so it is necessary for leaders to examine the appropriateness and effectiveness of their communication. The appropriateness of communication is evaluated in terms of the values of the organization, but appropriate communication also strives to transcend that value system. The organizational culture also constructs standards for assessing communication effectiveness. It can be measured in one of two ways: its conformance to a set of procedures that specifies how work is to be done or according to the end results it produces.

Leadership is an inherently complex process characterized by a wide range of possible behaviors performed in a wide range of situations in varying types of organizations. Only responsible leaders can manage well the vast number of possible communication behaviors that they may perform. Although leaders work to organize people toward collective action to achieve goals, they must at the same time strive to use appropriate and effective behavior as well as responsible and competent communication.

QUESTIONS AND APPLICATIONS

1. You are an organizational leader and an employee comes to you with a work-related problem. The employee is faced with a decision that could generate good profits for the company if it succeeds, but would be costly if it fails. You are asked to give the employee assistance in making the decision. How would you approach the situation and use competent communication in each of the following corporate cultures: the tough-guy macho culture; the work hard, play hard culture; the bet-your-company culture; the process culture; and the TQM culture?

2. You are in the midst of a leadership workshop that your company arranged for you to attend. Part of the workshop is on empowerment. This afternoon, a heated discussion took place over whether empowerment is effective or ineffective. As part of the workshop, you have been asked to write a one-page position paper entitled "The Limits of Empowering Behavior." What would be your position in the paper? Explain.

3. The local Chamber of Commerce is sponsoring a series of public debates in the community. The resolution that you have been asked to debate is as follows: Leadership communication in organizations should reflect and validate societal values. What would you say in this debate? What side would you take? Explain.

4. The theme of this book, first introduced in Chapter 1, is that leadership can only manage the obstacles it faces if it is as complex as its environment. Chapter 9 focuses on leadership communication and the idea that it is viewed as competent when it is appropriate and effective. Do you agree that, as leaders become more complex communicators, they are more likely to be viewed as competent? Why or why not? Is it possible for leaders to be too complex for their environment? Explain.

REFERENCES

Albrecht, T. L., & Hall, B. (1991). Relational and content differences between elites and outsiders in innovation networks. *Human Communication Research, 17*(4), 535–561.

Albrecht, T. L., & Ropp, V. A. (1984). Communicating about innovation in networks of three U.S. organizations. *Journal of Communication, 34,* 78–91.

Alderfer, C. P. (1972). *Existence, relatedness and growth: Human needs in organizational settings.* New York: Free Press.

Aldrich, H. (1979). *Organizations and environments.* Englewood Cliffs, NJ: Prentice-Hall.

Alsop, R. (1988, May 13). Advertisers put consumers on the couch: Research probes emotional ties to products. *Wall Street Journal,* p. 21.

Ancona, D. G. (1987). Groups in organizations: Extending laboratory models. In C. Hendrick (Ed.), *Annual review of personality and social psychology: Group and intergroup processes* (pp. 207–231). Beverly Hills, CA: Sage.

Ancona, D. G. (1990). Outward bound: Strategies for team survival in an organization. *Academy of Management Journal, 33*(2), 334–365.

Ancona, D. G. & Caldwell, D. F. (1988). Beyond task and maintenance: Defining external functions in groups. *Group and Organization Studies, 13,* 468–494.

Argyris, C. (1968). The nature of competence-acquisition activities and their relationship to therapy. In W. G. Bennis, D. E. Berlew, E. H. Schein, & F. I. Steele (Eds.), *Interpersonal dynamics: Essays and reading on human interaction* (pp. 546–566). Homewood, IL: Dorsey Press.

Argyris, C. (1986). Skilled incompetence. *Harvard Business Review, 64,* 74–81.

Argyris, C. (1988). Crafting a theory of practice: The case of organizational paradoxes. In R. E. Quinn & K. S. Cameron (Eds.), *Paradox and transformation: Toward a theory of change in organizations and management* (pp. 255–288). Cambridge, MA: Ballinger.

Ashby, H. (Director). (1980). *Being There* [Film]. Lorimar.

Ashby, W. R. (1960). *Design for a brain.* New York: Wiley.

Ashby, W. R. (1968). Variety, constraint, and the law of requisite variety. In W. Buckley (Ed.), *Modern systems research for the behavioral scientist* (pp. 129–136). Durham, NC: Duke University Press.

Avolio, B. J., Waldman, D. A., & Einstein, W. O. (1988). Transformational leadership in a management game simulation. *Group and Organization Studies, 13,* 59–80.

Bach, B. W. (1989). The effect of multiplex relationships upon innovation adoption: A reconsideration of Rogers's model. *Communication Monographs, 56,* 133–150.

Bachrach, P., & Baratz, M. (1962). Two faces of power. *American Political Science Review, 56,* 947–952.

Backof, J. E., & Martin, C. L. (1991). Historical perspectives: Development of the codes of ethics in the legal, medical, and accounting professions. *Journal of Business Ethics, 10,* 99–110.

Baird, J. E. (1980). Enhancing managerial credibility. *Personnel Journal, 50,* 1001–1002.

Barge, J. K. (1989). Leadership as medium: A leaderless group discussion model. *Communication Quarterly, 37*(4), 237–247.

Barge, J. K. (1990). *Task skills and competence in group leadership.* Paper presented at the annual meeting of the Speech Communication Association, Atlanta, GA.

Barge, J. K., Downs, C. W., & Johnson, K. E. (1989). An analysis of effective and ineffective leader conversation. *Management Communication Quarterly, 2*(3), 357–386.
Baron, R. A. (1991). Motivation in work settings: Reflections on the core of organizational research. *Motivation and Emotion, 15*(1), 1–8.
Barry, V. (1986). *Moral issues in business* (3rd ed.). Belmont, CA: Wadsworth.
Bartol, K. M. (1978). The sex structuring of organizations: A search for possible causes. *Academy of Management Review, 3,* 805–815.
Bass, B. M. (1985). *Leadership and performance beyond expectations.* New York: Free Press.
Bass, B. M. (1990a). *Bass & Stogdill's handbook of leadership* (3rd ed.). New York: Free Press.
Bass, B. M. (1990b). From transactional to transformational leadership: Learning to share the vision. *Organizational Dynamics, 18*(3), 19–31.
Bass, B. M., & Avolio, B. J. (1990). *Manual: The multifactor leadership questionnaire.* Palo Alto, CA: Consulting Psychologist Press.
Bass, B. M. & Avolio, B. J. (1993). Transformational leadership: A response to critiques. In M. M. Chemers & R. Ayman (Eds.), *Leadership theory and research* (pp. 49–80). San Diego, CA: Academic Press Inc.
Bass, B. M., Avolio, B. J., & Goodheim, L. (1987). Biography and the assessment of transformational leadership at the world-class level. *Journal of Management, 13,* 7–19.
Bass, B. M., Waldman, D. A., Avolio, B. J., & Bebb, M. (1987). Transformational leadership and the falling dominoes effect. *Group and Organization Studies, 12,* 73–87.
Bateman, T. S. (1986). The escalation of commitment in sequential decision making: Situational and personal moderators and limiting conditions. *Decision Sciences, 17,* 33–49.
Baxter, L. A. (1984). An investigation of compliance-gaining as politeness. *Human Communication Research, 10,* 427–456.
Benne, K. D., & Sheats, P. (1948). Functional roles of group members. *Journal of Social Issues, 4,* 41–49.
Bennis, W. G. (1993). *An invented life.* Reading, MA: Addison-Wesley.
Bennis, W. G., & Nanus, B. (1985). *Leaders: The strategies of taking charge.* San Francisco: Harper Collins.
Berry, P. (1983). Mentors for women managers: Fast-track to corporate success. *Supervisory Management, 28,* 36–40.
Blake, R. R. & Mouton, J. S. (1985). *The managerial grid III.* Houston: Gulf.
Blake, R. R., Mouton, J. S., & Allen, J. S. (1987). *Spectacular teamwork.* New York: Wiley.
Blake, R. R., Shephard, H. A., Mouton, J. S. (1964). *Managing intergroup conflict in industry.* Houston: Gulf.
Blank, W., Wietzel, J., & Green, S. G. (1986). Situational leadership theory: A test of underlying assumptions. *Proceedings of the Academy of Management.*
Blau, P. M. (1982). Structural sociology and network analysis: An overview. In P. V. Marsden & N. Lin (Eds.), *Social structure and network analysis* (pp. 273–279). Newbury Park, CA: Sage.
Bogadan, J. L. (1982). Paradoxical communication as interpersonal influence. *Family Process, 21,* 443–452.
Bormann, E. G. (1975). *Discussion and group methods: Theory and practice.* New York: Harper.
Bottger, P. C., & Yetton, P. W. (1988). An integration of process and decision scheme explanations of a group problem-solving performance. *Organizational Behavior and Human Decision Processes, 42*(2), 233–249.
Bourgeios, L. J. (1985). Strategic goals, perceived uncertainty, and economic performance in volatile environments. *Academy of Management Journal, 28,* 548–573.

Bowen, D. D. (1985). Were men meant to mentor women? *Training and Development Journal, 39*(2), 31–34.

Bowen, D. E., & Lawler, E. E., III (1992). Total quality-oriented human resources management. *Organizational Dynamics, 20,* 29–41.

Bowers, D. G., & Seashore, S. E. (1966). Predicting organizational effectiveness with a four-factor theory of leadership. *Administrative Science Quarterly, 11,* 238–263.

Boyatzis, R. R. (1982). *The competent manager: A model for effective performance.* New York: Wiley.

Bradac, J. J., & Mulac, A. (1984). A molecular view of powerful and powerless speech styles: Attributional consequences of specific language features and communicator intentions. *Communication Monographs, 51,* 307–319.

Bradac, J. J., Hemphill, M. R., & Tardy, C. H. (1981). Language style on trail: Effects of "powerful" and "powerless" speech upon judgments of victims and villains. *Western Journal of Speech Communication, 45,* 327–341.

Bradford, D. L., & Cohen, A. R. (1985). *Managing for excellence: The guide to developing high performance organizations.* New York: Wiley.

Brass, D. J. (1984). Being in the right place: A structural analysis of individual influence in an organization. *Administrative Science Quarterly, 29,* 518–539.

Brass, D. J. (1985). Men's and women's networks: A study of interaction patterns and influence in an organization. *Academy of Management Journal, 28,* 327–343.

Breen, P., Donlon, T. F., & Whitaker, U. (1977). *Teaching and assessing interpersonal competence—A CAEL handbook.* Columbia, NJ: CAEL.

Brockner, J. (1992). The escalation of commitment to a failing course of action: Toward theoretical progress. *Academy of Management Review, 17* (1), 39–61.

Brown, K. A., & Mitchell, T. R. (1986). Influence of task interdependence and number of poor performers on diagnoses of causes of poor performance. *Academy of Management Journal, 29,* 412–424.

Brown, M. H. (1985). That reminds me of a story: Speech action in organizational socialization. *Western Journal of Speech Communication, 49,* 17–42.

Burgoon, M., & Miller, M. (1990). Communication and influence. In G. L. Dahnke & G. W. Clatterbuck (Eds.), *Human communication: Theory and research* (pp. 229–258). Belmont, CA: Wadsworth.

Burns, J. M. (1978). *Leadership.* New York: Harper.

Calder, B. J. (1977). An attribution theory of leadership. In B. M. Staw & G. R. Salancik (Eds.), *New directions in organizational behavior* (pp. 179–204). Chicago: St. Clair.

Cameron, K. S., & Quinn, R. E. (1988). Organizational paradox and transformation. In R. E. Quinn & K. S. Cameron (Eds.), *Paradox and transformation: Toward a theory of change in organization and management* (pp. 1–18). Cambridge, MA: Ballinger.

Cartwright, C., & Zander, A. (1968). Leadership and performance of group functions: Introduction. In D. Cartwright and A. Zander (Eds.), *Group dynamics: Research and theory* (pp. 301–317). New York: Harper.

Case, J. (1993). A company of businesspeople. *Inc., 15* (4), 79–93.

Cheney, G. (1983). On the various and changing meanings of organizational membership: A field study of organizational identification. *Communication Monographs, 50,* 342–362.

Cheney, G., & Vibbert, S. L. (1987). Corporate discourse: Public relations and issue management. In F. M. Jablin, L. L. Putnam, K. H. Roberts, & L. W. Porter (Eds.), *Handbook of organizational communication* (pp. 165–194). Newbury Park, CA: Sage.

Chusmir, L. H. (1985). Motivation of managers: Is gender a factor? *Psychology of Women Quarterly, 9,* 153–159.

Chusmir, L. H. (1986). Personalized versus socialized power needs among working men and women. *Human Relations, 39,* 149–159.

Chusmir, L. H., & Parker, B. (1991). Gender and situational differences in managers' values: A look at work and home lives. *Journal of Business Research, 23,* 325–335.

Cody, M. J., & McLaughlin, M. L. (1980). Perceptions of compliance-gaining situations: A dimensional analysis. *Communication Monographs, 47,* 132–148.

Cody, M. J., & McLaughlin, M. L. (1985). The situation as a construct in interpersonal communication research. In M. L. Knapp & G. R. Miller (Eds.), *Handbook of interpersonal communication* (pp. 263–312). Beverly Hills, CA: Sage.

Coleman, T. L. (1990). Managing diversity at work: The new American dilemma. *Public Management, 72* (9), 2–5.

Conger, J. A. (1989). *The charismatic leader: Behind the mystique of exceptional leadership.* San Francisco: Jossey-Bass.

Conger, J. A. (1991). Inspiring others: The language of leadership. *Academy of Management Executive, 5*(1), 31–45.

Conger, J. A., & Kanungo, R. N. (1988). The empowerment process: Integrating theory and practice. *Academy of Management Review, 13* (3), 471–482.

Conrad, C. (1985). *Strategic organizational communication: Cultures, situations, and adaptation.* New York: Holt.

Cook, J., & Wall, T. (1980). New work attitude measures of trust, organizational commitment and personal need non-fulfillment. *Journal of Occupational Psychology, 53,* 39–52.

Corcoran, M. E., & Courant, P. N. (1987). Sex-role socialization and occupational segregation: An exploratory investigation. *Journal of Post Keynesian Economics, 9,* 330–346.

Cotton, J. L., Vollrath, D. A., Froggatt, K. L., Lengneck-Hall, M. L., & Jennings, K. R. (1988). Employee participation: Diverse forms and different outcomes. *Academy of Management Review, 13,* 8–22.

Crable, R. E., & Vibbert, S. L. (1986). Public relations as communications. Edina, MN: Bellweather Press.

Crenson, M. A. (1971). *The un-politics of air pollution: A study of non-decision making in the cities.* Baltimore: Johns Hopkins University Press.

Cronshaw, S. F., & Lord, R. G. (1987). Effects of categorization, attribution, and encoding processes on leadership perceptions. *Journal of Applied Psychology, 72*(1), 97–106.

Crouch, A. G., & Yetton, P. (1987). Manager behavior, leadership style, and subordinate performance: An empirical extension of the Vroom-Yetton conflict rule. *Organizational Behavior and Human Decision Processes, 39,* 384–396.

Cusella, L. P. (1980). The effects of feedback on intrinsic motivation: A propositional extension of cognitive evaluation theory from an organizational communication perspective. In D. Nimmo (Ed.), *Communication yearbook 4* (pp. 367–387). New Brunswick, NJ: Transaction Books.

Cusella, L. P. (1982). The effects of source expertise and feedback valence on intrinsic motivation. *Human Communication Research, 9*(1), 17–32.

Cusella, L. P. (1984). The effects of feedback source, message and receiver characteristics on intrinsic motivation. *Communication Quarterly, 32*(3), 211–221.

Cushman, D. P., & King, S. S. (1993). High-speed management: A revolution in organizational communication in the 1990s. In S. Deetz (Ed.), *Communication yearbook 16* (pp. 209–236). Newbury Park, CA: Sage.

Dance, F. E. X., & Larson, C. E. (1976). *The functions of human communication: A theoretical approach.* New York: Holt.

Deal, T. E., & Kennedy, A. A. (1982). *Corporate cultures: The rites and rituals of corporate life.* Reading, MA: Addison-Wesley.

Deaux, K. (1979). Self-evaluation of male and female managers. *Sex Roles, 5,* 571–580.

Dess, G., & Beard, D. (1984). Dimensions of organizational task environments. *Administrative Science Quarterly, 29,* 52–73.

DeTurck, M. A., & Miller, G. R. (1982). The effect of birth order on the persuasive impact of messages and the likelihood of persuasive message selection. *Communication, 11,* 78–84.

Dewey, J. (1910). *How we think.* Lexington, MA: Heath.

Dienesch, R. M., & Liden, R. C. (1986). Leader-member exchange model of leadership: A critique and further development. *Academy of Management Review, 11,* 618–634.

Downs, C. W., Johnson, K. M., & Barge, J. K. (1984). Communication feedback and task performance in organizations: A review of the literature. In H. H. Greenbaum, R. L. Falcione, & S. A. Helweg (Eds.), *Organizational communication: Abstracts, analysis, and overview* (pp. 13–47). Beverly Hills, CA: Sage.

Drake, B. H., & Moberg, D. J. (1986). Communicating influence attempts in dyads: Linguistic sedatives and palliatives. *Academy of Management Review, 11*(3), 567–584.

Drecksel, G. L. (1984). *Interaction characteristics of emergent leadership.* Unpublished doctoral dissertation, University of Utah, Salt Lake City.

Duhaime, I. M., & Schwenk, C. R. (1985). Conjectures on cognitive simplification in acquisition and divestment decision making. *Academy of Management Review, 10*(2), 287–295.

Duncan, R. B. (1972). Characteristics of organizational environments and perceived environmental uncertainty. *Administrative Science Quarterly, 17,* 313–327.

Eagly, A. H., & Johnson, B. T. (1990). Gender and leadership style: A meta-analysis. *Psychological Bulletin, 108* (2), 233–256.

Eagly, A. H., Makhijani, M. G., & Klonsky, B. G. (1992). Gender and the evaluation of leaders: A meta-analysis. *Psychological Bulletin, 111* (1), 3–22.

Eccles, J. P., & Hoffman, L. W. (1984). Sex role socialization and occupational behavior. In H. Stevenson & A. Siegel (Eds.), *Child development and social policy* (pp. 367–420). Chicago: University of Chicago Press.

Einhorn, H. J., & Hogarth, R. M. (1982). Prediction, diagnosis, and causal thinking in forecasting. *Journal of Forecasting, 1*(1), 23–36.

Eisenberg, E. M. (1984). Ambiguity as strategy in organizational communication. *Communication Monographs, 51,* 227–242.

Eisenberg, E. M. (1990). Jamming: Transcendence through organizing. *Communication Research, 17*(2), 139–164.

Eisenberg, E. M., & Goodall, H. L. (1993). *Organizational communication: Balancing creativity and constraint.* New York: St. Martin's Press.

Eisenberg, E. M., & Witten, M. G. (1987). Reconsidering openness in organizational communication. *Academy of Management Review, 12*(3), 418–426.

Emerson, R. H. (1962). Power-dependence relations. *American Sociological Review, 27,* 31–41.

Emery, F. E., & Trist, E. (1965). Causal texture of organizational environments. *Human Relations, 18,* 21–32.

Erez, M., & Rim, Y. (1982). The relationships between goals, influence, tactics, and personal and organizational variables. *Human Relations, 35,* 871–878.

Evans, M. G. (1970). The effects of supervisory behavior on the path-goal relationship. *Organizational Behavior and Human Performance, 5,* 277–298.

Fahr, J. L., Podsakoff, P. M., & Cheng, B. S. (1987). Culture-free leadership effectiveness versus moderators of leadership behavior: An extension and test of Kerr and Jermier's "substitutes for leadership" model in Taiwan. *Journal of International Business Studies, 18*(3), 43–60.

Fairhurst, G. T., & Chandler, T. A. (1989). Social structure in leader-member interaction. *Communication Monographs, 56,* 213–239.

Fairhurst, G. T., & Snavely, B. K. (1983). Majority and token minority group relationships: Power acquisition and communication. *Academy of Management Review, 8,* 292–300.

Fairhurst, G. T., Rogers, L. E., & Sarr, R. A. (1987). Manager-subordinate control patterns and judgments about the relationship. In M. McLaughlin (Ed.), *Communication yearbook 10* (pp. 83–116). Beverly Hills: Sage.

Falbo, T. (1977). Relationships between sex, sex role, and social influence. *Psychology of Women Quarterly, 2,* 62–72.

Farace, R. V., Monge, P. R., & Russell, H. M. (1977). *Communicating and organizing.* Reading, MA: Addison-Wesley.

Ferris, G. R. (1985). Role of leadership in the employee withdrawal process: A constructive replication. *Journal of Applied Psychology, 70,* 777–781.

Ferris, K. R., & Aranya, N. (1983). A comparison of two organizational commitment scales. *Personnel Psychology, 36,* 87–98.

Fiedler, F. E. (1964). A contingency model of leadership effectiveness. In L. Berkowitz (Ed.), *Advances in experimental social psychology* (vol. 1, pp. 149–190). New York: Academic Press.

Fiedler, F. E. (1967). *A theory of leadership effectiveness.* New York: McGraw-Hill.

Fiedler, F. E. (1978). The contingency model and the dynamics of the leadership process. In L. Berkowitz (Ed.), *Advances in experimental social psychology* (vol. 11, pp. 59–112). New York: Academic Press.

Fiedler, F. E. (1993). The leadership situation and the black box in contingency theories. In M. M. Chemers & R. Ayman (Eds.), *Leadership theory and research: Perspectives and directions* (pp. 1–28). San Diego, CA: Academic Press, Inc.

Fiedler, F. E., & Garcia, J. E. (1987). *New approaches to effective leadership: Cognitive resources and organizational performance.* New York: Wiley.

Filley, A. C. (1975). *Interpersonal conflict resolution.* Glenview, IL: Scott Foresman.

Filley, A. C., House, R. J., & Kerr, S. (1976). *Managerial process and organizational behavior* (2nd ed.). Glenview, IL: Scott, Foresman.

Fischer, C. (1982). *To dwell among friends.* Chicago: University of Chicago.

Fisher, A. B. (1992, September 21). When will women get to the top? *Fortune, 126* (6), 44–56.

Fisher, B. A. (1986). Leadership: When does the difference make a difference? In R. Y. Hirokawa & M. S. Poole (Eds.), *Communication and group decision-making* (pp. 197–218). Beverly Hills: Sage.

Fisher, C. D. (1979). Transmission of positive and negative feedback to subordinates: A laboratory investigation. *Journal of Applied Psychology, 64*(5), 533–540.

Fisher, L., Anderson A., & Jones, J. E. (1981). Types of paradoxical intervention and indications/Contraindications for use in clinical practice. *Family Process, 20,* 25–35.

Fisher, R., & Ury, W. R. (1981). *Getting to yes.* Boston: Houghton-Mifflin.

Fitt, L. W., & Newton, D. A. (1981). When the mentor is a man and the protégé is a woman. *Harvard Business Review, 59*(2), 56–60.

Fitts, W. H. (1970). *Interpersonal competence: The wheel model. Studies on the self-concept and rehabilitation,* Research monograph no. 2, Dede Wallace Center, Nashville, TN: W. H. Fitts.

Fleishman, E. A. (1957). A leader behavior description for industry. In R. M. Stogdill & A. E. Coons (Eds.), *Leader behavior: Its description and measurement* (pp. 103–119). Columbus: Ohio State University, Bureau of Business Research.

Fleishman, E. A., & Simmons, J. (1970). Relationship between leadership patterns and effectiveness ratings among Israeli foremen. *Personnel Psychology, 23,* 169–172.
Fleishman, E. A., Harris, E. F., & Burtt, H. E. (1955). *Leadership and supervision in industry.* Columbus: Ohio State University, Bureau of Educational Research.
Foote, N. N., & Cottrell, L. S., Jr. (1955). *Identity and interpersonal competence.* Chicago: University of Chicago Press.
Freeman, L. C., & Romney, A. K. (1987). Words, deeds and social structure. *Human Organization, 46,* 330–334.
French, J. R. P., & Raven, B. H. (1959). The bases of social power. In D. Cartwright (Ed.), *Studies in social power* (pp. 150–167). Ann Arbor, MI: Institute of Social Research.
Froelich, K. S., & Kottke, J. L. (1991). Measuring individual beliefs about organizational ethics. *Educational and Psychological Measurement, 51,* 377–383.
Frost, P. J. (1987). Power, politics, and influence. In F. M. Jablin, L. L. Putnam, K. H. Roberts, & L. W. Porter (Eds.), *Handbook of organizational communication* (pp. 503–548). Beverly Hills: Sage.
Frost, P., Moore, L., Louis, M., Lundberg, C., & Martin, J. (1991). *Reframing organizational culture.* Newbury Park, CA: Sage.
Gardner, J. W. (1990). *On leadership.* New York: Free Press.
Garland, H. (1984). Relation of effort-performance expectancy to performance in goal-setting experiments. *Journal of Applied Psychology, 69,* 79–84.
Gatewood, R. D., & Carroll, A. B. (1991). Assessment of ethical performance of organization members: A conceptual framework. *Academy of Management Review, 16*(4), 667–690.
Geier, J. G. (1967). A trait approach to the study of leadership in small groups. *Journal of Communication, 17,* 316–323.
Geldof, B. (1986). *Is that it?* New York: Penguin.
George, A. L. (1980). *Presidential decision making in foreign policy: The effective use of information and advice.* Boulder, CO: Westview.
Ghiselli, E. E. (1963). Intelligence and managerial success. *Psychological Reports, 12,* 898.
Gibb, J. R. (1961). Defensive communication. *Journal of Communication, 11,* 141–148.
Giddens, A. (1979). *Central problems in social theory.* Berkeley: University of California Press.
Gioia, D. A., & Poole, P. P. (1984). Scripts in organizational behavior. *Academy of Management Review, 9*(3), 449–459.
Glazer, M. P., & Glazer, P. M. (1986). Whistleblowing. *Psychology Today, 3,* 37–43.
Goldhaber, G. M. (1993). *Organizational communication* (6th ed.). Madison, WI: WCB Brown & Benchmark.
Gore, Wilbert L. (1983, October 17). *Industry Week,* pp. 48–49.
Gouran, D. S. (1986). Inferential errors, interaction, and group decision making. In R. Y. Hirokawa & M. S. Poole (Eds.), *Communication and group decision making* (pp. 81–92). Beverly Hills, CA: Sage.
Gouran, D. S. (1990). Evaluating group outcomes. In G. R. Phillips & B. Dervin (Eds.), *Teaching how to work in groups* (pp. 175–196). Norwood, NJ: Ablex.
Gouran, D. S., & Hirokawa, R. Y. (1983). The role of communication in decision-making groups: A functional perspective. In M. S. Mander (Ed.), *Communications in transition* (pp. 165–185). New York: Praeger.
Gouran, D. S., & Hirokawa, R. Y. (1986). Counteractive functions of communication in effective group decision making. In R. Y. Hirokawa & M. S. Poole (Eds.), *Communication and group decision making* (pp. 81–92). Beverly Hills, CA: Sage.
Gouran, D. S., Hirokawa, R. Y., & Martz, A. E. (1986). A critical analysis of factors re-

lated to decisional processes involved in the *Challenger* disaster. *Central States Speech Journal, 37*(3), 119–135.

Graber, D. A. (1992). *Public sector communication: How organizations manage information.* Washington, DC: Congressional Quarterly.

Graen, G. (1976). Role-making processes within complex organizations. In M. D. Dunnette (Ed.), *Handbook of industrial organizational psychology* (pp. 1201–1246). Chicago: Rand McNally.

Graen, G., & Ginsburgh, S. (1977). Job resignation as a function of role orientation and leader acceptance: A longitudinal investigation of organizational assimilation. *Organizational Behavior and Human Performance, 19,* 1–17.

Graen, G. B., & Scandura, T. A. (1987). Toward a psychology of dyadic organizing. In L. L. Cummings & B. M. Staw (Eds.), *Research in organizational behavior* (vol. 9, pp. 175–208). New York: JAI Press.

Gramovetter, M. (1973). The strength of weak ties. *American Journal of Sociology, 78,* 1360–1380.

Green, S. G., & Mitchell, T. R. (1979). Attributional process in leader-member interactions. *Organizational Behavior and Human Performance, 23,* 429–458.

Hackman, J. R., & Morris, C. G. (1975). Group tasks, group interaction process, and group performance effectiveness: A review and proposed integration. In L. Berkowitz (Ed.), *Advances in experimental social psychology* (vol. 8, pp. 45–99). New York: Academic Press.

Hall, D., & Nougaim, K. E. (1968). An examination of Maslow's need hierarchy in an organizational setting. *Organizational Behavior and Human Performance, 3,* 12–35.

Hall, F. S. (1991). Dysfunctional managers: The next human resource challenge. *Organizational Dynamics, 20,* 48–57.

Halpin, A. W. (1957). *Manual for the leader behavior description questionnaire.* Columbus: Ohio State University, Bureau of Business Research.

Hambrick, D. C., & Mason, P. A. (1984). Upper echelons: The organization as a reflection of its top managers. *Academy of Management Review, 9,* 193–206.

Hamner, W. C. (1979). Motivation theories and work applications. In S. Kerr (Ed.), *Organizational behavior* (pp. 41–58). Columbus OH: Grid.

Harper, N. L., & Hirokawa, R. Y. (1988). A comparison of the persuasive strategies used by female and male managers I: An examination of downward influence. *Communication Quarterly, 36,* 157–168.

Harris, L. (1979). *Communication competence: Empirical tests of a systemic model.* Unpublished doctoral dissertation, University of Massachusetts, Amherst.

Harvey, J. B. (1988). The Abilene paradox: The management of agreement. *Organizational Dynamics, 17,* 16–43.

Heath, M. R., & Bekker, S. J. (1986). *Identification of opinion leaders in public affairs educational matters and family planning in the township of Atteridgeville* (Research Finding Comm. N-142). Pretoria, South Africa: Human Sciences Research Council.

Hemphill, J. K. (1955). Leadership behavior associated with the administrative reputations of college departments. *Journal of Educational Psychology, 46,* 385–401.

Henning, M., & Jardim, A. (1977). *The managerial woman.* New York: Pocket Books.

Hersey, P., & Blanchard, K. H. (1982). *Management of organizational behavior* (4th ed.). Englewood Cliffs, NJ: Prentice-Hall.

Hewes, D. E. (1986). A socio-egocentric model of group decision making. In R. Y. Hirokawa & M. S. Poole (Eds.), *Communication and group decision making* (pp. 293–312). Beverly Hills, CA: Sage.

Hewitt, J. P., & Stokes, R. (1975). Disclaimers. *American Sociological Review, 40,* 1–11.

Hillerman, T. (1989). *Talking god.* New York: Harper.

Hirokawa, R. Y. (1985). Discussion procedures and decision-making performance: A test of the functional perspective. *Human Communication Research, 12,* 203–224.

Hirokawa, R. Y. (1988a). Group communication and decision-making performance: A continued test of the functional perspective. *Human Communication Research, 14*(4), 487–515.

Hirokawa, R. Y. (1988b). *The role of communication in group decision-making efficacy: A task-contingency perspective.* Paper presented at the annual meeting of the Central States Speech Association, Schaumburg, IL.

Hirokawa, R. Y. (1990). The role of communication in group decision-making efficacy: A task-contingency perspective. *Small Group Research, 21*(2), 190–204.

Hirokawa, R. Y., & Miyahara, A. (1986). A comparison of influence strategies utilized by managers in American and Japanese organizations. *Communication Quarterly, 34,* 250–265.

Hirokawa, R. Y., & Rost, K. (1992). Effective group decision making in organizations. *Management Communication Quarterly, 5,* 267–388.

Hirokawa, R. Y., & Scheerhorn, D. R. (1986). Communication in faulty group decision making. In R. Y. Hirokawa & M. S. Poole (Eds.), *Communication and group decision making* (pp. 63–80). Beverly Hills, CA: Sage.

Hoerr, J. (1985, April 15). A company where everybody is the boss. *Business Week,* p. 98.

Hogarth, R. M., & Makridakis, S. (1981). Forecasting and planning: An evaluation. *Management Science, 27*(2), 115–138.

Hosking, D. M. (1988). Organizing, leadership and skillful process. *Journal of Management Studies, 25* (2), 147–166.

Hosking, D. M., & Morley, I. E. (1988). The skills of leadership. In J. G. Hunt, B. R. Baliga, H. P. Dachler, & C. A. Schriesheim (Eds.), *Emerging leadership vistas* (pp. 80–106). Lexington, MA: Lexington Books.

House, R. J. (1971). A path-goal theory of leader effectiveness. *Administrative Science Quarterly, 16,* 321–339.

House, R. J. (1974). Path-goal theory of leader effectiveness. *Journal of Contemporary Business, 3,* 81–97.

House, R. J., & Dessler, G. (1974). The path goal theory of leadership: Some *post hoc* and *a priori* tests. In J. G. Hunt & L. L. Larson (Eds.), *Contingency approaches to leadership* (pp. 29–55). Carbondale: Southern Illinois University Press.

House, R. J., & Mitchell, T. R. (1974). Path-goal theory of leadership. *Journal of Contemporary Business, 3,* 81–97.

House, R. J., Filley, A. C., & Kerr, S. (1971). Relation of leader consideration and initiation structure to R and D subordinates' satisfaction. *Administrative Science Quarterly, 16,* 19–30.

Howell, J. P., & Dorfman, P. W. (1981). Substitutes for leadership: Test of a construct. *Academy of Management Journal, 24,* 714–728.

Howell, J. P., & Dorfman, P. W. (1986). Leadership and substitutes for leadership among professional and nonprofessional workers. *Journal of Applied Behavioral Science, 22,* 29–46.

Howell, J. P., Bowen, D. E., Dorfman, P. W., Kerr, S., & Podsakoff, P. M. (1990). Substitutes for leadership: Effective alternatives to ineffective leadership. *Organizational Dynamics, 19*(1), 20–38.

Howell, J. P., Dorfman, P. W., & Kerr, S. (1986). Moderator variables in leadership research. *Academy of Management Review, 11,* 88–102.

Hubbard, K. (1990). For new age ice-cream moguls Ben and Jerry, making 'cherry garcia' and 'chunky monkey' is a labor of love, *People Weekly, 34*(10), 73–75.

Huber, G. P., & Daft, R. L. (1987). The information environments of organizations. In F.

M. Jablin, L. L. Putnam, K. H. Roberts, & L. W. Porter (Eds.), *Handbook of organizational communication* (pp. 130–164). Beverly Hills: Sage.

Huerta, F. C., & Lane, T. A. (1983). Participation of women in centers of power. *Social Science Journal, 18,* 71–86.

Ilgen, D. R., & Knowlton, W. A. (1980). Performance attributional effects on feedback from superiors. *Organizational Behavior and Human Performance, 25,* 441–456.

Instone, D., Major, B., & Bunker, B. B. (1983). Gender, self-confidence and social influence strategies: An organizational simulation. *Journal of Personality and Social Psychology, 44,* 322–333.

Jablin, F. M. (1987). Organizational entry, assimilation, and exit. In F. M. Jablin, L. L. Putnam, K. Robert, & L. Porter (Eds.), *Handbook of organizational communication* (pp. 679–740). Beverly Hills: Sage.

Jablin, F. M. (1980). Subordinates' sex and supervisor-subordinate status differentiation as moderator of the Pelz effect. In D. Nimmo (Ed.), *Communication yearbook 4* (pp. 349–366). New Brunswick, NJ: Transaction Press.

Jacobs, M., Jacobs, A., Feldman, G., & Cavior, N. (1973). Feedback in the "credibility gap": Delivery of positive and negative and emotional and behavioral feedback in groups. *Journal of Consulting and Clinical Psychology, 41*(2), 215–223.

Jago, A. G. (1982). Leadership: Perspectives in theory and research. *Management Science, 28,* 315–336.

Janis, I. L. (1972). *Victims of groupthink: A psychological study of policy decisions and fiascoes.* Boston: Houghton-Mifflin.

Janis, I. L. (1982). *Groupthink: Psychological studies of policy decisions and fiascoes.* Boston: Houghton-Mifflin.

Janis, I. L. (1989). *Crucial decisions: Leadership in policymaking and crisis management.* New York: Free Press.

Janis, I. L., & Mann, L. (1977). *Decision making: A psychological analysis of conflict, choice, and commitment.* New York: Free Press.

Johnson, P. (1976). Women and power: Toward a theory of effectiveness. *Journal of Social Issues, 32,* 99–110.

Johnston, W. B., & Packer, A. E. (1987). *Workforce 2000:* Work and workers for the 21st century. Indianapolis, IN: Hudson Institute.

Jones, G. R. (1986). Socialization tactics, self-efficacy, and newcomers' adjustments to organizations. *Academy of Management Journal, 29,* 262–279.

Kanter, R. M. (1976). The impact of hierarchical structures on the work behavior of women and men. *Social Problems, 23,* 415–430.

Kanter R. M. (1977). *Men and women of the corporation.* New York: Basic Books.

Kanter, R. M. (1979). Power failure in management circuits. *Harvard Business Review,* July–August, 65–75.

Kaplan, R. E. (1984). Trade routes: The manager's network of relationships. *Organizational Dynamics, 12,* 37–52.

Katzell, R. A., & Thompson, D. E. (1990). Work motivation: Theory and practice. *American Psychologist, 45* (2), 144–153.

Kazdin, A. E. (1980). *Behavior modification in applied settings.* Homewood, IL: Dorsey.

Kelly, C. M. (1987). The interrelationship of ethics and power in today's organizations. *Organizational Dynamics, 16,* 4–18.

Kenny, D. A., & Zaccaro, S. J. (1983). An estimate of variance due to traits in leadership. *Journal of Applied Psychology, 68,* 678–685.

Kerr, S. (1977). Substitutes for leadership: Some implications for organizational design. *Organization and Administrative Sciences, 8,* 135–146.

Kerr, S., & Jermier, J. (1978). Substitutes for leadership: Their meaning and measurement. *Organizational Behavior and Human Performance, 22,* 374–403.

Kerr, S., & Slocum, J. W., Jr. (1981). Controlling the performances of people in organizations. In P. C. Nystrom & W. H. Starbuck (Eds.), *Handbook of organizational design,* (vol. 2, pp. 116–134). New York: Oxford University Press.

Kilmann, R. H., & Thomas, K. W. (1978). Four perspectives on conflict management: An attributional framework for organizing descriptive and normative theory. *Academy of Management Review, 3,* 59–68.

Kipnis, D., & Schmidt, S. M. (1988). Upward-influence styles: Relationship with performance evaluations, salary, and stress. *Administrative Science Quarterly, 33,* 528–542.

Kipnis, D., Schmidt, S., & Wilkinson, I. (1980). Intraorganizational influence tactics: Explorations in getting one's way. *Journal of Applied Psychology, 65,* 440–452.

Kirkpatrick, S. A., & Locke, E. A. (1991). Leadership: Do traits matter? *Academy of Management Executive, 5* (2), 48–60.

Klauss, R., & Bass, B. M. (1982). *Interpersonal communications in organizations.* New York: Academic Press.

Knutson, T. J., & Holdridge, W. E. (1975). Orientation behavior, leadership and consensus: A possible functional relationship. *Speech Monographs, 42,* 107–114.

Kotter, J. P. (1979). *Power in management.* New York: ANACOM.

Kouzes, J. M., & Posner, B. Z. (1990). *The leadership challenge: How to get extraordinary things done in organizations.* San Francisco: Jossey-Bass.

Krackhardt, D. (1990). Assessing the political landscape: Structure, cognition, and power in organizations. *Administrative Science Quarterly, 35,* 342–369.

Kram, K. E. (1985). *Mentoring at work.* Glenview, IL: Scott, Foresman.

Krefting, L. A., & Frost, P. J. (1985). Untangling webs, surfing waves, and wildcatting: A multiple-metaphor perspective on managing organizational culture. In P. J. Frost, L. F. Moore, M. R. Louis, C. C. Lundberg, & J. Martin (Eds.), *Organizational culture* (pp. 155–168). Beverly Hills, CA: Sage.

Kreps, G. L. (1980). A field experimental test and reevaluation of Weick's model of organizing. In D. Nimmo (Ed.), *Communication yearbook 4* (pp. 389–398). New Brunswick, NJ: Transaction Books.

Kretch, D., & Crutchfield, R. S. (1948). *Theory and problems of social psychology.* New York: McGraw-Hill.

Krone, K. J., Jablin, F. M., & Putnam, L. L. (1987). Communication theory and organizational communication: Multiple perspectives. In F. M. Jablin, L. L. Putnam, K. H. Roberts, & L. W. Porter (Eds.), *Handbook of organizational communication* (pp. 18–40). Beverly Hills, CA: Sage.

Kuhnert, K. W., & Lewis, P. (1987). Transactional and transformational leadership: A constructive/developmental analysis. *Academy of Management Review, 12,* 648–657.

Kunhardt, P. B., Kunhardt, P. P., & Kunhardt, P. W. (1992). *Lincoln: An illustrated biography.* New York: Knopf.

Landy, F. J. (1985). *The psychology of work behavior* (3rd ed.). Homewood, IL: Dorsey Press.

Landy, F. J., & Becker, W. A. (1987). Motivation theory reconsidered. In L. L. Cummings & B. M. Staw (Eds.), *Research in Organizational Behavior,* (vol. 9, pp. 1–38). New York: JAI Press.

Langer, E. J. (1983). *The psychology of control.* Beverly Hills, CA: Sage.

Larson, C. W., & LaFasto, F. J. (1989). *Teamwork: What must go right/what can go wrong.* Beverly Hills: Sage.

Larwood, L., & Blackmore, J. (1978). Sex discrimination in manager selection: Testing predictions of the vertical dyad linkage model. *Sex Roles, 4,* 359–367.

Latham, G. P., & Lee, T. W. (1986). Goal setting. In E. A. Locke (Ed.), *Generalizing from laboratory to field settings* (pp. 101–118). Lexington, MA: Lexington.

Latham, G. P., Erez, M., & Locke, E. A. (1988). Resolving scientific disputes by the joint design of crucial experiments by the antagonists: Application to the Erez-Latham dispute regarding participation in goal setting. *Journal of Applied Psychology* (monograph), *73*, 753–772.

Lawler, E. E., & Suttle, J. L. (1972). A causal correlational test of the need hierarchy concept. *Organizational Behavior and Human Performance, 7*, 265–287.

Lawrence, P. R., & Lorsch, J. W. (1967). *Organization and environment: Managing differentiation and integration.* Boston: Harvard University, Graduate School of Business Administration.

Lenney, E. (1977). Women's self-confidence in achievement settings. *Psychological Bulletin, 84*, 1–13.

Leon, F. R. (1979). Number of outcomes and accuracy of prediction in expectancy research. *Organizational Behavior and Human Performance, 23*, 251–267.

Leon, F. R. (1981). The role of positive and negative outcomes in the causation of motivational forces. *Journal of Applied Psychology, 66*, 45–53.

Levering, R., Moskowitz, M., & Katz, M. (1984). *The one hundred best companies to work for in America.* Reading, MA: Addison-Wesley.

Lewin, K., Lippitt, R., & White, R. K. (1939). Patterns of aggressive behavior in experimentally created "social climates." *Journal of Science Psychology, 10*, 271–299.

Liden, R., & Graen, G. (1980). Generalizability of the vertical dyad linkage model of leadership. *Academy of Management Journal, 23*, 451–465.

Lind, E. A., & O'Barr, W. M. (1979). The social significance of speech in the courtroom. In H. Giles & R. St. Clair (Eds.), *Language and social psychology* (pp. 66–87). Baltimore: University Park Press.

Locke, E. A. (1991). Goal theory versus control theory: Contrasting approaches to understanding work motivation. *Motivation and Emotion, 15*(1), 9–28.

Locke, E. A., & Latham, G. P. (1984). *Goal-setting: A motivational technique that works.* Englewood Cliffs, NJ: Prentice-Hall.

Locke, E. A., & Latham, G. P. (1990a). *A theory of goal setting and task performance.* Englewood Cliffs, NJ: Prentice-Hall.

Locke E. A., & Latham, G. P. (1990b). Work motivation and satisfaction: Light at the end of the tunnel. *Psychological Science, 1*(4), 240–246.

Locke, E. A., & Schweiger, D. M. (1979). Participation in decision making: One more look. In B. Staw & L. L. Cummings (Eds.), *Research in organizational behavior*, vol. 1, pp. 265–340. Greenwich, CT: JAI Press.

Locke, E. A., Motowidlo, S. J., & Bobko, P. (1986). Using self-efficacy theory to resolve the conflict between goal-setting theory and expectancy theory in organizational behavior and industrial/organizational psychology. *Journal of Social and Clinical Psychology, 4*, 328–338.

Lord, R. G., DeVader, C. L., & Alliger, G. M. (1986). A meta-analysis of the relation between personality traits and leadership perceptions: An application of validity generalization procedures. *Journal of Applied Psychology, 71*, 402–410.

Louis, M. (1980). Surprise and sense-making: What newcomers experience in entering unfamiliar organizational settings. *Administrative Science Quarterly, 23*, 225–251.

Makridakis, S. G. (1990). *Forecasting, planning, and strategy for the 21st century.* New York: The Free Press.

Mainiero, L. A. (1986). Coping with powerlessness: The relationship of gender and job dependency to empowerment strategy-usage. *Administrative Science Quarterly, 31*, 633–653.

Manz, C. C., & Sims, H. P. (1989). *Superleadership: Leading others to lead.* New York: Berkley Books.

March, J. G., & Simon, H. A. (1958). *Organizations.* New York: Wiley.

Margerison, C., & Glube, R. (1979). Leadership decision making: An empirical test of the Vroom and Yetton model. *Journal of Management Studies, 16,* 45–55.

Marini, M. M., & Brinton, M. C. (1984). Sex typing in occupational socialization. In B. F. Reskin (Ed.), *Sex segregation in the workplace: Trends, explanations, remedies.* Washington, D. C.: National Academy Press.

Marsden, P. V. (1987). Core discussion networks of Americans. *American Sociological Review, 52,* 122–131.

Marwell, G., & Schmitt, D. (1967). Dimensions of compliance-gaining behavior: An empirical analysis. *Sociometry, 30,* 350–364.

Maslow, A. H. (1970). *Motivation and personality* (2nd ed.). New York: Harper.

McClelland, D. C., & Boyatzis, R. E. (1982). Leadership motive pattern and long-term success in management. *Journal of Applied Psychology, 67,* 737–743.

McCroskey, J. C. (1982). Communication competence and performance: A research and pedagogical perspective. *Communication Education, 31,* 1–8.

McFall, R. M. (1982). A review and reformulation of the concept of social skills. *Behavioral Assessment, 4,* 1–31.

Metcalfe, B. M. A. (1982). Leadership: Extrapolating from theory and research to practical skills training. *Journal of Management Studies, 19*(3), 295–305.

Miller, K. I., & Monge, P. R. (1986). Participation, satisfaction, and productivity: A meta-analytic review. *Academy of Management Journal, 29,* 727–753.

Miller, V. D., & Jablin, F. M. (1991). Information seeking during organizational entry: Influences, tactics, and a model of the process. *Academy of Management Review, 16*(1), 92–120.

Misumi, J. (1985). *The behavioral science of leadership. An interdisciplinary Japanese research program.* Ann Arbor: University of Michigan Press.

Misumi, J., & Peterson, M. F. (1985). The performance-maintenance (PM) theory of leadership: Review of a Japanese research program. *Administrative Science Quarterly, 30,* 198–223.

Mitroff, I. I. (1978). Systematic problem solving. In M. W. McCall & M. M. Lombardo (Eds.), *Leadership: Where else can we go?* (pp. 129–143). Durham, NC: Duke University Press.

Monge, P. R., & Eisenberg, E. M. (1987). Emergent communication networks. In F. M. Jablin, L. L. Putnam, K. H. Roberts, & L. W. Porter (Eds.), *Handbook of organizational communication* (pp. 304–342). Beverly Hills: Sage.

Monge, P. R., Bachman, S., Dillard, J., & Eisenberg, E. (1982). Communicator competence in the workplace: Model testing and scale development. In M. Burgoon (Ed.), Communication yearbook 5 (pp. 505–528). New Brunswick, NJ: Transaction Books.

Monroe, C., Borzi, M. G., & DiSalvo, V. S. (1989). Conflict behaviors of difficult subordinates. *Southern Speech Communication Journal, 54,* 311–329.

Moore, G. (1990). Structural determinants of men's and women's personal networks. *American Sociological Review, 55,* 726–735.

Morgan, G. (1986). *Images of organization.* Beverly Hills, CA: Sage.

Mottaz, C. (1986). Gender differences in work satisfaction, work-related rewards and values, and the determinants of work satisfaction. *Human Relations, 39,* 359–378.

Mowday, R. T., Steers, R. M., & Porter, L. W. (1979). The measurement of organizational commitment. *Journal of Vocational Behavior, 14,* 224–247.

Mumby, D. K. (1987). The political function of narrative in organizations. *Communication Monographs, 54,* 113–127.

Mumby, D. K., & Putnam, L. L. (1992). The politics of emotion: A feminist reading of bounded rationality. *Academy of Management Review, 17* (3), 465–486.

Mumford, M. D. (1986). Leadership in the organizational context: A conceptual approach and its applications. *Journal of Applied Social Psychology, 16*(6), 508–531.

Nadler, D. A. (1979). The effects of feedback on task group behavior: A review of experimental literature. *Organizational Behavior and Human Performance, 23,* 309–338.

Nanus, B. (1992). *Visionary leadership.* San Francisco: Jossey-Bass.

Nathan, J. (Director). (1986). *In search of excellence* [Film]. A John Nathan and Sam Taylor Production.

Nicotera, A. M. & Cushman, D. P. (1992). Organizational ethics: A within-organization view. *Journal of Applied Communication Research, 20*(4), 437–462.

Nisbett, R. E., & Ross, L. (1980). *Human inference: Strategies and shortcomings of social judgment.* Englewood Cliffs, NJ: Prentice-Hall.

Noe, R. A. (1988). Women and mentoring: A review and research agenda. *Academy of Management Review, 13,* 65–78.

Norton, R. (1983). *Communicator style: Theory, applications, and measures.* Beverly Hills, CA: Sage.

Norton, R. (1988). *Lexicon of intentionally ambiguous recommendations.* Deephaven, MN: Meadowbrook.

O'Barr, W. M. (1982). *Linguistic evidence: Language, power, and strategy in the courtroom.* New York: Academic Press.

O'Reilly, C. A. (1977). Supervisors and peers as information sources, group supportiveness, and individual performance. *Journal of Applied Psychology, 62,* 632–635.

O'Reilly, C. A., & Roberts, K. H. (1977a). Communication and performance in organizations. *Proceedings of the Academy of Management, 37,* 375–379.

O'Reilly, C. A., & Roberts, K. H. (1977b). Task group structure, communication and effectiveness and three organizations. *Journal of Applied Psychology, 62,* 674–681.

Osborn, R. N., Hunt, J. G., & Bussom, R. S. (1977). On getting your own way in organizational design: An empirical illustration of requisite variety. *Organization and Administrative Sciences, 8,* 295–310.

Ouchi, W. (1981). *Theory Z: How American business can meet the Japanese challenge.* Reading, MA: Addison-Wesley.

Pacanowsky, M. (1988). Communication in the empowering organization. In J. Anderson (Ed.), *Communication yearbook 11* (pp. 356–379). Beverly Hills, CA: Sage.

Pacanowsky, M., & O'Donnell-Trujillo, N. (1983). Organizational communication as cultural performance. *Communication Monographs, 50,* 126–147.

Parker, V. A., & Kram, K. E. (1993). Women mentoring women: Creating conditions for connection. *Business Horizons, 36* (2), 42–51.

Patten, T. H. (1991/1992). Beyond systems—The politics of managing in a TQM environment. *National Productivity Review, 11,* 9–19.

Pearce, W. B., & Cronen, V. E. (1980). *Communication, action, and meaning: The creation of social realities.* New York: Praeger.

Perrow, C. (1984). *Normal accidents.* New York: Basic Books.

Peters, L. H., Hartke, D. D., & Pohlmann, J. T. (1985). Fiedler's contingency theory of leadership: An application of the meta-analysis procedure of Schmidt and Hunter. *Psychological Bulletin,* 97, 274–285.

Peters, T. (1987). *Thriving on chaos.* New York: Knopf.

Peters, T. (1989). The challenge for continuous learning. Speech given to the Fifth Annual Directors' Forum Conference, April 7–10, 1989, St. Petersburg, FL.

Peters, T., & Austin, N. (1985). *A passion for excellence: The leadership difference.* New York: Warner.

Peters, T. J., & Waterman, R. H. (1982). *In search of excellence.* New York: Harper.

Peterson, M. F., & Sorenson, R. L. (1991). Cognitive processes in leadership: Interpreting and handling events in an organizational context. In J. A. Anderson (Ed.), *Communication yearbook 14* (pp. 501–534) Beverly Hills: Sage.

Pfeffer, J. (1978). The ambiguity of leadership. In M. W. McCall & M. M. Lombardo (Eds.), *Leadership: Where else can we go?* (pp. 13–34). Durham, NC: Duke University Press.

Pfeffer, J. (1981). Management as symbolic action: The creation and maintenance of organizational paradigms. In L. L. Cummings & B. M. Staw (Eds.), *Research in organizational behavior* (vol. 3, pp. 1–52). Greenwich CT: JAI.

Pfeffer, J. (1990). *Managing with power.* Boston, MA: Harvard Business School Press.

Phillips, G. M. (1984). A competent view of "competence." *Communication Education, 32,* 25–36.

Phillips, J. S. (1984). The accuracy of leadership ratings: A cognitive categorization perspective. *Organizational Behavior and Human Performance, 33,* 125–138.

Phillips, J. S., & Lord, R. G. (1981). Causal attributions and perceptions of leadership. *Organizational Behavior and Human Performance, 28,* 143–163.

Phillips, J. S., & Lord, R. G. (1986). Notes on the practical and theoretical consequences of implicit leadership theories for the future of leadership measurement. *Journal of Management, 12*(1), 31–41.

Pinder, C. C. (1984). *Work motivation.* Glenview, IL: Scott, Foresman.

Podsakoff, P. M., & Todor, W. D. (1985). Relationships between leader reward and punishment behavior and group processes and productivity. *Journal of Management, 11,* 55–73.

Podsakoff, P. M., Todor, W. D., & Skov, R. (1982). Effect of leader contingent and noncontingent reward and punishment behaviors on subordinate performance and satisfaction. *Academy of Management Journal, 25,* 810–821.

Podsakoff, P. M., Todor, W. D., Grover, R. A., & Huber, V. L. (1984). Situational moderators of leader reward and punishment behaviors: Fact or fiction? *Organizational Behavior and Human Performance, 34,* 21–63.

Pondy, L. R. (1978). Leadership is a language game. In M. W. McCall, Jr., & M. M. Lombardo (Eds.), *Leadership: Where else can we go?* (pp. 87–99). Durham, NC: Duke University Press.

Poole, M. S. (1983). Decision development in small groups III: A multiple sequence model of group decision making. *Communication Monographs, 50,* 321–341.

Poole, M. S., & Roth J. (1989). Decision development in small groups V: Test of a contingency model. *Human Communication Research, 15,* 549–589.

Porter, L. W., & Lawler, E. E. (1968). *Managerial attitudes and performance.* Homewood, IL: Irwin-Dorsey.

Posner, B. Z., & Kouzes, J. M. (1988). Relating leadership and credibility. *Psychological Reports, 63,* 527–530.

Potts, M., & Behr, P. (1987). *The leading edge.* New York: McGraw-Hill.

Putnam, L. L. (1985). Bargaining as organizational communication. In R. D. McPhee & P. K. Tompkins (Eds.), *Organizational communication: Traditional themes and new directions* (pp. 129–148). Newbury Park, CA: Sage.

Putnam, L. L. (1986). Conflict and negotiation. Hallie Maude Neff Wilcox lecture, Baylor University, Waco, TX.

Putnam, L. L., & Poole, M. S. (1987). Conflict and negotiation. In F. M. Jablin, L. L. Putnam, K. Roberts, & L. W. Porter (Eds.), *Handbook of organizational communication* (pp. 549–599). Beverly Hills: Sage.

Putnam, L. L., & Sorenson, R. L. (1982). Equivocal messages in organizations. *Human Communication Research, 8*(2), 114–132.

Putnam, L. L., Van Hoeven, S. A., & Bullis, C. A. (1991). The role of rituals and fantasy themes in teachers' bargaining. *Western Journal of Speech Communication, 55*(4), 85–103.

Ragins, B. R. (1989). Power and gender congruency effects in evaluations of male and female managers. *Journal of Management, 15*(1), 65–76.

Ragins, B. R., & Cotton, J. L. (1991). Easier said than done: Gender differences in perceived barriers to gaining a mentor. *Academy of Management Journal, 34* (4), 939–951.

Ragins, B. R., & Sundstrom, E. (1989). Gender and power in organizations: A longitudinal perspective. *Psychological Bulletin, 105*, 51–88.

Rahim, M. A., Garrett, J. E., & Buntzman, G. F. (1992). Ethics of managing interpersonal conflict in organizations. *Journal of Business Ethics, 11*, 423–432.

Raushenberger, J., Schmitt, N., & Hunter, J. E. (1980). A test of the need hierarchy concept by a Markov model of change in need strength. *Administrative Science Quarterly, 25*, 654–670.

Rhodes, L. (1982, August). The un-manager. *Inc.*, pp. 34–46.

Rice, R. W. (1978). Construct validity of the least preferred co-worker score. *Psychology Bulletin, 85*, 1199–1237.

Ricillo, S. C., & Trenholm, S. (1983). Predicting managers' choice of influence mode: The effects of interpersonal trust and worker attributions on managerial tactics in a simulated organizational setting. *Western Journal of Speech Communication, 47*, 323–339.

Rim, Y., & Erez, M. (1980). A note about tactics used to influence superiors, co-workers and subordinates. *Journal of Occupational Psychology, 53*, 319–321.

Rimer, S. (1992, October 23). A Caprice that Chevy couldn't sell. *New York Times*, pp. 1, 18, Business Section.

Roberts, K. H., & O'Reilly, C. (1978). Organizations as communication structures: An empirical-theoretical approach. *Human Communication Research, 4*, 283–293.

Roberts, K. H., & O'Reilly, C. A., III. (1979). Some correlations of communication roles in organizations. *Academy of Management Journal, 22*(1), 42–57.

Rosen, B., Templeton, M. E., & Kichline, K. (1981). First few years on the job: Women in management. *Business Horizons, 24*, 25–29.

Saint-Exupéry, A. de. (1943). *The little prince.* New York: Harcourt.

Salancik, G. R., & Pfeffer, J. (1977). Constraints on administrator discretion: The limited influence of mayors on city budgets. *Urban Affairs Quarterly, 12*, 475–498.

Sayles, L. R. (1993). *Working leadership.* New York: The Free Press.

Schein, E. (1988). *Organizational culture and leadership.* San Francisco: Jossey-Bass.

Schein, E. (1991). The role of the founder in the creation of organizational culture. In P. Frost, L. Moore, M. Louis, C. Lundberg, & J. Martin (Eds.), *Reframing organizational culture* (pp. 14–25). Beverly Hills: Sage.

Schlueter, D. W., Barge, J. K., & Blankenship, D. (1990). A comparative analysis of influence strategies used by upper- and lower-level male and female managers. *Western Journal of Speech Communication, 54*(1), 42–65.

Schonberger, R. J. (1992). Total quality management cuts a broad swath—through manufacturing and beyond. *Organizational Dynamics, 20*, 16–28.

Schriesheim, C., & Kerr, S. (1974). Psychometric properties of the Ohio State Leadership Scales. *Psychological Bulletin, 81*(11), 756–765.

Schriesheim, C. A., & Von Glinow, M. A. (1977). The path-goal theory of leadership: A theoretical and empirical analysis. *Academy of Management Journal, 20*, 398–405.

Schultz, B. (1974). Characteristics of emergent leaders of continuing problem-solving groups. *Journal of Psychology, 88*, 167–173.

Schultz, B. (1980). Communicative correlates of perceived leaders. *Small Group Behavior, 11*, 175–191.

Schultz, B. (1986). Communicative correlates of perceived leaders in the small group. *Small Group Behavior, 17* (1), 51–65.

Schwartz, E. I. & Treece, J. B. (1992, March 2). Smart programs go to work. *Business Week*, pp. 97–105.

Schweiger, D. M., & Leana, C. R. (1986). Participation in decision making. In E. A. Locke (Ed.), *Generalizing from laboratory to field settings* (pp. 147–166). Boston: Heath-Lexington.

Schweiger, D. M., Sandberg, W. R., & Ragan, J. W. (1986). Group approaches for improving strategic decision making: A comparative analysis of dialectical inquiry, devil's advocacy, and consensus. *Academy of Management Journal, 29*(1), 51–71.

Schwenk, C. R. (1984). Cognitive simplification processes in strategic decision making. *Strategic Management Journal, 5*, 111–128.

Schwenk, C. R. (1988). The cognitive perspective on strategic decision making. *Journal of Management Studies, 25*(1), 41–55.

Scott, W. R. (1981). *Organizations: Rational, natural, and open systems.* Englewood Cliffs, NJ: Prentice-Hall.

Searle, J. (1969). *Speech acts: An essay in the philosophy of language.* Oxford: Oxford University Press.

Seibold, D. R., Cantrill, J. G., & Meyers, R. A. (1985). Communication and interpersonal influence. In M. L. Knapp & G. R. Miller (Eds.), *Handbook of interpersonal communication* (pp. 551–614). Beverly Hills, CA: Sage.

Shannon, C., & Weaver, W. (1949). *The mathematical theory of communication.* Urbana, IL: University of Illinois Press.

Sharfman, M. P., & Dean, J. W., Jr. (1991). Conceptualizing and measuring the organizational environment: A multidimensional approach. *Journal of Management, 17*(4), 681–700.

Shaw, M. E. (1981). *Group dynamics: The psychology of small group behavior.* New York: McGraw-Hill.

Sherman, S. (1993). A brave new Darwinian workplace. *Fortune, 127* (2), 50–56.

Shipper, F., & Manz, C. C. (1992). Employee self-management without formally designated teams: An alternative road to empowerment. *Organizational Dynamics, 20*, 48–61.

Shockley, P. S., & Stanley, C. M. (1980). Women in management training programs: What they think about key issues. *Public Personnel Management, 9*, 214–224.

Skinner, B. F. (1969). *Contingencies of reinforcement: A theoretical analysis.* New York: Appleton-Century Crofts.

Smircich, L. (1983). Concepts of culture and organizational analysis. *Administrative Science Quarterly, 28(3)*, 339–358.

Smircich, L., & Calas, M. (1987). Organizational culture: A critical assessment. In F. Jablin, L. L. Putnam, K. H. Roberts, & L. Porter (Eds.), *Handbook of organizational communication* (pp. 228–263). Newbury Park, CA: Sage.

Smircich, L., & Stubbart, C. (1985). Strategic management in an enacted world. *Academy of Management Review, 10*(4), 724–736.

Smith, K. K., & Berg, D. N. (1987). *Paradoxes of group life.* San Francisco: Jossey-Bass.

Smith, R., & Eisenberg, E. (1987). Conflict at Disneyland: A root metaphor analysis. *Communication Monographs, 54*, 367–380.

Snyder, M., & Swann, W. B. (1978). Hypothesis-testing processes in social interaction. *Journal of Personality and Social Psychology, 36*, 1202–1212.

Spitzberg, B. H. (1983). Communication competence as knowledge, skill, and impression. *Communication Education, 32*, 323–328.

Spitzberg, B. H., & Cupach, W. R. (1984). *Interpersonal communication competence.* Beverly Hills: Sage.

Spitzberg, B. H., & Cupach, W. R. (1989). *Handbook of interpersonal competence research.* New York: Springer-Verlag.

Spitzberg, B. H., & Hecht, M. L. (1984). A component model of relational competence. *Human Communication Research, 10,* 575–599.

Spivack, G., Platt, J. J., & Shure, M. B. (1976). *The problem-solving approach to adjustment.* San Francisco: Jossey-Bass.

St. John, B. (1989). *The Landry legend: Grace under pressure.* Dallas, TX: Word.

Stahl, M. J. (1983). Achievement, power and managerial motivation: Selecting managerial talent with the job choice exercise. *Personnel Psychology, 36,* 775–789.

Staw, B. (1983). Proximal and distal measures of individual impact: Some comments on Hall's performance evaluation paper. In F. Landy, S. Zedeck, G. J. Cleveland (Eds.), *Performance measurement and theory* (pp. 31–39). Hillsdale, NJ: Erlbaum.

Steiner, I. D. (1972). *Group process and productivity.* New York: Academic Press.

Stewart, L. P., & Gudykunst, W. P. (1982). Differential factors influencing the hierarchical level and number of promotions of males and females within an organization. *Academy of Management Journal, 25,* 586–597.

Stogdill, R. M. (1974). *Handbook of leadership.* New York: Free Press.

Stogdill, R. M. (1981). *Stogdill's handbook of leadership* (2nd ed.). New York: Free Press.

Stubbart, C. I. (1989). Managerial cognition: A missing link in strategic management research. *Journal of Management Studies, 26*(4), 325–347.

Sunnafrank, M. (1986). Predicted outcome value during initial interactions. *Human Communication Research, 13*(1), 3–33.

Tannebaum, R., & Schmidt, W. H. (1958). How to choose a leadership pattern. *Harvard Business Review, 36*(2), 95–101.

Terborg, J. R. (1977). Women in management: A research review. *Journal of Applied Psychology, 2,* 647–664.

Tichy, N. (1981). Networks in organization. In P. Nystrom & W. Starbuck (Eds.), *Handbook of organizational design* (vol. 2, pp. 225–249). New York: Oxford University Press.

Tichy, N. M., & DeVanna, M. A. (1986). *The transformational leader.* New York: Wiley.

Tjosvold, D. (1984). Effects of leader warmth and directiveness on subordinate performance on a subsequent task. *Journal of Applied Psychology, 69,* 422–427.

Tjosvold, D. (1991). *The conflict-positive organization.* Reading, MA: Addison-Wesley.

Tjosvold, D., Wedley, W. C., & Field, R. H. G. (1986). Constructive controversy: The Vroom-Yetton model and managerial decision making. *Journal of Occupational Behavior, 7,* 125–138.

Tompkins, P., & Cheney, G. (1985). Communication and unobtrusive control. In R. McPhee, & P. Tompkins (Eds.), *Organizational communication: Traditional themes and new directions* (pp. 179–210). Beverly Hills, CA: Sage.

Trempe, J., Rigny, A., & Haccoun, R. R. (1985). Subordinate satisfaction with male and female managers: Role of perceived supervisory influence. *Journal of Applied Psychology, 70,* 44–47.

Tung, R. (1979). Dimensions of organizational environments: An exploratory study of their impact in organizational structure. *Academy of Management Journal, 22,* 672–693.

Tversky, A., & Kahneman, D. (1974). Judgment under uncertainty: Heuristics and biases. *Science, 105,* 1124–1131.

Vecchio, R. P. (1982). A further test of leadership effects due to between-group variation and within-group variation. *Journal of Applied Psychology, 67,* 200–208.

Vecchio, R. P. (1987). Situational leadership theory: An examination of a perscriptive theory. *Journal of Applied Psychology, 72,* 444–451.
Vecchio, R. P., & Sussmann, M. (1991). Choice of influence tactics: Individual and organizational determinants. *Journal of Organizational Behavior, 12,* 73–80.
Veroff, J., Reuman, D., & Feld, S. (1984). Motives in American men and women across the adult life span. *Developmental Psychology, 20,* 1142–1158.
Vroom, V. (1964). *Work and motivation.* New York: Wiley.
Vroom, V. H., & Jago, A. G. (1978). On the validity of the Vroom-Yetton model. *Journal of Applied Psychology, 63,* 151–162.
Vroom, V. H., & Jago, A. G. (1988). *The new leadership: Managing participation in organizations.* Englewood Cliffs, NJ: Prentice-Hall.
Vroom, V. H., & Yetton, P. W. (1973). *Leadership and decision making.* Pittsburgh: University of Pittsburgh Press.
Wagner, J. A., III., & Gooding, R. Z. (1987). Shared influence and organizational behavior: A meta-analysis of situational variables expected to moderate participation-outcome relationships. *Academy of Management Journal, 30,* 524–541.
Waldman, D. A., Bass, B. M., & Einstein, W. O. (1987). Leadership and outcomes of performance appraisal process. *Journal of Occupational Psychology, 60,* 177–186.
Watzlawick, P., Beavin, J. H., & Jackson, D. D. (1967). *Pragmatics of human communication.* New York: Norton.
Wegner, A. (1991). Gore: An innovative philosophy. *Management Review, 80,* 5–6.
Weick, K. E. (1974). Middle-range theories of social systems. *Behavioral Science, 19,* 357–367.
Weick, K. E. (1978). The spines of leaders. In M. McCall & M. Lombardo, (Eds.), *Leadership: Where else can we go?* (pp. 37–61). Durham, NC: Duke University Press.
Weick, K. E. (1979). *The social psychology of organizing* (2nd ed.). Reading, MA: Addison-Wesley.
Weick, K. E. (1980). The management of eloquence. *Executive, 6,* 18–21.
Weick, K. E. (1988). Enacted sensemaking in crisis situations. *Journal of Management Studies, 25*(4), 305–317.
Weick, K. E. (1989). Organized improvisation: Twenty years of organizing. *Communication Studies, 40*(4), 241–248.
Wellmon, T. A. (1989). Conceptualizing organizational communication competence. *Management Communication Quarterly, 1*(4), 515–534.
Wiley, M. G., & Eskilson, A. (1982). The interaction of sex and power base on perceptions of managerial effectiveness. *Academy of Management Journal, 25,* 671–677.
Wilson, S. R., & Putnam, L. L. (1990). Interaction goals in negotiation. In J. A. Anderson (Ed.), *Communication yearbook 13* (pp. 374–406). Beverly Hills, CA: Sage.
Winter, D. G. (1988). The power motive in women—and men. *Journal of Personality and Social Psychology, 54,* 510–519.
Wong, P. T. P., Kettlewell, G., & Sproule, C. F. (1985). On the importance of being masculine: Sex role, attribution, and women's career advancement. *Sex Roles, 12,* 757–769.
Wood, R. E., & Bandura, A. (1989). Social cognitive theory of organizational management. *Academy of Management Review, 14,* 361–384.
Wood, R. E., Mento, A. J., & Locke, E. A. (1987). Task complexity as a moderator of goal effects: A meta-analysis. *Journal of Applied Psychology, 72,* 416–425.
Wright, J. W., II, Hosman, L. A. (1983). Language style and sex bias in the courtroom: The effects of male and female use of hedges and intensifiers on impression formation. *Southern Speech Communication Journal, 48,* 137–152.
Wyatt, N. (1993). Organizing and relating: Feminist critique of small-group communica-

tion. In S. P. Bowen & N. Wyatt (Eds.), *Transforming visions: Feminist critiques in communication studies* (pp. 51–86). Cresskill, NJ: Hampton Press.

Yukl, G. (1989). Managerial leadership: A review of theory and research. *Journal of Management, 15*(2), 251–289.

Zabel, D., & Avery, C. (1992). Total quality management: A primer. *RQ, 32*(2), 206–216.

Zaleznik, A. (1992). Managers and leaders: Are they different? *Harvard Business Review, 70,* 126–135.

Zorn, T. E. (1991). Construct system development, transformational leadership and leadership messages. *Southern Communication Journal, 56*(3), 178–193.

Acknowledgments (*continued from copyright page*)

Box 5.4, adapted with the permission of The Free Press, a division of Macmillan, Inc. from *Crucial Decisions: Leadership in Policymaking and Crisis Management* by Irving L. Janis. Copyright 1989 by The Free Press.
Table 6.1, courtesy of the Society for Psychological Study of Social Issues.
Figure 6.1, courtesy of JAI Press, Inc.
Figure 6.2, reprinted with permission of Cambridge University Press.
Box 6.1, courtesy of *Academy of Management Review.*
Box 7.3, courtesy of Chuck Lamar.
Box 8.1, reprinted by permission of Sage Publications, Inc.
Table 8.1, adapted by permission of Jossey-Bass, Inc.
Excerpt from the motion picture *Being There* (United Artists, 1979), by Jerzy Kosinski, adapted from his novel, *Being There* (Bantam Books, Copyright © 1985), with permission of the estate of Jerzy Kosinski. All rights reserved.

INDEX